City Girls

City Girls

The Nisei Social World in Los Angeles, 1920–1950

VALERIE J. MATSUMOTO

OXFORD
UNIVERSITY PRESS

OXFORD
UNIVERSITY PRESS

Oxford University Press is a department of the University of Oxford.
It furthers the University's objective of excellence in research, scholarship,
and education by publishing worldwide.

Oxford   New York
Auckland   Cape Town   Dar es Salaam   Hong Kong   Karachi
Kuala Lumpur   Madrid   Melbourne   Mexico City   Nairobi
New Delhi   Shanghai   Taipei   Toronto

With offices in
Argentina   Austria   Brazil   Chile   Czech Republic   France   Greece
Guatemala   Hungary   Italy   Japan   Poland   Portugal   Singapore
South Korea   Switzerland   Thailand   Turkey   Ukraine   Vietnam

Oxford is a registered trademark of Oxford University Press
in the UK and certain other countries.

Published in the United States of America by
Oxford University Press
198 Madison Avenue, New York, NY 10016

Library of Congress Cataloging-in-Publication Data
Matsumoto, Valerie J.
City girls : the Nisei social world in Los Angeles, 1920–1950 / Valerie J. Matsumoto.
pages cm
Includes bibliographical references and index.
ISBN 978–0–19–975224–9 (hardback); 978–0–19–065520–4 (paperback)
1. Japanese American women—California—Los Angeles—History—20th century.   2. Japanese
Americans—California—Los Angeles—History—20th century.   3. Japanese Americans—Cultural
assimilation—California—Los Angeles.   4. Female friendship—California—Los Angeles.   5. Teenage
girls—California—Los Angeles.   6. Los Angeles (Calif.)—Social conditions—20th century.   I. Title.
F869.L89J339 2014
973'.04956—dc23
2013040044

*This book is dedicated to the Nisei women
who built networks of friendship,
pushed social boundaries,
and danced.*

CONTENTS

ACKNOWLEDGMENTS

As I researched the networks of urban Nisei youth, I too benefited from the assistance and encouragement of community and scholarly networks. Many, many people have helped me and I apologize to anyone I have inadvertently omitted.

This project was sparked by the Nisei members of the Center for Japanese American Studies (CJAS) in San Francisco. After completing my Ph.D. dissertation about the history of a Japanese American farming community in the Central Valley of California, I was invited by the CJAS to give a talk about the childhood of rural Nisei in the 1930s. I sketched the routines of dawn-to-dusk work and education that framed the experiences of farm youth, noting racial constraints, the expectations of strict Issei parents, and romantic dreams influenced by radio and Hollywood. Afterward, the CJAS members asked if I had heard about the prewar lovelorn advice columns (*Nisei* lovelorn advice columns?!) and pen-pal club news in the San Francisco ethnic newspapers. Coming from a family with rural roots myself, I had had no idea. As they proceeded to top each other's stories of urban Japanese American youth activities before World War II, the tantalizing vision of a hitherto-unsuspected world flashed before me.

Oral history and personal records have been crucial to this project. For generously sharing their experiences and helping with my research, I thank Rose Honda, Mary Nishi Ishizuka, Esther Takei Nishio and Shig Nishio, Setsuko Matsunaga Nishi, Fumiko Fukuyama Ide, Mary Oyama Mittwer, Vicki Mittwer Littman, Joe Oyama, Lily Oyama Sasaki, Yasuo Sasaki, Kay Komai, Toyoko Kataoka Kanegai, Aiko Herzig-Yoshinaga, Sumi Hughes, Sophie Tajima Toriuchi, Elsie Uyematsu Osajima, Wakako Yamauchi, Noriko "Nikki" Sawada Bridges Flynn, Ikuko Kiriyama, Toshi Nagamori Ito, and William W.T. Hiroto. Gwen Muranaka, J.K. Yamamoto, Janice D. Tanaka, Kiyo Knight, Stefani Chisholm, Mia Rankin, and Melanie Nagahiro kindly assisted in my hunt for images.

For their insightful comments on my manuscript, I am indebted to Sachi Matsumoto, Vicki Ruiz, Jessica Wang, Ruth Bloch, Peggy Pascoe, Mary

Rothschild, and Bernice Zamora; two anonymous readers also provided critical feedback. Vicki Ruiz deserves a medal for reading so many drafts in the midst of her own pressing duties; her work and that of Peggy Pascoe and Judy Yung have especially helped me to think about the multiple roles of Nisei women within and outside the ethnic community. For her amazing editing, I am deeply grateful to Susan Ferber.

My life and research have been enriched by colleagues Ruth Bloch, Muriel McClendon, Melissa Meyer, Kate Norberg, Janice Reiff, Miriam Silverberg, Sharon Traweek, Jessica Wang, Joan Waugh, Mary Yeager, Emily Abel, Sharon Bays, Karen Brodkin, Carole Browner, Sandra Harding, Carollee Howes, Sondra Hale, Katherine King, Keith Camacho, Andrea Goldman, Toby Higbie, Lane Hirabayashi, Marilyn Alquizola, Marjorie Kagawa-Singer, Jinqi Ling, Bill Marotti, Gary Nash, Geoffrey Robinson, Alexander Saxton, Bruce Schulman, Tritia Toyota, David Yoo, Henry Yu, Min Zhou, Becky Smith, and Craig Manning. For their encouragement and sage advice, I thank Estelle Freedman, Victor Becerra, Ellen Brigham, Yvette Huginnie, Alice Killian, Ruthanne Lum McCunn, Greg Robinson, and Joyce Trifiletti.

For the opportunities to gain feedback on my work, I am grateful to Eileen Boris, Xiaojian Zhao, the Department of Feminist Studies, and the Department of Asian American Studies at the University of California, Santa Barbara; Ikuko Kiriyama and the Japanese American Historical Society of Southern California; Rosalyn Tonai and the National Japanese American Historical Society; and Roy Imazu and the Japanese American Community Center in Pacoima, California.

The perspectives of Japanese scholars have added important dimension to Japanese American studies and to my research. For the opportunities to present my work in Japan, I thank the Japanese Association of American Studies and the Organization of American Historians, Natsuki Aruga, Yoshiko Takita, Teruko Kumei, Noriko Shimada, Masako Iino, Fumiko Fujita, Rieko Ohki, Kikuyo Tanaka, Mariko Takagi-Kitayama, Yoko Tsujimoto, Eriko Yamamoto, Hiroshi and Ikumi Yanagisawa, and Rumi Yasutake.

My project received crucial support from the UCLA Asian American Studies Center directors Don Nakanishi and David Yoo; Asian American Studies Department chairs Lane Hirabayashi and Cindy Fan; History Department chairs Edward Alpers, David Myers, Teo Ruiz, and Richard Von Glahn; Christine Littleton, Vice Provost for Faculty Diversity and Development; and Dean of Social Sciences Scott Waugh. Many thanks!

I am grateful to the John Randolph and Dora Haynes Foundation for a research grant and to the University of California, Davis Humanities Institute for a year as a scholar in residence that aided my development of this project.

For helping me access a wide array of archival treasures and secondary sources at the UCLA Charles E. Young Research Library, I thank the staff of Special

Collections; Norma Corral, the Asian American Studies bibliographer; Diane McMorris and the staff of the Microfilm Reading Room; Charlotte Brown of the University Archives; and the expert sleuths of the Reference section. Special thanks are due to Marjorie Lee, head of the Asian American Studies Center Library and Reading Room, who provided crucial support and camaraderie. I am deeply grateful to the staff at the Japanese American National Museum, including Marie Masumoto, John Esaki, Clement Hanami, Margaret Wetherbee, Tomi Yoshikawa, Yoko Shimojo, Greg Kimura, Chris Paschild, Maria Kwong, Jane Nakasako, Sojin Kim, Brian Niiya, Darcie Iki, Daniel Lee, and Glen Kitayama. The archival staff of the library at California State University, Northridge introduced me to a terrific collection of YWCA documents. Seizo Oka, founder of the Japanese American Library in San Francisco, opened the first window into the prewar Nisei world through the pages of the *Shin Sekai* newspaper.

For their unflagging support, I thank the staffs of the UCLA Asian American Studies Center and the Asian American Studies Department: Russell Leong, Mary Kao, Glenn Omatsu, Arnold Pan, Tam Nguyen, Marjorie Lee, Meg Thornton, Betty Leung, Melanie de la Cruz-Viesca, Irene Soriano, Ann Chau, Sarah Chong, Meng-ning Li, Barbra Ramos, Ming Tu, Gena Hamamoto, Stacey Hirose, Barrett Korerat, Kenneth Kuo, Kehaulani Vaughn, Jessie Singh, Anne Bautista, and Natalia Yamashiro-Chogyoji.

Warm thanks to the graduate students who helped with this research: Stacey Hirose, Rumi Yasutake, Kristen Lee, Alfred Peredo Flores, and Rachel Shuen.

I have benefited from the research and collegiality of many scholars, including Roger Daniels, Eiichiro Azuma, Gary Okihiro, Gordon Chang, Mark Dean Johnson, Karin Higa, Angela Oh, Randy Sakamoto, Jennifer Helgren, and Lon Kurashige. Greg Robinson generously shared with me a copy of *Gyo-Sho*. Jennifer Malia McAndrew kindly allowed me to read her dissertation. Martin Manalansan and Robert Ji-Song Ku offered thoughtful reflections on the food-ways portion of this research.

My father Terry Teruo Matsumoto gave me my first childhood glimpses of Little Tokyo and central Los Angeles: the curtained booths and Cantonese dishes of the Far East Café on First Street; the old produce market on Central Avenue where so many Issei and Nisei toiled; fresh maguro eaten at a sushi bar. This was the start of my seeing the area as a place of both work and leisure delights. For introducing me to other Japanese American communities and for their support, I am also grateful to Eileen Aiko Matsumoto and Janice Fujii.

My Nisei mother Sachi Fujii Matsumoto grew up in then-rural East Oakland in northern California, where her family engaged in truck farming. When I first told her about the dances, parties, and outings I found detailed in the prewar ethnic newspapers, she exclaimed, "I just knew those city kids were having more fun than we were!" Despite her distance from urban pleasures and excitement, my mother has given me the greatest insight into the lives of the young Nisei. She reflects the dedication, creativity, and generosity that have infused Nisei women's activities, past and present.

Permissions

I am grateful to the following journals and presses for permission to adapt material from my previously published articles:

Apple Pie and *Makizushi*: Japanese American Women Sustaining Family and Community, in Robert Ji-Song Ku, Martin F. Manalansan IV, and Anita Mannur, eds. *Eating Asian America, A Food Studies Reader.* © 2013 New York University.

Desperately Seeking 'Deirdre': Gender Roles, Multicultural Relations, and Nisei Women Writers of the 1930s. *Frontiers: A Journal of Women Studies* 12, No. 1 (1991); and Japanese American Women during World War II, *Frontiers: A Journal of Women Studies* 8, No. 1 (1984). By permission of University of Nebraska Press.

Japanese American Girls' Clubs in Los Angeles during the 1920s and 1930s, in Shirley Hune and Gail M. Nomura, eds. *Asian/Pacific Islander American Women, An Historical Anthology.* © 2003 New York University.

Japanese American Women and the Creation of Urban Nisei Culture in the 1930s, in Valerie J. Matsumoto and Blake Allmendinger, eds. *Over the Edge: Remapping the American West.* © 1999 by the Regents of the University of California. Published by the University of California Press.

Nisei Daughters' Courtship and Romance in Los Angeles before World War II, in Jennifer Lee and Min Zhou, eds. *Asian American Youth: Culture, Identity, and Ethnicity.* © 2004 Routledge. By permission of Taylor and Francis Group.

Redefining Expectations: Nisei Women in the 1930s. *California History, the Magazine of the California Historical Society* (Spring 1994). © 1994 by the Regents of the University of California. Published by the University of California Press.

I thank Rutgers University Press for permission to use a poem by Mitsuye Yamada, "My Home Town This Earth," *Camp Notes and Other Writings* (1998), and fiction excerpts from Hisaye Yamamoto, "The Brown House," "Life among the Oil Fields, A Memoir," "Yoneko's Earthquake," and "Seventeen Syllables," *Seventeen Syllables and Other Stories* (1988).

City Girls

Introduction

In 1926 Akatsuki Sakano, an irate (and presumably older) Nisei man, wrote to the editor of the English-language section of the Los Angeles *Rafu Shimpo* newspaper to complain about "these slick, knock-'em-dead sheiks and these painted, red-hot shebas that strut about the streets of Little Tokio." Although he included men in his tirade, he singled out women's bodies and fashion. Sakano criticized the Nisei women as "short-skirted baby dolls with their artificial rose-bud lips and their languishing, mascara'ed eyelashes" who "arrogantly displayed" their "knock-kneed, bowshaped, overgrown limbs." He expressed dismay that these "sheiks and shebas" were "respectable members of the churches and even Sunday School teachers and leaders of their young people's societies."[1]

Viewing the youth clubs as just a "rendezvous for amorously inclined males and females," Sakano offered a blistering critique of the proliferation of Nisei organizations.[2] He began with what he called the "little kids" clubs—probably junior high school level—and then moved on to the high school girls' clubs, the co-ed social service groups, women's athletic clubs, church-related youth leagues, and even those sponsored by the Young Women's Christian Association (YWCA) and the Young Men's Christian Association (YMCA). On the college level, he blasted the Japanese Student Christian Association as well as a Nisei sorority and fraternity.[3] Sakano's lengthy diatribe certainly brought into view the existence of an impressive array of clubs. In 1936 writer Joe Oyama reported that in Los Angeles there were "some 66 second generation Japanese organizations, whose members range from 18 years of age and up" and 104 such groups in southern California.[4] Had Oyama included the clubs for younger boys and girls, the figure would have been even higher. Indeed, the *Rafu Shimpo* estimated in 1940 that there were some 400 Nisei youth organizations in southern California.[5]

Stung by Sakano's criticism, the Nisei women quickly leaped to the defense of their clubs. Lily Satow—poet, "ace basketballer," and later a Japanese YWCA secretary—decried Sakano's knowledge of the young people's clubs as very superficial. She also suggested that "The most probable explanation for his vituperative attitude is that the poor fish must have been disappointed in love, perhaps by one of the very 'painted, short-skirted, bow-legged shebas' whom he so strongly condemns."[6] Another woman wrote, "To my mind, he's a fogey-faced dumb nit-wit wot ain't gotta chance with the so-called shingled Shebas." The writer, who defiantly identified herself as "A Sheba," went on to assert that the network of Nisei youth clubs in outlying communities served as "the only means of getting young folks together."[7] In fact, Japanese Americans and other racial-minority youth were excluded from many extracurricular high school and college organizations, such as social fraternities and sororities; isolated rural Nisei particularly lacked opportunities for socializing. "A Sheba" also suggested that group activities might exert social control in checking romantic impulses. As she put it, "Are not such clubs an aid in keeping young folks from pairing off, as is the tendency where there aren't any clubs?"[8] As Sakano suspected, the Nisei organizations facilitated mixed-sex socializing and courtship; however, reflecting the sentiments of "A Sheba," such club events were peer monitored and offered a much wider range of activities.

FOCUS

This book recovers and explores the forgotten world of urban Nisei girls' ethnocultural networks in California. By the 1920s Nisei girls' clubs had taken root in Los Angeles and provided a key venue in which young urban women could claim modern femininity, an American identity, and public space.[9] These groups served as a bulwark against racial discrimination, offering a bridge between the immigrant community's expectations of young women and the lure of popular culture. Through their organizations, second-generation Japanese American women gained access to recreation, cultural education, social skills, and lead-

ARG.

ership training, attending religious youth conferences and making field trips to museums and businesses. Clubs promoted friendship, teamwork, and social service among young women, while also facilitating their pursuit of courtship and romantic love. Tracing the everyday activities of urban girls highlights the roles they have played in bridging the cultures of their ethnic community and mainstream society, whether introducing new foods and rituals to family and neighbors or dancing in kimono at civic events. Their social bonds would endure beyond their teenage years and would prove valuable during the World War II incarceration and postwar rebuilding. Both before and after the war, Japanese American women's ethnocultural networks provided vital support, understanding, and a measure of agency for youth who faced racial and economic barriers to full participation in American society.

Japanese imm. & settlement

Japanese immigration and settlement in the U.S. West had been inflected by nativist discrimination, legal restrictions, and tense U.S.-Japan diplomatic relations. Like the Chinese before them, the Issei (Japanese immigrants) faced the opposition of an immigration exclusion movement fueled by racism, political expediency, and fear of economic competition.[10] In 1908 the United States and Japan negotiated the "Gentlemen's Agreement," which cut off the flow of laborers from Japan, but contained a crucial loophole that permitted the entry of family members of Japanese already resident in the country. The next decade would see the peak of Japanese women's immigration, as wives reunited with their husbands, and brides journeyed to new homes with men who had returned to Japan to marry. They came seeking economic opportunity, adventure, and sometimes a fresh start, as in the case of Ura Sawada, who in 1920 escaped a hometown scandal through marriage to an Issei farmer in southern California.[11] An estimated half of the immigrating women were, like Sawada, "picture brides" who met their new husbands for the first time at the dock. The Immigration Act of 1924, which prohibited the entry of most Asians, ended the influx of Japanese and signaled the triumph of the exclusionist movement.[12]

Nonetheless, with the arrival of women, Japanese American communities— and the population of second-generation youth—grew faster than those of other early Asian immigrant groups on the West Coast.[13] The presence of the U.S.-born Nisei deepened their parents' stakes in this country, despite the obstacles confronting them in every arena of life.

Both Issei and Nisei faced a battery of discriminatory laws and quotidian hostility. Ineligible for naturalization, the Issei could not vote.[14] Several western states, led by California, passed alien land laws to prevent Japanese and other Asians from owning or leasing agricultural land.[15] California also joined a number of western states in passing antimiscegenation statutes barring people of Asian and African descent from marrying whites.[16] Throughout the West, racial housing covenants enforced residential segregation, limiting the areas where people of color and Jews could live. Although the Nisei, as citizens by birth, had voting rights and could hold title to land, they were subject to antimiscegenation laws and housing covenants, as well as to discrimination in the job market and in public facilities. These very real restrictions shaped the lives of Nisei women as they came of age in southern California.

Because they were often excluded from school clubs and extracurricular activities during the two decades before World War II, many young Japanese Americans turned to their peers for camaraderie and recreation. Nisei clubs spread rapidly along the Pacific coast in cities such as Seattle, San Francisco, and San Diego. Los Angeles, home to the largest population of Japanese Americans, boasted the most extensive youth networks. In addition to the church- and Y-sponsored clubs, young people formed organizations to study Japanese culture, promote Nisei literature and art, develop their dramatic and musical talents, and play sports. Reflecting the lively social world developed by the urban youth, the 1938 holiday issue of the *Rafu Shimpo* noted that there had been only one day (July 20) in the entire year on which no Nisei club had scheduled an event.[17] On some days, young Nisei could choose from among 10 to 15 different activities.[18]

From the 1920s to the mid-1930s, clubs were primarily an urban phenom-
enon, as public transportation and neighborhood settlement patterns put social
and recreational activities within the reach of Nisei girls and boys. A club meeting
or movie might be a short streetcar ride away or within walking distance. Even
though many teenagers helped out in family businesses, they were more likely
to have leisure time than the rural Nisei, whose farm labor stretched from dawn
until past dusk. By the late 1930s, though, youth clubs in rural communities
had also increased considerably, many of them rooted in the local Nihongakko
(Japanese language and culture schools).[19] Still, city youth had access to a smor-
gasbord of cultural, social, and educational activities of which many of their rural
cousins could only dream.

As Akatsuki Sakano sensed with alarm, the spread of Nisei clubs was connected with significant shifts in young women's behavior. The Nisei women's
bobbed hair, flapper attire, and pursuit of romantic love represented the hallmarks of the Modern Girl who emerged around the world during the 1920s and
1930s.[20] In addition to changes in dress and hairstyle, black and white women
formed vigorous club movements, through which they sponsored cultural events
and advocated civic reforms, usually to protect women and children. As growing numbers of young middle-class women began to attend college and pursue
careers, the "New Woman" emerged, much to the alarm of conservatives who
predicted the disintegration of the family and the American character.[21] Both
feminists and conservatives were disconcerted by the flamboyant appearance of
the flapper, who seemed to combine personal independence and income with
extravagant consumer spending, lack of social responsibility, and overt displays
of sexuality.

The appeal of modernity, defined as American, captivated youth in Los
Angeles's Little Tokyo, as well as in Tokyo, Japan. In both settings the "moga"
(modern girl) and her male counterpart the "mobo" (modern boy) excited interest as they "strut[ted] back and forth" along the streets.[22] A few weeks after the
Rafu Shimpo published Sakano's letter, a Nisei woman, Mrs. K.S. Inu, contributed an article on her own perspective after five years of living abroad, including
a year in Japan. She attributed generational conflict in Japan to the eagerness of
youth "to adopt American customs and ideals" and criticized the Nisei for being
"swept in the same whirl pool of desire and doing." She linked the pursuit of
modernity, Americanness, and consumption, calling it a tragedy that "we are so
mad at the business of becoming Americanized or ultra-modern that our better
judgment or the guidings of our elders have flown to the winds. As a result we
are acquiring the very latest, fastest, and wildest in this jazzy age and think that
it is American!"[23] Indeed, the *Rafu Shimpo's* advertisements for transformative
face creams and sleek dresses display the reach of gendered consumer culture
into the ethnic enclave.

Mrs. Inu's reference to the "latest, fastest, and wildest" encompassed not only commodities, but also new modes of socializing, for her chief warning concerned the dangers of "dancing without moderation verging on madness."[24] Like Sakano, though in a more temperate tone, she drew a connection between clubs and heterosexual interaction, suggesting that dancing had become a preoccupation of the Nisei organizations. This, of course, was part of their attraction for youth.

Socializing

For the second-generation Japanese Americans, class status and racial barriers restricted access to the accoutrements of fashionable modernity and commercialized leisure.[25] Most Nisei daughters, like many women of color, contributed to the family economy, whether through paid or unpaid work, and had little disposable income. Even if they could afford it, their access to commodified leisure proved limited because many restaurants, movie theaters, hotels, and other recreational facilities refused to serve racial-minority people. In addition, their embrace of romantic love and personal choice caused conflict with immigrant parents whose marriages had been arranged and who sought to instill in their daughters traditional feminine virtues of quiet obedience and restraint. Daughters faced greater parental control and surveillance than sons, since maintaining a chaste reputation was a marker of family respectability within the ethnic community. In this light, peer-monitored club participation offered both a haven from racial exclusion and a parent-approved way to sample some of the pleasures of popular culture.

limitations

Nisei youth organizations constituted part of the flowering of girls' and boys' clubs across the country, particularly in urban areas, propelled by new ideas about "adolescence" as a stage in life. The first organizations—the YMCA and YWCA—were established in England and moved to the United States in the 1850s and 1860s. By the end of the nineteenth century the Y had founded segregated ethnic branches for African Americans, Native Americans, and Chinese Americans. In the early twentieth century other national organizations took root, such as the Camp Fire Girls, the Girl Scouts USA, the YWCA's Girl Reserves movement, and the B'nai B'rith Girls.[26] In the 1920s a host of African American girls' clubs also formed, many as junior auxiliaries of African American women's organizations.[27] Nisei girls' clubs varied in their affiliations: In addition to the YWCA, some were sponsored by local Christian churches and Buddhist temples, while others began as independent groups formed by neighborhood friends or, like the Chi Alpha Delta sorority, by schoolmates.

idea of "adolescence"

Despite the enthusiastic participation of racial-minority girls and boys in the growing youth organizations and activities of the early twentieth century, they have been largely absent from histories of adolescence, which have mainly focused on mainstream white culture. The histories of immigrant families have also tended to overlook the roles of adolescents in shaping ethnic cultural

HISTORIOG.

ARG.

practices. Examining the club activities of Nisei girls reveals their multifaceted influence within the Japanese American family, from embracing American holidays to pushing the boundaries of feminine propriety within the ethnic community. Their work and leisure pursuits make visible the ways in which their social lives both aligned with and diverged from those of their white and other racial/ethnic peers.[28] Fumiko Fukuyama Ide, for example, was the editor of the Belmont High School newspaper as well as an active member of groups such as the French Club and the Ephebians, but much of her socializing took place within the Nisei circles of the Tartanettes, a girls' club affiliated with the Union Church in Little Tokyo, and Boy Scout Troop 379 to which her brothers belonged.[29] Although levels of interracial acceptance and animosity varied in schools and neighborhoods throughout southern California, the burgeoning network of Nisei clubs reflected the need for a welcoming social space.

In California, Japanese American girls, like other Asian American young women, developed lively social worlds with other club members within their own ethnic community. In San Francisco, Chinese American girls flocked to the Chinese YWCA and groups such as the Square and Circle Club or the Mei Wahs, a renowned basketball team.[30] In the smaller Chinese American community of Los Angeles, the Chinese Girls Glee Club, the Mei Wah Club, the Kuan Ying Girls Club, and the YWCA-affiliated Lowa Girls Club channeled young women's energies into sports and social service. Initially formed to support China war relief efforts in 1938, the award-winning Mei Wah Girls Drum Corps met weekly to practice in Chinatown parking lots and dazzled crowds at many civic events and parades.[31] Ronyoung Kim's novel *Clay Walls* suggests that Korean American girls in Los Angeles also enjoyed club activities before World War II—the teenaged character Faye and her friends in the Mugunghwa Club looked forward to Friday night dancing with their male peers in a Korean community hall.[32] Common threads of recreation, community service projects, and co-ed socializing wove through the fabric of Chinese American, Japanese American, and Korean American young women's club activities during the 1920s and 1930s. With the largest numbers, Nisei girls' organizations were particularly visible in southern California.

Tracing young Nisei women's clubs reveals linkages between prewar and postwar Japanese American histories, long obscured by the community's forced uprooting and incarceration during World War II. The experience they gained in forming peer groups—including leadership training, planning and hosting social events, carrying out community service projects, fund raising, and learning teamwork on and off the court—contained the seeds of postwar rebuilding. Indeed, as sociologist Evelyn Nakano Glenn suggests, women have "emerged over time as prime movers in the organizational life" of the ethnic community.[33]

ARG.

The quotidian practices of Japanese American girls reflect their engagement *Ruiz– "cultural coalescence"* in what historian Vicki Ruiz has termed "cultural coalescence"—the process by which, to the extent permitted by societal and familial circumstances, first- and second-generation individuals have improvised, adapted, and maintained cultural forms, from everyday customs to holiday festivities.[34] This concept is particularly useful for considering the multiethnic landscape of prewar south- ern California. In the process of cultural coalescence, the immigrant Japanese community and dominant European American society were primary sources for Nisei youth, but they also interacted with members of other ethnic groups, dancing with Mexican American schoolmates and savoring foods introduced by African Americans and other neighbors, for example. As a child living in Boyle Heights in East Los Angeles, Rose Honda learned about tortillas from the Mexican neighbors who called her "Rosita"; to shop, her mother "would walk us up to Brooklyn Avenue to the Jewish stores." "So at an early age," Honda said, "I believe I was exposed to a few different cultures."[35] Both Nisei girls and boys engaged in cultural coalescence, but because of women's role as culture bearers, their choices had particular impact in shaping Japanese American families and communities. Like other ethnic women, Japanese American women did much of the work of maintaining ethnic traditions, such as organizing holiday celebra- tions and preparing food.[36] Examining Nisei women's activities reveals the ways *ARG.* in which they created and adapted cultural forms in their daily interactions with family, friends, teachers, classmates, and neighbors within the constraints of the Great Depression and regional race relations.

Making claims to modern femininity in the prewar United States was espe- cially complicated for women of color. For example, while expressing his dis- approval of young women's provocative appearance in Little Tokyo, Akatsuki Sakano displayed his internalization of white standards of beauty, remarking that if the Nisei shebas "had halfway straight legs, no one would raise a kick" about their short skirts.[37] This stinging comment references the gendered and racial- ized insult sometimes aimed at Nisei girls by Nisei boys—but not vice versa— about having "daikon ashi," legs like thick white radishes, with the implied comparison being the stereotypically longer, straighter, and more attractive legs of European Americans. Young Nisei women defied such racial pigeonholing, not only through their choice of fashions, but also by dancing, competing in sports, embracing ideals of romantic love, and seeking access to public space, activities facilitated by their networks. Nisei girls' clubs served as important *ARG.* spaces of ethnocultural peer association in which girls could claim modern femi- ninity and American status while continuing to serve their families and com- munities. Maintaining cordial ties with Issei elders and institutions—through cultural performance, social service, and representing the ethnic community at civic events—remained important to Nisei women, despite generational synthesis

tensions. For young, urban Japanese American women, the most viable synthesis of the Modern Girl and the good musume (daughter) might well have been the Nisei club girl.

During the prewar period, relatively few Japanese American women were active in traditional electoral politics, although some older Nisei women were involved in political organizations—for example, senior journalist Ruth Kurata served as charter president of the Japanese American Young Democratic Club in 1938.[38] The exclusion of the noncitizen Issei from the voting booth hampered second-generation engagement. The youth of the Nisei (whose average age at the start of World War II was 18) and the immigrant community's expectations regarding the appropriate behavior of daughters also limited their participation. However, if one defines as political the development of alternative places of belonging in the face of racial exclusion and interprets efforts to participate in popular youth culture as the claiming of public space in dance halls, skating rinks, and theaters, then urban Nisei girls' clubs can be considered "political." In their clubs young women gained leadership training and organizing experience that would prove useful in the postwar reconstruction of Japanese American communities and, in the 1970s and 1980s, would help to mobilize the Japanese American movement for wartime redress and reparations.

The Japanese American newspapers in Los Angeles constituted a crucial source for recovering girls' organizations. In 1926, the first letter to the editor of the *Rafu Shimpo*'s fledgling English-language section came from a Nisei girl, part of the growing second-generation readership targeted by the ethnic press. Cora Kaoru Asakura welcomed the Nisei-focused section with delight, saying, "I hope we may put our club news in it too."[39] Announcements and coverage of club activities quickly filled the English-language pages of the *Rafu Shimpo*—the oldest Japanese American newspaper in Los Angeles, established in 1903—and its rival, the *Kashu Mainichi*. The *Kashu Mainichi*, which became known for its strong literary features, had an English-language section from its founding in 1932.[40] Coverage of girls' club news and youth reportage distinguished the Nisei-edited English sections from the Japanese-language sections geared to the Issei.

From the beginning of the Nisei-run English-language sections, women served as editors, journalists, columnists, and literary contributors, as well as readers. The *Rafu Shimpo*'s first English-section editor was Louise Suski, a member of the Blue Triangles and the co-ed Japanese Student Christian Association.[41] The *Rafu* regaled readers with richly detailed accounts of Nisei club meetings and athletic events, as well as offering a forum for Nisei literary efforts and discussion of topics relevant to the second generation. Ongoing conversations about women's roles generated particularly lively, sometimes heated, reader responses. Judging from the contributors to and content of the English-language sections, the prewar readership appears to have consisted primarily of high school and college age Nisei.

Youth activities continued to fill the pages of the ethnic press during the World War II incarceration and postwar resettlement. Every camp had its own newspaper, subject to varying degrees of control by the administrators of the War Relocation Authority. The *Manzanar Free Press*, the *Poston Chronicle*, and the Amache camp newspaper, the Granada *Pioneer*, provide glimpses of life within camps where many Japanese Americans from southern California were sent. After Japanese Americans were permitted to return to the West Coast, the *Rafu Shimpo* resumed publication in 1946, including a one-page English-language section—a fraction of its prewar peak of eight pages.

Oral history interviews and memoirs also constitute rich sources for the experiences and insights of Japanese American women.[42] The Nisei's memories bring to life prewar activities and Issei enterprise. For example, Esther Takei Nishio described the unusual economic niche of her parents, who started carnival concessions at the Venice Amusement Pier, offering a variety of games, including one "where you threw baseballs at milk bottles to win a prize, and...a shooting gallery where you shot corks at candy bars and knocked them off the shelf." Venice, California, was then "a glamorous place" with a grand ballroom and a dragon slide. As a child, Nishio "used to be on the pier all the time, because I was too young to be left home alone. So I'd be playing inside the booth. When there was music at the grand ballroom, I'd go in and dance....My friends and I would get to ride on all the rides for free....."[43] The joy of club outings and parties also surfaces in the oral histories of women such as Fumiko Fukuyama Ide, whose dance card was always full in her high school years. During the 1930s, Ide and her club, the Tartanettes, learned to organize socials with scant resources: "It wasn't very elaborate because none of us had any money to do that. We made our own invitations. And we always had punch." Adept at the foxtrot, waltz, and swing, she remembered, "We really danced up a storm!"[44] The Nisei's recollections also shed light on the challenges of facing racial barriers, from the Great Depression to postwar resettlement, and the range of women's work in sustaining families and communities.[45]

World War II uprooting and incarceration not only dashed many Nisei dreams and shattered Japanese American communities, but they have also overshadowed the vitality of Little Tokyo and other prewar ethnic enclaves. Recovering Nisei girls' clubs reveals the intricacy of the second generation's negotiation of roles—as cultural mediators, workers, and ethnic representatives. The first half of this book examines prewar club life, focusing on organizations during the 1920s and 1930s. Chapter 1 places the growth and significance of urban girls' clubs within the context of the expectations of immigrant parents and West Coast race relations. Through their organizations, Nisei daughters gained entry to a broader world, interacting with boys' clubs and Nisei from other regions as well as attending interracial and interethnic gatherings. Chapter 2 explores the multifaceted role of young Nisei women as cultural agents, both within and outside the ethnic enclave. Japanese American foodways, cultural performance, courtship, and family rituals reflect their influence. Chapter 3 focuses on a rich strand of women's involvement in organizing second-generation networks, tracing the endeavors of Nisei women poets, fiction writers, essayists, and columnists to create a distinctive ethnic and generational literary voice.

Women's networks and skills were severely tested during wartime incarceration and resettlement. Throughout the war years, as Chapter 4 chronicles, Nisei women continued to participate in clubs and do a range of work—as teachers, nurses' aides, farm laborers, secretaries, domestic workers, and factory operatives—within the bleak confines of the camps and in new terrains in the Midwest and East. Chapter 5 charts the postwar return of Japanese Americans to southern California, showing how women's organizational ties and experience as well as their labor proved critical to rebuilding families and communities.

Urban Nisei women's organizational affinities constitute a strong vibrant thread throughout the decades of this study. Girls and young women formed ethnocultural networks to counter racial discrimination and exclusion. They supported kin and community through myriad activities, many of them sponsored by Japanese American youth clubs: During the Great Depression their charitable efforts ranged from donating food baskets to needy families and holding benefit dances to sewing nightgowns for orphans. Of course, group membership afforded access to an enticing range of (mostly) parent-sanctioned mixed-sex social and leisure pursuits linked with modern femininity.

One of the numerous young urban Nisei women who found camaraderie and recreation through a 1930s peer network was Aiko Herzig-Yoshinaga, a leader in the postwar redress movement. She recalled, "Having joined a group of other girls in the neighborhood to form a social club, *The Junior Misses*...gave us girls opportunities (and excuses) to get together with other Nisei boys' clubs." A YWCA Girl Reserves club, the Junior Misses enjoyed jitterbugging as well as beach picnics and sports. She noted, "The girls' clubs had names such as the *Debutantes* and *Queen Esthers*, while the boys' clubs were named *Mustangs, Knights, and other manly names.* We held volleyball, baseball games, and held dances to get to know the boys."[46] Her immigrant Japanese parents disapproved of single couples dating, but allowed her to socialize with other young men and women in group activities.

Herzig-Yoshinaga's memories of childhood and adolescence, like those of many second-generation Japanese Americans in southern California, reflect prewar racial boundaries. Although most of her classmates were European American, her friends were Japanese American.[47] "My days at Los Angeles

High School were, on the whole, a good experience," she wrote, "despite a feeling (on my part, at least) of not being truly a part of the primarily white student body population."[48] This sense became a painful realization when the school principal announced to her and the other Nisei in the 1942 graduating class that they did not deserve to get their diplomas because "your country bombed Pearl Harbor."[49] Navigating between the racial constraints of the larger society and the gender-role expectations of Japanese immigrant elders, many Nisei daughters—especially urban girls like Aiko Herzig-Yoshinaga and the Junior Misses—found rapport and understanding in ethnocultural youth organizations. As club members, cultural mediators, and workers they helped shape prewar enclaves in southern California and forged enduring networks of friendship.

1

The Social World of the Urban Nisei

As a young teenager in Los Angeles in the early 1930s, Kay Kyoko Moritani Komai joined the Blue Circles, a popular YWCA Girl Reserves group. Born in 1920 in Berkeley, California, Komai was raised in Los Angeles by a devoted aunt and uncle; her uncle worked as a gardener and her aunt as a domestic for a white family in Beverly Hills.[1] Despite her adoptive parents' financial losses in the 1929 stock market crash, Komai's main memories were not of Depression Era privations, but of the round of activities she enjoyed in a Nisei girls' club. She and her friends first joined the Girl Scouts, which met at the Centenary United Methodist Church, a Japanese congregation.[2] By the time she was in ninth or tenth grade, the girls had become Blue Circles, affiliated with the Girl Reserves movement of the YWCA. Averaging between 15 and 20 members, the Blue Circles played basketball and softball, coached by young men from the Nisei boys' clubs, who turned out to cheer them on at games.[3] They also organized parties at roller-skating rinks and enjoyed outings to the YWCA's Eliza Cottage, a Hermosa Beach house. As Komai happily recalled, dancing was a favorite pastime. The Blue Circles were "social butterflies," delighting in "exchanges" with various Nisei boys' clubs such as the Sequoias from the All People's Church: The girls would serve punch and cookies, and the boys would bring the record player and records. The boisterous Blue Circles had a reputation for being fun and noisy, always talking and laughing the loudest, as well as having the best refreshments.[4]

Throughout the 1920s and 1930s, Japanese American young women's ethnocultural organizational affinities gave rise to numerous groups such as the Blue Circles. They flourished in southern California to such an extent that the Nisei club girl became a recognizable "type." Many of the more than 300 Nisei youth clubs listed in the *Rafu Shimpo*'s 1937 holiday club directory were girls' groups.[5] By the eve of World War II, the *Rafu Shimpo*'s estimates of the number of Nisei youth organizations ranged from 400 to 600, with young women swelling the number.[6] They were so prominent a feature of the Japanese American social landscape that the *Kashu Mainichi* profiled the female club member in its New Year's issue for 1941. The article attributed the large number of girls'

organizations in "Li'l Tokio"[7] to the influence of the YWCA, in fact interchangeably using the terms "typical nisei club girl" and "typical nisei 'Y' girl." Stated the journalist, "Out of the thousands of girls who come into direct contact with the Japanese YWCA, many belong to the 29 affiliated 'Y' clubs in this city or to the WAU (Women's Athletic Union) where they find uninhibited outlet[s] for their social and athletic activities."[8] A host of other institutions, primarily Buddhist and Christian churches, also sponsored young women's organizations, co-ed groups, and boys' clubs.

This chapter explores how Nisei girls and young women found in their clubs a haven from racial discrimination and parental pressures, as well as a place to gain skills. To understand the importance of their clubs, it is necessary to examine the social world of the second generation—the expectations of the immigrant community, the influence of school and church, the racial barriers they faced, the economic responsibilities they shouldered, and the enticing leisure pursuits offered by city life. Peer networks facilitated young women's access to new opportunities for recreation, leadership training, and romance. Many forged in these groups lifelong bonds of friendship and understanding. As of 2000, the Blue Circles continued to meet once or twice a year, their loud happy laughter still attracting attention whenever they got together at a restaurant.[9]

Investigating Nisei club activities in the 1920s and 1930s reveals a range of interactions among members of different ethnic and racial groups. Even in an era of racial discrimination, the Japanese American community was not completely isolated from mainstream American culture. Although exclusionary practices largely fueled the formation of ethnic youth organizations, the Nisei clubs facilitated social and athletic exchanges with white and other ethnic youth groups and exposed members to non–Japanese American guest speakers and public institutions. Studying young women's groups reveals how they not only challenged but also sometimes reinforced the racial dynamics of the era. Developing their own strong networks enabled them to counter segregation and to interact with a range of white and other racial-ethnic girls, often members of sister organizations. However, reportage of their events also shows their acceptance of some racial stereotypes, particularly regarding African Americans.

Within their clubs, Nisei daughters pushed the boundaries of gender behavior expected by their immigrant parents, while also maintaining some traditional gender roles. For example, they engaged in flirting and Western-style couples' dancing, of which many Issei elders disapproved. Indeed, young women often took the initiative in organizing mixed-sex social activities such as dances. At the same time, they routinely prepared the food for social events with boys' clubs.

As Kay Komai's account suggests, club social events created an accepted space for urban Nisei courtship.[10] The second generation neared adulthood influenced by notions of heterosexual romance and individual choice celebrated on the silver screen and in music and magazines. They also faced constraints from both the expectations of their immigrant parents—virtually all of whom had had arranged marriages—and the racial strictures of the larger society, in the form of California miscegenation laws banning marriages between whites and people of African or Asian descent.[11] In this context, Nisei youth clubs offered a comfortable peer-monitored environment in which to meet potential partners. Group activities protected young women's reputation within the ethnic enclave while providing opportunities for flirtation, courtship, and mixed-sex recreation.

Club activities often facilitated young women's participation in cultural coalescence. The Nisei's social and recreational pursuits, their games, dances, attire, music, and food, reflect their process of selecting and adapting cultural forms from an array of models in multiethnic southern California. Young women's choices would become highly visible to peers and elders in the growing Japanese American communities in Los Angeles.

"The Land Where the Eyes of the Nisei Are Focused"

By the second decade of the twentieth century, Los Angeles had become the major population center of Japanese Americans in the United States. The Census Bureau recorded 8,641 living in Los Angeles County in 1910. By 1930 the number had grown to 35,000, of whom half were U.S.-born Nisei. As Joe Oyama, a Nisei writer, observed in 1936: "Los Angeles is to the Japanese what Harlem is to the Negro, San Francisco is to the Chinese, Stockton to the Filipinos, and Hollywood to the Mid-Western girl."[12] A year later, Nisei journalist Bill Hosokawa echoed him, calling it "the coming town for the second generation."[13]

Japanese American neighborhoods and businesses formed in many parts of southern California, reflecting patterns of work and residential segregation. In Los Angeles County the trade in Japanese American–grown fruit and vegetables fueled a thriving wholesale produce market (a $26 million business) as well as numerous fruit, grocery, and dairy stores. Early communities took shape in the neighborhoods of Virgil Avenue (northwest of downtown), 10th Street (west of downtown), and West Jefferson Street—the "Southwest" area—home to a large African American enclave. At least half the Japanese men worked as day laborers and gardeners in Hollywood and the Wilshire area.[14] A settlement in the Sawtelle area of West Los Angeles furnished the landscape gardeners who tended estates in Westwood, Beverly Hills, and Bel Air. In the Boyle Heights area of East Los Angeles, a community took root as Japanese established plant nurseries and farms. In the south bay, Gardena—which remains a Japanese American center—also developed as an agricultural and gardening settlement. A Japanese

American fishing and cannery community formed on Terminal Island across from San Pedro. Because racial discrimination barred Japanese from buying or renting homes in more desirable areas, Japanese enclaves were often located near commercial or industrial sites and frequently in proximity to African American and Mexican American neighborhoods.[15] For example, Fumiko Fukuyama Ide grew up on Adams, 26 blocks south of her father's hardware store in Little Tokyo; Japanese, Italian, Chinese, African American, and Greek families lived on the street, with a German butcher, a Chinese store, and a Jewish-owned drugstore.[16]

The hub of these diverse communities was Little Tokyo, or "Li'l Tokio"[17] as it was often then written, a cluster of stores, restaurants, barber shops, hotels, and homes in downtown Los Angeles, centering on First Street between Alameda and Los Angeles Streets. Bookstores, bathhouses, ethnic newspapers, confectionery and tofu shops, photographers' studios, department stores, and other businesses supplied the needs of Japanese immigrants and their children. Passersby stopped for bowls of steaming nabeyaki-udon or chop suey at small cafes in the winter, and in the summer went to the Iwaki fountain to cool off with Cokes and ice cream sodas. Women bought vegetables and Japanese kitchen staples and eyed enticing arrays of colorful fabric. On Saturdays and Sundays, hundreds filled the seats of the Fuji Theatre to see films from Japan. Here farm families came on weekends to shop, job-seekers headed to employment agencies, and both Issei and Nisei attended church and club meetings, danced, gambled, and went to movies, theater performances, and music recitals with friends. During the Great Depression, nightlife dwindled in the Japanese American urban center, which became "a village where the sidewalks are rolled up and taken in at ten o'clock."[18] Nevertheless, the lights of Little Tokyo and Los Angeles continued to shine with elusive promise. As Poppy Yama, a Nisei writer, rhapsodized: "Neons of the brightest hue, and golden cobwebs of lights strung out in a riot all over the city. As if the stars of the midnight heavens had tumbled down upon earth, the dark sky is a bright smiling mirror."[19]

The prospect of living in this bustling, vigorous community thrilled Nisei newcomer Mary Korenaga, who initially viewed Los Angeles as "the land of opportunity and fortune, the land of eternal sunshine and flower, and the land where the eyes of the Nisei are focused."[20] To Korenaga and many of her peers, city life glittered with the allure of modernity and excitement; equally appealing was the urban Nisei's reputation for accomplishment and sophistication. After a while Korenaga found her dreams of paradise fading in the face of the rambling, decentered city and her discovery that the local second generation seemed less extraordinary than she had expected. Nevertheless, she took delight in the busy Japanese American community and, as a newspaper columnist and poet, she became one of the second-generation women who documented and critiqued the dynamics of the lively youth networks in southern California.

From the perspective of one Nisei male journalist, the demeanor and recreational activities of Nisei girls of southern California distinguished them from their counterparts in other regions. In 1939 he characterized them as friendly, athletic, fond of movies, and less conservative than their northern California or East Coast sisters, whom they greatly outnumbered. He wrote, "The sunshine and...the many opportunities to indulge in outdoor sports makes the young ladies more carefree and sociable. This is especially true at dances, in outdoor activities and other socials." He also noted with approval the prevailing fashions: "As to dress, the flashy sweaters and skirts of Southern California cannot be equalled. The sportswear blends with the carefree atmosphere and gay spirit."[21] His description beguilingly reflects the greater access to leisure pursuits and thriving peer networks of urban Nisei youth in southern California.

Generally speaking, the Nisei were a very young group. In 1930, the bulk of the second generation in Los Angeles County were under 21 years old. In 1934, a journalist reported that the majority of Nisei in the United States were between the ages of 15 and 18.[22]

Although these young women generally reflected the spirit of California youth, they experienced more traditional Japanese arrangements at home. Fathers held the supreme position within the Japanese immigrant family. Immersed in work, and often much older than their wives, they were sometimes rather distant figures. Children tended to be closer to their mothers, who carried primary responsibility for childrearing and disciplining. Believing that education was vital to social mobility, the Issei admonished the Nisei to study hard and excel academically. They also sought to instill in their children a sense of filial piety (oyakoko), which included the notion of achievement bringing family honor.[23]

Birth order and gender affected the experiences of the Nisei. Older children carried the burden of greater familial responsibilities. Daughters were usually subject to stricter supervision and had to do domestic chores from which their brothers were exempt. Most of the second generation spoke Japanese with their parents and English with their siblings, friends, and teachers. They grew up synthesizing the Japanese customs of their parents, American mainstream culture, and other ethnic cultural elements, from Chinese food to Mexican piñatas.

Public schools constituted the primary vehicle conveying mainstream culture to Nisei children.[24] Interacting with teachers and non–Japanese American classmates introduced them to ideals of democracy, citizenship, and individualism, as well as to U.S. holidays and middle-class WASP etiquette. When the regular school day ended, their parents sent them to Japanese-language school (Nihongakko) to learn about Japanese language and culture.[25] Many Nisei resented having to go after public school hours and on weekends. Rose Honda recalled, "Being Japanese meant that I had to go to Japanese school, and I couldn't join any of the clubs at Nora Sterry School."[26] Nisei social activities often revolved around school and church. As Setsuko Matsunaga Nishi said, "I felt that...most Nisei lived in two worlds: The world of school—many of them were very involved in the social life of their high schools—and also the social world related to their church. And I think it was mainly through religious institutions or athletic groups that they were connected to the Japanese."[27]

Like the schools, Buddhist and Christian churches constituted core institutions for many Nisei, serving as important social and spiritual centers within the ethnic community. More than a superficial sign of assimilation, the growth of Nisei networks within Japanese American churches reflects the efforts of Nisei Buddhists and Christians to carve out a distinctive niche, reinforcing generational and ethnic ties.[28] Because they moved in different social circles through their churches, the Nisei Christians and Buddhists appear to have had little interaction outside of school. Mary Nishi Ishizuka, whose Buddhist parents did not object to her attending a Christian church, "didn't see any kind of conflict" between followers of the two religions. She observed that the Nisei tended to socialize mostly with members of their own church "because they had social activities. And people joined that church because of the social activities."[29] In the prewar era, a majority of the Issei and Nisei held Buddhist affiliation.[30] However, more Japanese on the West Coast converted to Christianity than in Hawai'i.[31]

Christianity held great appeal for many Nisei, who came to see it as the religion of Americans as well as an avenue to opportunities for recreation and socializing.[32] As a child, Mary Nishi Ishizuka was initially attracted to a Japanese Presbyterian church because "it was fun."[33] Her parents, busy with work, had little time for the kinds of trips arranged by her Sunday school teacher to the observatory and other places.

Nisei girls and Issei women may also have been attracted to Christianity because of somewhat broader latitude for female activity. While studying a rural Japanese American enclave in 1931, sociology student Marion Svensrud observed a "marked difference" in Christian and Buddhist homes with regard to the position of Issei women: "The Christian homes seem to be more Americanized in this respect, and more consideration and freedom is evident."[34] Embracing Protestant ideals of fellowship and virtue did not mean surrendering Japanese cultural heritage, but it may have enlarged women's social sphere.[35] Religion as well as city life appear to have fostered change in Issei gender relations and family hierarchy.

Because of the existing structure of youth organizations associated with Protestant churches—notably the YMCA and YWCA—a large portion of the Nisei girls involved in clubs were Christian. There were also active Buddhist youth groups, but they lacked the support of a well-established, widespread institutional framework. Strict Issei parents—Buddhists and Christians alike—were more likely to allow daughters to participate in youth activities held under church auspices. Rose Honda said, "I mainly stuck to the activities at the [Japanese Methodist] church, because, as far as my mother was concerned, as long as the church...was doing the activity, she just felt, 'Well, they'll be all right.'"[36]

The leisure time of girls like Rose Honda was subordinate to family responsibilities. Whether they lived on a farm or in the city, Japanese American children provided vital labor. City girls often helped operate family businesses within the Japanese American enclave, waiting on restaurant customers or stocking the shelves of a grocery store. In the Sawtelle enclave of West Los Angeles, Rose Honda and her sister aided their mother with her pansy nursery, transplanting seedlings and digging up plants for customers.[37] Living in seaside Venice, young teenager Esther Takei Nishio helped her parents with their Venice Amusement Pier concessions, working on weekends in a game booth or as a cashier at the octopus ride.[38] Girls' chores also included housework and supervising younger siblings.

Economic survival and advancement often drew on the work of all family members. Fumiko Fukuyama Ide and her brothers, for example, regularly swept clean their father's hardware store on First Street in Little Tokyo. Every week, Fumiko walked through Filipino Town to Main Street to deliver the store earnings to the Farmers' & Merchants' Bank. On the floor above the hardware store, her mother sewed dresses for the Tomio Company Department Store; Fumiko helped by stitching hems and making belts.[39] After her mother taught her to sew when she was in junior high school, Fumiko was also expected to make all of her own clothes, pieced from her mother's fabric remnants, used flour sacks, and discount yardage from the May Company. Her parents' hardware and dressmaking businesses supported not only the nuclear family but also a paternal grandmother and young uncle who came from Japan to live with them, and later an unrelated Kibei schoolboy, a Nisei who returned to the United States after being educated in Japan.[40] Collective effort sustained the family.[41]

Despite their work, the urban Nisei were more likely to have free time and greater access to commercialized leisure activities than their rural peers. Living in the city afforded them mobility. Libraries and parks were often within walking distance; other youth activities were a streetcar ride away. Mary Nishi Ishizuka, whose first home adjoined her father's flower shop in Hollywood, said, "I was an adventurous type, I would go on my own, on my bicycle everywhere, or I would take the streetcar and go to the plunge [pool]."[42] As a young teenager Fumiko Fukuyama Ide regularly roller-skated from her home south of Little Tokyo to her friend May Tomio's home in West Adams to learn tap dancing.[43]

Movies were a popular recreation for many Issei and Nisei. With their parents, the second generation watched samurai adventures, and with their siblings they followed the exploits of cowboy heroes. In West Los Angeles, Rose Honda saw

Japanese films with her parents at the Japanese school on Corinth and went with Nisei friends to American movies at the Tivoli Theatre (now Laemmle's Royal Theatre) on Santa Monica Boulevard. She was a fan of both Shirley Temple and Japanese movie star Shirley Yamaguchi.[44] Teenage girls looked forward to the movies of screen idols like Deanna Durbin, Claudette Colbert, Clark Gable, and Tyrone Power.

To urban and rural Nisei alike, the radio was "all important." Mary Nishi Ishizuka recalled that reading and radio were the only entertainments at home.[45] Although "everybody listened to the radio for all the news," she said, "primarily we listened to music. They had the 'Hit Parade', and we knew all of the well-known songs of the day."[46] The radio transmitted Japanese as well as American popular culture. Rose Honda listened to Japanese music and news on the radio as well as American programs.

Like their non–Japanese American peers, the urban Nisei loved to dance. Although only girls learned odori (traditional Japanese dance), both sexes practiced the foxtrot and waltz. Setsuko Matsunaga Nishi remembered jitterbugging at lunchtime mixers in the high school gym. She and her brother Ernest learned to dance using mail-ordered footprint patterns from the Arthur Murray Dance Studio. Fumiko Fukuyama Ide first went with her brothers to the dances held by their Boy Scout Troop 379. Later she attended dances organized by her club, the Tartanettes, and other Nisei groups. She remembered, "We had one every weekend practically."[47]

Urban Nisei girls' schedules were also filled with training that reflected mixed expectations of domestic competence and accomplishment in the cultural arts. Issei mothers like Setsuko Matsunaga Nishi's started early: "One of the things she did was to have us stand by her side while she cooked, so that we would learn to cook. Also, when we were very little, before we went to pre-school, she taught us calligraphy."[48] In addition to learning to cook, sew, knit, and crochet, many second-generation girls took piano lessons; some, like Aiko Herzig-Yoshinaga, studied ballet and tap-dancing. The movies whetted their interest. Fumiko Fukuyama Ide remembered, "When I was a small child…the Meglin Kiddies and Shirley Temple were the idols for us young girls. And we all wanted to dance."[49] Urban daughters attended classes in Japanese arts such as ikebana (flower arranging), odori, tea ceremony, and Japanese musical instruments such as the koto and shamisen.[50] By contrast, boys were encouraged to learn the martial arts of judo and kendo (fencing).[51] Second-generation girls varied in their enthusiasm for these pursuits, but the Issei took pride in their performance of Japanese songs and dance at weddings, kenjinkai (prefectural association) picnics, and other community events. Girls' cultural performance reflected favorably on a family's social status in the ethnic enclave.

Second-generation daughters and sons were brought up with an awareness of being under scrutiny from both the Issei and mainstream society. As Seattle Nisei Monica Sone wrote, the propriety her mother tried to instill meant that when critical Issei elders were present children "must not laugh out loud and show our teeth, or chatter in front of guests, or interrupt adult conversation, or cross our knees while seated, or ask for a piece of candy, or squirm in our seats."[52] Rose Honda said, "It was so emphasized that we listen, and...respect other people, and don't talk back.... We were never to bring shame to the family."[53] The Nisei were cautioned that their behavior would reflect on the larger ethnic enclave as well. Mary Nishi Ishizuka recalled being expected to "be on our best behavior because we didn't want to bring shame to the Japanese community."[54]

Girls faced more rigorous monitoring than did their brothers. Like Sone, they found that Issei teachers and community leaders wished to mold them into "an ideal Japanese o-joh-san, a refined young maiden who is quiet, pure in thought, polite, serene, and self-controlled."[55] Not surprisingly, a 1939 survey of Issei and Nisei revealed that the majority believed that Nisei boys almost always had more freedom in the home than the girls.[56]

Adolescents and young women felt even more keenly the weight of expectations of proper female behavior. In 1934, one rebellious high school student in San Francisco bemoaned the limitations of "Girls who walk the usual tread of life all planned by society and family" and described a dreary round of domesticity, concluding that for women, "Life is a matter of surpressing [sic]."[57] She made it clear that fear of community scrutiny enforced compliance: "We do our darnest [sic] to keep our self free from gossip. Anything different even in a form of an experiment will cause a riot among the sneeking [sic], whispering gossip-front."[58] Although her outspoken defiance may have been unusual, her awareness of social pressure was not. As Setsuko Matsunaga Nishi recalled, "appearances were terribly important" in the ethnic community.[59]

The pressure on daughters increased as they entered adolescence—and neared marriageable age—because girls' behavior was a marker of family respectability and social status within the ethnic community. Nisei "girls are under much stricter supervision than are the boys," observed sociologist Robert Ross in 1939, adding, "Only a certain class of immigrants allow their daughters to mix freely with members of the opposite sex."[60] This was the case in other immigrant communities too. Historian Judy Yung found that Chinese immigrant parents also "were more concerned about regulating their daughters' sexuality than their sons', of protecting their daughters' virginity and the family's upright standing in the community."[61] Similarly, historian Vicki Ruiz noted that, in the prewar Mexican American community, a "family's standing...depended, in part, on women's purity."[62] Unwed Nisei girls who became pregnant were often sent to

Japan, or their children might end up in Shonien, the Japanese orphanage in Los Angeles.[63]

Japanese immigrant parents and community held high expectations for the second generation, although their aspirations for sons and daughters often differed. On arrival in the United States, the Issei discovered that their racial position overrode class; regardless of their diverse class origins, they shared similar experiences of being treated "like pariahs."[64] On the West Coast and in Hawai'i, Japanese immigrants made great efforts, individually and collectively, to try to improve their status. In Hawai'i, they strove to escape the confines of plantation labor.[65] The Issei in California shared these goals, especially for their children, stressing education and industriousness, which they hoped would lead to good jobs and secure middle-class lives.

Such dreams proved elusive, particularly during the Great Depression, when many Issei struggled to eke out a living. In 1937, a sociology student from Japan observed of the southern California Japanese Americans, "Except for a score of successful Japanese farmers and business men, the majority of the Japanese are poor, but, on the whole, they are not in abject poverty."[66] Rose Honda said, "I think my mother wanted to be more middle class, but she couldn't financially. It was a struggle—it was a real struggle."[67] Married to a gardener, her mother worked as a seamstress as well as a farm and produce-market employee in order to give her two daughters clothing, toys, and cultural training. She paid for Rose to take classes in ikebana, odori, watercolor painting, and the dreaded piano lessons. Through resourceful, ceaseless work, Taka Takebe Honda strove to provide her daughters with the comforts she had enjoyed as a doctor's child and to cultivate in them accomplishments that would signal their middle-class female status to both the ethnic and mainstream society.

Nisei daughters as well as sons were urged to excel in school, perceived as a key to social mobility, but the Issei tended to stress education for boys, particularly with regard to higher education.[68] With some exceptions, limited family resources were more likely to be used to send sons to college than daughters. Ross's 1939 survey revealed that the southern California Issei deemed high school education "sufficient for their daughters."[69] Chinese American women in Los Angeles faced similar obstacles, as parents often privileged the education of sons.[70] These patterns mirrored gendered educational expectations in the larger society also, although more white women were likely to pursue schooling. The Nisei youth embraced their parents' valorization of education, but not the priority placed on boys—in contrast, they believed that both sons and daughters should enjoy educational opportunities.[71] Immigrant parents and their daughters sometimes had differing notions about the kind of education most appropriate for young women, with some Issei favoring language and cultural training in Japan intended to groom them for marriage.

Difficulties in communication may have magnified generational differences, particularly in the urban setting. Robert Ross viewed language as the most serious problem between the Japanese immigrants and their children. In 1939 he observed that the Issei were unable "to convey to their offspring their inner thoughts."[72] He added, "The language problem is more acute between parent and child in the city than in the country."[73] A young Nisei male college graduate attributed this to "the complex and highly commercialized life in the cities."[74] The urban second generation were "provided with far more recreational facilities to take them away from home and parents. Parents, on the other hand, are ever too busy to care about their children's every detail and let them do as they choose."[75] The work routines of urban Issei and the enticements of city life appear to have had impact on intergenerational communication. Of course, living in urban southern California also offered both the Issei and their children more opportunities to participate in both ethnic culture and popular culture. Japanese immigrants not only took part in church activities, art and poetry clubs, and prefectural association gatherings, but also attended Japanese and Western movies and musical performances; in Little Tokyo they had access to Japanese and Chinese restaurants, Japanese groceries, books, and magazines. Despite some overlap, parents and children tended to move in different leisure spheres oriented to their peers.

Not surprisingly, the social mingling of Nisei girls and boys—especially at dances—became a key area of generational conflict. In both southern California and Hawai'i, Japanese parents' complaints focused mainly on the dress and behavior of girls, reflecting their double standard for sons and daughters.[76] The Issei and their children disagreed over allowing mixed-sex youth activities as well as clashing over who should make decisions regarding Nisei marriage.

Once she reached her twenties, a second-generation woman faced increasing pressure to marry. Parental expectations were reinforced by those of other Issei elders. A writer for the San Francisco Hokubei Asahi related the "typical case" of a 24-year-old college-educated Nisei woman who had "staved off four proposals to her father by 'friends' of comparatively unknown or personally repulsive men." These suitors were likely to be Issei and much older than the Nisei woman. According to the author, "The matter becomes worse because of the girl's age, which is a terrible age for an unmarried Japanese daughter to be still on her father's hand—people are already beginning to ask what is the matter with her that she cannot secure a husband." He added, "She is not alone—there are hundreds like her in the same situation."[77] In southern California, Robert Ross noted, "Up until very recently many young girls were being married, by family decree, to older men, very often Japan-born, with whom they have very little in common."[78]

As Nisei girls grew older, they also faced economic pressure, as the needs of immigrant parents sometimes took precedence over their own wishes, particularly during the lean years of the Great Depression. Filial duty forced some second-generation women to put aside their own aspirations, as in the case of Haruko Sugi Hurt. With her elderly husband unable to find work, Haruko's mother supported the family by doing home nursing, massage, and garment piecework. Haruko had dreamed of pursuing higher education, but her mother told her, "We can't afford college. We've been looking forward to having you help us economically."[79] After taking a sewing class, Haruko made dresses for the Kurata Department Store and then shifted to domestic work.

Nisei women often juggled a range of jobs. In the 1930s Mary Oyama, who had spent several years as a social worker in Spokane, Washington, rejoined her parents and siblings in Los Angeles, where an endless round of laundry, house cleaning, sewing, mending, darning, cooking, and ironing consumed much of her time.[80] Although occasionally helping with the family cosmetics business and lending a hand at a brother's store, Mary, who, in her late twenties faced parental pressure to marry, also continually looked for jobs, which were hard to come by in the Little Tokyo community and even harder to find outside. Mary Oyama Mittwer, Esther Takei Nishio, Fumiko Fukuyama Ide, Rose Honda, and Haruko Sugi Hurt exemplify the many second-generation Japanese American women in southern California who contributed to the prewar family economy through wage-paid or unpaid labor in family businesses and households.

From the 1920s through the 1940s, racism limited the Nisei's social horizons as well as their economic opportunities. Despite their U.S. citizenship and immersion in American culture, the second generation faced racial barriers that would spur many to turn to peer networks for friendship and support. Growing up in Gardena, California in the 1920s, Haruko Sugi Hurt would walk home from school with a white classmate. Rosemary never invited her in, nor did it occur to Haruko to invite her to visit either. "In school they were very friendly," Haruko said, "but there was absolutely no social contact with any—at least from my experience—non-Japanese families and their children."[81] She accepted this as a matter of course until, after graduating from high school, she was snubbed by another former classmate, someone she had spoken to for years. Spotting her on the street one day, Haruko called out a greeting, only to watch the woman jerk her head and walk away. "See, outside of school the Caucasian families didn't want to have anything to do with us," Haruko realized with shock.

Even those who did not experience racial prejudice in their neighborhood or at school were aware of residential segregation. Mary Nishi Ishizuka, whose family moved from Hollywood to the Sawtelle community in West Los Angeles just before the war, said that "above Montana [Avenue], we couldn't even find a place to live. They would never show us real estate in that area." Japanese Americans could only reside in sections "like this area of Santa Monica, or in the Virgil district. And we wouldn't think of finding something in Brentwood or Bel Air.... So there were definitely areas that we felt uncomfortable in."[82] Japanese Americans faced restrictions not only in where they could live and work, but also in the extent to which they could participate in California's well-publicized leisure culture.

By the 1920s, as the delights of mass culture and public amusements enticed growing numbers of young urban men and women throughout the country, southern California had already become a leisure capital. Tourists as well as locals flocked to sun themselves at the beaches, sporting a tan as a new emblem of health and attractiveness; the more daring frequented the gambling boats that operated along the coast. They kicked up their heels at dance halls and partied at nightspots such as the Cocoanut Grove in the Ambassador Hotel. They could shimmy to jazz at the Cotton Club or attend classical music concerts at the Hollywood Bowl. They thrilled to the exploits of the likes of Douglas Fairbanks, Mary Pickford, and Charlie Chaplin at movie palaces such as Grauman's Egyptian Theater in Hollywood. At the Venice Pier they rode on the roller coaster and tried to win prizes at game booths like those run by Esther Takei's parents.

However, not everyone was welcome at those sunny beaches. Like the prewar job and housing markets, the beaches, eateries, hotels, and public amusements were not equally accessible to racial-minority people in southern California. Exclusionary practices often mirrored patterns of residential segregation. For example, from 1912 to 1927 Bruce's Beach, founded by Willa and Charles Bruce, was the only resort open to African Americans, and nearby Peck Pier was the only amusement pier to accept them. As rising property values signaled the area's growing desirability, the City of Manhattan Beach forced out the local black community, and the Ku Klux Klan drove away African American beach-goers, who were then relegated to "the Inkwell," a blacks-only section of the Santa Monica Beach.[83] African Americans, Mexican Americans, and Asian Americans were excluded from many public golf courses and swimming pools. In 1925, the Los Angeles Playground Commission officially mandated racial restrictions at swimming pools; some barred outright people of color, including Asians, whereas others admitted them one afternoon per week. Although segregation of public pools was ruled illegal in Los Angeles in 1931, it persisted through the 1940s.[84]

Encountering hostility and discrimination in public facilities, many Nisei were painfully aware of racial boundaries. Katsumi Hirooka Kunitsugu, a Nisei woman whose family lived in East Los Angeles in the late 1930s, recalled a prevailing sense that "everyone was against you except for school where people were more open-minded and tolerant.... Once you step outside of school, you go to—say, the Four Star Theater, you want to see *Young Mister Lincoln*, and you could only sit in the balcony." Many movie theaters restricted racial-minority customers to poor seats far in the back or in the balcony.[85] Some restaurants refused them service. Katsumi recalled, "You go into just any old restaurant, and sometimes the waitresses wouldn't serve you. They don't tell you to get out, they just never came around to take your order."[86] Such discrimination was one of the factors that made Chinese restaurants such as San Kwo Low and Far East in Little Tokyo popular settings for prewar kenjinkai (prefectural association) gatherings, wedding receptions, and after-funeral meals.[87] Even though her parents could afford to dine at places outside the ethnic enclave, Mary Nishi Ishizuka remembers that the family only went to the Far East: "I don't think it was so much the cost, but...they were probably afraid to go to [other] restaurants—they might not have served us."[88] Although race relations varied in different neighborhoods and districts of southern California—ranging from inclusive schools such as Roosevelt High School in East Los Angeles to institutions such as Pasadena City College where racial/ethnic youth felt unwelcome in extracurricular clubs—most Japanese American youth faced the realities of discrimination and exclusion from an early age. In this respect, their experiences mirrored those of their counterparts in Hawai'i; despite a more tolerant climate in the islands, the same racial hierarchy structured social relations in Hawai'i and on the West Coast. As historian Eileen Tamura states, "White supremacy was assumed among European Americans in both places."[89] In the arena of leisure as in work, navigating racial boundaries—determining where they were and were not welcome—was tricky and demoralizing.

Given the pressures they encountered within and outside the ethnic community, Nisei girls and single women found much-needed camaraderie and peer-group understanding in a wide array of urban Japanese American organizations. They were excluded from college sororities and fraternities, as well as from clubs in some high schools. Barred from taking part in many of the social activities of the majority culture, the Nisei by the 1930s had established a broad network of organizations within their ethnic communities.[90]

Nisei Girls' Clubs

In 1941 the *Kashu Mainichi* spotlighted the "typical Nisei club girl" in its holiday issue. The unidentified journalist drew a critical but not unsympathetic portrait of her as a spirited young woman who enjoyed the pastimes of urban youth culture: "She likes to talk, dance and go to the shows."[91] Club activities were a regular feature in the club girl's life: "Gossip she loves, but confines it usually to her monthly club meetings and teas." The effort to keep personal information within the channels of her closest peer networks suggests the young Nisei woman's awareness of the Japanese American community's expectations regarding the behavior of Nisei daughters, as well as mindfulness that "the scandal mongers are ready to distort her reputation." The club girl appeared unengaged in political issues, though she was capable of discussing "the latest best-seller, democracy and leadership, and (or) how to win friends and influence 'dates.'" This assessment may reflect more about the gendered power dynamics of prewar Nisei politics, the dismissive attitude of the presumably male Nisei journalist, and the youth of the club girl than about her degree of superficiality or seriousness.[92]

Regardless of how they were perceived by outsiders, the Nisei women clearly saw themselves as Americans. As the journalist concluded, "With her youthful outlook, the typical nisei club girl has striven to do things in the American Way...any way which is the opposite of the traditional Japanese Way."[93] Although this blanket statement overlooks the many Japanese cultural activities fostered by girls' clubs, it suggests the appeal of mainstream middle-class gender ideology for young urban Nisei women as they tried to define themselves, from the Jazz Age through the Great Depression, and then in the tense atmosphere of approaching war. In Los Angeles, one of the key vehicles for Nisei girls' synthesis of models of femininity was the YWCA.

Both Christian and Buddhist churches fostered girls', boys', and co-ed clubs, not to mention the Girl Scouts and Boy Scouts, but YWCA-sponsored activities were particularly widespread. In 1926, "Katy," a Nisei male columnist for the *Rafu Shimpo* observed, "The work of the Y.W. is well known. Their activities are ever helpful to the women of this community, and the effects of their work are unconsciously felt more or less by every woman of the Japanese community in the Southland."[94] The YWCA sponsored a wide array of clubs for Nisei girls as well as practical classes for their Issei mothers; these efforts, although indeed helpful, show the limits of the Y's vision of interracial cooperation.

The structure of the YWCA-affiliated Nisei clubs shows how the YWCA sought to include racial-minority girls without challenging racial lines. By the 1910s, YWCA leaders had concluded that "the most different groups—such as industrial girls, Negroes, the foreign-born—would not be reached by the Association without special efforts related to their own life-experiences and cultural backgrounds."[95] Their "special efforts" to reach Japanese American girls seem to have mirrored their practices with regard to African American and Chinese American young women, for whom they established separate branches in ethnic communities.[96] There were "Oriental" branches—subdivided into Chinese American and Japanese American groups—in at least two cities, Los Angeles and San Francisco.[97] This establishment of segregated ethnic-branch clubs mirrors the delineation of racial boundaries before World War II.

The beginnings of the Japanese YWCA are difficult to unravel, as various records give different dates. The "Japanese YWCA" in Los Angeles began in 1922, according to a pamphlet put out by the organization.[98] However, from the 1941 Annual Report of the Japanese YWCA, it appears that the group had its roots in an earlier body "formed for Japanese women and children by a group of foresighted ministers and friends" in 1912.[99] In 1916 the *Los Angeles Herald* announced the opening of a Japanese Young Women's Christian Union "to meet the needs of Oriental maids in Los Angeles" and added that classes in domestic science, childcare, English, and dress-making would be offered.[100] The *Herald* also noted the involvement of Michi Kawai, the national secretary of the Japanese YWCA in Japan.[101] By this time, there were 130 women, probably all Issei, affiliated with the Japanese YWCA in Los Angeles.[102]

In 1921 the Japanese YWCA opened a downtown office and hospitality center; by 1941 it was located on the third floor at 312 East First Street in Little Tokyo. In keeping with the YWCA's concern for urban workers, the Japanese YWCA also ran a dormitory, the Magnolia Residence at 2616 East Third Street, purchased in 1922, which provided housing for single women as well as a meeting place for club socials; by 1940, it accommodated 14 girls who had come to Los Angeles for work or study.[103]

In addition to the formation of ethnic-branch clubs, a second development greatly influenced the organization of Nisei girls' clubs: the fast-growing YWCA Girl Reserves (GR) movement, begun in 1918, aimed to enlist seventh- and eighth-grade school girls, junior high school and older high school adolescents, and the younger women in industry and business.[104] The first Japanese GR club formed in 1918 and by 1926, there were five such clubs in Los Angeles.[105] The aim of the movement was to help girls build character and contribute to society, as reflected by the GR emblem: a blue triangle within a circle, the three sides of the triangle representing mind, body, and spirit, and the circle symbolizing the world. (The names of two of the GR clubs—the Blue Triangles and the younger Blue Circles—mirrored these symbols.) The emphasis of the GR movement on "the developing of program out of the needs and desires of the group rather than as a standardized pattern" [106] may have made it particularly adaptable to the Nisei girls who flocked to join, picking individual names for their GR clubs and choosing their own activities for the year.[107] This adaptability may similarly have drawn other racial-ethnic girls, as did the vibrant New York YWCA movement among African American women.[108] The Nisei girls of Los Angeles, like the African American girls of New York, were eager to join this "fun club," which offered opportunities to hike, skate, hold parties, and go on outings.[109] The Japanese American girls also learned handicrafts, played sports, and planned social-service projects.

The GR's dramatic candlelight ceremonies appealed to Nisei girls. The 1926 initiation of new members concluded a joint meeting of the T.M.T.M. Girl Reserves and the S.O.F. Girl Reserves with candlelight, the "most impressive event of the evening," reported the *Rafu Shimpo*. "The officers of both clubs formed one side of a triangle in front of the fireplace and the members came

marching in to the tune of 'Hymn of Lights.'" One of the girls explained the significance of the candle: "The warmth meaning friendship, its brightness meaning honor, its steady glow meaning purpose, and its radiance meaning faith."[110]
The popularity of the GR ceremonies may have inspired other groups to develop
similar rituals. For instance, in December 1938, the Senshin Temple branch of
the Young Women's Buddhist Association announced a candlelight installation
ceremony to honor its new officers.

Another development important to Nisei girls' clubs was the founding of
the YWCA's International Institutes, designed to reach immigrant women and
their U.S.-born children. The first was established in 1910; by the mid-1920s
there were 55 International Institutes in cities across the country, including Los
Angeles.[111] By the 1930s the International Institute in Boyle Heights had become
a bustling center for young women's club activities, including the Japanese
YWCA branch in southern California.

For Nisei girls and their mothers, the International Institutes offered a space
conducive to cultural coalescence, owing to their unusual dual emphasis on
pluralism and integration. Influenced by Louis Adamic and other proponents
of cultural pluralism, they did not aim for the complete assimilation of immigrants, but sought to facilitate the newcomers' adjustment to American society; they simultaneously promoted ethnic cultural retention and pride, not
only among immigrants but also their U.S.-born children.[112] In line with this
thinking, the International Institutes' staff members included immigrant and
second-generation women "nationality workers" who were usually college educated and had social work training, as well as familiarity with ethnic cultures
and languages.[113] The Institutes' goals took concrete form in ethnic culture and
general education classes, the sponsorship of "nationality clubs," and the hosting of interethnic pageants and handcraft exhibits.[114] Serving multiple ethnic
groups, the International Institute in Boyle Heights mirrored these aspirations,
as attested by the countless Japanese YWCA events and interethnic festivals held
there throughout the interwar years.[115]

A profile of Maki Ichiyasu, a dynamic, warmly remembered Nisei adviser,
suggests that the Japanese YWCA, like the International Institutes, also sought
to hire "nationality workers." Ichiyasu "grew up with the 'Y,'" starting as an
"enthusiastic Girl Reserve" in San Francisco. After high school, she attended
Mills College, where she majored in economic sociology.[116] She began working
as an adviser to Los Angeles Nisei girls in July 1934; by 1940, the "ever sympathetic and helpful" Ichiyasu was employed as the executive secretary of the
Japanese YWCA, serving as adviser and confidante to nearly 500 Nisei girls.
Fumiko Fukuyama Ide appreciatively recalled Ichiyasu and Sophie Tajima, the
Girl Reserve secretary: "Maki and Sophie . . . were great influences in our lives as
Tartanettes, because they're the ones that we looked up to. And they're the ones

that arranged all this fun stuff for us."[117] Many of the Japanese YWCA staff were Japanese American, especially by the end of the 1930s.

The Japanese YWCA, under the guidance of Maki Ichiyasu, Sophie Tajima, and an all-Japanese American Committee of Management by the late 1930s, aimed to train young women to become "the leaders of tomorrow!" As their pamphlet announced:

> The Japanese YWCA is doing its part in the preparing of young people for the responsibilities they will be expected to carry as they grow older. The program of the Y.W.C.A. is planned to meet a girl's needs from youth to maturity, from the time she is a junior high school student until she goes to university or enlarges her interest in the Business or Industrial Department of the 'Y'. The girl is also trained for club advisership and for leadership as a member of a committee or board.[118]

This aim of fostering women's organizational skills distinguished the YWCA from its brother organization, showing, as historian Joanne Meyerowitz asserts, how "the YWCA challenged patriarchal prerogatives in ways that the YMCA did not."[119] Nisei girls rotated as club officers, learned to plan events and raise funds, represented their clubs at conferences, and showcased their talents through public performances. In this respect, the Japanese YWCA—together with many other prewar girls' and co-ed clubs—laid the groundwork for urban Nisei women's active involvement in a variety of community organizations in the postwar period.

The flexibility of its programs, a dazzling array of activities, and the presence of energetic role models attracted many Nisei girls to the YWCA; in 1940, the Japanese YWCA claimed to serve directly 1,800 girls annually, with influence extending to a larger number.[120] Like young Chinese American club women in San Francisco, the Japanese American "Y" members enjoyed a broadened social life, developed leadership skills, and took part in community service.[121] The Japanese YWCA was part of a pantheon of Nisei youth organizations with similar character-building aims, including the network of Buddhist youth clubs, the Young Women's Buddhist Association (YWBA) and the Young Men's Buddhist Association (YMBA). However, judging from ethnic-press coverage, the YWCA had particularly high visibility and impact within the prewar Japanese American community in southern California.

The reflections of two Tartanettes—a GR club affiliated with the Union Church in Little Tokyo—make clear the significance of the Japanese YWCA in providing supportive leadership and access to a larger world. Fumiko Fukuyama Ide recalled that the YWCA advisers were regarded as "part of the family. We never thought of them as dictating anything that we did, but they were always there.... They were very helpful and they were important because

:ept us all busy. They kept us together."[122] The YWCA also served as a
e between the ethnic enclave and mainstream society. Setsuko Matsunaga
Nishi, who won a 1939 YWCA-YMCA oratorical contest with a speech on
"What the YWCA Means to Me," said, "Our parents didn't have connections
into the larger community. So that, in a way, the YWCA Tartanettes and the
YWCA meant a linkage into a larger American social world of young women."
And for "Nisei who also had an active life in a larger community of school
and their professional interest" groups, the Tartanettes offered "a good way to
maintain some linkage to the Japanese American community."[123]

As these reflections suggest, the Nisei youth groups served a variety of functions. They were a means of social control, but peers rather than parents often
directed the organizations. Nisei sociologist Harry Kitano noted that "although
the Issei periodically attempted to control them," the groups "were usually
guided by the Nisei themselves. The youngsters were left pretty much alone, to
make mistakes, to try new things, and to translate their understanding of large
community models in ways that could be of use to them."[124] This varying degree
of supervision (or lack thereof) may reflect the growing independence of the
Nisei and their ability to utilize group membership to negotiate between the
ideals of Issei elders and mainstream society—another key function. Linked
with this mediating role, the clubs facilitated access to leisure pursuits—within
the flexible framework of the YWCA and other youth organizations—the urban
second generation found appealing. For young Nisei women who, like their
Mexican American sisters "sought to reconcile parental expectations with the
excitement of experimentation," youth clubs afforded a heady opportunity.[125]

These groups constituted an important alternative for Japanese American
children excluded from European American clubs or unable to assume leadership positions in them. "If we hadn't had these ethnic organizations to join,"
Yoshiko Uchida wrote, "I think few Nisei would have had the opportunity to
hold positions of leadership or responsibility. At one time I was president of
the campus Japanese Women's Student Club, a post I know I would not have
held in a non-Japanese campus organization."[126] The name of the first Japanese
American Girl Reserves club reflected their sense of inclusiveness: the
T.M.T.M. GR Club stood for "the more, the merrier."[127] Within such groups,
Nisei members received reinforcement of generational and ethnic identification, as well as opportunities to define themselves and their own interests.

Girls' Clubs and Cultural Coalescence

The variety of names chosen by young Nisei women for their clubs reveals
the wide array of cultural forms on which they drew and suggests their

drawing on Ruiz's concept of "cultural coalescence"

identifications, adaptations, and dreams. In a nod to the cachet of European culture, some selected French names: the Demoiselles (Los Angeles) and Les Jeunes Filles (Venice). The Swansonettes (Gardena) evoked the glamour of movie star Gloria Swanson, whereas the Queen Esthers (Hollywood), affiliated with both the M.E. Church and the YWCA, chose a biblical heroine as their symbol. Although few if any Nisei daughters could hope for the kind of social debut anticipated by elite white women, they could claim for themselves the title of Debutantes. Others preferred the tantalizing mystery of initials, like the S.O.F. (Service, Opportunity, Friendship) Girl Reserves and the J.U.G. (Just Us Girls) of Norwalk. Some names referenced Japanese ethnic heritage, as in the case of the Sumire Kai (violets club) of Santa Monica and the Sakura Shojo Kai (cherry blossom young girls' club) of Palos Verdes. Others, such as the Nipponettes (Long Beach), illustrated the creative hybridity of the Nisei world. Japanese American club names—humorous, cryptic, aspirational, hybrid—reflect how the urban second generation imaginatively selected from among the diverse cultural elements that were part of their daily lives.

A number of clubs chose names that referenced a racial/ethnic group not their own. Several YWCA groups such as the Toquiwas, the Loha Tohelas, and the Tres Arrowians adopted names that the Nisei (and the YWCA) regarded as American Indian in origin. In 1930, upon learning that their "locality was discovered as an Indian reservation when it was first settled," a newly formed West Los Angeles GR group chose "a significant Indian name" from a list "presented to the girls" at the previous meeting. They unanimously selected the name "Ekolela," which meant "to continue to grow."[128] This decision may have stemmed from a YWCA GR tradition; however, the diversity of names among Nisei GR clubs indicates considerable latitude of choice. Although the popularity of so-called "Indian" names among an array of mainstream boys' and girls' organizations and high school athletic teams in this era (and on into the 1950s) reflects both romanticization and appropriation, the appeal of an Indian name to Nisei daughters suggests an additional element: the desire to claim American identity by identifying with an incontestably native group that shared the Japanese Americans' non-white status.

Club membership facilitated cultural coalescence, as young women's groups provided socialization in both ethnic and mainstream culture. Some, like the Sumire Kai, a junior women's club, met to learn about the history of Japan and the intricacies of Japanese etiquette. A similar group, the Shira-yuri (white lily) club of Long Beach, vowed to speak only Japanese at their meetings. The Norwalk J.U.G. Girls' Club included in its activities twice-monthly classes in formal Japanese flower arrangement,[129] whereas the Blue Triangles decided to "take up etiquette both Japanese and American," starting with the latter.[130]

Women's organizations also reinforced some traditional gender roles, drawing on both mainstream and Japanese practices, as in the case of classes to teach
young women domestic skills. For example, the Japanese YWCA in 1927 offered
lessons in "household arts," which included sewing and Japanese cooking. As
the YWCA announced, "Everyone gets tired of eating the same thing every day.
Here is a chance to learn some new culinary art."[131] Handicrafts such as basketry,
batik dying, linoleum-block printing, and scrapbook making also proved to be
popular.

The Nisei girls' clubs provided a forum in which to explore peer-group and
intergenerational issues, as well as to participate in a range of activities common
to groups such as the Girl Scouts. For example, the Junior Girl Reserves conference in 1932 included in its schedule swimming, hiking, handicrafts, nature
study, music, and outdoor sports. The featured topics of discussion reflected
the influence of popular culture: "What the Boyfriend Thinks?" "What is 'It'?"
and "What We All Think of Dancing?"[132] The leaders also hoped to facilitate
intergenerational understanding by offering discussions of mother-daughter
relations. Mother-daughter ties were honored at annual banquets (paralleled
by father-son affairs) by a number of clubs, particularly the YWCA affiliates.[133]
The Inter-Club Council also held an annual GR Family Tea at the International
Institute "to acquaint the parents with the meaning and activities of the Girl
Reserves Club."[134]

Another aspect of cultural coalescence can be seen in the way organizations
introduced the Nisei to American holidays unfamiliar to their immigrant parents.
For example, club Halloween parties became an attraction for children and adolescents across southern California. In 1926, the *Rafu Shimpo* recorded a round
of Halloween parties held by "Schools, Clubs, Churches, including Catholics,
Protestants and Buddhists...."[135] The Maryknoll Girls received large headlines
for their "Halloween merriment" at the St. Francis Xavier School auditorium,
where the costumed girls played games, bobbed for apples in a tub of water,
and ate treats such as home-made fudge. The dance performance they enjoyed
reflects a mixture of ethnic and mainstream influences: One girl "was prevailed
upon to render a pretty little Japanese dance, which she performed with much
grace....Another wee bundle of nerves, masquerading as a Hollywood sheik,
presumably, managed to twist herself into various shapes and designs in her
endeavor to present her own conception of the Charleston."[136] Club celebrations
of Thanksgiving, Christmas, and Valentine's Day also facilitated the Nisei's participation in mainstream American holidays.

From early on, popular elements of Mexican American cuisine and customs figured in the mix of cultural forms from which the Nisei drew, as a co-ed
Christmas party hosted by the Blue Triangle Girls revealed in 1926. The highlight of the evening was the breaking of a piñata, which was described as "an

old Mexican game which is filled with candy, fruits, nuts, and small pickens."[137] Given the close proximity of racial/ethnic communities in southern California, it is not surprising that Japanese American youth activities incorporated a range of cultural influences and adaptations.

Recreation

The Nisei organizations enabled the second generation to take part in a wide range of recreational activities, some for girls only and others co-ed. Picnics and beach outings were a staple for southern California clubs. For example, in September 1927 the Cherry Club, composed of the older girls at the Buddhist Nishi Hongwanji Temple, met for "one of the snappiest picnics ever held by the members of this club," whereas the younger girls in the Poppy Club looked forward to spending a "day at East San Pedro, where they will enjoy the day on the water as well as in the water."[138] YWCA club members and their advisers took advantage of their access to the YWCA's Eliza Cottage at Hermosa Beach for short stays. The T.M.T.M. girls' weekend at Eliza Cottage featured swimming and "a bonfire on the sand, where good eats were masticated between each song."[139] A few months later another group of girls spent a week at the cottage, their daily schedule filled with housecleaning, morning worship, a business meeting, games, and swimming. At night the girls entertained each other with programs such as "a roaring comical skit entitled 'Jemima and Her Beaus.'"[140] After a final "tamale feed"—evidence of the influence of regional cuisine on the Nisei palate—they returned home with "a nice coat of tan and many thrilling stories to tell their folks."[141]

Club outings also introduced Nisei girls and young women to local cultural institutions and to public spaces with which few of their parents were familiar or had leisure time to visit. Through clubs they gained access to sites they might have hesitated to approach alone. For example, the Emba Girl Reserves made a trip to the Southwest Museum in Pasadena, "where they visited all of the rooms open for exhibition. Through the courtesy of one of the guides, who happened to be a friend of Miss Doris Palmer, temporary secretary at the International Institute, the girls were able to see the closed room where the exhibitions are arranged." They found particularly interesting "the latest excavations from Arizona" and the "Oriental room."[142] Nisei clubs also visited local businesses. An "educational tour" took the S.O.F. Girl Reserves and their sponsor, Mrs. Leech, to the Alfred Ice Cream Plant. As one happy Girl Reserve reported, "'Pop' took us on a tour of the plant. He showed us how they made Eskimo pies, sundaes, bricks, and last but not least ice cream....When the tour was ended the man presented each of us with two Eskimo pies." Buoyed by this experience, on the way home they saw Olson's Bakery and "expecting to get free bread we offered to inspect their plant for them. We saw every process of bread making. When we got out we did not have any bread so we unanimously voted that we would not visit it again. Oh, how passionate!" She added philosophically, "Well, good luck next time at the Holsum's Bakery. We expect to go on more educational tours in the future."[143]

Girls also enjoyed club sports. Baseball and basketball teams abounded for all ages and drew enthusiastic crowds. Athletic events fostered a range of friendly interaction among the Nisei, strengthening women's networks.[144] In this vein, the *Rafu Shimpo* anticipated that "When the Triangle Club girls from Santa Barbara come to Los Angeles to play against the Senior girls of Union Church it will mean the meeting of old friends again. They will meet both on and off the courts."[145] Games also provided opportunities for young women and men to socialize. Kay Moritani Komai recalled that she and her friends in the Blue Circles enjoyed the attention of the Nisei boys' club members who would show up to coach their teams and watch them play.[146]

Sports provided opportunities for congenial interethnic interaction as well. In March 1928, the Blue Triangle Girls played the YWCA "Russian Girls" basketball team, losing to their taller opponents.[147] Afterward, "the two teams had supper together.... Vocal solos by members of both clubs enlivened the spirit of the girls during the supper. The two teams decided to have a return game in the near future."[148] Next, the Blue Triangles played against the African American "Student Club of the Twelfth Street Center," again losing. The *Rafu Shimpo* reported, "Although the game was a hard fought one, the taller colored girls were at an advantage with their height and they managed to keep the ball most of the time."[149]

In sports, the Nisei women's sometimes aggressive maneuvering belied stereotypes of demure and fragile Asian maidens. They proved to be enthusiastic, and sometimes rough, competitors on the baseball diamond or the basketball court. For example, in a practice game between the S.O.F. Girl Reserves and the Blue Triangle quintet, a sports reporter observed with some ambivalence, "Unlike a good, honest-to-goodness, feministic casaba game many fouls, personal, technical, and otherwise and roughness filled the game. The referee failed to call most of the fouls. Just the same, the game was exciting, not barring the bumping, shoving, pushing, walking, running and many other tactics used by both sides."[150] The reporter also drew attention to the skills of competitors, noting Mabel Aratani's "clever footwork" and the "wonderful shots made by Rosemary Matsuno."[151] The extensive sports coverage in the ethnic press shows that women, as well as men, won admiration for athletic prowess.

Sports, particularly basketball, proved popular among second-generation Chinese American girls as well during the 1930s. In San Francisco, the only

Chinese American women's basketball team, the Mei Wahs, garnered acclaim for their athletic skill, playing against white teams in a city league and against Chinese American boys, as well as other Chinese American girls.[152] In Los Angeles, the Mei Wah Club and the Lowa Auxilliary Girls' Club, a YWCA Girl Reserve group, organized basketball teams that competed with each other and against other local teams.[153] The place of sports in the round of Nisei girls' club activities seems similar to that of the Mei Wah Club, which aimed to "maintain friendship through our athletic, social, and philanthropic activities."[154] It appears that, because of their greater numbers, the Nisei girls' clubs were able to develop more extensive intra-ethnic networks for athletic competition.

The groundswell of young women's interest in sports gave rise to an umbrella organization for athletic competition. In 1935, 20 girls "met at the Japanese Y.W.C.A. office to mother [a] Japanese girls' basketball league" that quickly grew into the Women's Athletic Union (WAU), a female counterpart to the all-boys Japanese Athletic Union (JAU), organized earlier.[155] In its first year, 17 teams and 245 members joined the WAU, participating in baseball, basketball, swimming, tennis, ping-pong, and volleyball.[156] The WAU boasted a membership of nearly 500 young women by 1939.

Perhaps reflecting its YWCA roots, the WAU was marked by a focus on inclusiveness and character building, emphasizing "sportsmanship rather than victory."[157] Unlike the JAU, the WAU chose not to present trophies for its championships; instead, a "niche on the Sportsmanship Plaque [was] considered a higher honor among the girls than a questionable victory and championship."[158] The WAU also fostered inclusiveness by encouraging "the use of greater numbers of players to allow less talented girls to enjoy the game. Through this participation, friendships will arise hand in hand with good clean sports."[159] Thus the WAU sought to channel competitive energy into teamwork and the forging of warm ties among young women. Nisei girls also cultivated these linkages through inter-club activities.

Strengthening Nisei Ties

Many of the Nisei's club activities strengthened broader second-generation bonds, especially among the sister clubs of the YWCA. The Nisei clubs frequently held joint meetings, for which the usual program included "a guest of honor or speaker to draw the thoughts of all present into the same channel."[160] For example, when the Tartanettes gathered on November 12, 1938 to hear "Miss Evangelina Abellera, Girl Reserves secretary from the Philippine Islands" speak about her travels, they invited the Cubs, Archerettes, Embas, and Tri-U Girl Reserves to join them.[161] The girls' clubs sometimes planned joint outings to Eliza Cottage and often collaborated on major events like the "family teas" at the International Institute. As Fumiko Ide said, "through the Tartanettes, we met all these other groups.... We had socials together. And we all went to [church] conferences."[162]

Attending an array of conferences, many sponsored by religious groups, also brought Nisei young women together. In 1933, for example, some 250 delegates—including a contingent from southern California—were expected to attend the Seventh Annual Conference of the North American Federation of the Young Women's Buddhist Association, held in San Jose. This conference, which also included some male delegates, was geared to training Sunday school teachers.[163] The Japanese YWCA regularly sent members to a range of conferences for high school students, young women in business, and college students. Women were also highly visible at the regional and statewide conferences of co-ed organizations such as the Young People's Christian Federation and the Japanese Student Christian Association.

Group events not only reinforced ties among young women's organizations, but also sometimes between girls' organizations and boys' clubs, which were often brother clubs in the YMCA. Staging benefit programs often required combining club resources and energies. Such jointly organized events display the mélange of popular culture elements that appealed to the Nisei, as well as offering glimpses of racial and gender dynamics. For instance, in 1926 the S.O.F. Girl Reserves worked with two boys' clubs—the Hi-Y (YMCA) and the Oliver Club—to put on a successful "Gymnasium Benefit Program."[164] The S.O.F. members presented a skit about "a woman who needed a cook...describing the character of each applicant." This performance suggests middle-class gender-role aspirations, since Japanese American women in the 1920s, 1930s, and 1940s were more likely to be domestic workers than to employ them. In addition to drama and dance performances, the program included a "Minstrel Act" for which members of the male Oliver Club, "painted up like 'darkies', sang a few songs." Participation in a minstrel act reflects how these Nisei men, in claiming American identity, drew on and perpetuated the stereotyping of African Americans that proliferated in popular culture.[165] Although they fostered generational and community ties, Japanese American club activities both contested and reinforced boundaries of race and gender.

Dances and socials were favorite collaborative club projects. As S. Frank Miyamoto observed in 1939, the socials, "which the Nisei generally organized totally independent of Issei supervision since the latter had little concept of how such events were fashioned in America, were often settings for the Nisei's first experience with boy-girl relations."[166] The Nisei were enthusiastic about their socials, sometimes making elaborate preparations. For instance, when the Japanese Girl Reserves Inter-Club Council held a party to honor its high school graduates in 1938, the seven affiliated girls' clubs took responsibility for different aspects of the social, the Embas and Cubs planning decorations, the Loha-Tohelas taking care of the invitations, Les Serrelles organizing games, Tri-U handling music, and the Tartanettes and Archerettes providing refreshments. Eight boys' clubs were invited to the social.[167]

Such occasions provided opportunities for heterosexual flirtation within a controlled environment, as in the case of a 1926 party given by the Hi-Y boys for the Girl Reserves and their adviser, Mrs. Leech. The evening ended with a Victorian parlor game, "Forfeits," during which "Jimmy Nakamura had to disclose the way he made his living when he was compelled to make love to a girl in order to get back his dime. Tom had a hard time getting out of the double handcuff with Seiko (a girl)."[168] A trip to the Eliza Cottage on the beach also offered groups like the Tartanettes chances for flirtation—as Setsuko Matsunaga Nishi remembered, "We got to invite boys to join us for activities there. The idea was to try to invite the most attractive guys you knew."[169] With regard to romantic heterosexual relations, the Nisei clubs provided ample opportunities for socializing and courtship, within the context of monitored events—sometimes regulated by peers—that reinforced group ties and standards of behavior.

Box lunch socials, popular in the late 1920s, also reveal the Nisei clubs' cultural adaptation, combined opportunities for flirtation and fund raising, and reinforcement of conventional gender roles. This fund raising practice, probably transplanted in California by white migrants from the Midwest, showcased and commodified young women's domestic skills. Young men purchased not only the food but also the company of the maker. In 1926, in order to raise money to install showers (for the boys) at the Japanese M.E. Church gym, the Epworth League youth held a box lunch social. "All girls who plan to attend," the *Rafu Shimpo* reminded, "are earnestly asked to bring box lunches. These will be auctioned, so make something enough for two."[170] The reporter underscored assumed differences in male and female appetites. "Remember, even if you are a light-eater, boys always have a big appetite."[171] In 1931, the All Around Girl Reserves held a highly successful Valentine Box Lunch social, raising more than $60 to send delegates to an annual GR summer conference. By this time, dancing had become a feature of the Nisei box lunch social, expanding the opportunity for male-female socializing and flirtation. The Valentine social ended with "each boy dancing with the fair maker of his lunch."[172] Illustrating how club events facilitated a range of interethnic interactions, the All Arounds and their guests danced to the music of the African American "Stevedore" orchestra.

The reportage of club events reveals how such organizations established and sometimes gently pushed the boundaries of socially sanctioned activities for Japanese American girls, from charitable endeavors to recreation. The Nisei embraced certain pursuits of the Modern Girl: male-female socializing and the search for romantic love. The growing popularity of dances throughout the pre-war years provides an example of changing cultural mores. The Issei and Nisei held very different views of this pastime, as reflected in a *Rafu Shimpo* colum-nist's 1929 definition of "Dance": "To first generation: hugging set to music. To second generation: Highest type of social interaction."[173] By 1936, journalist Bill Hosokawa declared, "Not more than half a decade ago, dancing was looked upon as next to sin by many of the first generation. Invariably they associated danc-ing and the second generation problem.... But times doth change. Any young person now that doesn't dance is practically a social outcast."[174] In this respect, generally speaking, city youth had greater latitude than their rural peers.

Club meetings gave girls a chance to demonstrate and learn new dances. The 16 girls at an M.O.M. Club meeting in Riverside in 1928 enjoyed an exhibition of a Hawaiian dance, waltz, foxtrot, Charleston, and "the latest dances." The eve-ning was spent "in teaching the girls who did not know how to dance."[175] Clubs scheduled more and more dance practices "to satisfy the inner yearning of so many nisei young people to become blue-blooded 'rug-cutters'" adept at "shag-gin', half-timing" and "jitter-bugging."[176] The Blue Circles held regular practice sessions, sometimes inviting a Nisei boys' club. Because the Centenary Church did not permit dances on the premises, they would meet at the homes of vari-ous Blue Circles; this allowed the girls' parents to meet the young men and thus allayed parental anxiety about the respectability of the gatherings.[177] Club advis-ers also served as chaperones for formal dances held at rented halls.

Nisei women took the initiative in planning, regulating, and maybe even in attending dances, as a stern admonition to southern California gate-crashers indicated in 1931: "Men and women who walked in without invites at the last Blue Triangle dance are getting into hot water and the sooner their crusts melt away the better."[178] Leap Year dances planned by the Blue Triangles and Chi Alpha Delta received special notice from the *Kashu Mainichi* in January 1932: "Already two dances are scheduled for February for the benefit of the supposed-to-be stronger sex by the weaker sex."[179] The Cherry Blossom and Nadeshiko Club of nearby Gardena also planned to sponsor jointly a Leap Year dance. The repeated mention that dances would be "strictly invitational" suggests their success in attracting Nisei youth.[180] Such heterosexual couples dancing would have been unheard of by the Nisei's immigrant parents and still incurred their disapproval in rural areas.

Nisei attitudes about club dances reflect the second generation's sense of appropriate behavior for young women and men; within the ethnic community as in the larger society, a sexual double standard prevailed. Girls were subject to more surveillance, and boys bore the major expense of furnishing transportation and paying for dance admission fees and refreshments afterward. In 1933 the YMCA distributed questionnaires about dancing to 16 groups—nine women's clubs, six men's groups, one co-ed—of high school age and older. The respondents' prescriptions focused primarily on Nisei daughters. Revealing the greater vulnerability of a young woman's reputation, they said that girls "should by all means notify their parents with whom they are going to the dance. For the boys this is not absolutely necessary."[181] Girls should be home at 1:00 a.m., or by 1:30 at the latest; no curfew was given for boys.

The polled groups differentiated between younger and older adolescents in what they considered acceptable and appropriate behavior. Perhaps bearing in mind the kind of tone they wished to set at their social events, they sternly warned, "It is not advisable for young people under 16 years of age to attend these community dances." They also felt that it was "better for younger Nisei to go to dances in groups rather than in single couples."[182] Issei parents were more likely to permit attendance if their daughters had the additional check of peer chaperonage; this measure may also have provided girls with some buffering from awkward situations and sexual pressures. Young women's close networks were critical to their gaining access to youth social events and also assisted in the maintenance of their respectable standing within the ethnic community.[183]

Dances peaked in popularity among the Nisei in the late 1930s. In 1937, there were more than 130 dances or socials sponsored by the senior Nisei clubs.[184] The vast majority were financially successful fund raisers, with "bids," or entrance fees, ranging from "the very 'steep' $2.50 to the proletariat 25 cents per couple."[185] In 1938, 64 public dances drew avid Nisei jitterbuggers and waltzers, in addition to "over 100 socials and various benefits, bazaars and carnivals, at which dancing was one of the drawing cards."[186] Clubs vied to secure good orchestras that would attract Nisei rug-cutters. The number of dances mushroomed to the point of eliciting calls for regulation of scheduling to avoid conflicts.[187]

By the end of the decade, dances were rivaled in popularity only by roller-skating parties, both of them primary fund raisers for the Nisei clubs. Skating parties were highly profitable, as the *Rafu Shimpo* observed in 1937: "Entailing no actual expense other than newspaper advertising and all derived from tickets sold chalked up as pure profit, the cash which came rolling in was phenomenal. From two to six hundred young people attended every party, which meant $20 profit, at the least, at 10 cents per head."[188] The increase in "skatefests" was attributed to the increasing number of clubs for younger Nisei, as well as the general rise in enthusiasm for roller skating in southern California, perhaps stimulated by publicity received by the Hollywood Rollerbowl in movie magazines.[189] The most popular Nisei venue was the Shrine Rink in Los Angeles where groups such as the Junior Misses "had good times skating to live organ music."[190] Whether on skates or in their dancing shoes, the urban Nisei enjoyed fancy footwork with their friends throughout the prewar period.

Showcasing Nisei Creativity

The youth clubs in southern California, as in San Francisco and Seattle, stimulated and showcased a wide range of Nisei artistic and entrepreneurial creativity.[191] In addition to the pantomimes, singing, skits, and dance exhibitions they staged to entertain fellow club members, the girls' organizations put on a variety of programs attended by parents, peers, and the larger ethnic community. For instance, for a national Buddhist conference in 1927, the entertainment included the Los Angeles YWBA's diligently rehearsed four-act Japanese play "Itamiya Sodo," a tragedy revolving around greed, murder, and retribution.[192] In this pre-television era, such plays and musicals were popular community events.

Another YMWBA (Young Men's and Women's Buddhist Association) production illustrates the Nisei's imaginative selection and synthesis of cultural elements. In May 1932 at the Nishi Hongwanji Auditorium, they staged "Tsumano Atae" ("Price of a Wife"), an adaptation of Ibsen's *Doll House*. The famous "Nora" became the Japanese "Noro," asking her husband, "Do you mean to say that you bought me for $500?"[193] Perhaps feeling that the overcast, rainy Pacific Northwest weather provided a more appropriate atmosphere for Ibsen's play, it was set not in southern California but in Seattle.

The Nisei clubs provided opportunities for young women to produce their own original material as well. In the summer of 1940, for example, the westside Toquiwa girls staged "the stirring melodrama, 'Virtue is Triumphant.'" The *Rafu Shimpo* reported, "An original play, written by the girls themselves, it was complete with the traditional hero, heroine, villain and vamp."[194]

The countless girls' club performances and projects announced in the Japanese American newspapers reflect the tremendous outpouring of Nisei creative energies in the 1920s and 1930s. Within their organizations, young women found a congenial space in which to exercise their imaginations and skills. Depression-era budgetary constraints and inter-club competition challenged them to "make do" in style. Much of their ingenuity was channeled into fund raising programs—whether cleverly themed dances, carnivals, musical variety programs, or cookie sales—to support their annual round of activities, to send delegates to conferences, and to fuel social-service efforts.

Community Service

In addition to their social functions, many of the Nisei organizations had a community service component. For some, it was a priority. This can be seen in the name of the S.O.F. Girl Reserves, which stood for "Service, Opportunity, and Friendship."[195] Girls in such groups tackled a range of projects within the Japanese American community. For example, the newspaper reported in 1933 that the "Cherry Blossom Girls have purchased the material and are now making 'nighties' for all of the girls in the Japanese Children's Home," a local orphanage.[196] The Japanese Children's Home, or Shonien, received much-needed support from the Nisei clubs that, in the same year, launched a fund-raising drive to expand the facilities.[197]

Club social activities tended to dominate in the ethnic press, as the *Rafu Shimpo* noted, whereas community service, although impressive, received less publicity.[198] The newspaper drew attention to the contributions of "nearly 50 Nisei organizations" to the Japanese Community Chest drive in 1938.[199] Young women received special recognition: "Most outstanding were the girls' groups in the Y.W.C.A. organization, which responded 100 per cent."[200]

The young women's clubs regularly collected food and toys for needy families at holiday time. In 1928, the Blue Triangles, for whom this became an annual activity, gave a large Thanksgiving basket "to the Takenouchi family which consists of a widowed mother and five children" and a second basket to "the Uyeda family where the wife is bed-ridden and the husband is unable to work and keep house at the same time."[201] During the difficult Depression years, Nisei groups continued to make efforts to ease the plight of families struggling to make ends meet.[202]

Even recreational activities like dancing provided opportunities for social service. Of five spring dances announced in 1932, three were "benefit dances." Admission to the Savings Association dance required "three large cans of food, preferably Japanese."[203] Later in May, the Blue Triangles lured the light of foot to their "cabaret style" benefit dance with the promise of waltz and foxtrot contests and live music to be furnished by Dave Sato's Wanderer Orchestra. Through such measures the Nisei responded to community needs while enjoying the "excitement of experimentation."

Service activities also reveal ethnic club and community interactions with the larger society. Although it was their main focus, the Nisei did not limit their social-service efforts to the Japanese American enclave. For example, in 1934 a range of Issei and Nisei musicians and dancers performed in a Little Tokyo benefit program to raise funds for the Los Angeles Philharmonic Orchestra. As the *Rafu Shimpo* announced, the program would include an intermission during which "some 40 girls, dressed in beautiful kimonos, will dance down the aisles doing various kind of ondos (Japanese dances)."[204] The money raised from the 25- and 50-cent tickets would be presented to the orchestra fund as "the contribution of the Japanese community."[205] This program reflects Issei and Nisei endeavors to take part in larger civic projects in southern California.

As war approached, the Nisei organizations continued their service activities. For example, Mrs. T. H. Yamasaki proudly declared in the Japanese YWCA Annual Report of 1941:

> As the Japanese Branch we give good service to our community. We helped to sell 500 U.S.O. pins which were 50 cents each. We assisted the local [Japanese American] Citizens League in many ways during its recent 'Nisei Festival' week. Our girls helped to make ticket boxes to put in the votes for the Queen Contest. When they invited [European] American friends to the banquet, our girls ushered and served as hostesses, and when the Inter-racial group had a tea party at the Exposition Park, our girls served tea in Japanese kimonos.[206]

Nisei clubs benefited the community in a range of ways, some material and others less tangible. They raised funds for the needy through bazaars, carnivals, movies, talent shows, and dances, as well as distributing food, clothing and gifts at holiday times.[207] They provided entertainment and opportunities to socialize, for non-affiliated Nisei as well as for their members. And they helped in "cementing Japanese-American friendship outside of the Japanese community."[208]

Interethnic and Interracial Activities

As Yamasaki's report and the sports news suggest, the Nisei youth clubs provided some opportunities for interethnic and interracial interaction. Club dances offer glimpses. For example, at the 1931 Blue Triangle Mid-Season Frolic, Oko Murata, a Blue Triangle member, was "crowned as Queen of the festival by Walter Browne Rodgers, featured player of Universal Studio."[209] The participation of a European American actor at a Nisei dance was unusual, but not the presence of white, African American, or Chinese American musicians. For their Cord and Gingham Dance in the same year, the Queen Esthers engaged the Majestic Mandarins, a ten-piece Chinese American orchestra whose "jazz music was well received."[210] The reportage of two other dances, although not club-sponsored events, draws attention to the existence of interethnic relations in daily life as well as leisure. A Chinese American group, The Celestians, sponsored a dance for Chinese American and Japanese American youth to mark their debut as a jazz orchestra. Five musicians in the eight-piece ensemble were already familiar to the Nisei in Little Tokyo, as members of "the Lem family of Lem's Café, prominent café located in the heart of the Japanese community."[211] When an "oriental sport dance" was held "to create a better feeling of friendship" between Chinese Americans and Japanese Americans, the Rafu Shimpo noted,

"This is one of the few dances to which the Japanese people as a whole have been invited to attend. In the past, many Japanese individuals have been invited to various Chinese dances."[212] The dance floor, whether at the International Institute or a Knights of Pythias hall, also constituted a site for interethnic encounters.

Joint club activities occasionally brought together young women of various ethnic backgrounds, often under the auspices of church-sponsored events. The YWCA and the International Institute were particularly active in promoting these occasions. As Judy Yung has found, the Girl Reserves afforded a rare venue for Chinese American girls to interact interethnically and interracially.[213] Such was also the case for their Japanese American counterparts. In 1926 the members of the Japanese High School Girl Reserves Club of the Union Church attended a "rally" at a boarding school for Mexican girls. More than 200 girls attended, including European American girls from Los Angeles Presbyterian churches. As their part of the rally, the Nisei girls dressed in kimonos and sang songs in Japanese.[214] In the same month, the T.M.T.M. Girl Reserves entertained 15 European American girls from Hollywood at a meeting whose theme was "Friendship."[215]

The Nisei clubs also sent delegates to conferences with which they were affiliated as "ethnic branches." For example, in 1928, 15 delegates from the YWCA's International Institute attended the Southern California Girl Reserves Conference in Hollywood. This delegation included seven Nisei and "representatives from the Russian, Mexican, Armenian and the Neighborhood [probably African American] groups...."[216] The Nisei attendees, it was noted, "would stay at some [European] American home during the two nights of the conference."[217] Such conferences offered chances for both interethnic and interracial contact.

Interracial understanding was the theme of a women college students' conference, held annually among "the stately pines and snowy sand dunes" of Asilomar, California, in 1926. The 10 Japanese American delegates from organizations such as the JSCA and the YWCA spent 10 days with 400 other students from Arizona, California, Nevada, and Utah. Attendee Lily Satow reported, "Besides the usual hikes, athletic tournaments, marshmallow roasts, midnight feeds, etc., the days were filled with lectures, chapel services, discussion groups, and intimate heart-to-heart talks," all intended "to give each girl a better understanding of herself and her fellowmen" as well as to strengthen her fellowship with God.[218] Satow particularly took note of conference leaders who spoke on issues of race: The "only Negro public school teacher in California" made "a powerful appeal for inter-racial justice." A "government research student from Mexico" showed film footage and "helped the girls to take a sane view of the Mexican situation." Dr. Yamato Ichihashi, a Stanford University professor, gave five lectures that "disclosed the truth about the Orient and in some cases startled his hearers by his candid revelations."[219]

This conference simultaneously provided opportunities for cross-ethnic discourse and recreational activities and for the strengthening of Nisei ties. According to Lily Satow, the Japanese American delegates from northern and southern California and Hawai'i met almost daily for their own private discussion group.[220] At such conferences, often sponsored by Christian youth organizations, young Nisei women came into contact with peers and elders of other racial/ethnic groups, gaining opportunities to discuss issues of race and gender and enjoying exposure to an even wider range of cultural practices.

Nisei Clubs on the Eve of War

In 1940, the *Rafu Shimpo* announced the presence of "nearly 400 active nisei organizations" in southern California.[221] By this time many of the senior Nisei clubs shared a common pattern: "Their activities form an endless cycle—the inevitable annual elections; the installation of officers, usually calling for an exclusive ceremony and dance; bi-weekly or monthly meetings for business or informal socials and an annual benefit to raise funds to carry on these activities."[222] The younger Nisei were no less busy, as the schedule of events planned by the girls' Emanon Club in Santa Monica for December 1939 through August 1940 illustrates. In December the members worked on a Christmas basket for the Shonien and looked forward to a party at the Aramaki Chop Suey. Their planned activities included skating, a snow hike, a wild flower outing, a "weenie bake," and several socials.[223] Every season offered plentiful opportunities for urban young women's engagement in club events.

The proliferation of youth organizations prompted the *Rafu Shimpo* to ask, "Are they necessary?" Journalist Sadae Nomura assessed their role in the lives of three cohorts of urban Nisei and concluded that clubs were "desirable and useful as well as necessary."[224]

Nomura painted a vivid picture of the lively "teensters." The typical 15-year-old girl and boy excelled scholastically: "[D]espite their hard-boiled, extremely-Americanized attitudes, they still have enough Japanese in them to respect and look up to their teachers." The girl is more mature than the boy, but "you can't tell him so." They were at different stages in their attitudes toward the opposite sex: "For the past few years" the Nisei girl "has had a definite interest in the opposite sex, and is subject to sporadic crushes. She loves to dance, with a special weakness for jitterbugging." By contrast, the Nisei boy is indifferent to girls, although his outlook is liable to change shortly. Both the boy and girl were "completely engrossed in their respective clubs."

Nomura viewed the clubs as "healthy, wholesome" outlets for youthful energy. Meetings provided girls with opportunities for self-improvement; for boys, athletics were paramount. Within their organizations, the young Nisei learned "to develop their minds and talents with talks and discussions led by older people, lessons in handicraft, in etiquette, in developing personalities, in morals, etc." These lessons, she suggested, supplemented what was learned at school and at home.

After high school, club life provided escape from the daily rigors of the "working Nisei." Nomura noted their milestones: "She voted for the first time this year, while he became of draft-age last year." Both women and men entered the wage-paid work force early, facing limited opportunities: "She is a secretary to a nisei lawyer in Li'l Tokio, which she has been for the past two years, ever since she graduated from business school. He is working in a fruit stand, not because he likes it especially well, but it pays well, compared to a lot of white-collar jobs, and besides, there is nothing else to do." Clearly, the Nisei played a role in the family economy, as well as enjoying some disposable income: "Most of their earned income goes into their family, but what is left for them is used most eagerly— hers for clothes, mostly, and his for the all-important dates." As the single young women and men slogged through their daily grind, Nisei clubs served as their "one outlet and major interest.... At times when their work becomes too, too boring and unbearable, the prospect of a session with 'the girls' or 'the boys'... is always something to look forward to."

The Nisei clubs continued to provide camaraderie for the married urban second generation. These older women and men were the "pioneers in the nisei world": "It was they who had to break in the Issei to the American way of life. They had to convince their parents that clubs were an essential part of the young people's lives—that dancing was a traditional American custom and perfectly correct—that it was all right to go out on dates." Like the Chinese American second generation, the Japanese American youth played an important part in "socializing their parents to a different behavioral pattern." [225] However, according to Nomura, the Nisei clubs had an influential role in a process of two-way socialization:

> Through their leaders, they [the Nisei] were kept from going too extremely American, so much so that they might have become too far alienated from their parents.... They were made to realize that their Japanese heritage worked for their own good in many ways; that things Japanese were not necessarily old-fashioned and "wrong."

In Nomura's words, the clubs emerge as a crucial mediator between children and parents, facilitating the Nisei's understanding of the Issei and appreciation of ethnic culture, as well as their adoption of mainstream recreation and ideas.

Although still a "vital part of their lives," the clubs to which the married Nisei belonged may have differed from the organizations of their school years. Nomura suggested that the young adults had outgrown the "Girl Reserves and [YMCA] Comrade clubs." Indeed, once girls graduated from high school, they could not technically be Girl Reserves, but often continued to meet with the same group of friends, sometimes under a new name, sometimes affiliating themselves with a YWCA branch for young working women. For example, the T.M.T.M. Girl Reserves decided to become the Blue Triangles after graduation; likewise, the older cohort of the Hollywood Queen Esthers in 1937 began meeting under the new name "Fifteen Little Working Girls."[226] Nomura described the young married Nisei woman as typically belonging to "a group that was one of the most active in the earlier thirties. Most of the group are either married or have been going steady for years. They're all working, except the ones with children." The young married Nisei man was likely to have joined "an organization that is largely civic in character," whose activities "boost him both materially and spiritually."

Nomura's 1940 article, written after more than 15 years of mushrooming Nisei club growth, indicated that same-sex organizational affiliations—at least for the urban second generation—retained significance even for married women and men. Nomura was adamant that the "clubs have not diminished in importance with their growth into full womanhood and manhood.... The clubs have become a vital part of their lives in making their existence well-rounded and wholesome." [227]

Not all Nisei leaders agreed with Nomura's positive view of the Japanese American youth clubs. Throughout the 1930s, occasional grumbling from older Nisei about the frivolity of club social activities surfaced in the ethnic newspapers. By 1940, as U.S.-Japan tensions increased, some community pundits were critiquing the notion of Nisei-only clubs. Uneasy about their conspicuous separation from mainstream organizations and overlooking the racial barriers that gave rise to it, they urged the second generation to seek admission to non–Japanese American clubs as well as to integrate their own. Sam Hohri, who called the Nisei "over-clubbed," targeted for abandonment the "Japanese club in schools," of which he said, "We're the only racial group that extensively fosters them." Instead he urged the Nisei to join interethnic and interracial school organizations, which in fact some Nisei did in high schools with more inclusive and diverse populations, such as the Roosevelt and Belmont High Schools. This, he felt, would allow the Nisei not only to "extend their appreciation of their fellow Americans and v.v. [vice versa], but would further their interests in other pursuits—develop possible life interests instead of being sadly limited to rounds of dances, skating parties and conferences."[228] After the bombing of Pearl Harbor on December 7, 1941 and the outbreak of war between the United States and Japan, Warren Tsuneishi criticized not only "exclusive Nisei churches, Nisei clubs, and the Nisei Citizens League [Japanese American Citizens League]" but also the Nisei press, which he felt "'exclusivizes' the Nisei and cuts down his social horizon."[229] Tsuneishi glossed over the racial barriers that Nisei often faced in trying to join mainstream organizations and put the onus on the shoulders of the second generation to break through them: "we feel that someone has to break the ice somewhere—and it might as well be we who are hard-headed, thick-skinned, and inclined to laugh off the 'discrimination', 'prejudice', etc., which we are bound to encounter."[230] Indeed, he charged that by forming exclusively Japanese American groups, the Nisei "actively discriminate against Negroes, Chinese, Filipinos, Mexicans, and Caucasians."[231] He noted that his views had aroused antagonism, not from the "greater [white] group, our neighbors," who he lauded for their "agreeableness and democratic-ness," but from the Nisei themselves. As Akatsuki Sakano had learned 14 years earlier, the second generation held strong attachments to their clubs.

Nevertheless, older Nisei continued to sound this theme, as hostility against Japanese Americans grew and their situation became increasingly tenuous. Mary Oyama Mittwer, a prolific writer and energetic organizer, wrote, "After more than 15 years of active participation in the Japanese and nisei community activities, we have arrived at the identical conclusion arrived at by Warren Tsuneishi and Charles Kikuchi.... We do not believe in 'Japanese' clubs, organizations, Y.M.C.A.'s, churches and even the J.A.C.L."[232] Overlooking as Tsuneishi had the segregationist policies of institutions such as the YMCA, YWCA, and many churches, Oyama similarly urged the second generation to join or form integrated groups. She cited examples from among the co-ed organizations of more senior Nisei:

> ...the Nisei Democrats affiliated with the Caucasian American group and are now the Twentieth Century Club. The Writers group dropped the word "Nisei" and have admitted Caucasian Americans into membership. We hope to see them soon affiliated with the larger body of the American Writers group.[233]

The glare of war intensified Japanese American vulnerability, and in this harsh light their actions can be seen as desperate attempts to integrate themselves into the larger body politic and to counter the forces that were moving to tear them from it. As Oyama Mittwer presciently wrote, "We are entering the Era of a Great Change in our nisei and Japanese community."

Immediately after Pearl Harbor, uncertainty and curfews curtailed Nisei club activities; dances and socials were canceled as inappropriate under the circumstances. The newspapers urged Japanese American women to become involved in the war effort, for, as the *Rafu Shimpo* proclaimed, "This is no time for nisei girls to remain shy, reticent, modest o[r] coy as the women of still-socially feudal Japan are. The slow Americanization of our new immigrant community must be speeded up."[234] The girls' clubs responded, channeling their energies into knitting and sewing clothing for the armed services, taking first-aid courses, and collecting food for the needy in the community. By the end of December, in order to bolster spirits, the YWCA clubs resumed their activities, which they restricted to daytime affairs, unless chaperonage and blackout precautions could be arranged for evening meetings and socials. As Sophie Tajima, the Group Work Secretary, charged the advisers of the 35 affiliated clubs of the Japanese YWCA, "we have the responsibility of keeping high the morale of our members and of our community.... Remember that we are ... trying to help develop character strong enough to live today and far-visioned enough to plan for the post-war reconstruction."[235] A number of clubs began to schedule modest activities such as sports practices, but for the most part, they busied themselves supporting the war effort. Louise Suski reported on December 28, 1941 that "All girl's clubs are now taking up civilian defense work, mostly through the Japanese Y.W.C.A."[236]

The "Great Change" that Mary Oyama Mittwer foresaw would prove to be far more drastic and devastating than anyone imagined. As Japanese Americans were uprooted from their homes and neighborhoods, the social networks they had forged in earlier decades would be severely tested in the crucible of wartime incarceration and resettlement.

2

Shaping Japanese American Culture

The wedding guests who gathered at the Japanese Union Church on the evening of December 8, 1928 listened to the familiar tune "I Love You Truly" as they awaited the bridal party. When the wedding march sounded its cue, two small flower girls came down an aisle, followed by a ring bearer, four bridesmaids, and a maid of honor, gowned in pastel taffeta and carrying bouquets. The focal point was the bride, Rosemary Matsuno, who appeared in a snow-white satin dress and a long veil crowned by a headdress of orange blossoms. Along the other aisle marched four Nisei ushers and behind them the groom, Justus Sato, with his best man. In accordance with mainstream custom, they drew far less attention than the bride and her entourage.

After a short ceremony conducted in Japanese, the couple rushed to a festively decorated reception room where their friends showered them with congratulations. A European American representative of the YWCA's International Institute chaired the reception, at which celebratory speeches were made as well as thanks given to the guests, as was customary at a Japanese wedding. The guests enjoyed light refreshments served by the Blue Triangles—the bride's club—and a musical program showcased local Nisei female talent, two singers and a pianist.

Following the nuptial script that the urban Nisei knew by heart, as the musical program ended, the newlyweds dashed from the church to a waiting automobile to make their getaway. The only glitch was the bride's throwing her bouquet skyward—it fell on the sidewalk and was retrieved, as expected, by a young Nisei woman. Then Rosemary and Justus departed amid the cheerful clatter of tin cans tied to the car.[1]

From the first strains of the wedding march to the tossing of the bridal bouquet, the format of the Matsuno-Sato wedding—the church site, the music, the attire, the focus on the bride and her attendants, and the guests' familiarity with all of these elements—reflected urban Nisei adoption of American mainstream customs and popular culture. Although Nisei weddings like this one differed dramatically from the unions of the Issei in Japan, the conducting of the ceremony in Japanese as well as the thanks given to the guests on behalf of the newlyweds also show the Nisei's acknowledgment of their parents and the immigrant community. The newspaper's explanation of the thanks giving as part of a "Japanese wedding" suggests that some of the second generation may already have become more accustomed to mainstream nuptial conventions. Second-generation girls and young women took an active part in synthesizing such customs.

This chapter examines how, within and outside the ethnic enclave, Nisei women played significant roles as agents of culture, adapting mainstream and other ethnic cultural practices while maintaining and sometimes contesting Japanese customs. Second-generation women were attracted by aspects of modern American femininity that offered greater freedom of choice and expression; they also selectively affirmed elements of Japanese culture filtered through the immigrant community. Women were the most visible arbiters of social etiquette, serving as conduits of the manners expected in the Japanese American community and in mainstream settings, dispensed through advice columns. Similarly, women sustained their ethnic culture by preparing Japanese dishes, while also broadening the Japanese American palate by adopting European American, Chinese American, and Latino cuisine. Girls and young women were also called upon to represent the ethnic community at civic and school events, wearing kimono and performing Japanese songs and dance— something not expected of their brothers. This role caused increasing tension by the time war became imminent. The image of a traditional Japanese maiden, perceived as "exotic" and "foreign" by the larger society, conflicted with the modern American femininity Nisei women sought to claim. The newspaper coverage of fashion, beauty culture, and movies reflects their engagement with popular culture. Women quickly adopted mainstream female rituals such as wedding showers that affirmed both ties of female friendship and romantic heterosexual love. Nisei patterns of mixed-sex socializing, courtship, and marriage show their embrace of mainstream practices, while taking measures to ensure the propriety expected by the immigrant community. However, subversive elements of women's culture reveal that they sometimes critiqued western romantic ideals as well as the authority of Issei parents. Through their continuing role in the family economy, women supported Japanese values of filial piety and obligation, though their choices were limited by racial discrimination and Depression-era stringencies.

Women's choices proved influential in shaping Japanese American culture, not only on festive occasions but also in daily life.[2] For the urban second generation, everyday life involved learning to traverse multiethnic neighborhoods, Japanese American institutions, and mainstream schools and businesses. It was often Nisei women who provided guidance for their peers in demystifying the etiquette of the immigrant community and the dominant society.

Nisei Women as Social Arbiters

Second-generation women served as keen social arbiters, dispensing a wide range of advice through the Japanese American newspapers. Both men and women aired their opinions in the English-language sections, often under the cover of pseudonyms like "Madame Nadeshiko."[3] In 1931 the *Rafu Shimpo* editors remarked on the "super-abundance" of young columnists, which they linked to the "Americanization" of the second generation. In other words, they associated the glut of writers with a trend publicized in the mainstream press: Americans, hungry for the intimate connections and fresh ideas previously provided by the exchange of personal letters, were turning to newspaper columnists for the same comfort.[4] There were fewer female than male editors and reporters, and women's roles in the English-language newspapers remained circumscribed, with men more often enjoying the privilege of writing unrestricted columns.[5] However, the wide array of Nisei advice columns was written largely by and for women.

The urban second generation, trying to please their parents as well as navigate the unfamiliar waters of mainstream middle-class social convention, could turn to such advice columnists for guidance. In the *Kashu Mainichi*, Emiko Hashira responded succinctly to male and female readers' questions such as "Should a girl repair her makeup in public?" and "Should the boy serve the girl with refreshments at a social?"[6] Indeed the Nisei were targeted for a great deal of general advice in the newspapers, from hints not to say anything if they found an insect in their food, to stern admonitions such as "Avoid strong tea and coffee, evil companions, lewd conversations, and corrupt and vicious novels."[7]

"Madame Nadeshiko," "Miss Etiquette," and others provided clues to proper behavior within the immigrant community. In 1933 a crusty advice maven railed at the Nisei for the "unpardonable sins" of failing to greet one's hosts, using the telephone without permission, and lounging "in all sorts of ungodly positions in davenports, chesterfields, or easy chairs with a gigolo-ish lounge lizard attitudes [sic]!"[8] Taking for granted urban amenities and superiority, she gave advice tailored both to Issei expectations and the varying language skills of Nisei boys and girls: "Upon leaving your friend's home say, 'go-men ku-da sai' (preferable to the rustic 'kon-nichi wa') or say 'o-jama ni a-gari ma shita.' If you cannot speak Japanese say, 'How do you do, Mrs. Saito' or 'Good evening, Mr. Yamada'..."[9]

Sometimes the discourse on manners reflected the Nisei's involvement in interracial as well as intraethnic relations. In 1936 "Miss Etiquette," for example, urged the Nisei to send thank you notes promptly, citing the unfortunate tardiness of a "well-known Japanese girls' organization" that sent a "bread-and-butter" note "practically a month after borrowing an American lady's home and garden for a meeting and a dinner."[10]

Columnists devoted considerable space to boy-girl socializing and courtship, addressing situations from multiple perspectives. After a Nisei boy wrote to ask the proper way to approach a girl for a dance, "Miss Etiquette" not only made it the subject of her column but in subsequent weeks held forth on how a hostess at a dance might deal with "wall-flowers" and also how a young woman might become the "belle of the ball," or, failing that, when she should give up and go home.[11] Likewise, men and women were counseled on appropriate holiday gifts for friends of the opposite sex and for family members. "Miss Etiquette" warned single women against giving clothing or jewelry to men, recommending books and advising that home-made candy and fruit cake "are always welcome—provided you are a good cook."[12]

The *Rafu Shimpo* also offered more intimate advice for second-generation readers, who were not always comfortable discussing such matters with their parents or sometimes lacked the command of Japanese to do so. In the 1920s the newspaper regularly carried reprinted articles on nutrition, communicable diseases, and sex education. From a moralistic series of stories put out by the American Medical Association for young readers, Nisei could learn about boys' nocturnal emissions, girls' menstrual cycles, and the dangers of venereal disease.[13] By 1940 a woman physician, Dr. Megumi Y. Shinoda, offered medical advice in "Among Us Women." Her frank columns provided detailed information on issues such as childbirth, athlete's foot, varicose veins, and baby health. She introduced Nisei women to procedures like episiotomy, which she presented as a beneficial surgical technique not available to the midwives who attended Issei deliveries.[14]

Through advice columns and other writings, Japanese American women helped to shape the nascent Nisei social world. From their articles readers learned how to interact with the Issei and with middle-class European Americans, as well as how to behave with peers at dances and socials. Women similarly sustained and expanded Japanese American customs in the culinary arena.

Food and Foodways

Nisei gender roles, as well as women's efforts to maintain ethnic cultural practices and their experimentation with other cultural influences, were particularly evident in the culinary realm. In accordance with Western and Asian gender roles, girls and women prepared most of the food for Japanese American gatherings, which constituted a major area of unpaid female labor. Food figured largely in the Nisei world, whether prepared for a family holiday or a group fund-raising event. No 1920s reportage of an outing, meeting, wedding, or club social was complete without a reference to the "good eats" that were enjoyed. From early on, urban women showed interest in European American and other ethnic cuisines.

Culinary experimentation engaged Issei women such as Mary Nishi Ishizuka's mother, who excelled at both Japanese and western cooking. Mary remembered fondly the "bottles and bottles of root beer that she made for us,"[15] her wonderful tsukemono (pickles) and sukiyaki, as well as corn chowder. Urban Japanese women encountered new dishes through jobs as domestic workers in white households, through their Japanese friends, and from neighbors. For example, Setsuko Matsunaga Nishi's mother learned from an African American neighbor how to bake deep-dish apple pie. Taka Honda attended adult classes in English and cooking at the Nora Sterry School, where she learned how to prepare a Thanksgiving dinner; her repertoire included pumpkin pie and peanut butter cookies.[16] Many kept up with the latest Japanese recipes through women's magazines such as *Shufu no Tomo,* and those with English skills consulted American cookbooks such as *The Joy of Cooking.*

Both Nisei daughters and Issei mothers were eager to improve their culinary skills, as reflected by the popularity of cooking classes in the Japanese American community. The Japanese YWCA taught "Japanese and western style culinary art," and the Midori Kai, an "Uptown Ladies Club," advertised lessons in baking and making pudding as well as in Japanese cookery.[17] Girls' organizations also sometimes included cooking lessons in the round of their activities. In 1928 the young women of the Blue Triangle Club favored culinary training over handicrafts and etiquette.[18]

These cooking classes were often explicitly aimed at preparing women for their anticipated roles as wives and mothers. With marital harmony in mind, the Midori Kai proclaimed the household art of cooking a necessity for every wife and mother; wives were invited to attend their classes so that "their husbands will always want to eat at home."[19] The *Rafu Shimpo* similarly encouraged women to take the Japanese YWCA's Japanese cookery classes, saying, "Girls, here's one way you can make your husbands happy. They may be tired of ham and eggs every morning."[20] A decade later, a forum of Nisei college students in northern California reported that men believed cooking skills essential for women and that most of the women in attendance were majoring in home economics or taking cooking classes. All present agreed that "we shall want both American and Japanese cooking in our homes."[21]

By the mid-1930s, the Nisei women appear to have been most interested in three areas of cuisine: Japanese, "American," and Chinese. In this, they both reflected and bucked the larger trend of the homogenization of the national diet stemming from the growth of giant food companies, technologies of preservation and distribution, and a flood of culinary advice dispensed via radio, cookbooks, and newspapers.[22] At this time the regional model deemed emblematic

of American cuisine shifted from New England to the Midwest—a shift that may
have been hastened in California by the influx of Midwestern migrants in the
early twentieth century.[23] To the Nisei, "American" food seemed to mean the
kind of meat-and-potatoes fare popular among transplanted Midwesterners. In a
1936 special supplement, the *Rafu Shimpo* focused on the three favored categories. They took pains to distinguish between "Real Tempura" and "Occidental
fritters," and to explain how "Original Sukiyaki" differed from the "U.S. Variety."[24]
This may indicate not only the Nisei women's interest in preserving cultural
practices and flavors, but the introduction of certain Japanese dishes—such as
sukiyaki—into broader West Coast dining. As the newspaper predicted blithely,
"It won't be long before the American people will come to adopt Japanese dishes
in their homes."[25]

Women's culinary experimentation and improvisation stimulated the development of hybrid forms that became part of Japanese American cuisine. A recipe for pakkai (sweet-and-sour spare ribs) reflected this hybridization: among
the ingredients were katakuriko (Japanese starch made from dogtooth violets),
shoyu (soy sauce), green chili pepper (an element of regional Mexican American
cuisine), and a can of pineapple, hinting at the labor migration routes that
Chinese and Japanese settlers pursued from Hawai'i to the continental United
States.[26] In the process of cultural coalescence, Japanese immigrants and their
children drew on a rich array of culinary traditions in the multicultural landscape
of the U.S. West.

The urban setting offered the Nisei opportunities to try new dishes. Fumiko
Fukuyama Ide recalled how, as a junior high school student, for the first time, she
bought a dish of macaroni and cheese at the cafeteria: "I loved it! I never knew
such things existed." On the way home from studying at the downtown Central
Library, she and her friends would stop at the Thrifty Drugstore for cherry cokes
and ice cream sodas. A special treat was a jaunt to the Pig 'N Whistle—"THE
dessert place to go to"—which introduced her to delights such as mocha chocolate cake and carrot cake.[27] Varied cultural influences and the integration of a
round of Japanese and U.S. holidays can be seen in the array of recipes in the
Kashu Mainichi. In the spring of 1938, for example, home cooks could find
instructions for dishes including a Ukrainian Easter dessert, Kashiwa mochi (a
sweetened rice confection) for Japanese Boys' Day, Mother's Day angel food
cake, and German potato salad to serve fifty.[28] City families living in or near an
ethnic enclave were more likely to have access to—and to be able to afford—a
range of Asian and western ingredients.

In the early 1940s, the *Rafu Shimpo's* recipe section—by then a regular feature—reflected Nisei women's continuing interest in both Japanese cultural practices and culinary diversity. For instance, a discussion of tsukemono (Japanese
pickles), without which a "Japanese meal is never complete," might share the

page with recipes for cream sponge cake and baked lemon pudding.[29] The Nisei were also encouraged to try "'Good neighbor' dishes from south of the border," such as "Enchilada Luncheon Pie" and "Mexican Chicken," though they were so heavily adapted to the mainstream U.S. (and possibly Japanese American) palate that it is questionable whether a Mexican cook would recognize their origin.[30] Reflecting the second-generation girls' club activities, the newspaper offered "sure fire" cookie recipes for "your next club tea" or for the club cookie sales that had become "quite the fad these days."[31]

The preparation and consumption of food became a bonding experience for Nisei girls, particularly as part of their group activities. Together, they experimented with making foods unfamiliar to their parents, like seafoam candy and fudge; they cemented ties of gender and generation at club teas and "progressive dinners" during which each course would be served at a different club member's home. They often utilized their cooking skills on behalf of their organizations, holding box-lunch socials and bake sales. Their food preparation also retained significance in the family realm.

From the mid-1920s to the Second World War, traditional holiday food held deep importance for Japanese Americans, urban and rural. Chinese American women also cooked special holiday foods signifying wishes for health, wealth, and longevity. The planning and presentation of such festive dishes and other rituals remained female responsibilities, part of women's work of maintaining kinship ties.[32] Issei and Nisei women played a crucial role in preparing the symbolic dishes vital to the celebration of family, community, and shared ethnicity.

A central New Year's food—rice cakes—entailed elaborate, often communal preparation, called "mochi tsuki." Rose Honda recalled that relatives and friends would gather a few days before New Year's for the festive occasion. Her mother would soak and steam sweet glutinous rice, which would then be dumped into a large concrete mortar. The men would take turns pounding it rhythmically with wooden mallets, two at a time, while the women would wet the mochi. When it had reached a smooth consistency, the women would remove the rice and quickly shape the hot, sticky mass into small round rice cakes. Everyone who came to help with the mochi tsuki would take a portion home. Saving some for their New Year's soup, Rose's family would toast the fresh mochi and eat it with soy sauce and sugar, or a mixture of kinako (toasted soybean flour) and sugar.[33]

Observed on January 1, New Year's Day—Oshogatsu—was the major holiday for Japanese Americans, whose ways of celebrating varied somewhat depending on the region of Japan from which they had come. For most, it was imperative to have a fresh start for the New Year, with a clean house and a bath the previous night. Since no work was supposed to be done on that day, women spent hours beforehand preparing a range of symbolic dishes invoking health and good fortune for the coming year. Most Japanese families began New Year's

Day with ozoni, a clear soup in which rice cakes floated, symbolizing prosperity. When people visited their friends to share good wishes for the new year, they enjoyed a feast prepared by the Issei and Nisei women of the household, which might include mame (sweetened black beans, a homonym for "health"), kazunoko (herring roe, symbolizing fertility), kimpira (spicy strips of burdock root), kamaboko (steamed fish cakes), nishime (a cooked vegetable dish), makizushi (rolled sushi), inarizushi (rice in soy pouches), and yokan (a sweet bean confection).[34]

Over the course of the prewar period, the coverage of ethnic holiday food in the newspapers reflected the coming of age of the second generation. As youngsters, the urban second generation enjoyed a mixture of New Year's observances. As Nellie Nimura wrote in a 1931 New Year's greeting to the editor of the *Rafu Shimpo*, "I'm getting a quite a dose of this Japanese American harmony idea. Danced just about all night of New Year's Eve a la Americain style and getting up early the same morning to eat historic 'o-zoni' and other antiquated foods."[35] She slept through the rest of the day, rising in time to hear the score of the football game. Her letter suggests that she lived in her parents' household as a daughter—perhaps a younger daughter—who was not required to do any of the New Year work. Nimura's breezy attitude about holiday harmony may have suffered a serious challenge when her turn came to face the tasks of preparing the ozoni and all the "antiquated dishes" she so readily ate.

By the end of the 1930s, the swelling ranks of the Nisei matured and increasing numbers of second-generation women began to shoulder primary responsibilities in their parents' and their own households. As Nisei handled more of the food preparation, the *Kashu Mainichi* and the *Rafu Shimpo* relayed the significance of the special New Year's dishes as well as the instructions for making them.[36]

By this time there appeared obvious tensions arising between the time-consuming work of producing Oshogatsu food and urban Nisei inclinations to celebrate the holiday in more Western fashion. In 1941, a journalist reported, "With each new year, the traditional Japanese-style New Year's Day with its dishes after dishes of Japanese food becomes more outmoded. The young folks don't see much sense in wasting the precious New Year's Eve hours in working over a hot stove for foods they'd just as soon do without, while the issei parents are beginning to agree with them."[37] Nevertheless, traditional recipes were reprinted for the benefit of Nisei whose parents "feel that New Year's wouldn't be New Year's without kazunoko, omochi and the rest."[38] Of course, many of the second generation did enjoy eating ozoni, sushi, and yokan. However, given the labor involved in preparing these foods, the desire to please the Issei and a sense of filial duty clearly became major factors in Nisei women's decisions about how to celebrate the New Year.

Second-generation girls and women quite literally nourished their communities, preparing the food for a wide variety of private and public events, ranging from club socials and church fund-raisers to weddings. They cooked staple foods like rice and holiday dishes laden with symbolism; at the same time they also introduced other cuisines into the ethnic community, adapting flavors to suit Japanese American tastes. Not only did they provide many of the "good eats" for Japanese American organizations, they occasionally introduced Japanese food to groups outside the community.[39] In the 1930s, for example, when sukiyaki became a trendy dish in southern California, Nisei girls prepared it for their own parties and were also called upon to cook and serve it for interethnic college organizations and European American society events.[40] Within and outside the ethnic enclave, women often provided symbolic linkages to Japanese culture.

Representing the Ethnic Community

Nisei girls, more than boys, were expected to represent the ethnic community at school festivals and civic events. This meant putting aside their regular clothes and donning Japanese kimono with ornate obi (sashes). They were usually called upon to serve tea or to perform traditional Japanese songs and dances. For example, in 1933 Nisei girls took part in an "International Day" celebration at the YWCA's International Institute in Boyle Heights. As a reporter noted, the Nisei girls participated in "bringing the color of the Cherry Blossom Isles to the afternoon."[41] On the one hand, such performances can be viewed as an affirmation of immigrant ethnic culture. On the other hand, they also illustrate how the second-generation Japanese Americans were often "typecast" as exotic and foreign, rather than recognized as homegrown Americans.[42] This complex role, a striking contrast to the image of the Modern Girl, reinforced stereotypes and made Nisei daughters increasingly uncomfortable as war approached.

From the 1920s on, Nisei girls clad in "picturesque" kimonos served as highly visible community representatives at an array of civic events.[43] In 1926, forty "Cherry Blossom Girls"—twenty from the YWCA, ten from the Higashi Hongwanji Buddhist Temple, and ten from a private teacher—were slated to perform at the "Festival of Nations," a pageant organized to support the work of the Council on International Relations and to "present in a dramatic way scenes that reveal accurately the life of the people in their respective countries."[44] Despite their American birth and upbringing, Nisei women were often identified as being from Japan. In 1928 ten Nisei girls danced in the Roosevelt High School's "All-Nations Festival" held to raise funds for equipment for the Girls' Gymnasium. The *Rafu Shimpo* reported without irony, "Native girls of many nations, wearing their costumes, will give their country's dance at this time."[45]

It could be argued that a costume and dance more representative of the urban Nisei girl might have been a drop-waisted dress and the foxtrot. Nevertheless, the prevailing public image of them may well have been that of the exotic maiden in colorful Japanese robes and sash.

The second-generation women's ethnic-cultural performance adds a gendered twist to the idea of the Nisei's potential role as a bridge of understanding between the United States and Japan. This metaphor, initiated by the Issei, was adapted by some of the second generation as they tried to navigate between the expectations of mainstream society and their ethnic enclave.[46] Although most of the second generation lacked the Japanese cultural knowledge needed to fulfill such a role, this notion remained a potent motif in Nisei discourse from the mid-1920s through much of the 1930s.[47] Part of its appeal lay in the prospect of a significant part that might be played by the Nisei, many of whom struggled with generational and racial issues in addition to economic uncertainty and political vulnerability. It was with an eye to U.S.-Japan tensions—and the Nisei situation—that Miyoko "Mickey" Shimizu, an Emba Girl Reserve and the winner of the 1933 Southern California Japanese YMCA oratorical contest, proclaimed, "Even today…with the dawn of the Pacific era, the peoples of the different races are not on the terms they should be." This she attributed to white domination of, and discrimination toward, "colored groups."[48] Shimizu delineated the mindsets of the Nisei within the framework of their subordinate position in U.S. society:

> Because we are physically Oriental and since many fellow Americans of the white races do not consider us as equals, the attitude of most of us is that we should live closely together and organize within ourselves a self-sufficient unit. There are others of us who feel that for our own good as well as the best interests of all others, we should at the same time endeavor to break into American society.[49]

cultural bridge

She proposed that the second generation could help to alleviate the international (and perhaps the local) problem by serving as "the medium through which Japan and America will understand each other." The role of the cultural bridge was frequently delegated to young Nisei women in the prewar period, particularly on the U.S. side.

Nisei women in kimono occasionally served as intermediaries in formal U.S.-Japan encounters. A few days after Shimizu took first place in the oratory contest, the *Kashu Mainichi* announced that "Maids of Lil' Tokio on Japanese Ships Help to Bridge Real Friendship."[50] One hundred Nisei girls "dressed in beautiful kimonos"—and under the eye of chaperone Mrs. Mogi—entertained and served as interpreters for 150 U.S. midshipmen and 200 midshipmen of the Japanese Naval Training Squadron during an afternoon tea on the deck of the Iwate. The midshipmen "exchanged cards and personal views on the naval problems with much discussion on the customs of the country," no doubt aided by the Nisei young women who, the *Kashu* reported, helped to add the "Color and Atmosphere of Cherry Blossom Land."[51] Nisei men were noticeably absent from this occasion. On board the battleship Iwate, young women were not only expected to provide a Nisei bridge of understanding between "Japan" and "America," but also to facilitate friendly relations between two groups of military men.

As war approached, this public role caused increasing discomfort for some Nisei, particularly as it was requested by European American organizations. In an interethnic religious forum, Reverend Donald Toriumi, Y.P. (Young People's) pastor of the Los Angeles Presbytery, lamented, "We wish to be treated like the rest of the Americans, and yet we are not....Yes, even when we are invited to church gatherings and racial and Americanization meetings, the amazing fact is that, in many instances, we are asked to come dressed in our 'native' costumes, sing Japanese songs and teach the people the secret lores of Oriental culture."[52] This burden weighed heavily on Nisei women, as Toriumi explained: "Upon inquiring, I have found that most of the girls do not care to wear these Japanese kimonoes [sic]. Many of the cute and quaint Japanese songs you have heard were doll songs and other children's songs learned in preschool days. The secret lores that you have heard were, in many cases, frantically gathered, and thrown into some kind of presentable shape and were given by people who kept their fingers crossed and hoped that no one would ask any embarrassing detailed questions."[53] Toriumi's words conjure images of young Nisei women hastily gleaning bits of information from Issei mothers and then uneasily relaying them to white audiences desiring to hear Oriental secrets imparted by exotic "Others." No doubt some Nisei women enjoyed or took pride in ethnic-cultural performance, but they differed in their level of comfort with it and experienced tensions surrounding this role by 1941.

The image of the Nisei daughter in kimono, though read somewhat differently, was important symbolically in the ethnic community as well. Rose Honda and her sister, in elaborate makeup and kimono, danced at Japanese school programs, wedding receptions, and kenjinkai picnics. Young women in kimono were often the highlighted dancers at Buddhist commemorations of the birth of Buddha (Hana Matsuri, or the Flower Festival), observed in April. A poem written in honor of an early Flower Festival parade described how "Dancing maidens with picturesque fans / Bring recollections of old Japan."[54] Such dancers could also herald civic improvements: To celebrate the new street lights on East First Street in 1927, Little Tokyo held a "Big Fiesta" at which "Many Japanese girls will appear in dance numbers."[55] Though female dancers were still predominant, ethnic community celebrations were more likely to showcase Nisei men and women in a range of performances, both Japanese and western.

Still, even in Japanese American settings, women were more likely to appear in Japanese attire than men. When the co-ed Janus Club of college-age Nisei attended a benefit program at the International Institute, "the Janus girls by far outshined the rest [of the guests]. In their beautiful Japanese gowns, they proved to be the main attraction on the spacious floor."[56] Their male peers did not don traditional Japanese garb.

Nisei girls in kimono became part of long-term efforts to attract both Japanese American and mainstream customers to Little Tokyo. Young women's club members provided support for the JACL-run Nisei Week festival (still in existence), which was initiated in 1934 by Issei merchants who sought to lure the second-generation to patronize their businesses. Under the auspices of the JACL, the festival began as a vehicle utilizing "biculturalism"—the display of Japanese cultural arts in tandem with mainstream elements such as a beauty contest and parade—to appeal to both Japanese Americans and European Americans.[57] Nisei women served as the welcoming face of the ethnic community: wearing kimono, they greeted and served tea to visitors, competed in the Nisei Week queen contest, walked the runway in fashion shows, and performed as musicians, singers, and dancers.[58] Women were excluded from the male-dominated leadership of the festival despite the crucial nature of their participation.[59]

The cover photo of the *Rafu Shimpo*'s holiday issue for 1940 displayed a shift in cultural emphasis. Over armfuls of flowers, the Nisei Week queen and princesses beamed at the reader, resplendent in tiaras and ball gowns. Above the photo, and beneath a patriotic eagle head and flag-emblazoned shield, was an inscription proclaiming "God bless America/Our Home, Sweet Home!" and identifying the American status of the women.[60] Clearly, the Nisei women's role as ethnic representatives was a complicated one. As war approached, the appearance of the kimono-clad Japanese maiden was increasingly at odds with the images of modern femininity promoted in popular culture.

Fashion, Beauty Culture, and Consumption

For urban Nisei women, adopting mainstream fashions and pastimes became a way to claim and demonstrate American feminine identity.[61] Since the rise of advertising and mass media in the early twentieth century, women have been targeted for the sale of cosmetics, clothing, movies, home furnishings, and food. Living in the film capital of the world, under the pervasive, intertwined influence of the entertainment and advertising industries, the second generation was surrounded by the dazzling imagery of popular culture. The reach of mainstream newspapers, magazines, radio, and film in the 1920s and 1930s made the latest consumer goods and popular icons appealing and familiar to a national audience, including Nisei girls like the protagonist of a Hisaye Yamamoto short story, "A Day in Little Tokyo." When a family beach outing is preempted by a sumo tournament, Chisato Kushida kills time in Little Tokyo by buying a newspaper, reading the "funnies" and poring over pictures of Marlene Dietrich and Jeannette MacDonald. Chisato wishes she had stayed home to listen to "the weekly fairy tale from New York City [on the radio], with kids like Billy and Florence Halop and Albert Alley always perfect in every story."[62] Finally she begins to sing the Cream of Wheat advertising jingle, which she knows by heart.

Although some Issei and older Nisei might deplore the urban second generation's embrace of popular culture and particularly Modern Girl styles, the Nisei were, in fact, following in their parents' footsteps. When Japanese immigrants disembarked at the turn of the century, anxious to fit in with American society, often their first act was to buy Western clothes. Newly arrived wives were whisked off to stores by their husbands to make a speedy transition from kimono and sandals to hats, high-necked dresses, corsets, bustles, brassieres, panties, and laced-up shoes. In a 1937 retrospective article about life in Little Tokyo 30 years earlier, Uchikoshi Arao, with tongue in cheek, linked this outer transformation with changes in women's status among the Issei:

> In the period which was to witness the granting of women's suffrage and extension of other privileges to them, probably the groundworks for the gradual subjugation of husbands were laid down with the adoption of the feminine style which required their wearing the atrocious corsets. At any rate, Japanese husbands must have sensed the inkling of the collapse of their position when they were forced to get down on their knees to help their good women fasten and unfasten the girdles while the wives sucked [in] their breath.[63]

Although later oral history accounts have relayed the challenges of women's adjustment to the more confining Western garments, Arao assessed the transition as a rapid one: quickly "casting aside kimonos, Nipponese women took to American style like the proverbial ducks to the pond."[64] For the Issei newcomers, Western dress signified their modernity and their desire to be accepted in American society.

Their offspring were no less eager to appear modern; the urban Nisei girls and boys avidly followed mainstream styles. The up-to-date sheiks and shebas of 1920s Los Angeles paraded their finery on First Street, the Broadway of Little Tokyo.[65] As the irate Akatsuki Sakano detailed in his 1926 letter to the *Rafu Shimpo*, even the respectable church-going Nisei youth leaders had adopted these fashions. Although he criticized the sheiks for their "sloppy 37-inch

ballooners," it was the "painted red-hot shebas" who inspired his outrage, sporting bobbed hair, short skirts and, to complete the flapper look, "two different
shades of scarlet on their lips and cheeks, and another on the tips of their ears."[66]
Though the examples he singled out may not have been normative, Sakano's
letter suggests that flapper fashion was not just a fringe fad but accepted more
broadly among urban Nisei.

To social pundits and worried parents of the 1920s, the fashions, pastimes,
language, and sexual candor of European American middle-class youth appeared
to be a harbinger of social disintegration. Many of their anxieties focused on
the flapper, a potent symbol of the changes in young urban women's attitudes
and manners. Their hairstyle, dress, cosmetics, smoking, and dancing were read
by elders as provocative and troubling expressions of sexuality.[67] Although they
were not the wanton revolutionaries their parents feared, college youth of the
twenties did expand the possibilities of women's behavior and create new social
patterns.[68] As Sakano's letter and subsequent newspaper reportage show, urban
Nisei youth were eager participants in this process.

By 1933, European American journalist Gilbert Brown observed that the
"new generation of Los Angeles Japanese is completely Americanized, in costume, manners and looks." As Sakano had, Brown focused his attention on
the Nisei women, but with a more positive tone. "Japanese girls of high school
flapper age," he wrote, "wave their hair, wear collegiate sweaters and slacks,
Gibson-girl puffed sleeves—everything their western sisters do. They have the
stamp of America—and Hollywood—on their features and their apparel."[69]
Brown's words reflect both the Nisei women's immersion in popular culture, and
the distinctions that were still drawn between them—as "Japanese"—and their
"western sisters."

New fashions spread quickly within the urban Japanese American community, as shown in ethnic newspaper advertising. Department stores such as
the Tomio Company displayed the latest clothing and accessories; the Ginza
Beauty Salon, the Nisei Beauty Salon, and a host of others sought to entice
customers with specials on permanents and finger-waving. A wide array of
cosmetics promised allure. As *La Opinion* sought to entice Mexican American
women consumers, so too the *Rafu* and the *Kashu* targeted female readers.
Fashion news from the mainstream press purveyed the newest styles, their
appeal often underscored by photos of glamorous Hollywood actresses such
as Rita Hayworth and Norma Shearer modeling them. For those whose fashion desires were limited by budget, especially during the Great Depression, the
Little Tokyo stores ran yard-goods advertisements depicting elegant women
poring over pattern books or selecting fabric. By the late 1930s, Elizabeth
Ataka, Chiduyo Imoto, and other Nisei women penned fashion and beauty
advice tailored to their peers.

Girls and women were targeted as the primary consumers, usually through the kinds of merchandise depicted in the advertisements for dolls, hosiery, undergarments, hats, and dresses. One 1926 Tomio Company ad eschewed pictures in favor of straight text, reading emphatically:

> Mother!!
>> I Want Over Coats.
>> I Want Dresses.
>> I Want Hats.
>> I Want Shoes.
>> I Want Underwears.
>> I Want Stockings.
>> I Want Purses.
>> I Want????
> What Else—Sister?
>> Lets go TOMIO Pickout.[70]

Men garnered a secondary share of the merchants' attention. "Clothes make the man," declared the *Rafu Shimpo* in 1934, urging the "Beau Brummels" of Lil' Tokio to patronize a new Nisei store, Y. Kashiwagi & Son.[71] The store advertisement next to the article showed a man in dress-up attire, smiling as an elegant woman leaned forward to place a boutonniere in his lapel. "This isn't anything to what our clothes will do," the Kashiwagis promised, suggesting that the style and irresistibility of their suits might endow the wearer with similar qualities.[72] Columnist Mitzi Sugita noted that men as well as women dressed with the desire of looking attractive to the opposite sex: "Every woman knows that there is nothing that can compare with the male ego. It is fashion that forces men to shave every day. Fashion dictates the width of his trousers, the cut of the coat and many details."[73]

Although Nisei men might wish to enhance their appeal, women's bodies and appearance remained a greater focus for both sexes.[74] As Chiduyo Imoto warned female readers in her cosmetology column, "Your face is your fortune to a large extent. Miladies especially the college co-eds and Miss Sorority, your lovely complexion may result" in more "bids for winter parties."[75] Such admonitions spoke to Nisei girls' hopes and fears. They joked about "calorific" food and worried about being teased for having "daikon ashi" (legs like thick white radish). Some, accustomed to the measuring stick of western beauty, found their features wanting, like Lily Tanaka (age 14), who lamented in a poem "My Flat Japanese Nose":

> Some day, for my sake
> My folks may let take
> A operation—

On my flat Japanese nose!
People look upon it
As they pass by
Giggle and laugh,
And say my! my!
Now do you blame me when I sigh?
O, my flat Japanese nose!...[76]

Chiduyo Imoto sought to channel such anxieties into the use of cosmetic rem-
edies, reassuring the Nisei that "every Lady of Fashion knows that natural beauty
is rare" and thus, "Every woman is the architect of her own beauty."[77] Dangling
both carrot and stick, she directed them to consult with a beautician like herself
and to utilize the appropriate procedures and products: "There has to be cooperation for greater beauty results... or that charm of loveliness will vanish."[78]

Girls not only learned about cosmetics from the ethnic and mainstream press
and movies but also from authorities within—and sometimes from outside—
the ethnic community. In 1931, the Young Women's Buddhist Association of
the Nishi Hongwanji Temple went to the Angel Beauty Salon for a demon-
stration by the proprietor, Mrs. Matsumoto; afterward, Mr. Oyama (presumably of the Oyama Cosmetics Company) gave a lecture on color harmony
and chemical contents in cosmetics.[79] Beauty experts also visited their clubs.[80]
One of the famed Westmore Brothers came to a Tartanettes meeting and used
then-president Fumiko Fukuyama Ide as a model, piling her hair high and making her up in Hollywood style.[81] Setsuko Matsunaga Nishi also recalled how
Nisei poet Loretta Chiye Mori, working as a cosmetics demonstrator, showed
the Tartanettes how to apply eye makeup.[82] In the interwar years, Nisei daughters, like countless other American women, sought to tap the transformative
potential of makeup, promoted by the fast-growing mass-market cosmetics
industry.[83]

Japanese and Japanese American cosmetics firms did good business competing with mainstream brands. The Oyama Cosmetics Company in Los Angeles
produced products for men and women, including an "Ideal Beauty Cream,"
that could be used as a powder base for foundation or after shaving.[84] One of
the tactics that made such businesses successful was their practice of sending
Japanese American sales representatives to visit potential customers in outlying rural communities. Issei prolabor writer Haru Matsui accompanied a cosmetics saleswoman on her rounds to "rural farmhouses and fishing villages near
Los Angeles" and reported on the strong response: "When beautiful make-up
creams and powders were spread out in a bare, unornamented room in a farm-
house, then the smile anticipating town-going-day shone like a bright sunray on
the faces of the young farm mistresses."[85] Strict though rural families might be

about women's use of cosmetics, the influence of beauty practices and popular culture still filtered into the countryside.

Some rural Nisei girls tried to emulate their urban peers, but faced challenges in doing so. The advice directed at second-generation "Sweet Sixteens" by "Mrs. Grundy of Hick-Town" in 1931 consisted of a long list of prohibitions such as not wearing tight dresses and short skirts, not shaving their eyebrows, not reading trashy magazines, and not being overly friendly with "strange boys from L.A." At the end, Mrs. Grundy declared that this litany was aimed at "the hick-town girl[s], who try to ape their big city sisters." She concluded flatly, "It can't be done, for hick-town parents are rigid and narrow."[86] However, the influence of popular culture had made inroads among rural Nisei. In a cautionary 1937 tale of a small-town girl who succumbed to the "deadly fever" of "Hollywood Madness," Buddy Uno first introduced the doomed protagonist Sophie Katano as having skipped church to sprawl on the front lawn poring over movie magazines, filling herself with Hollywood gossip and carefully studying each fashion note and picture.[87] Poor Sophie's path to perdition was cobbled with Tinseltown dreams.

The trashy magazines of which "Mrs. Grundy" and Buddy Uno warned were just one source of the Hollywood imagery and news that captivated so many Nisei from a young age. As the *Kashu Mainichi* reported, "girls of high school age [in Little Tokyo] are most exacting about their hair styles which they copy from movie, magazine and rotogravure specimen of American beauty."[88] Both the mainstream and ethnic press—whether *La Opinión* or the *Rafu Shimpo*—carried movie reviews, Hollywood gossip, and stars modeling the latest fashions, often debuted in film.

Indeed, the *Kashu Mainichi* and the *Rafu Shimpo* did a great deal to stoke Hollywood fever, presenting numerous columns devoted to the entertainment industry. Readers could learn about the movie business in Japan from Taijin Tsuda's "Klieg Lights," as well as the latest developments in U.S. film-making. They could savor tantalizing tidbits about the stars' lives, from domestic details like Betty Grable's learning to use a washing machine as a new bride, to elite luxuries like Dolores Del Rio's sedan floor being covered in gray karakul fur.[89] They could find synopses of films playing at the Fujikan and other Japanese American theaters as well as at mainstream theaters. They read short reviews by fellow Nisei and drew inspiration from articles about first- and second-generation celebrities.

Movie-going was a favored leisure activity among the city Nisei. In 1933 columnist Roku Sugahara commented on its popularity among the young women: If asked, "would you like to go to a show? Nine out of ten Nipponese damsels will say 'yes, kind sir.' The other will nix the idea because she saw the show at a preview."[90] He opined, "There's no getting around it that our local lassies like the movies. In most every home you'll see film mags scattered around, well thumbed and well-studied." He drew the same connection as Buddy Uno, though less censoriously: "Thus we see the Garbo complex, the Dietrich slacks, the Gaynor innocence, the Joan Crawford lips, Blondell vivacity, the Harlow humidity and so on down the list, in our Lil' Tokio."[91] Nisei women not only went to the movies on dates, as Sugahara's account implies, but also made it a girls' group activity, as in the case of the Rho Sigma Rhos who planned a joint movie outing with the Kayans and the Kalifans, sister clubs in the Japanese YWCA.[92]

Nisei discussions about fashion and cosmetics, as well as fads like gum chewing and cigarette smoking, reflect more than women's participation in popular trends; they also show their staging of the debate over the boundaries of sanctioned female behavior and appearance among their peers. For example, in a newspaper column on lipstick, Alice Suzuki poked fun at romantic imagery: "In olden times ladies used their ring for the seal of true love, but modern women leave their red lip-prints on the cheeks of the gallant knights—which have caused many heartbreaks and trips to Reno." Although she warned against the excessive use of "loud" red, she concluded by asserting women's right to employ cosmetic enhancement: "it is imperative that ladies must have lip-sticks and indulge in them."[93]

Subverting both racial stereotypes and flapper incursions into male prerogative, Suzuki's writing reveals ambivalence, even as she stakes claims to broader parameters of acceptable behavior for "modern women." Critiquing the exoticized, belittling imagery often applied to Asian and Asian American women, she notes, "In this day and age when women are no longer the dainty little creatures that used to flutter about like butterflies, it is not surprising to see them acquiring the habits of the male in landslide fashion. Take smoking, for example.... What is good for the men should be good for the women." She concludes, however, by declaring, "And now that we have granted the point that it is all right for women to smoke, may we suggest that they try smoking Havana cigars and be real, real men, or try a pipe—and smell like one."[94] Her words convey the sense of smoking as unfeminine, a prevailing sentiment within the prewar Japanese American community. To the end of the 1930s, the ambivalence continued about what smoking signified for women. A 1938 short story about rowdy Nisei behavior at a dance included a flirtatious, fickle girl whose overture to the protagonist was a purred "Will you give me a cigarette, Spud darling?"[95] A month later, another fictional Nisei hero at a dance met a new love when she asked him for a smoke; by contrast, she was portrayed as a smart sophisticated individual, dutifully supporting her mother and younger brother.[96] These two female characters reflect different aspects of what was hoped and feared of the Modern Girl: attractive independence and wanton behavior. Playwright Wakako Yamauchi has remarked that smoking was one of the things that "nice girls" didn't do.[97] Perhaps because of this, fewer Nisei women than men became regular smokers. But a number of them were certainly experimenting with such hallmarks of the flapper.

With the arrival of war, Nisei women, like other Americans, displayed their patriotism in their attire. As Louise Suski observed in 1940, "In women's clothes today the patriotic colors of the flag are used as color schemes. It is fashionable to wear red, white and blue in all clothes from the sport outfit to evening gowns."[98] Chiduyo Imoto noted that women were keeping abreast of politics and war as well as popular culture, talking about "the new trend in hat brims and about how to seize the Dardenelles [sic]." Her fashion advice applied the metaphor of a successful military campaign to romance, given new urgency by men's imminent departure for war: "Every girl is feeling the pinch...competition is increasingly acute." She gave tips for securing the affections of men in uniform and urged readers to "Be sure to look pretty when he's on leave" in order to carry out their own victorious "feminine maneuvers."[99]

Female participation in popular culture was complicated for nonwhite women by the multiple pressures they faced within the family, the ethnic community, and the larger society.[100] At times, Nisei daughters, like their Mexican American sisters, struggled to negotiate between powerful mainstream notions of modernity and romance, on one hand, and the feminine ideals inculcated by parents reared in Meiji-Era Japan, on the other.[101] As they endeavored to integrate popular and parental values, they introduced a range of gender-role issues into the Japanese American community. The tensions between competing notions of womanhood emerged most clearly in the discourse over romance, courtship, and marriage.

Courtship and Romance

Urban Nisei women were eager participants in the new modes of mixed-sex socializing that had taken shape as courtship in the United States moved from the private to the public sphere and dating became a widespread practice.[102] Movies, magazines, radio shows, and songs influenced the expectations of youth across the country, including the second-generation Japanese Americans. So engrained was the ideal of romance that the notion of arranged marriage, as one second-generation columnist described, was unthinkable to many of those Nisei "who have sat with their mouth open during tense romantic scenes on the screen; those who are addicted to true confession magazines and motion picture periodicals; those who have pored over the Freudian Gospel or attempted to read the precepts of companionate marriage; those who go romantically on automobile joy-rides."[103] At the same time, Nisei daughters were also acutely aware that within the tightly knit immigrant community, female behavior and family reputation were closely linked. The practices of Nisei courtship—and the eligibility of potential partners—were also affected by the structure of prewar

ARCa.

race relations on the West Coast. [Given these factors, a great deal of Nisei romantic socializing and courtship occurred—or at least began—within the monitored setting of youth-club activities and in the context of young women's strong, extensive peer networks.

It is difficult to ascertain how many of the urban Nisei went on dates in the 1920s. Younger boys and girls often attended dances and socials in the company of a same-sex group, arriving and leaving together. Older Nisei were more likely to have the parental approval and financial wherewithal for heterosexual-couple social activities. *Rafu Shimpo* reportage of the 1920s suggests that city life and access to cars gave some of them chances to conduct their courtship away from the eyes of parents or club advisers. In 1926 a serialized poem—"The Evolution of a Flapper"—described how a love-struck couple took advantage of automobility to go on a date in a popular seaside city:

> One dreamy night
> Her sheikie took her
> Out to Venice near the bay
> And there they danced
> And there they flirted
> Beneath the moon's soft ray.[104]

The car was a critical vehicle for heterosexual romance, as a number of Julia Suski's one-panel comics in the *Rafu Shimpo* reflected. Below the picture of an Asian-looking woman with a blasé expression ran the caption, "Gertie sez: I would have enjoyed the ride last night if we had found a parking place."[105] The next week's panel echoed the same theme. Although the captions may have originated outside the ethnic community, the sentiments they expressed were familiar to the second generation. The concern of Issei parents and older Nisei indicates that these practices were not confined to mainstream youth or newspaper wit. One columnist in 1927 commented that dances often led to problematic consequences such as "Surreptitious dates, the ride back home . . . and a score of other complications. . . ." He hinted at the heat of youthful passions, the opportunities afforded by intimate car rides, and a sense of inevitability about both. His emphasis on the containment of young women conveys the sexual double standard and also, perhaps, the active role some Nisei shebas played in romantic socializing.

Worries about the behavior of Nisei sons and daughters—particularly daughters—prompted the hosting of numerous social-hygiene and health-education speakers at girls' club meetings and church gatherings. For example, in 1933, Mrs. Olds, a "noted lecturer on social hygiene," gave a talk at the International Institute on sex education for high school girls.[106] Sometimes teachers provided instruction, as when the Loha Tohelas gathered in 1937 to hear a Jefferson High School teacher give a talk on "Personal Hygiene" and "Boy and Girl Relations."[107] It is not clear what impact these efforts had on the second-generation girls, but the caption of a Julia Suski drawing hinted at sly rebuttal. Beneath the image of three glamorous Asian American women was a dialog:

LOU-LIA—Some terrible things can be caught from kissing.

DORITA—I believe it. You ought to see the poor fish our Aggie caught.[108]

What Aggie caught from kissing was not a "social disease" but a lackluster suitor. While aware of the former, urban Nisei girls may have been more concerned about the latter. Despite their adoption of the fashions and some of the pastimes *ARG.* of the flapper, Nisei women—along with their peers and elders—set limits on the carefree sensuality associated with the Modern Girl. Japanese American girls, like their Mexican American and Chinese American sisters, were under pressure to maintain a chaste reputation within the tightly knit immigrant community and thus subject to greater surveillance than their brothers; premarital sexual intercourse was a line that few crossed in the prewar period.

By the mid-1930s, the components of a Nisei date had become well estab- *Nisei date* lished: The young man would drive to the woman's family home to pick her up. (Boys lacking access to a car cringed at the prospect of asking a girl to travel by streetcar.) Then they might go to see the latest movie at the Carthay Music Box, or join their friends at a Nisei club dance, or go to one of the public ballrooms of the Southland. Afterward, they would repair to a cafe for refreshments, for which the male was expected to pay.[109]

The familiarity of urban Issei parents with the Nisei youth clubs may have smoothed the way for one-on-one dating. Fumiko Fukuyama Ide remembered, "The first dances I went to were with my brother at the 379 Boy Scout Troop's dances." Fumiko's parents knew the young men she dated, often friends of her older brothers. She went on dates to movies, museums, a skating rink, the Griffith Observatory, and also to the Palomar, where couples dined and danced to the big band music of Harry James, Tommy Dorsey, and Glenn Miller.[110]

Setsuko Matsunaga Nishi, who attended the J.H. Francis Polytechnic High School in downtown Los Angeles and then the University of Southern California, often dated young men from school. They would go dancing at the Hollywood Palladium or occasionally to nightclubs such as the Trocadero on Hollywood Boulevard. "The Nisei could go to most places," she noted, "but weren't always treated nicely." Movies were the most popular activity; they also went to plays, concerts at the Hollywood Bowl or in Little Tokyo, or to see athletics in the park. Afterward they might go to the Brown Derby or drive to the beach for a walk.[111]

interracial dating

Nisei women who dated interracially were careful to be discreet. Setsuko Nishi and her sisters, who went out with both Japanese American and white men, tried to avoid being seen by members of the ethnic community. "Dick Vernon, the president of the [high school] student body would invite me out on dates," she recalled, "and we'd go to dances and things like that." While at USC, she also dated a white student whose father—active in the American Legion— became furious and forbade him to see her. Nevertheless, he persisted, even visiting her at the Santa Anita Assembly Center after the Japanese Americans had been incarcerated. She also went out with Nisei like Joe Oyama, who took her to her first union meeting, and Frank Chuman, who was a law student at USC when she was there.[112] Setsuko's parents may have been more accepting of her interracial dating because they knew she was not interested in a serious relationship. "The guys I went out with knew that we could be good friends, but that was it," she said. "Somehow I had the early idea that it would cut off other possibilities and friendships. And there were too many interesting and exciting things out there, so I wasn't going to make any commitments."[113]

From time to time, especially during the Depression era, a few male columnists grumbled about the high cost of dating. John Fujii reported that a group of second-generation men were appalled at "the extravagance of their sisters," lamenting that the Nisei women, "though aware of the financial plight of the men, heartlessly want to go to this place and that place—to buy this and that. The men usually shoulder the burden and—as one fellow puts it—we get very little out of it."[114] This complaint perhaps also reflected the boundaries of permissible premarital sexual behavior among the second generation. In 1938, columnist Bean Takeda detailed male expenditures to meet what he felt were urban girls' expectations: "High-powered cars, costly corsages, too many dances, redundant 'pig-stand' treats, and even expensive nightclubs."[115] Despite the issue of expense, which varied according to the age of the Nisei and the venue of entertainment, there is no sign of any slackening in the pace of second-generation recreation and courtship.

ARG.

Dances provided some opportunities for interethnic and interracial socializing. As Joe Oyama observed in 1936, "Los Angeles dances are more cosmopolitan than San Francisco, Sacramento, San Jose, Fresno, Salinas, or Berkeley dances. Here you will always see a handful of Caucasians dancing with Japanese girls or the other way around." The diversity of participants reflected that of southern California's population:

> Sometimes a tall handsome Mexican will drag a petite Nipponese maiden to some high school club dance. Beautiful blonde Russian girls come with husky Japanese boys. Koreans are numerous—with only a sprinkling of Chinese.

"Once in a blue moon," according to Oyama, African American men might "appear in the middle of the floor in the stag line." He reported, "There is little prejudice, in fact no prejudice at all against these other races 'intruding,' for the nisei boys are too busy cutting each other's throats."[116] However, mixed couples were not welcome at all public venues, as Oyama described five years later: "[F]our of us, including one Caucasian American fellow, went to a certain ballroom in Ocean Park. We had heard before that mixed dancing (Whites with Orientals) was not allowed." The rumors were confirmed when one of the Nisei women and her white escort "stormed out of the ballroom explaining that they had been insulted." One of the aspects of the incident that most angered the Nisei woman was that, at the time, "a nisei couple was standing behind her giving her a very disdainful and reproachful look."[117] Oyama's observations reflect the range of opinion among the urban Japanese Americans with regard to the boundaries of acceptable interracial socializing. He himself argued that the Nisei should not seek to avoid such racial discrimination but should fight it. His writing also shows how the Nisei, like other racial-minority youth in the West, had to navigate a terrain in which the boundaries might vary in rigidity, depending on circumstances. Although some casual interracial dating did occur, most of the Nisei, mindful of the strong preferences of the Japanese American community as well as the legal restrictions of the larger society, searched for a romantic partner within their own ethnic group.

Nisei women not only fueled but also sometimes challenged Western con- *love* ceptions of love. Even while attesting to the popularity of heterosexual romantic ideals, one Los Angeles columnist, "Mme. Yamato Nadeshiko," deplored their impact. Her critique also underscored the effectiveness of mainstream media as a vehicle for these rosy notions. She felt that "seeing too many movies" and "reading too many novels" had caused Nisei women to harbor unrealistic dreams of "tall stalwart sons of men, bronzed by desert's noonday heat and whipped by bitter rain and hail. Hearts of gold, strength of steel, romantic Romeos." She warned women not to wait for a "Sir Galahad" but to recognize the "everyday heroes [who] exist all about us."[118] Another columnist who identified herself as "a deb" similarly mused, "The trouble with us is—we build too many air castles. And we pick on a man, the dream of our teens as the 'one and only'—who not only seems sincere, but can do no wrong. But that's being over romantic and over idealized. Sort of dangerous, don't you think?" She advised her peers "to be hardboiled towards love" because "we're just bound to undergo some of its misfortunes."[119] Her admonition transmitted not only caution about, but also an expectation of, romantic love.

What did the urban Nisei women expect of their Nisei Galahads and Romeos? A 1938 *Rafu Shimpo* article presented a list of qualities that local co-eds hoped to find in a "dream spouse": The boys had better be well groomed, sophisticated, manly or athletic, fluent in Japanese and English, loyal, sensible, sincere, considerate, cheerful, generous, tolerant, responsible, and good-looking. At this point in the litany, the writer warned, "Fellows, you're not perfect yet. You've also got to have ambition, be financially secure,... have a terrific I.Q., be a one-woman man, faithful, and have the same interests."[120] In addition to cosmopolitan bilingualism, they incorporated the Japanese considerations of educational background and family heritage. Whether or not the co-eds truly expected to locate a paragon with all of these attributes, their wish list reflects the influence of mainstream middle-class values as well as the criteria important to their parents.

And what did the Nisei campus men hope for in their dream girl? A 1931 account of a "bull session" among Japanese American men at UCLA revealed that they, like their female counterparts, had been influenced by mainstream ideals:

> Perhaps most of the girls would like for a husband with the strength of a Samson, the sex appeal of Casanova, the wisdom of Socrates, and the personality of a Mussolini. Usually they want too much. *The same is true of the boys.* They want a Clara Bow, a Cleopatra, and a Portia all rolled into one.

This columnist concluded in the same vein as Mme. Yamato Nadeshiko: "But we're mortals and we must get to accept humans with their weaknesses and faults."[121] A prudently anonymous poem of 1939 expressed both Hollywood dreams and pragmatism with regard to the "Nisei Girl":

> Madeleine Carrol is a glamourous [sic] blonde
> And of her pictures I'm very fond;...
>
> ...
>
> And Linda Darnell isn't bad
> But, of course, she can't be had.
> Yet, the NISEI GIRL I'd rather squeeze
> 'Cause she has curves below her knees.[122]

Jesting aside, because of ethnic-community preference and miscegenation laws, the vast majority of Nisei searched within their own ethnic peer group for husbands and wives.

Like their mothers and most U.S. women then, Japanese American women expected a future centering on marriage and family. In contrast to Issei women, they expected their marital relations to be based on romantic attraction and individual choice—the hallmarks of mainstream ideals—as well as duty. Unlike their parents, they considered happiness "the first and last object of any marriage" and dreamed of finding true love.[123]

Given these values and hopes, it is not surprising that urban second-generation women increasingly challenged the practice of arranged marriage in favor of "love marriage." Like her friends, Setsuko Nishi expected to choose her own spouse, and she found a quick way to scotch any match-making efforts: "Whenever they [other Issei] made any inquiries,...I would say [to my parents], 'If I hear about any kind of arranging of marriage, I will marry whomever I'm going out with at the moment.' "[124] Nisei women, who had less veto power over the choice of marital partners than Nisei men, wrote frequently to Nisei advice columnist "Deirdre" to rail against arranged matches; heated debates among readers often raged for weeks in the popular San Francisco newspaper column.[125] In a 1934 article in the *Kashu Mainichi*, Mary Korenaga passionately decried such unions, asking rhetorically if Nisei should allow themselves to "become a breeding machine to which we are forced by the third party merely for the purpose of keeping the world populated? Are we to lose emotions which we have harbored merely to become a human mechanism on the order of the common ant?" "No!!" she declared, "A thousand times, No!"[126] The priority Korenaga placed on individual choice and romantic love mirrors the Nisei's embrace of mainstream ideals of companionate marriage.[127]

Many urban Nisei were in step with the shift to new ideals of romantic love and sexual fulfillment by the 1920s from Victorian codes of marriage.[128] Women bore the chief responsibility for such relationships and were the most vulnerable if unions failed, since their social status and economic security hinged on marriage.[129] Sex-role differentiation persisted in marriage, with husbands expected to be the family breadwinners and wives nurturing homemakers.[130] Both women and men were supposed to find within companionate marriage the emotional support that they had previously found most often with members of their own sex.[131] Although the urban Nisei youth maintained same-sex networks as well as participating in mixed-sex organizations, they shared these romantic heterosexual expectations.

The shifting role of the baishakunin (marriage brokers) reflects the Nisei embrace of love marriage and their negotiation of the formalities expected by their parents. In 1939, sociology student Robert Howard Ross described the baishakunin as go-betweens who "make all of the arrangements pertaining to the wedding of two young people, acting as intermediaries for the two families whose representatives are to be joined in wedlock."[132] Ross's survey of the two generations showed strong Nisei opposition to the use of baishakunin.[133] The role of the go-between became increasingly nominal. A Japanese university student remarked, "Among the niseis, the baishakunin is usually chosen after the couple has decided to get married—the purpose is defeated."[134]

It is impossible to know exactly how many prewar Nisei marriages were arranged and how many were romantic unions. It was rare that the newspapers revealed such information, as did this announcement of the 1928 engagement of a young woman from San Luis Obispo, "The young couple shyly confessed that it was a love match."[135] Even in this case, official matchmakers were listed. It was equally unusual to read, as the *Rafu Shimpo* announced in 1937, that the betrothal of Yaye Tokuyama and journalist Noboru "Brownie" Furutani "was arranged in traditional Japanese manner."[136] Even though urban Nisei were increasingly finding their own spouses, baishakunin—usually older married couples—were routinely mentioned in the last lines of prewar wedding announcements. This may have reflected the second generation's accommodation of their Issei parents by adopting the conventional Japanese forms rather than the full practice.[137] In 1936, a Los Angeles Nisei columnist reported that the second generation "prefer to have baishakunins perform the minor duties and leave the matter of selection to the individual."[138] For some Nisei, the possibility of arranged marriage may have offered a fallback plan. One second-generation girl said, "I want to marry the man I fall in love with, but if I should not meet that man, I shall have a 'go-between' and be married according to our Japanese custom."[139] More research is needed to discern how the baishakunin custom was adapted to fit the circumstances of life in America.

Ironically, the dominant society not only broadened but also constrained Nisei marital choices, which were made within the framework established by state codification of racial discrimination. Like their mothers, Nisei women retained values of duty and obligation and most expected to marry men of their own racial-ethnic group. This stemmed not only from the strong preference of the Japanese American community, but also from the even stronger opposition of the dominant society. In 1880 California's miscegenation law was amended to include Asians. The marriage of a white person to a "Negro, mulatto, Mongolian or Malay" was illegal until the overturning of the law in 1948. By the 1930s, fourteen states—including Arizona, California, Idaho, Montana, Nebraska, Nevada, Oregon, Utah, and Wyoming—had miscegenation laws aimed at Asian immigrants and their children.[140] When the author of "Nisei Girl" wrote that actress Linda Darnell "could not be had," Japanese American readers would know that her unattainability stemmed from both status and race. In the arena of marital choice, as in other social and economic arenas, the Nisei remained highly conscious of the boundaries of race and gender.

The few interethnic and interracial marriages that did occur garnered attention in the Japanese American press. Publicized Asian-interracial matches on the East Coast—where miscegenation laws did not target Asians—often involved educated elite European Americans and Japanese Americans in university settings. On the West Coast, intermarriages were more likely to occur between Japanese American women and Chinese or Filipino American men. Given the dearth of women in the Filipino immigrant community, a number of men—often living and working in proximity to Japanese American enclaves—turned their attentions to Nisei daughters. Rural Issei reacted to such matches with disapproval. In the 1930 case of Felix Tapia and Alice Saiki, who had met in the Stockton pool hall of Alice's father, a starry-eyed elopement ended in anguish: Alice returned to her parents' home for what was to have been a short stay and was never seen again by her distraught husband, who believed her parents had sent her to Japan.[141] Some of the urban Nisei adopted a more tolerant attitude toward intermarriage. In 1933 journalist Larry Tajiri critiqued the stigmatization of interracial unions and the acute pressures such couples faced from "the attitude of the community as a whole."[142] Given the disapproval of the immigrant enclave and the legal restrictions of the dominant society, the number of interracial matches was small. As Kay Nishida observed in 1935, "On the Pacific Coast there have been a number of international marriages lately in which scions of the samurai joined their nuptial destinies with Chinese, Caucasians, and Mexicans. But they are, as a whole, rarities." Nishida predicted with foresight, "Among the future third and fourth generation people, this should not be so."[143]

In the prewar era, the children of these unusual interracial marriages often had difficulty finding acceptance in either the immigrant or mainstream society. The history of the See family illuminates the complex position of mixed-race children in the Los Angeles Chinatown.[144] Margaret Uchiyamada, a frequent literary contributor to the *Kashu Mainichi*, described her experiences as the daughter of a Japanese father and an Irish mother. "Sometimes I feel like the Bat in Aesop's fable," she wrote, "which [was] neither bird nor beast but what it found most convenient at the time and was in the end, either, both, and neither." Hers was a "strange heritage but a rich one," which included listening to Japanese and Irish fairytales, and eating corned beef and cabbage and Japanese dishes with equal gusto. Uchiyamada also recounted the pain of being excluded from a white friend's birthday party, and how her blood boiled when neighborhood rowdies called her "Chink" or "Jap." Like Nishida she foresaw future change, but personal experience tempered her optimism, leading her to conclude, "the way of the pioneer is hard, the struggle bitter, the fight long, that the path of those who follow may be easier."[145] In the prewar years, deterred by external legal sanctions and ethnic community preferences, few Nisei pursued such matches.

Also suggesting the strength of ethnic community control, the prewar divorce rate among the Nisei was lower than the national average. In 1938 it was estimated that one out of ten Nisei marriages would end in divorce, as compared to one out of six for the nation at large.[146] Although divorce was stigmatized among the Japanese American community as in the larger society, shifting mainstream attitudes had begun to affect Nisei thinking. Columnist T. Roku Sugahara reported that the Nisei "believe in the merits of divorce to be used when necessary."[147]

With the hope of preventing divorce among the Nisei, youth leaders made efforts to educate the second generation. In this spirit the YMCA sponsored a 1940 lecture series on "Preparation to Marriage," including a panel discussion by prominent Nisei couples on "the practical aspects of marriage."[148] The low rate of divorce among the Nisei suggests the power of ethnic community pressure, the retention of some Japanese values, and Depression era economic limitations. At the same time, their increasing rejection of arranged marriage signals Nisei women's valorization of individual choice and romantic love.

Rituals

The Nisei women's enthusiasm for mainstream female rituals reflects their romantic expectations of companionate marriage and the importance placed on attaining the roles of wife and mother. Like their mainstream peers, many Nisei girls dreamed of starring in an elaborate wedding that would highlight this momentous transition in their lives. The care they took in planning the details of the celebratory rituals mirrors the significance of the step.

For the prewar Nisei, wedding festivities began with the announcement of the engagement, which might be made at a party or women's club tea. Rosa Ando, for example, surprised the members of the Japanese American Chi Alpha Delta sorority with her news at a party in 1930: "The announcement was revealed through favors. A kewpie doll placed in a flower bearing the names of the betrothed couple made known the fact."[149]

The female ritual of the wedding shower proved popular among the Nisei from the 1920s. Although both Buddhist and Christian Nisei held showers, the Christians, with more exposure to European American advisers and customs, may have encountered this custom first. Such might have been the case for Harumi Okafuji and her fiancé Masayoshi Omura, who in 1927 were honored with a party by thirty Nisei members of the Japanese Union Church. The pair was "showered" with kitchen utensils.[150] What seemed unusual about this shower was the presence of men, including Omura.

In the ensuing years, wedding showers quickly became the exclusive domain of women, often organized by the bride-elect's club or by her women friends. Typical was a shower given by the Blue Triangles for Rosemary Matsuno after their club basketball practice. While the girls ate sandwiches and fruit, a note was passed to Rosemary "telling her to look in a bookcase. Here she found a package and a note. Each note gave her directions to another spot. In this way she found all the gifts."[151] The often elaborate planning of wedding showers reinforced the solidarity of female support networks as well as the sense of the importance of the impending marriage. The categories of wedding showers—kitchen, linen, glassware, and china showers—underscored women's responsibility for the domestic sphere.[152] In addition to providing young couples with material assistance, such rituals reflected the expectation that middle- or upper-class urban couples would form their own households and nuclear families.[153]

Like the showers, weddings evidenced the adoption of mainstream western *weddings* practices in terms of romantic emphasis, the focus on the bride and her attendants, their attire, the format of the ceremony, and the music. They presented a marked contrast to the weddings of those Issei parents who married in Japan. Of course, newspaper accounts tended to spotlight the nuptials of the urban middle and upper class within the ethnic community. Not all Nisei were Christian; the press also recorded a number of marriages celebrated with Buddhist and Shinto ceremonies. However, the western "white wedding" quickly spread among the urban Japanese Americans.[154] The 1927 wedding of Chiyo Otera and Thomas Sashihara, attended by 500 guests, provides an illustration.

Like many European American couples, Otera and Sashihara chose to marry in June and in a church. Like most mainstream couples, they had a "white wedding," which had become the U.S. standard. A celebration of romantic love, this ritual featured a white dress and decor symbolic of the bride's sexual purity.[155] Otera, a popular club member, wore a white satin gown and was attended by Nisei bridesmaids, flower girls, and a ring-bearer.[156]

The couple's strong ties to local Nisei society were reflected by the reception that followed the short ceremony. The Young People's Society of the church served the refreshments, and among those who gave congratulatory speeches was Lily Satow, an active YWCA member. The reception gave Nisei performers an opportunity to shine, including acclaimed soprano Kyo Inouye who sang "Oh Promise Me," a song repeated at countless Nisei and other weddings in the 1920s and 1930s.[157]

Like many of their peers—if they could afford to do so—Otera and Sashihara embraced another middle-class western tradition and Victorian legacy: the honeymoon. The wedding guests pelted the newlyweds with rice before they left for Yosemite, a popular honeymoon site for southern California Nisei.[158]

The celebration of this marriage did not end with the newlyweds' departure. About forty of their Nisei friends attended a homecoming party in their honor after they returned. This gathering reflects as much about the strength of urban Nisei social ties as about class. It also shows how the Nisei blended mainstream and ethnic elements, playing American and Japanese games, dancing, and enjoying refreshments provided by a committee.[159] The format of these festivities also evidences the influence of club events in setting the pattern for other Nisei social occasions.

By the end of the 1930s, the Nisei wedding had become fairly standardized. It was often a white wedding, the mark of modern urban couples. Traditional

Shinto rites declined. Depression era concerns about cost may have helped to hasten the spread of the simpler, relatively less expensive Western-style wedding.[160] Many Buddhists also adopted parts of the white wedding. For example, in 1933 Yone Tomio, a UCLA graduate and a daughter of the Tomio Department Store family, was married in a white gown and with a full complement of attendants. At the end of the outdoor ceremony performed by a Buddhist priest, a Nisei woman sang "I Love You Truly."[161] Whether the ceremony was Christian, Buddhist, or Shinto, the wedding party usually included the family and friends of the couple as well as the baishakunin. Afterward, guests usually attended a reception. Depending on pocketbook and preference, the receptions ranged from "simple intimate gatherings in the church hall to hearty banquets at Little Tokyo's 'china-meshi' [Chinese food] establishments."[162] San Kwo Low and Manshu Low were favorite sites for such celebrations.

Not surprisingly, the next ritual to take its place in Nisei women's circles was the "stork shower," a celebration invented in the 1930s.[163] Although the shower originated among middle-class and affluent women, it rapidly spread among women of every class, race, and region.[164] Announcements for baby showers appeared in the Japanese American newspapers more frequently by the end of the decade, heralding the arrival of the Sansei, or third generation. Like wedding showers, they were usually hosted for the expectant mother by her female friends, often members of her club. As in the case of a 1938 celebration held by the Hollywood YWBA for a former member, the format also paralleled that of the wedding shower: Following the "opening of the many beautiful gifts, the evening was spent in games and entertainment."[165] Baby showers, like betrothal announcements and wedding showers, served as signifying rituals through which Nisei women supported each other and shared the joy of major life stage transitions.

Work: Three Roads and None Easy

In the arena of work young Nisei women continued to affirm Japanese values of filial piety and obligation, while beginning to move into new fields. However, racial barriers, gender inequities, and economic competition during the Great Depression constricted their opportunities. Like their Issei mothers, they did an enormous amount of work—both paid and unpaid—to sustain families. Just as they expected to marry, many urban Nisei women also expected to help in a family business or to enter the wage-paid workforce. As adults, they—like other racial-ethnic and working-class women—faced limited job prospects made grimmer by the fact that work outside the home was rarely a choice and more often a necessity. In the prewar period, three narrow paths led urban Japanese American women to jobs within the ethnic community, work outside the enclave, or— for a minority—the pursuit of opportunities in Japan. One writer termed them "Three Roads and None Easy."[166]

Like their Chinese American peers, most Nisei found that in the larger job market, factors of race (and in the case of women, gender) outweighed their education and English proficiency.[167] In a 1933 *Los Angeles Times* interview, UCLA student Alma Matsumoto summed up the situation: "This question of prejudice bobs up most alarmingly when we are planning our vocations. You can imagine how restricted our choice is, if we stay in America. We can't teach. There is room for only a few Japanese doctors and lawyers, business men and bankers. We may work in an oriental restaurant or a curio store, and of course we can farm or sell vegetables in a grocery."[168] Educated women and men alike faced a discouraging paucity of jobs, which led to a competitive scramble for the more desirable positions in the ethnic enclave.

The responses of 72 women to Robert Ross's 1939 questionnaire about Japanese American generational relations offer insight into Nisei girls' vocational aspirations. Like most American women of this period, they expected to fulfill the role of "homemaker," although in the case of the Nisei it was unlikely to preclude other work. Despite a variety of obstacles, Japanese American women dreamed of entering the feminized fields of secretarial work, nursing, teaching, and librarianship. Traditionally feminine businesses such as dressmaking, millinery, and cosmetology—highly visible in Little Tokyo—attracted some; an interest in costume design may have been prompted by proximity to Hollywood. The more daring mentioned professional dancing and dance instruction, perhaps inspired by the examples of urban Nisei performers lauded in the ethnic press.[169] Nonetheless, securing a position in any of these fields proved challenging during the 1930s.

In the prewar period few Nisei women become professionals. A *Rafu Shimpo* writer in 1940 attributed this to women's eschewing long years of study in favor of beginning to earn money right away, but gender and racial discrimination may have been a stronger deterrent.[170] For example, there was only one female attorney in Little Tokyo, and at least one Nisei remembered that during the prewar period, this pioneering lawyer had to work as a secretary. California racial barriers prevented Nisei from becoming public school teachers, one of the two key areas of feminized professional work that opened to U.S. women in the early twentieth century.[171] Japanese American women, however, did make inroads into nursing and a few as doctors, both of them primarily serving an ethnic clientele.

Women who succeeded in attaining professional status made an impression on their peers, as a second-generation male writer described in 1933. He had visited a friend who was worried about his ill son and had called a doctor, while the child's mother waited anxiously. "I wondered idly…as to who this doctor

was," the writer recounted. "I thought that the doctor must be indeed a wonderful presence of a man that the parents asked only that he should come to be
reassured." To his surprise, the physician was a young Nisei woman who quickly
calmed the parents and ministered to the sick boy. His final vision of her was one
of confident, competent female authority: "She stood, now, bag in hand ready to
depart; smiling, poised, completely self-possessed and having the dignity of true
womanhood."[172] That the doctor's competence mirrored the traditional female
role of family caregiver may have facilitated the writer's perception of its compatibility with "true womanhood."

A small number of Nisei women filled the needs of ethnic professionals and
merchants for secretaries and clerks. In 1939 Robert Ross noted a transition in
their status and signs that women were beginning to challenge gender inequity
in the ethnic workplace: "They are not pushed into the background as much
as they were formerly. Of late they are demanding recognition and have been
showing that they are equal to men in many respects, especially in the uptown
business houses of the Japanese section of Los Angeles."[173] Some women, like
Yoshiko Hosoi Sakurai, channeled their skills into a family business. After graduation from high school, she worked with her parents to operate Mansei An, a
popular Little Tokyo udon (noodles) and sushi shop.[174] Others worked as nurses,
seamstresses, waitresses, and beauticians within the ethnic economy.

Cosmetology, Chiduyo Imoto declared, was a field open to the Nisei, and
one in which they could be successful serving either an ethnic or racially mixed
clientele. She said frankly: "While many lucrative businesses are for all practical purposes closed even to nisei girls of marked intelligence cosmetology today
offers a wide-open opportunity for individual advancement and independence.
The country's third largest industry, pioneered by women and today filled with
women of great ability in all lines of its fields should appeal to the nisei miss as
a profession."[175]

The "pulchritude business" boomed in prewar Little Tokyo. As the *Kashu
Mainichi* reported in 1940, the urban Issei and Nisei women frequented beauty
salons in equal numbers, with the average Japanese American girl getting her
first permanent upon entering high school and visiting "the beauty salon about
once a week for a shampoo and a finger-wave."[176] Beauty culture became a significant area of entrepreneurship for urban Nisei women, as it was for other
women of color.[177] Japanese American women, like their African American and
Mexican American sisters, probably also considered cosmetology jobs more
appealing than domestic or factory work.[178] Delmar Umeko "Meshan" Azeka,
who started the Ginza Beauty Salon with her sister in 1934, was among the
first Japanese Americans in the business. In 1938, there were more than twelve
Japanese-owned and operated beauty salons in the Little Tokyo area, all managed by women.[179]

Domestic work—the least attractive option—proved the most readily available labor outside the urban Japanese American enclave, as the "Help Wanted" ads in the Japanese American newspapers reflected. Mary Oyama's younger sister Lillie worked as a live-in domestic for a European American employer, while also attending art classes. Such domestic work constituted the primary area of nonagricultural wage-paid labor for Issei and Nisei women.[180] In 1937, T. Ellen Kunisaki, writing about work opportunities in the San Gabriel Valley of southern California, reported that women on average left home to take domestic service positions. These jobs abounded, for "there are not enough girls to fill the demands of American neighbors who earnestly seek Nipponese girls as housemaids and companions."[181] In 1941, the Japanese YWCA in San Francisco estimated that two out of every five young women worked in domestic service.[182] This pattern persisted. During the war, the greatest number of jobs advertised in the incarceration camps were domestic positions in the Midwest and East recently vacated by black, Latina, and white women flocking to better-paid defense and industrial work.

At least a few women, like Fumiko Fukuyama Ide, found skilled jobs outside the ethnic enclave. Fumiko entered the clerical field, although it was not what she had intended. Having served as editor of the Belmont High School newspaper, she hoped to pursue a career in journalism: "But my mother wanted to send me to Japan, so I had this period where I did other things before the plans were finalized before the war. And my brother said, 'If you know...typing and shorthand, you'll always have a job.'" With one typing class under her belt, she took a civil service test and got a position in the records department of the County General Hospital. She worked a shift from midnight to morning, afterward taking a streetcar to the Metropolitan Business School to attend a course in Gregg shorthand. After class, "I came home and slept, and dated...and went to work again at night."[183] Clerical skills would prove critical to her finding jobs during the war and after.

It is difficult to estimate how many Nisei women and men decided to seek their fortunes in Japan. Judy Yung notes that more second-generation Chinese Americans than Mexican Americans or Japanese Americans set their sights on working in their parents' homeland.[184] The ongoing discussion of opportunities abroad in the Japanese American newspapers of Los Angeles and San Francisco suggests that at least some gave it serious consideration, particularly if they had good Japanese-language skills. A 1926 interview with a Nisei collegian specializing in secretarial work underscores the limitations of the U.S. job market. She said, "After I graduate, what can I do here? No American firm will employ me. All I can hope to become here is a bookkeeper in one of the little Japanese dry goods stores in the Little Tokyo section of Los Angeles, or else become a stenographer to the Japanese lawyer here."[185] Instead she planned to go to Japan where a job in a large shipping company awaited her. Two of her Nisei women friends also intended to journey to Japan to teach English. In 1933, UCLA co-ed Alma Matsumoto expressed the hope of going into "oriental-American trade" where she could use both her familiarity with America and her "sketchy knowledge of Japan."[186]

How these Nisei fared in Japan appears to have hinged a great deal on their Japanese language skills, according to the Japanese YWCA Education Secretary for the foreign-born in Tokyo, Miya Sannomiya.[187] Sannomiya, herself second generation, reported in 1934 that the approximately 500 young Nisei men and women in Tokyo had found themselves "virtually folks without a country," accepted neither as foreigners nor as Japanese. She observed that the Nisei, "who should, by appearances, be Japanese but who are not by language, customs, education, and all social contacts" did not receive the warm welcome extended to other foreigners.[188] Poor language ability particularly limited their prospects, though it might be mitigated, in the case of women, by typewriting skill.

A small, yet highly visible group of Nisei turned their ambitions toward pursuing careers in entertainment and the performing arts in Japan. Thwarted by racial barriers in the United States, some found a warm reception abroad. In 1932 the *Kashu Mainichi* reported that singer Agnes Miyakawa, violinist Alice Katayama, and pianist Lillian Katayama were "creating a sensational hit in the winter musical debut," and that Kyoko Inoue had gotten a role in a Japanese movie. Concluded the editor, "Japan is indeed the land of opportunity for the second generation who are talented in some special line of endeavor."[189] The majority of Nisei women and men in the younger cohorts, however, cast their economic lot with the land of their birth.

The search for jobs lay at the heart of the "Nisei problem" confronted by female and male alike. Women faced barriers of race and gender in seeking jobs outside the ethnic community. It was the unusual Japanese American who found employment in a mainstream business. It was a mark of this rarity that when Nobuko Suzuki was hired by the Fifth Street Store in 1937, the *Rafu Shimpo* ran a photo and an article. Suzuki, a Sansei who was hired to serve Japanese-speaking customers, commented, "There is no class or racial discrimination in the store and one can feel immediately at home."[190] She, and the Nisei men and women who became professionals, were a minority. More commonly, they found jobs— often not commensurate with their education—within the ethnic economy. Many men worked at the produce market, or at fruit and vegetable stands, or at plant nurseries; others entered farming or learned chick sexing, the work of sorting newly hatched chickens to retain the future egg-laying females and discard the males.[191] Urban young women tended to do unpaid work in family businesses, or to find positions as clerks, secretaries, nurses, waitresses, beauticians, or domestic workers. Some, disappointed by the poor prospects, sought better

"Nisei problem"

opportunities in Japan. Whether single or married, second-generation women continued to contribute to the family economy; as workers they brought income and broadening trends of female employment into the Japanese American community.

* * *

Nisei girls and young women played dynamic, complex roles as cultural agents within and outside the ethnic enclave from the Jazz Age through the Great Depression. They grew increasingly ambivalent about performing as ethnic community representatives in kimono, an image that contrasted sharply with the modern American femininity popularized in media and advertising. Though attracted to the greater freedom, romantic ideals, and rituals of the middle-class mainstream, some were critical of what they viewed as an unrealistic glorification of romantic love. Under the watchful eyes of the immigrant community, and well aware of the restrictions they faced within the framework of West Coast race relations, they experimented with cultural forms, introducing popular mainstream and other regional elements into the ethnic enclave while adapting aspects of their parents' customs. As Kimi Kanazawa put it, they were "taking parts of both American and Japanese cultures to fit our own situation."[192] This messy, exuberant, and variable process of cultural coalescence is visible in their advice columns, culinary endeavors, fashion, social gatherings and courtship, expectations and rituals of marriage, and work.

Sounding the Dawn Bell

Developing Nisei Voices

On the evening of October 7, 1934, 11 Nisei writers and poets—seven women and four men—gathered for dinner to discuss the formation of a second-generation literary organization. Mary Oyama, prolific columnist, poet, and youth club worker, reported, "For the first time ever, creative nisei writers sat down together at one table." In this heady company, spirits were high and hard to contain, as Oyama attempted to "steer the irrepressibles" into serious dialogue, aided by Chiye Mori and Lucile Morimoto. "To the versatile and talented Chiye much of the credit is due," said Oyama, "for serving as the stimulus toward awakening the interest and the ambitions of the pen-inclined nisei."[1]

The gathering constituted a cross-section of Los Angeles Nisei talent. Acclaimed poet Bunichi Kagawa, then married to Chiye Mori, was the one Issei present. Teru Izumida, "lovely and distinctive in a Grecian-looking green gown," was a modern dancer as well as a poet and essayist. Carl Kondo, a fiction writer and poet who ran a typewriter-repair shop in Little Tokyo, added "laconically business-like comments to the discussion." Lillie Oyama, Mary's younger sister and the one artist present, tried to stifle her laughter at the witty remarks of Margaret Uchiyamada, whose lively humor distracted poet James Shinkai, seated next to her.

Kashu Mainichi editor, sports writer, and columnist Larry Tajiri expressed his regret that he was leaving Los Angeles just when this group was forming. One of the founders of the Little Tokyo Players, a theater group, Tajiri had always devoted attention in his column to Japanese American writers and artists as well as to politics, race relations, and life in Little Tokyo. Now headed for a new job at the San Francisco *Nichibei Shimbun* (Japanese American Newspaper), he said, "I might have been able to help you put out your publication."[2]

"That's right too—it's a pity that you're leaving us," declared poet Ellen Thun, "but our loss will be your gain. You deserve a change, and all our best wishes go with you." As Oyama explained, Thun was "the adopted daughter of our writing family," as she was "the only literary-minded young person of the Korean nisei, and has cast her lot with the Japanese-American writers—lest she be lonesome."[3] She and the rest of the group, and indeed many other Nisei, were frequent contributors to the *Kashu Mainichi's* literary section.

By the end of the evening, they had decided to put out a bi-monthly publication to showcase second-generation articles, fiction, poetry, and essays, which would be submitted to an editorial board of three. Chiye Mori, Mary Oyama, and Carl Kondo were chosen as the editors for the first issue. The organization, which by 1940 was known simply as the Nisei Writers Group, became a focal point and catalyst for efforts to create a distinctive second-generation literary voice.

A well-documented example of the intense engagement of second-generation Japanese Americans in peer organizing, the Nisei Writers Group reveals the dynamic roles played by women in forging literary networks. In southern California, the core cluster of second-generation literati of the 1930s—including Mary Oyama Mittwer and Chiye Mori—tended to be somewhat older and more educated than the members of clubs such as the Tartanettes and Blue Circles. However, as evidenced by the Nisei press—the key vehicle for second-generation literary production—there was overlap. During a time of racial exclusion, the ethnic press served a vital function in coordinating, publicizing, and promoting second-generation events, networks, and artistic expression. For instance, the *Rafu Shimpo's* English-language section from its inception was intertwined with youth group activities through editor Louise Suski, who had been an enthusiastic participant in Nisei girls' clubs and sports. As both columnist and adviser, Mary Oyama Mittwer vigorously supported youth organizational events, to which she was often invited. The younger Nisei submitted poems and essays to the press, as well as their club news. Some of the literati, like dancer Teru Izumida, were involved in multiple forms of artistic expression, which drew them into multiple organizations. Youth clubs and specialized-interest groups fostered Nisei creative efforts in literature, music, theater, and dance, offering an avenue for their participation in the energetic cultural arts scene in Little Tokyo. The Nisei Writers Group exemplifies how, in the context of racial barriers, the second generation simultaneously tried to develop their own institutions and forms of expression, while also endeavoring to gain access to the mainstream audience—both efforts in which young women took part.

Nisei women were active and influential in all spheres of creative expression, especially in literary circles. They wrote passionate poetry and humorous ditties, penned romantic and social realist fiction, reviewed new books and music, composed analytical essays on literature, and aired their opinions in a plethora of newspaper columns. They debated the roles of women and the "Nisei problem" (limited economic opportunities because of racism in the job market and the small size of the ethnic enclave), waxed lyrical over the beauty of nature, and lamented the trials of love. Some, like Mori and Oyama, also provided inspiration and encouragement for aspiring writers, working to develop a network of second-generation literati. Oyama particularly made efforts to stimulate Nisei interest in and interaction with writers from the mainstream and other ethnic communities; she maintained the vision of a larger world in which the Nisei might find a place, ceaselessly endeavoring to broaden their social and artistic horizons. This chapter examines women's vital engagement in Little Tokyo's art scene and especially in the creation of a Nisei literary world. The lives of three key figures—Mary Oyama, Chiye Mori, and Hisaye Yamamoto—offer insights into the workings of writers' networks and the ongoing discourse facilitated by the ethnic press. Nisei literary efforts constituted part of a broader upsurge of music, theater, dance, and art activity in prewar Little Tokyo. The writers' search for role models and intense debate over Nisei literature reveal a number of inter-ethnic influences in the process of cultural coalescence.

Beginnings

In 1934, Toyo Suyemoto, a scholar as well as a poet, assessed the promise of Nisei literary efforts. She stated:

> The second generation Japanese, as a group, realize that in our complex environment, the youthful literati of our race have much to accomplish. As yet, there has been only the foreshadowed evidence of greater things to come, for we are still in the embryonic stage of literary development. Our lot is by no means simple, for differentiation of thoughts and ideals lie between the first generation and our own, between our occidental acquaintances and ourselves, necessitating an interpretation, written expression.

Suyemoto believed that, in the process of gaining the maturity and experience necessary for literary achievement, "The second generation literati are gradually building a world entirely our own; constructing a structure belonging wholly to ourselves, simply by mastery of prose-writing and poetry."[4] Throughout the 1920s and 1930s, a flood of poetry, essays, fiction, and letters by second-generation women and men contributed to this construction of a lively Nisei world. Denied access to mainstream publishing by racism as well as by inexperience, they turned to outlets within the ethnic community.

The ethnic press, which stretched along the West Coast from Los Angeles to Seattle, offered a crucial forum for the development of the Nisei writers, publishing their fledgling efforts in literary sections that became regular features. The *Kashu Mainichi* became a particularly notable literary showcase for the second generation, including writers such as Mary Korenaga, Chiye Mori, Mary Oyama, Toyo Suyemoto, and Hisaye Yamamoto. Within a peer community facilitated by the English-language sections, the Nisei struggled to define themselves in relation to both their parents' generation and the larger society. In the process, they established an energetic literary conversation that crossed the United States and spanned the Pacific.

Women took vigorous and sometimes leading roles in literary networks. In 1940, *Current Life: The Magazine for the American Born Japanese* ran an article on "Who's Who in the Nisei Literary World," profiling 15 men and nine women, including Mary Oyama, Lucile Morimoto, and Hisaye Yamamoto.[5] They and many others published prolifically in the Japanese American newspapers, experimenting with form and content. Some adopted a flippant, bold jazz style; Hisaye Yamamoto poked fun at lyric convention in humorous poems with Latin titles, and Toyo Suyemoto limned her subjects in formal rhymed verse, stating:

> …all that I can give to you
> Is simple speech of everyday…
> Words stripped and stark like life and death
> Wherein you stand midway.[6]

Writing in a variety of styles on eclectic themes and drawing on popular culture as well as elements of classic literature, women enthusiastically engaged in the effort to express ethnic, generational, and gendered experiences. Their writings also reveal the influences of the overlapping worlds through which they moved in daily life.

Examining three second-generation writers of southern California illuminates women's ambitions, their experimentation with genre, and their significant roles in creating and maintaining literary networks. Within the community of Nisei writers, Mary Oyama Mittwer, Chiye Mori, and Hisaye Yamamoto emerged as central figures, as poets, fiction writers, and columnists. The next section briefly introduces their lives and work.

"Sincerely Yours, Mary Oyama"

A broad, inclusive vision characterized Mary "Molly" Oyama Mittwer's instrumental role in organizing and nurturing Nisei artistic efforts. A spirited writer herself, Oyama—as one of the older Nisei—became something of a literary den mother, seeking out second-generation talents and enthusiastically drawing them into a literary network. At the same time, she prodded them to mingle with European American and other ethnic writers; her home became a center for such ethnically mixed social gatherings.

Mary Oyama was born in Petaluma, California on June 19, 1907, the oldest daughter in a family of six children. Her brother Joe Oyama, also a writer, credited their well-educated Issei mother in large part for instilling literary interests in her children. A nurse who received military honors for her service during the Russo-Japanese War, their mother had been an avid reader in her youth, devouring the works of Washington Irving, Tolstoy, Dostoevsky, and the Bible. She married an innovative Issei man, Oyama Katsuji, who worked as a gold miner, plantation laborer in Hawai'i, cook, and tamale peddler before establishing in 1922 the first Japanese-owned cosmetics company in the United States. He first concocted his cosmetics at home, using his wife's kitchen utensils that, to the dismay of the Oyama children, made their food taste like perfume. Katsuji marketed his wares throughout California as well as in Hawai'i, selling face cream to Japanese immigrant women and hair pomade to Filipino men. In 1932 the family moved their business from Sacramento to Los Angeles.[7]

According to her brother Joe and her daughter Vicki Littman, the encouragement Mary received from European American teachers nurtured her confidence and writing skills. She graduated from the Sacramento High School in 1925 and then graduated as a deaconess from the Methodist Girls Training School, a missionary institution in San Francisco, in 1928.[8] She served as a social worker in Spokane, Washington, and then in Los Angeles, migrating south in the early 1930s to rejoin her family. She also studied journalism at the University of Southern California. In Los Angeles, she continued to work with youth organizations, while developing as a prolific writer for a host of Japanese American newspapers across the state, as well as for the San Francisco-based *Current Life: The Magazine for the American Born Japanese*. Attracting a string of admirers, she married at the age of 30, quite late for a Nisei. This change prompted a humorous senryu poem, "Lines to Myself," published under the name "Marry Oyama":

> Do
> Not write:
> "Love's a Bore"—
> Such lying words, repeat
> No more. Live and Learn![9]

Her husband, Frederick Mittwer, a handsome radio operator for the *Kashu Mainichi*, was a Japan-born man of European and Japanese parentage. He, too, began to write a column, entitled "RCA," reviewing new records for the *Kashu Mainichi*. While they lived in the Boyle Heights section of East Los Angeles, Joe Oyama recalled, "they rented a house formerly occupied by Yamatoda, the Tokyo Club gangster, who fled to Mexico. The house had a moat around it and gun turrets imbedded in the doors."[10] By the time of the war they had bought their own home in City Terrace, a nearby neighborhood. They had two sons, Richard, born in 1939, and Edward, born in 1941; their daughter Vicki was born in 1944 during their incarceration at the Heart Mountain camp in Wyoming.

Mary Oyama was a highly popular advice columnist, writing under the pseudonym "Deirdre" for the San Francisco *Shin Sekai-Asahi* from 1935 to 1941.[11] She reached a wide readership through the "I'm Telling You Deirdre" column, as evidenced by the letters and postcards sent from all areas of California, Colorado, Idaho, Illinois, Michigan, Nevada, Oregon, Texas, and Washington. Women comprised the majority of writers to the column until 1937, when Deirdre reported that the letters she received were equally divided between men and women. Cities, small towns, and rural districts were all equally represented in her incoming mail. Some of the issues of concern to Deirdre's readers were "boy and girl relations," the "Nisei problem," intergenerational conflict, careers, marriage, and etiquette. Like the other Nisei advice mavens, she tried to demystify the social conventions of the middle-class European American world, as well as counseling her readers regarding Issei expectations of correct behavior.

Although Deirdre addressed a variety of general issues that were not gender specific, the bulk of her writing was aimed at female readers. She admonished young women to avoid "little white lies" and false sophistication and advised that men preferred "good sports" to "davenport sirens" or "reclining Cleopatras." Her advice to Nisei women was mixed, perhaps reflective of the ambivalent position of middle-class European American women in the larger society during the interwar doldrums of feminism. On the one hand, she extolled the importance of finding one's life work; on the other, she bluntly asserted that "brainy women are not as accepted as brainy men" and must therefore conceal their intelligence. Deirdre's advice giving was complicated, moreover, by the fact that she was directing it to ethnic minority women in a society that imposed limitations on their opportunities and aspirations.

Oyama's writings and her life illustrate the tensions confronting Nisei women who dreamed of careers as well as marriage. Writing in the guise of "Deirdre," she encouraged ambitious readers to strive for both, but she also permitted herself to grumble that "Housewives Have No Spare Time" in a 1939 column, a complaint Betty Friedan would later examine in *The Feminine Mystique*. "Domesticity," Oyama found, "seems to allow less time for self-improvement...than regular routine work outside.... As hard as I'm toiling around the house, my folks complain and think that I'm not doing enough. It's aggravating, really."[12]

Despite her many duties and activities, Oyama managed to produce a staggering amount of poetry, fiction, book reviews, essays, letters to the editor, and a number of columns, including a *Kashu Mainichi* column, "Sincerely Yours" and by the eve of the war, a daily letter in the *Rafu Shimpo*. In her writings she pushed for more political involvement by "Alice Nisei" as well as for harmonious interracial relations and women's pursuit of independence and personal goals.

Oyama always read widely, as she encouraged her peers to do. Her book reviews sought to persuade the Nisei of the riches to be found between the covers and to reassure them of accessibility. In a 1936 review, for example, she wrote, "The eccentric Japanese-German, Sadakichi Hartmann, poet-art critic, philosopher, and once uncrowned king of San Francisco's Bohemia, wrote *Japanese Art* for the average lay person. This book, therefore, is not too technical and it is easy, simple reading for such as you and I."[13] She also tried to broaden the Nisei's interests beyond the confines of the ethnic enclave. One of her "Sincerely Yours" columns covered Merejekowski's biography of *Leonardo da Vinci*; Lauren Gilfillan's *I Went to Pit College*, a sociology student's investigation of life in the Pennsylvania coal mines; *The Dance of Life* by Havelock Ellis; short stories by D. H. Lawrence; Robert Graves's autobiography, *Goodbye to All That*; *The Forty-second Parallel* by John Dos Passos; and William Faulkner's *Light in August*.[14]

Like many of her peers, Oyama experimented with tone and subject in her poetry and peopled her fiction with both Japanese American and white characters. Her 1934 short story "The Glass Broke" focuses on the inner turmoil of a young woman, Mara, who at a dance inadvertently learns that her wild behavior may cause her social ruin.[15] The characters appear to be European American, but the story is ambiguous, perhaps deliberately, omitting last names and other ethnic markers. By the latter 1930s, Oyama's stories mainly centered on Issei and Nisei protagonists. Her 1938 short story "The House on the Hill," for instance, recounted a picture bride's memories of her departure from Japan and arrival in America. Fingering the brown silk-brocade purse her brother gave her when she left triggered her reverie. She recalled how she and the cousin she had married set off from San Francisco for their rural home, traveling:

> ...on a strange American wagon pulled by a large American horse which to the new little Takamura-san seemed much larger than any of the horses which she had seen back in Japan. And here another engulfing wave of nostalgia throbbed within her like a dull but persistent pain from an old wound which has been opened again. So far away.

When at last the hot, uncomfortable journey ends, the picture bride sees that her husband has brought her to a large inviting house on a hill and begins to smile in anticipation. When he points to a dingy shack on the side of the house and announces, "This is our home," she is in shock, feeling the disappointment experienced by many picture brides whose husbands turned out to be less successful than they had led the women to believe:

> Her home. Not—this one, but—that—one. Tiredness overwhelmed her. Her vision blurred. Oh weary, weariness! He was saying, "The big house is the boss', we're lucky to have the camp-house nearby his place as it's cooler up here. Let's go in," as he led the way into the unpainted shack. She followed, wordless.[16]

The story implies not only the long years of hardship and the many houses in which she has lived but also Takamura's resilience and the satisfactions she has found. At the close, she puts the worn purse back in the old trunk when she hears the voices of her family, home for lunch, calling her.

Oyama also tackled contemporary political themes in her creative writing. In 1934, she won first prize in a playwriting contest sponsored by the Players of San Francisco. Her play, "Our Great Adventure," presented the emotions of a group of Nisei college students upon the announcement of war between the United States and Japan.[17] The subject she chose for her script may reflect the tensions of the second generation, who sometimes felt wrenched between their parents' ways and expectations, and those of the larger society. In retrospect, it seems an eerie rehearsal for 1941.

"Emblems"—Chiye Mori

Loretta Chiye Mori, lauded by Mary Oyama as the key motivator of the Nisei literary movement, early developed a reputation as a writer and artist, although she was best known for her poetry. Born in 1915 and raised in Long Beach, California, she won recognition for her art and her literary contributions to student publications while attending the Long Beach Polytechnic High School. The *Kashu Mainichi* proudly announced, "Her work has appeared in Scholastic and other national publications. 'Civilization', a narrative poem, won a Carnegie award."[18] As a teenager Mori wrote a column entitled "Philosophical Hash" for the *Kashu Mainichi*. Writing under the byline "Loretta C. Mori," at the outset in 1932 she assured her readers that "no personal grievances will be hung out to dry in this column. No, this will be a column upholding a mansion of Thought, and no clothes dummy. In other words, your red flannels and ventilated socks will not be threadbare for having been bared to the boring gaze of the bored public." Knowing her audience, she added impudently, "And if anyone aims any rotten eggs at us, we threaten to publish the size of their shoes."[19]

A bold and steady contributor throughout the prewar period, Mori often explored romantic impulses in her poems, declaring:

> Let me drink deep the cloying ecstacy [sic]
> From the upturned petals of passion's lips
> For the bloom may wither in the drooping light
> And I may not pass this way again.[20]

She also linked the personal and the political in her writing. In 1932 Mori directly addressed the vulnerability of the Nisei in her poem "Japanese American."[21] She likened them to:

> Clay pigeons traveling swiftly and aimlessly
> On the electric wire of international hate
> Helpless targets in the shooting gallery of political discord
> Drilled by the clattering shells
> That rip toward us from both sides.[22]

Her striking imagery conveys the powerless position of the second generation, finding no sure haven in either country.

After a courtship sparked by an exchange of poems, Mori married Bunichi Kagawa in March 1933 and moved to the San Francisco Bay area, his home. She continued to be a leading figure in Nisei literary networks, writing poetry and essays and doing pencil illustrations for the *Kashu Mainichi*. Following this short-lived match, in 1938 Mori married the son of the actor Sojin Kamiyama. It appears that she returned to southern California and for a while found work as a cosmetics demonstrator; Setsuko Matsunaga Nishi remembers her showing the Tartanettes how to apply eye makeup.

Mori, who began to write as "Chiye Mori" by 1933, wrote poetry as well as a *Kashu Mainichi* column—called "Emblems"—on poetics. At the outset in 1934, the 19 year old presented a stern assessment of the adolescent state of Nisei literature:

> There has not yet appeared on the literary horizon a single nisei
> writer who has developed to a mature state of mind. That is, a
> writer who has graduated from the acutely adolescent wondering
> stage or the excessively dramatic and attitudinal period.

She believed that the Nisei "must write with a feeling of time in his bones, with a consciousness of the law of change, of the entire span of human and traditional history behind him."[23] She tried to utilize her column to this end, starting with a discussion of Ben Johnson's "Drink to Me Only with Thine Eyes."

Mori also focused on newer poetic forms. She vigorously defended free verse (her most often-chosen form) from its detractors in pithy terms, while conceding that the "laxity and sloppiness" of many writers merited critique. However, she charged, "To reject free verse itself because of its miserable protagonists would be somewhat like spurning religion because of one tippling parson." She called for balance and care in composition, asserting that

> The material should be proportioned gracefully. In judging feminine
> beauty there is no hard and fast rule to tell how long the leg should
> be, how slim the waist, or how large the head. The measurements
> of the brow does not matter if it is in proportion with the rest of the
> body. It matters little whether a poem be cast in the sonnet pattern,
> in quatrains or in free verse if the material is effective within the limits
> of the method.

Rather than being a form lacking in rigor, Mori contended that "the fetters that accompany the free verse method are almost as binding as those imposed by rime and metre. In a way, it is a greater task to build a free verse poem with integral form than to work within the defined boundaries of an established form."[24] Mori's distinctive, influential poems clearly reflect her own rigor as well as insight. Through her essays, fueled by a passion for poetic expression and informed by her understanding as a practitioner, Mori contributed to the literary discourse among the second generation.

"Don't Think It Ain't Been Charmin'"—Hisaye Yamamoto DeSoto

One of the most distinctive Nisei voices was that of Hisaye Yamamoto DeSoto, who, like Chiye Mori, began writing and publishing as a teenager. She is the single most acclaimed Japanese American writer and perhaps the most studied. Many of her stories reflect the experiences of rural Japanese American families like her own; because of the restrictions of the California Alien Land Laws, they moved a number of times before settling in Oceanside, in southern California. Born in 1921, Yamamoto loved reading from an early age, growing up with European fairytales as well as the stories of Momotaro and Urashima Taro.[25] Like her Nisei peers, she enjoyed poring over Superman and Batman comic books, listening to the swing music of Tommy Dorsey and Glenn Miller on the radio, and going

to see American and Japanese movies. In the summer, when she had no access
to the school library, she recalled that she began "to look forward to the English
sections of the Japanese-language newspapers with a feeling of having found my
element."[26] She "faithfully followed" Nisei writers such as Mary Oyama Mittwer
and her brother Joe Oyama, Dr. Yasuo Sasaki, Toyo Suyemoto, Carl Kondo, and
others.

At the age of 14 Yamamoto began to write for the *Kashu Mainichi*, first using
the pseudonym Napoleon, "as an apology for my little madness—and then
growing bolder and signing my very own name. For a writer must possess an
enormous ego, absolutely certain that he is the greatest writer of the century
and absolutely certain that the most important thing in life is to communicate
his vision."[27] She eventually wrote a regular column in the *Kashu* under the titles
"Napoleon's Last Stand," "Don't Think It Ain't Been Charmin'," and "Small Talk."
She also collected rejection slips from mainstream magazines, while serving
on the yearbook staffs of the Excelsior Union High School and the Compton
Junior College and garnering praise from her English teachers. During her
World War II incarceration in Arizona, she wrote and served as an editor for
the *Poston Chronicle*, the camp newspaper. Her "Small Talk" continued in camp
and survived the war to reappear in the *Los Angeles Tribune* and the *Kashu*. Her
fiction found receptive mainstream and Japanese American audiences in the
postwar years. Four of her pieces were included in Martha Foley's annual lists
of "Distinctive Short Stories," and one was selected for *The Best American Short
Stories* of 1952.

Yamamoto's wry humor and sardonic eye found expression in poetry and
essays. She often poked fun at social convention and glossy facades, as in this
cinquain, "OF MILADY'S ART:"

> I see
> A painted face
> Stunning upswept hair
> Where
> Are you?[28]

Her target was romantic heartache in "OF A PRAGMATIST":

> She refused
> His proposal
> He supped heartily
> On a steak smothered
> With onions.[29]

Her prewar columns in the *Kashu* often included the world of her family—especially her brothers—and mundane life, slyly flecked with glints of social commentary. For example, in a rumination on possible New Year's resolutions, each of which Yamamoto proceeded to sabotage, she considered "telling littlest brother Yuke the truth when he gets inquisitive about the facts of life." For instance,

> the next time he asked us what shenanigans were, we wouldn't tell him they were little brown worms that taste good with sugar and French dressing. We'd tell him they were little brown worms that make you sick when you eat them, even with sugar. And when he asked us what social slop was once more, this time we wouldn't tell him that…high school kids get fed a bowl of social slop garnished with candied shenanigans to give them energy for their afternoon studies. We'd tell him truthfully that the kids get a bowl of social slop without candied shenanigans, and that social slop served plain was the awfullest-tasting mess. But it's no fun telling the truth.[30]

Yamamoto also skewered expectations of female behavior and, in particular, notions of the demure Nisei woman. This, she telegraphed, she most certainly was not, as her final New Year's resolution revealed:

> As a crowning touch to our perfection we could subtract ourselves from our cussing, or at least learn to blush convincingly when we do it. We could learn to say oh, my goodness gracious and frankly like [journalist] Kenny Murase instead of using phrases and four-letter words even sailors would be horror-stricken and aghast at. Why, we could become a wonderfully courteous lady if we put our mind to it. Ohellyes.[31]

The stunning punch line has long been a Yamamoto trademark.

In her literary pursuits, Yamamoto may have been following in the footsteps of her mother, a senryu poet whose work was published in the ethnic newspapers, but in the Japanese-language section. Like Yamamoto's mother, many Issei wrote poems, forming groups that produced traditional Japanese haiku, tanka, and senryu, short poems about everyday life. They published their own poetry magazines as well as submitting their poems to the ethnic press.[32] Japanese women and men of all ages and classes composed senryu, a form that retained popularity during and after the war.[33] In her fiction, Yamamoto, too, illuminated the quotidian lives of the Issei and Nisei.

Yamamoto's best-known story, "Seventeen Syllables" (1949), provides glimpses of immigrant literary activity through a rural Issei mother's passion for haiku writing and discussion, as perceived by her Nisei daughter Rosie.[34] After the day's work of picking and boxing tomatoes is finished, Tome Hayashi (the mother) becomes "an earnest, muttering stranger who often neglected speaking when spoken to and stayed busy at the parlor table as late as midnight scribbling with pencil on scratch paper or carefully copying characters on good paper with her fat pale green Parker."[35] Poetry writing is clearly popular: When friends visit, the group is "bound to contain someone who was also writing *haiku*," and the poets invariably become rapt in "comparing ecstatic notes."[36]

"Seventeen Syllables" also maps the language boundaries between many of the Issei and Nisei. The story begins with the Nisei daughter pretending to understand her mother's poems, which she cannot fully appreciate because of her limited Japanese language ability. For Rosie, "English lay ready on the tongue but Japanese had to be searched for and examined, and even then put forth tentatively (probably to meet with laughter)."[37] The communication between mother and daughter is hampered on both sides: "Rosie knew formal Japanese by fits and starts, her mother had even less English.[38] Because of these limitations, although both Issei and Nisei were publishing their creative writing in the prewar ethnic press, probably few read the work of the other generation.

Yamamoto's fiction has particularly delineated the multicultural flavor of prewar life in both city and country. The repertoire of treats to be enjoyed in Little Tokyo included Eskimo Pies purchased on the street and popular China-meshi (Chinese food) as well as sushi and Japanese confections. Living in Redondo Beach among the oil fields, Yamamoto's family stocked up on Japanese staples such as rice, soy sauce, miso (fermented soybean paste), green tea, red pickled plums, and ginger, also buying "bread from the Perfection Bakery truck that came house-to-house, fish and tofu and meat from the Italian fish man who would break off wieners from a long chain of them and give them to us as treats."[39] With rich detail Yamamoto delineates the joyful labor-intensive communal process of making New Year's rice cakes (mochi-tsuki) and her childhood memory of the enticing candy assortment—Abba Zabbas, jawbreakers, licorice whips—at a small local grocery store.[40]

Her writing is remarkable in its reflection of the spectrum of interethnic relations, never clichéd or contrived, always complex, rendered with her distinctive blend of irony and compassion. Yamamoto shows that the early Japanese American communities were not completely isolated but sustained everyday contacts, whether in the form of a visiting Korean herbalist or a gambling den run by Chinese Americans for men of many races. Such interaction is present in many of her stories, although it varies in intensity and impact, ranging from tragic collisions to camaraderie and love.

Yamamoto's fiction presents not only Japanese American and European American relations but also the interchange among Asian Americans, and between them and other minorities. Sometimes the meeting ground is love, as in "Seventeen Syllables," in which young Nisei Rosie Hayashi has a crush on Jesus Carrasco, the son of the Mexican family hired to help with the harvest, or in the story "Epithalamium," which traces the marriage of an idealistic Nisei to an alcoholic Italian American sailor. In "Yoneko's Earthquake," a Filipino hired hand wins the hearts of both Nisei daughter Yoneko and her mother.

In the interstices of these relations, Yamamoto makes the reader aware of the social tensions that pit ethnic groups against each other and suggests that even those often stereotyped are not immune from labeling others. For example, Yoneko's father chastises her for wearing fingernail polish by saying, " 'You look like a Filipino',... for it was another irrefutable fact among Japanese in general that Filipinos in general were a gaudy lot."[41] The Issei gambler in "The Brown House" is horrified when he discovers that, in the course of a police raid on the gambling den, an African American has taken refuge in his car. The African American man, unaware of Mr. Hattori's reaction, draws on another kind of stereotype in a thank you that leaves his unwitting benefactor dumbfounded and exhibits Yamamoto's characteristic blend of humor and irony: "He had always been...a friend of the Japanese people, he knew no race so cleanly, so well-mannered, so downright nice."[42]

Besides probing the ties between Issei and Nisei, husbands and wives, Yamamoto's stories are time capsules that capture prewar life, making details of food, games, and physical surroundings inextricable from the characters. For example, the list of mouthwatering dishes that once graced Kazuyuki Matsumoto's New Year's table serves to emphasize the emptiness of his later years. Such descriptions stitch together the patchwork quilt of the childhood of the young Nisei characters in Yamamoto's fiction.

The writings of Yamamoto and her literary sisters reveal the energy, playfulness, and determination with which the second generation addressed issues of gender, race, and generation. Their poetry, essays, and fiction show Nisei women's experimentation with literary forms as well as with different images of femininity, as idealized in the ethnic community and debated in the larger society. Their writings also chart the complex multilayered landscape of their generation.

Creative Ferment in Little Tokyo

The literati were part of a much larger groundswell of Nisei creativity in the 1920s and 1930s. As the ethnic press showed, the urban second generation poured their free time into an array of activities, including music, theater, art, and dance. YWCA and YMCA groups staged productions and Nisei organizations formed specifically to promote the performing arts. It appears that those immigrant parents who could afford to do so provided early support for these activities.

The announcements of recitals in the *Rafu Shimpo* suggest that a fair number of urban Issei parents valued musical education for their children—especially daughters—and could cover the expense of purchasing instruments for them, as well as paying for their lessons. Julia Suski, a talented musician and the older sister of *Rafu Shimpo* editor Louise Suski, became in 1928 the "latest person to join the large staff of music teachers" in Little Tokyo. By way of advertising her services, the *Rafu* noted that "Japanese people seem to take a great interest in piano" and commented on the steady rise in pupils. Julia offered classes at the Nanka Music Store on San Pedro Street as well as in students' homes.[43]

Born circa 1902, Julia was the eldest of seven children in the influential and accomplished Suski family. Their Issei father P. M. Suski had been a portrait photographer in San Francisco until the earthquake of 1906 destroyed much of the city. He and his family then moved to Los Angeles, where he worked by night at the *Rafu Shimpo* and pursued college studies by day, finally earning a medical degree at the University of Southern California. As a doctor he practiced in the Little Tokyo community, serving a multiethnic clientele, including Mexican Americans who lived in the area. During World War II, while incarcerated at the Heart Mountain camp in Wyoming, he continued to serve as a physician at the camp hospital. Partly at his instigation, the *Rafu Shimpo* started an English-language section in 1926; he drafted his daughter Louise, then a physical education student at UCLA, to become the first editor. Louise would draw upon Julia's artistic as well as musical skill. In the 1920s Julia Suski was already an acclaimed musician, the "pianist of the local Japanese Symphony Orchestra." Perhaps she turned to teaching partly in order to pay for her own studies with Homer Grun, a "well known pianist and composer."[44] Julia also performed frequently for community events; in addition, she often accompanied singers and instrumental soloists.

The symphony orchestra to which Julia Suski belonged was a young group that practiced at the Japanese Reformed Church in Little Tokyo. By 1932 the members included Aiko Tashiro, a pianist recently arrived from New York, cellist Josef Michiyoshi Kono, and Arthur Yuba, a "young violinist from Venice; rain or shine, he comes traveling over 25 miles to be with the group."[45] It was a mark of their commitment that many of the musicians endured long commutes for rehearsals. With two Chinese American young women participating, a *Kashu Mainichi* reporter mused that the group was unconsciously "developing a racial good will through music."[46]

In the late 1920s and 1930s, the urban ethnic enclave was part of a lively, cosmopolitan circuit for visual and performing arts. Little Tokyo music programs featured visiting as well as local talents. For example, on June 26, 1931, operatic soprano Agnes Yoshiko Miyakawa and cellist Josef Michiyoshi Kono appeared at the Nishi Hongwanji temple in a concert sponsored by the *Rafu Shimpo*.[47]

Reflecting the popularity of music in the ethnic community, an audience of several hundred (who paid $1.50 per ticket) gathered to hear the Sacramento singer who had just returned after "a successful season with the National Theatre Opera Comique in Paris."[48] Julia Suski accompanied both singer and cellist.

Miyakawa's repertoire and costuming reflected her cultural negotiations as a Nisei opera singer in the prewar period. Gauging her audience and displaying her versatility, she presented "a well-balanced program of French, Italian, English and Japanese songs," including, as all Japanese American sopranos did, a song from "Madame Butterfly."[49] She coordinated her outfits with the music, performing her first French song in a pink dress with rhinestone trim, switching to an "old-fashioned powder-blue gown with white lace" for a selection from the opera "Manon," and then donning a "beautiful white kimono with lavender iris" embroidery for her Japanese numbers.[50] The *Rafu* reviewer deemed "Comin' Through the Rye," one of her encore songs, "especially good" but devoted the most attention to the Japanese music and Madame Butterfly performance: "The audience seemed to appreciate her Japanese songs. Her aria from the opera 'Madame Butterfly' was loudly applauded as she sang and acted the part of the unfortunate Japanese girl."[51] Probably owing to racial barriers in the United States, Miyakawa became one of a number of Nisei performers who pursued wider career opportunities in Japan during the 1930s.

Another Nisei woman who aspired to a concert career was Setsuko Matsunaga Nishi. As a student at the J. H. Francis Polytechnic High School in downtown Los Angeles, she took classes in music composition, theory, and pipe organ, with a major field in liberal arts and music. She continued this major at the University of Southern California, pursuing music for three years until the outbreak of war.[52] Setsuko gave small solo concerts, including a well-attended recital at the Whittier Women's Club, and occasionally would perform a piece at a music club. Along with musicians such as Royden Susumago, the Nisei pastor at the Union Church, pianist Terry Hirashiki, opera singer Tomi Kanazawa, and baritone George Seno, she also belonged to a Japanese American music club that held concerts.

Such performances contributed to the vibrancy of the prewar community and, particularly in the case of local artists, awakened hopes with regard to their cultural potential. In 1933, for example, the English-language section editor of the *Kashu Mainichi* enthusiastically welcomed the establishment of a new drama society in Little Tokyo. He proclaimed, "From this group, we hope, the new ideas and new groups will develop to become a dynamo of intellectual energy for the future Americans of Japanese ancestry."[53]

The Lil' Tokyo Players and their northern California counterpart, the San Francisco Players, both formed in 1933. In Los Angeles, an assortment of Nisei contributed their energies to the fledgling group. One of their first productions was a pantomime play, "The Age of the Gods," adapted from the Japanese story of the creation of the world. The director, Joe T. Hirakawa, translated the tale and *Kashu Mainichi* journalist Larry Tajiri added additional dialogue. The large cast included columnist Alice Suzuki, singer Melba Yonemura, and musician Clara Suski. The Lil' Tokyo Players offered Nisei thespians opportunities to appear in mainstream plays, perhaps partly due to a lack of Japanese American-generated material.[54]

Aspiring Nisei actors also took part in numerous youth-club and church-sponsored plays, such as the Japanese YWCA's 1936 production of "Love Pirates of Hawaii," with an all-girl cast of 50.[55] In a drama directed by YWCA head Maki Ichiyasu at the Union Church around 1939, Setsuko Matsunaga Nishi played the mother of sons fighting on opposite sides in a war.[56] Many of the members of the Lil' Tokyo Players appeared in these performances; Clara Suski and Larry Tajiri, for example, had roles in the Japanese YMCA's staging of the prison drama "The Valiant."[57]

Nisei daughters also appeared in programs of traditional Japanese theater, with a gendered twist: The popular Shojo Kabuki (Little Girls' Kabuki) troupe performed classical Japanese drama, but instead of following the convention of all-male casting, young girls filled all the roles. In May 1927, a record crowd showed up to see the nine girls—then ranging in age from five to eight years—give a "perfect performance" at the Nishi Hongwanji Buddhist Church Hall. "All of these little girls are famous for their Japanese dancing," reported the *Rafu Shimpo*, adding that the troupe had previously performed for both "the Japanese public" and "Americans."[58] The girls demonstrated great crossover appeal: "Wherever they appear they prove to be a huge success."[59] As troupe member Toyoko Kataoka Kanegai remembered, these performances required tremendous discipline to memorize the lengthy scripts and stylized choreography.[60] Audiences may have initially been drawn by the novelty of seeing kabuki plays enacted by girls, but the popularity of the group, which toured in Japanese American communities in California and Hawai'i, was sustained by strong, polished performances.[61]

Film

A small number of the Nisei in southern California aspired to careers in film, but racial barriers and stereotyping made their chances of big-screen success even slimmer than for other star-struck youth of the era. Roku Sugahara, an avid movie fan, observed the cinematic ambitions of local Japanese Americans and mused glumly, "Usually no roles for Japanese except as a butler."[62] Sinister Chinese characters, he added, were the favorites; for the most part, Japanese Americans waited in the ranks of extras, hoping for even bit parts.

A few Nisei women managed to gain a toehold in the industry, such as Toshia Mori. Chosen Wampus Baby star for her work in "Bitter Tea," as Larry Tajiri reported, Mori "continued to set the pace for Nipponese misses on the American screen under the Columbia banner. 'Blondie Johnson' and 'Fury of the Jungle' contained two unusual bits by the exotic Los Angeles Japanese girl."[63] Tajiri also noted Iris Yamaoka's appearance in "Esquimo" as well as a role in "Hell 'n High Water" that "gave her a chance at portrayal a bit longer than the average allotted an almond-eyed emoter on Hollywood's sound stages."[64] Tajiri's examples echo Sugahara's assessment of the limited opportunities available to the Nisei. In the prewar period, racial discrimination prevented all but a few Asian Americans from pursuing careers in film; even the most successful, like Anna May Wong and Philip Ahn, faced a dearth of roles beyond the exotic or servile stereotypes.[65]

Art

Southern California boasted a busy prewar Japanese American art scene, with exhibitions featuring the work of artists from Japan as well as local Issei and Nisei.[66] Japanese American families came to have wedding photos taken at the Little Tokyo studio of Toyo Miyatake, one of the Issei photographers whose pictures won acclaim in international salons. The ethnic newspapers publicized the visits and shows of notable Japanese painters like Noboru Foujioka and Tsuguharu Foujita, both arriving from Paris, as well as Issei like the San Francisco Bay area artist Henry Sugimoto. A number of local Nisei also gained notoriety, such as Hideo Date and Benji Okubo, who often exhibited with their friend Chinese American artist Tyrus Wong.[67] Nisei men in art and architecture formed a group called the Ateliers.[68]

Gyo Fujikawa was notable as one of the few Nisei women professional artists to emerge. She was born in Berkeley in 1908 to an Issei farmer and an aspiring social worker; the family subsequently moved to San Pedro in southern California.[69] Like writers Chiye Mori and Hisaye Yamamoto, Fujikawa attained early recognition for her talent, winning a Los Angeles Opera Association poster contest as a teenager. She received training at the Chouinard Art Institute, and after returning from a year of art study in Japan, became an instructor there. She designed covers for *Westways* magazine and created fabric designs for national manufacturers such as Ever-Fast Fabrics, Julliard Fabrics, William Cohen, and Adler & Adler. Fujikawa also painted murals and designed department store displays before getting a job in the promotions department at Disney Studios; there, as Elaine Woo reports, she "worked on her first book, based on the movie 'Fantasia', and went on to design others under Walt Disney's watchful eye."[70] It is a measure of her success that Fujikawa was one of four featured speakers at a Japanese American Commercial Artists' Conference held in 1940. She gave practical advice to the Nisei who hoped to pursue careers in commercial art:

> While art cannot be placed in the same category as more academic studies, and "degreed", the average training is three or four years. And because it is essentially a medium of expression, the importance of ideas cannot be over-emphasized. Basic, fundamental training, however, is a very necessary factor in preparing for a career in this field.[71]

On the cusp of war, Fujikawa's work for Disney took her to New York, where she settled. There she enjoyed a long career, which included writing 46 children's books and illustrating nine more, as well as designing stamps for the U.S. Postal Service.[72] *Babies* (1963), her best-selling depiction of multiethnic tots, remains in print today.

Other Nisei women became regular illustrators for the English-language sections of the Japanese American newspapers, although they did not pursue careers in art. Chiye Mori drew pencil sketches and Lillie Oyama made linoleum block prints to accompany stories in the *Kashu Mainichi*. Julia Suski also penned beautiful, witty single-panel comics for the *Rafu Shimpo*'s English-language section, while her younger sister Clara contributed fashion drawings that appeared on the comics pages of the *Rafu* in its early years.

Julia Suski was a gifted artist whose work was well received beyond the ethnic enclave. She served as the art editor for *Wampus*, the official magazine for the University of Southern California, and her drawings appeared in periodicals such as *Life, Judge,* and *College Comics.*[73] One of her projects included illustrating a magazine put out by and for the Nisei college students in southern California. Her subjects in the *Rafu* occasionally included men, but were more usually young women, glamorously and fancifully attired, chatting together about fashion, scandal, human foibles, and romance and its pitfalls. Although many of the women she portrayed appeared to be white, she also created images of women who appeared Asian American; one bore a resemblance to actress Anna May Wong, who grew up in the nearby Los Angeles Chinatown. A few of her pictures depicted events within the ethnic community. Although Julia Suski considered herself more of a musician than an artist, her drawings constitute some of the rare prewar images created by a Nisei woman, conveying the tart humor of the day and the mixture of cultural influences that shaped the experiences of second-generation youth.

Dance

Dance was another avenue of creative expression for urban Nisei girls, who had far more opportunities than their rural peers to learn a range of forms, from traditional Japanese odori to ballroom and swing dancing. Practitioners of traditional dance performed for both the immigrant enclave and non–Japanese American audiences; even from a young age they were often called upon to provide symbolic representation of the ethnic community. For example, in 1927 five of the girls in the Shojo Kabuki troupe took part in an international program enjoyed by thousands at the Los Angeles Philharmonic. "Many favorable comments were heard" about the kimono-clad Nisei girls, whose "graceful motions appealed to the whole audience." At age seven or eight, they were already seasoned performers who had "appeared before the public a number of times, and now feel at home on any stage."[74] Studying dance, whether odori or ballet, enabled urban Nisei girls to develop poise and confidence in public presentation.

Little Tokyo also boasted modern dancers, such as Thelma Shizuko Okajima and Teru Izumida. Izumida was one of the four daughters of a Buddhist priest of the Higashi Hongwanji temple in Los Angeles. She began as a pharmacy student at the University of Southern California, graduating in 1929, but shifted to dance, studying with Michio Ito as well as with Bertha Wardell and Jose Fernandez, and learned traditional Japanese odori from Madame Izutsuya. As she stated before a 1936 performance at her alma mater, "In my creative work I have attempted a harmonious fusion of the orient and the occident. Free body movements are combined with the fragility of the arms in motion, yielding greater beauty than the tradition-bound classical dance." One of her new dances was based on a tanka—a Japanese 31-syllable poem—written in the twelfth century:

> I do not know
> Will he be true
> But since the dawn
> I have had as much disorder in my thoughts
> As in my black hair.[75]

Izumida included in the program her regular suite of Chinese, Burmese, and Javanese dances. Her work also incorporated experimental elements: according to the *Kashu*, "Enthusiastic fellow artists who have been following her progress in the art world are especially waiting to see her 'Wailing Song', a dance which will use a speaking accompaniment."[76]

Like Chiye Mori, Toyo Suyemoto, and other Nisei writers, Izumida attempted to educate her peers about her art form, creative dancing. It appears that some of her fellow Nisei, although comfortable on the ballroom dance floor, were baffled by modern dance. She wrote, "They ask me, 'But what does it all mean?' Or they utter a cryptic, 'Deep stuff', and shrug their shoulders." She sought to provide reassurance: "They have only to realize that greatness of simplicity is world famed in all arts. And what is more simple than the human emotions? Creative dancing is a thing of the emotions."[77]

In another example of cultural coalescence, Izumida championed the potential of combining Asian and Western dance elements. Her exemplar was her teacher, the famous Japanese dancer Michio Ito, who in the early 1930s had a studio in Little Tokyo where he practiced "a blend of the Orient and the Occident."[78] His choreography may have held particular appeal for her as a Nisei. "The rise of the second generation" interested her, she mused, given her "awareness of the advantages of heritage in the face of social disadvantages." She saw the advantages as "the oriental philosophic mind combined with an instinctive appreciation of art," that is, the "growth of the logical creative mind." Issues of race were submerged in her delicate definition of the disadvantages as "social barriers of misunderstanding caused mainly by a desire for personal gain."[79] Ultimately, she tried to impress upon her readers that they were heirs to a "gifted heritage" of adaptability as well as creativity.

More of the second generation—like Aiko Herzig-Yoshinaga, May Tomio, and Fumiko Fukuyama Ide—may have been attracted to less high-brow forms of dance. Perhaps enticed by the movies of Fred Astaire and Ginger Rogers, not to mention Shirley Temple, a number of Nisei enrolled in ballet, tap, and toe dancing classes at the local Dave King and Mae Murray School of Dance. "Of the two hundred and some pupils at the school," the *Kashu* reported in 1936, "among them several Hollywood film stars, none have shown more effort to master intricate steps than the young nisei…"[80]

The young dancers may also have drawn inspiration from Nisei performers like Fumi Kawabata and the Takahashi sisters, Helen and Dorothy. Kawabata began her career on stage in Los Angeles as "a gangling girl in her teens, and yet a veteran before the footlights." By the mid-1930s she had become a popular revue star in Japan, "singing Japanese 'blues' songs in the typical American cabaret manner."[81] In 1934 the Takahashis visited the Los Angeles Orpheum as part of an "Oriental revue" company; Helen sang the blues and Dorothy did a jazz dance. They next danced with Paul Jew as the "Three Mah Jonggs," and then Dorothy and Paul—who married—performed as a duo, billed as "Wing and Toy." By 1940 *Current Life* called them "one of the outstanding Japanese stage troupes now performing on the American vaudeville circuit."[82] Like the aspiring Nisei actors, the dancers and musicians also faced daunting racial barriers, exacerbated by the economic competition and stress of the Great Depression, to building careers as performers.

With this in mind, in 1933 second-generation musicians, dancers, and singers in southern California formed the Harmony Club, intended to serve as both a professional and social organization. The movement was instigated by a group of Nisei men and women already experienced in radio and stage work, including

Melba Yonemura and Mitsuya Yamaguchi. The chairman Joe Shimada said, "All second generation Japanese who are interested in this type of work are cordially invited to join this group."[83]

The *Kashu Mainichi*, under the editorship of Larry Tajiri, heralded the burgeoning creative efforts of the second generation with enthusiasm tempered by practicality. A 1933 editorial deemed the Nisei's interest in the arts, as exemplified by the increasing number of music recitals, "an encouraging sign for the second generation needs outstanding artists just as much as leaders in business and professions like medicine, dentistry and law." The writer proclaimed in ringing tones, "We, who have behind us the glorious culture of Japan, cannot afford to neglect the arts" but added on a more cautionary note, "To be sure, it may prove difficult for second generation people to earn their bread from music, painting and writing; but that should not deter us from developing whatever talent we possess in those fields." The gender-neutral terms of the editorial also suggest the visibility and significance of women as well as men in the creative endeavors of the southern California Nisei. With touching hope of eventual success, the editorial recommended the wisdom of maintaining a day job, saying, "Therefore, until we become masters, it may be wiser to develop it in our spare time."[84] Given the racial and economic obstacles they faced, as well as the pressure of parental expectations, it is not surprising that many Nisei with creative aspirations were indeed forced to relegate artistic pursuits to their leisure hours. Still, they continued to write and perform, to debate and dissect—they were each other's most appreciative and severe critics—fueled by the sense that they had a distinctive perspective to contribute to their community and to the larger society.

Promoting and Debating a Nisei Vision

Driven by this conviction, Nisei literati launched a number of creative writing journals in the 1930s, including *Reimei*, edited by Yasuo Sasaki in Utah, and *Shukaku*, a quarterly magazine published by the Southern California Poets, an Issei and Nisei organization.[85] A Buddhist youth journal, *Bhratri*, also included creative writing. Similarly, the Los Angeles Nisei writers' group began a publication called *Leaves* as a vehicle for second-generation literature and art.[86] Rather than showcasing local talent, they aimed to include Nisei from far and wide. As Carl Kondo explained in 1935, "The Literary club of Lil Tokio wants it understood that the pages of its magazine, 'Leaves' is open to all writers regardless of distance." The members, he said, "do not wish it to be merely a club organ but to have a real purpose, such as bringing the Japanese psychology forth for the American people to understand."[87]

In 1936, the Nisei writers' group moved to upgrade *Leaves* by merging it with *Gyo-Sho*, another quarterly publication. *Gyo-Sho* (Dawn Bell), edited by Eddie Shimano and sponsored by the English Club at Cornell College, made its debut in June 1936. For a subscription rate of one dollar per year, readers were promised "a real printed literary magazine, not a mimeographed copy, which will contain the works of The Writers as well as that of other Nisei writers."[88] After *Gyo-Sho* appeared, a social was held in honor of Shimano, a Nisei writer and artist from Seattle, with an interethnic mix of guests including Chinese Americans, Japanese Americans, and European Americans.[89]

The cover and title of *Gyo-Sho* signaled the transnational vision of the editor. On the cover, designed by Shimano, was a linoleum cut of a Japanese temple bell, with the title at the top, emblazoned in Japanese characters (kanji) that were echoed near the bottom by the romanized spelling of "Gyo-Sho." Shimano explained that, like a temple bell struck to herald the start of a new day, Gyo-Sho—meaning "dawn bell"—was intended to "announce to the world a new day, symbolizing the awakening of the Nisei."[90] He declared, "And like the reverberations of the temple bell, it will be heard universally, high birth or low, European ancestry or Asiatic."[91]

Striking the familiar note of the cultural bridge, Shimano expressed hope that the Nisei would someday "bridge the chasm between the cultures of the East and the West." Mindful of the challenges Japanese Americans faced, he wrote, "Struggling against economic, social, and racial problems, seeking self-expression in a language alien to their parents but a generation removed, called foreigners by their Caucasian fellow-men, the Nisei...are earnestly striving for a means of expressing their unique Japanese-American individualities."[92] Although Shimano did not elaborate on the nature of these unique individualities, he seems to have believed they were rooted in Japanese cultural traditions inherited from the Issei, including an aesthetic sense and an "awareness of cosmic forces," perhaps a reference to Shinto beliefs. As he saw it, the mission of *Gyo-Sho* was to help the Nisei "to attain full articulateness in self-expression and thereby to contribute to American culture the artistic simplicity and the symbolism of the Orient."[93]

Shimano did not draw any connection or comparison, but his goals somewhat paralleled those of the guiding lights of the 1920s Harlem Renaissance, later also called the New Negro Movement. Although he did not clearly define what might be unique about Nisei experiences, he felt that the second generation had something significant to contribute to American culture. The "new day" and Nisei awakening that he anticipated call to mind the emergence of the "New Negro" and a dynamic spirit of self-expression heralded by Alain Locke, an influential critic in the African American arts movement, who asserted that African Americans' artistic contributions would lead to recognition and acceptance in society.[94] Shimano, too, hoped that the gifts of Nisei creativity would reach a wide, appreciative audience beyond the ethnic community.

The vehicle of Shimano's ambitions was a 24-page journal presenting the poems, fiction, and short prose of 10 Nisei, with the addition of a translated Japanese story.[95] Six writers were female—Molly (Mary) Oyama, Toyo Suyemoto, Amy Tomita, Teru Izumida, Ellen Thun, Mary Korenaga—and four were male—Eddie Shimano, Ambrose Amadeus Uchiyamada (brother of Margaret), Jack McGilvrey (John McGilvrey Maki), and translator Eiji Tanabe (*Kashu Mainichi* editor). The 11th, Teru Ito, was probably a woman, but this is unclear.[96] Of the four stories included, three were written by women exploring a range of themes: the civic duty of the second generation, the struggle of a misunderstood artist, and dynamics among women in a Japanese family. In all three works, young women protagonists grappled with differences between how they were perceived by others and how they identified themselves—an issue of keen concern to the second generation.

Mary Oyama produced the one piece in *Gyo-Sho* that explicitly addressed racial dynamics from the point of view of a Japanese American character. A young Nisei woman's first trip to the voting booth marked her "Coming of Age" in Oyama's short story.[97] This work could be read as a how-to guideline, coaxing nervous Nisei to participate in the electoral process; it also suggested how interracial relations framed the political actions of second-generation youth. From the outset, the protagonist Sumiko thinks about how the white people at the polls may perceive her, expecting that they will misidentify her as younger than her age and as Chinese: "They always did."[98] The author contrasts how Sumiko identifies herself: "How were they to know that Sumiko wasn't even Japanese?" Although she is an American, she worries about not being recognized as such: "Wonder what they'll think—a 'Jap' girl coming to help elect the governor of the state?" Sumiko has heard that in some localities "young voters of Japanese extraction were subjected to a lot of unnecessary cross examination."[99]

Nisei readers might draw reassurance from the difference between Sumiko's anxieties and her actual reception at the polls: Two Jewish children campaigning nearby cheerfully urge her to support their candidate; a matronly poll worker smiles and matter-of-factly hands her a ballot. Even though no one can see her in the voting booth, Sumiko still feels self-conscious about how she will be perceived as a citizen. She deliberates before each name, lest the poll workers think that she had "voted without any judgment or wisdom on the matter." Finished at last, she marches away, satisfied that she has discharged "the important duty of a good American citizen."[100] The happy ending of this story hinged not on the outcome of the election, but on Sumiko's experience of having her American identity validated by participation in the political process.

In Ellen Thun's short story "Sketch," an unnamed woman art student clings fiercely to her own sense of aesthetics, despite being dismissed by her classmates as an "Affected monster."[101] The briefly limned dynamics of the atelier might have resonated with some Nisei writers frustrated by lack of recognition or understanding of their work, or of their emerging, still sketchy vision. When the teacher glares at the woman's charcoal drawing and questions her depiction, she defends it like "a savage mother protecting her young." After the teacher moves on, the young artist takes her materials and leaves, thinking, "I know what I want to do. Reality and technique were merely eyes. Then there was the mind.... The mind alone created. How much more important."[102] The sudden sense that she will dare to realize "the perfection at her finger's tips" fills her with elation and transforms her perception of her surroundings, no longer cheap and shabby.

Thun portrayed her main character, unidentified except for sex, as a woman with an unconventional vision. She thinks herself stronger than her classmates: "I can see ugliness and I'm not afraid. Even a little beauty..."[103] She flees the class, rashly or not, unwilling to subordinate her sensibility. Perhaps like some of the youthful Nisei writers, this character might lack experience and honed skill, but not a sense of her creative potential—a potential she believes can be fulfilled by pursuing her own notion of beauty.

Mary Korenaga's story, set in rural Japan, focused on the realm of family relations and particularly the ties among women. For Korenaga, this was an imagined setting, since she did not visit Japan until after World War II. However, hers was an informed imagination—a family member has speculated that this story may have grown out of Korenaga's relationship with her grandmother, who shared with Mary her experiences in Japan. The protagonist of "Chiyono" is a heartsick young woman working in a rice paddy. The story delineates the conflicting family obligations that Chiyono must weigh and also the nonverbal communication between her and the sister-in-law with whom she is at odds. Chiyono has just returned from three weeks spent caring for an ill sister. The presumably older brother with whom she lives gave permission, but his wife excoriates Chiyono for neglecting her duty to them. Deeply upset, she responds silently by going out to weed the rice, working like an automaton. Later, her sister-in-law also sends a nonverbal message: Chiyono's small nephew arrives with a lunch basket filled with her favorite foods. This "mute appeal" is magnified by the news that the sister-in-law is making sushi for dinner and afterward the whole family will attend a shibai (dramatic performance).[104] Chiyono is overjoyed by the prospect of these special treats that convey acknowledgment of her labor for the family.

"Chiyono" reflected the *Gyo-Sho* aim of welcoming a diverse audience—the author and editor clearly anticipated the needs of readers unfamiliar with the Japanese language. When Japanese words appeared, they were followed by parenthetical explanations: "Obachan" (auntie), "ne" (aren't you), "shibai" (a play, drama), and "osushi" (a delicacy made of rice and vegetables).[105] Nowhere else in *Gyo-Sho*—except for the explanation of the title and the definition of "Nisei"—do Japanese words appear.

Despite the ambitions Eddie Shimano voiced in his foreword, one would be hard-pressed to determine what might be uniquely Japanese American in most of the *Gyo-Sho* writings. The featured poems explored various shades of romantic disillusionment and philosophical musings, none of them addressing experiences particular to the Nisei, except for Teru Izumida's mention of Japanese dance. It would be difficult to ascertain whether this selection mainly reflected Shimano's tastes, or whether it was representative of the submissions he received. Without the contributions by Mary Korenaga and Mary Oyama, *Gyo-Sho* might have resembled a mainstream college literary publication.

In the assessment of reviewer Carl Kondo, the first issue of *Gyo-Sho* was a worthy beginning, but "the writings of the representative group of Nisei authors and poets express a stirring which has yet to see the light of the promised dawn."[106] Striving to balance his reservations with attention to notable features, Kondo focused his critique on what he perceived as the general absence of a Nisei voice. With a few exceptions, he felt that

> The others speak in occidental voices, no two the same, yet one in viewpoint. They do not see the American scene as other races do; what they see is tinged with the color of what they, themselves, are. The product is unsatisfactory when it is remembered that the efforts of the writers were to voice the surging flow of their generation, the Nisei.

As exceptions to this "occidentalized" tone, Kondo cited Teru Izumida's poem about dance and singled out Mary Oyama's "Coming of Age," in which he saw the beginning of a "new approach to literature typically Nisei." Such writing, he believed, would portray the struggles and environment of the second generation without bias and "narrate what is ordinary and American, yet Nisei because it will be saturated in the psychology of the Nisei."[107]

The Nisei, in their search to cultivate a Japanese American approach to literature, cast about for role models. The accomplishments of other Japanese Americans were hailed with pride, as when a Seattle Nisei woman Setsuko Kashiwagi sold a novel about Japanese American family life in the future to the Judson Press of Philadelphia, or Kimi Gengo's book of poetry *To One Who Mourns at the Death of the Emperor* was published in New York City.[108] They also looked to other ethnic-minority writers for inspiration. Their choices reveal the cultural diversity of the West Coast and provide clues as to how they thought about themselves as racial/ethnic Americans. Mary Oyama, in a series of interviews for the *Current Life* magazine, presented other ethnic Americans and the children of immigrants to stimulate her readers. One such potential role model was Leon Surmelian, a writer Oyama described as "An Armenian Nisei," whose articles about the "second-generation problem" of the Armenian Americans reminded her of the "Nisei problem." Upon learning that Surmelian lived in Hollywood, Oyama promptly invited him and several Japanese Americans to her house for a "bull session." "Over the tea-cups and rice-cookies," as she put it, "everything under the sun was discussed: Buddhism, Christianity,...the Nisei, interracial marriage, racial background of the Japanese people, Protestantism, Catholicism."[109] Oyama relayed Surmelian's sympathy with the Japanese Americans and the "Nisei problems," which she viewed as "really the common problems of all racial minority groups here in the United States."[110]

Oyama's writing reflected her strong concerns regarding multicultural relations. She never tired of trying to push her readers to "mix" socially with non-Japanese and to politicize her readers—as people of color and as citizens. For example, in July 1941, she interviewed the Italian American writer John Fante whom she called "a Nisei like the rest of us, as he was born in the United States."[111] Oyama deftly drew attention to another interethnic issue by focusing the article on a story by Fante that had appeared in the *Saturday Evening Post*.[112] The story, centering on a Filipino man, had met with strong criticism from the Filipino American intelligentsia. Fante sheepishly admitted to Oyama that he had, indeed, learned more about Filipinos *after* he wrote the story.

William Saroyan presented an even more impressive second-generation model. His life was a literary Horatio-Alger success story: Born in central California, the Armenian American Saroyan spent some time in an orphanage after his father's death, and as a teenager left school to work as a telegraph messenger. Another telegraph job enabled him to move to San Francisco, where he steadily pounded out short stories, beginning a meteoric career as a best-selling fiction writer, Pulitzer Prize–winning playwright, and screenwriter. Saroyan became a cosmopolitan figure whose orbit included New York, London, Paris, and Hollywood.[113]

Saroyan held particular appeal for the Nisei writers, who mentioned him frequently. Writing for *Current Life, The Magazine for the American Born Japanese* in 1940, Kenny Murase noted qualities with resonance for the Nisei: "in spite of his very American enthusiasm and vitality, there is still much of the East in Saroyan," the legacies of his immigrant father and story-telling grandmother.[114] Saroyan sent direct encouragement to the readers of *Current Life* in 1941, assuring them that "each of us is a Nisei," as well as predicting the "emergence of an outstanding Japanese-American writer."[115] Perhaps in response to rising tensions on the West Coast, Saroyan obliquely referred to racial and ethnic barriers as "a subtle opposition" that he knew "very personally." However, he downplayed them, stating that they were not "special" or different from the opposition faced by a poor man or an artist.[116] His proposed solution placed the burden on the Japanese Americans: "Let us make our heaviest demands upon ourselves and extend our greatest understanding toward everybody else." Saroyan's perspective appeared in May of 1941; within a matter of months, the Nisei and their parents would be the targets of unsubtle, special opposition, and no amount of understanding on their part would have the slightest effect on their fate. But in this moment before the storm, they could take heart from his urging: "The life of the Japanese in California is rich and full of American fables that need to be told to other Americans...they must be written by those who lived them in order to become a part of the whole American life."[117] Words of support from such an acclaimed author must have meant a great deal to Nisei writers.

The Nisei's attraction to Saroyan and Fante as models reflects the history of immigration and interethnic relations in the U.S. West. Many Armenians and Italians had settled in California at the turn of the century when the majority of Japanese arrived. For a brief period, the Armenians had shared the legal kinship of being categorized as "Orientals" in California. The success of Fante, Saroyan, and Surmelian as second-generation writers held out hope that Japanese Americans, too, might find acceptance on a larger literary stage. The early African American presence was smaller and the Harlem Renaissance had been a primarily Eastern regional development. Also, prejudice against African Americans may have prevented some Japanese Americans from viewing them as models to emulate.

Although some of the themes of the Nisei literary movement resonated with the impetus and issues of the Harlem Renaissance, there were vast differences. The Japanese American endeavor was far younger and smaller, lacking patronage, institutional infrastructure, and established senior leaders such as Du Bois. The second generation's efforts to create their own literary publications (*Leaves, Gyo-Sho*, etc.) fizzled out in the unpropitious climate of the Great Depression; World War II certainly cut short the early flowering of their creative work, including the promising magazine *Current Life*.

Gender dynamics constituted another key difference. The Nisei literary movement appears to have been less male-dominated than the Harlem Renaissance— women such as Mary Oyama Mittwer, Toyo Suyemoto, and Chiye Mori played active roles as artists, leaders, and organizers. Perhaps the best-known Nisei fiction writers today are, in fact, two southern California women, Hisaye Yamamoto and Wakako Yamauchi, who had been friends since they met in camp.

Of the southern California Nisei literati, Mary Oyama appears to have had the greatest interest in African American and other ethnic writers, whose work she publicized among the Japanese Americans. According to her family, Oyama initiated correspondences with a number of literary figures, including F. Scott Fitzgerald and Nelson Algren. One of the authors she befriended in this way was Chester Himes, an African American urban-realist writer of the post–World

War II era.[118] Himes and his wife Jean spent the war years in the Oyama-Mittwer home in East Los Angeles, where he wrote his first book.[119] In 1946, Mary Oyama recalled how Jean Himes welcomed the family back: "Our Negro American friend Jean, who had been living in our house the years we had been away, was in the kitchen picking up the last of her belongings. She greeted us warmly as we walked dazedly toward the living room, which seemed like a golden dream. 'Don't stand there, Mary! Sit down! After all, this is *your home!*'"[120] Through her newspaper columns, her friendships, the groups she supported, and the social gatherings she organized, both before and after the war, Oyama continually sought to advance interethnic and interracial contact among the Nisei.

Clearly Nisei writers looked both within their own community and out into the larger society for inspiration in grappling with the articulation of a distinctive American ethnic perspective. In this process, throughout the 1930s, they fiercely debated the potential and shortcomings of Nisei literature. Some, like Ujinobu Konomi, telegraph editor of the *Kashu Mainichi*, referred to the rich legacy of Japanese artistic expression and asked, "Are there not even a handful of youths among the nisei who have something to write on their own?" In a 1933 essay, Konomi suggested that, because of their racial location and ethnic-cultural heritage, the second generation were well situated to create art:

> They have perfect English; they have an environment more compli-
> cated than that of the average white youth. Their problems are far more
> profound, intense, poignant and abound in possibilities than those of
> the white man. And the artistic heritage of the Nisei must be adequate
> to carry all these ideological burdens with true artistry.

Konomi believed in what he called the "literary mission of the nisei," which he saw as something more than an aspect of a cultural-bridge role: "Let us forget all the banalities about 'bridging the Pacific' and 'promoting better understanding between America and Japan'. Art has a mission that transcends venal instrumentality."[121]

Perhaps in response to Konomi's query, one Nisei writer cited the comparative youth of the second generation as the reason they had yet to produce any great literature, although many "have shown gleams of future promise." In his judgment, they lacked the knowledge and experience "to write with any distinctive style; that is, to weld Oriental themes into the Occidental, to present a work that is truly American, yet with a definite influence of the Japan from which they have received their heritage."[122] Toyo Suyemoto encouragingly predicted that as the second generation matured, wisdom and perceptivity would enrich their writing.

Suyemoto continued to provide encouragement, a year later referring to the high hopes for the Nisei literati. She reported that as yet "no attempts have been made to picture in prose or verse the panoramic view of the nisei environment in America, nor of the first generation and their racial problems."[123] This she again attributed to the youth and inexperience of the second-generation writers, whom she likened to "observers on the outside of a fortified wall, not the dwellers within the citadel."[124] Her metaphor, although made in reference to life stage, carries resonance as a description of the Japanese Americans' marginal position as ethnic outsiders to the daunting fortress of the mainstream literary establishment.

The ranks of the critics and the volume of their complaints about Nisei writing increased in the mid-1930s. Some had grown impatient waiting for the second generation to produce substantial literary works that reflected Japanese American experiences. As Shin Kobayashi said, "Long awaited, long publicized especially in the California circles is the Great Nisei Novel: that is, a written record of the ideals, the hurts, the inwardly felt sense of injustice, and sometimes a sense of futility that wells up within those young folk of alien extraction during their passage through life." What most frustrated Kobayashi was the Nisei writers' focus on white characters, and their (to his mind) unrealistic depiction of Japanese Americans. He complained that the second generation "not infrequently write of something which they have never experienced, which gives a sense of artificiality to their writing which no mastered stylist among them can avoid." He also found the Japanese American characters unsatisfactory: "At best, the writings have some substantial Nipponese names as Hanako or Kimi, but they behave like a character out of True Confessions or the Saturday Evening Post!"[125] In this vein, a safely anonymous critic dismissed Nisei writing as "largely imitative," lamenting, "It is pulp magazine detective yarn, it is the Sunday supplement [romantic] triangle story, it is the latest racketeering writeup in the daily tabloids...in a word, it is anything but nisei."[126] The subjects and genres chosen by the young Nisei writers, although infuriating to their critics, demonstrate their engagement with U.S. popular culture and its impact on them. They may not all have written what they knew, but they certainly tried to write what they themselves enjoyed reading. Their literary efforts and the responding critique make clear the complexities of endeavoring to develop a distinctive ethnic voice in the face of an elite canon of high literature and the encompassing seductions of popular media.

Some Nisei writers felt stung by the vehement criticism. Johnnie Aisawa, author of "The Woman Speaks" column in the *Kashu Mainichi*, assailed the anonymous critic for his spitefulness, saying, "in the words that he did not write but felt nevertheless one knew that he was poking fun at those of us who have hope and faith in the ability of the Nisei to succeed."[127] She urged the critics to be more generous, quoting Mary Oyama—"our chief feminine penman"—"Give the Writers a Break!"[128]

Oyama, who had written an earlier defense of the experimental efforts of the Nisei literati, considered the criticism seriously. She responded to charges that the Nisei did not write "beautifully" by drawing appreciative attention to the work of writers she placed in the vanguard of Nisei literati, including Chiye Mori, Toyo Suyemoto, and Ellen Thun. Although a warm supporter of second-generation creative endeavors, Oyama was not uncritical of herself or others, realizing that "we all have a long way to travel before we reach any high standard of literary writing." For herself, she admitted feeling sheepish and humble after surveying her old files: "Personally we can tell you of how we almost blush to see some of the 'junk' we used to write just a year or so ago." She agreed with Shin Kobayashi and Richard Kawagishi that "the Nisei could most authentically and accurately write about life as it was being lived in the limited confines of the small Nisei world; and that strangely enough this angle is the least touched upon by Nisei writers." She also reflected that she, too, was one of the many "who had been glibly penning stories and such about occidental characters and shying away from Japanese and particularly Nisei characters."[129]

Oyama's explanation of why she had mainly peopled her fiction with white characters revealed her own sense of the Nisei's immersion in and embrace of mainstream culture. About her "occidental characters" she wrote:

> We used to write about them because naturally we understood them better than Japanese or Nisei characters. Being so completely Americanized, it was easier to write about Americans and occidentals because we understood their psychology better than that of the Japanese or Nisei psychology.

This "peculiar and distinctive Japanese and Nisei psychology," Oyama felt, was difficult to grasp or articulate. Consequently, "Oriental or Nisei characters were too exaggeratedly 'Japanesey' or too Americanized; they were not truly 'Nisei-ish' enough." Therefore she decided

> to wait until we thoroughly understood our own people, our own generation; and until we had mastered enough of the fundamental technique of effective writing, before we embarked upon the challenging task of depicting a true-to-life Nisei or Japanese character.

This, she said, was why "we, personally, up to this time confined ourselves to occidental heroes and heroines; we were experimenting."[130] Living up to her words, Oyama increasingly presented Japanese American characters in her fiction, whether an Issei picture bride or Nisei celebrating the New Year in a rural community.

Oyama's articles on behalf of the Nisei writers apparently effected a temporary cease-fire on the part of the critics, according to Johnnie Aisawa, but "it seems that our captious ones merely took time out to think up more acrimonious criticisms." Aisawa reported, "Yes, La Reine Mary [Oyama] informs that letters coming in now are more caustically, more perniciously critical than ever before." Aisawa called for more constructive comment: "Don't just write and say you're rotten, you shouldn't be writing for the paper because you're dull and uninteresting, please tell our columnists what you want."[131]

Nisei women energetically continued to take up cudgels—or pens—in defense of second-generation literary efforts. Poet and columnist Mary Korenaga issued a passionate "Counterblast to Carping Souls" in 1937, excoriating the small-mindedness and prudery of critics. No Nisei had yet produced any literary masterpieces, she acknowledged,

> But every time when a spark of genius is seen in some young rising writer, upon whom the weight of preserving the nisei life might have to rest, a flood of condemnation overwhelms him from all sides. Condemnation, not from the authorized critics of that time or any time, but from the narrow groping group of idiots who think it is their divine duty to tell the young author and all those who dare to print his work that hell and all its infernal heat is waiting for them, all because (they claim) the subject was of a shady nature. They forget, or never knew, that the literary work is not a book of moral codes but rather beauty of nudeness.[132]

By this time, Mary Oyama's impression was that Nisei literature was in a static state, "with no noticeable backward lagging or any remarkable step forward." She and some of the other literati wondered what the next step might be, and what the future would bring. "We have yet to produce a nisei William Saroyan who will loom up in the American literary horizon," she observed. "It will be interesting to watch if the much bull-sessioned over Great Nisei Novel will be written by one of our fellow nisei within the next decade or so."[133]

The Los Angeles Nisei literati continued to write and to meet, usually at Mary Oyama Mittwer's home. After the outbreak of war between the United States and Japan, they moved quickly to join the war effort and also to try to represent the realities of their situation to their fellow Americans. At a meeting on December 22, 1941, the writers and artists gathered "to clarify the loyalty, integrity, and ability of the nisei as Americans fighting for freedom, and to present the unhappy situation of discrimination, unemployment, and social and economic insecurity in which the nisei and issei are placed." Although affirming their patriotism, they also sought to draw attention to the racial inequities that predated the bombing of Pearl Harbor and intensified afterward.

The group envisioned publicizing the "positive position of the nisei in national defense" through an ambitious national effort making use of radio, documentaries, movies, and newspapers. Several members worked on a script for their first project, a dramatic presentation of the Nisei's position after the declaration of war to be aired in the "Fight for Freedom" broadcast over KFWB in January 1942. For the second project, they contemplated making a documentary film about the Japanese in and around Los Angeles. A third project involved analytical and dramatic materials about the second generation that would be forwarded to the Youth Division of the Office of Civilian Defense in Washington, D.C. They had hopes that the First Lady might be sympathetic to their cause. George Watanabe, who worked on this undertaking with Chico Sakaguchi, stated, "Mrs. Franklin D. Roosevelt is interested in the nisei problem as a youth and minority problem and especially appointed the Youth Division to deal with various racial and minority questions such as the unemployment, psychological maladjustments of youth and the extension of democracy to racial groups as a democratic right of all Americans."[134] Soon thereafter, as another measure to demonstrate their desire to be accepted in the larger society, the Nisei writers' group integrated their organization, inviting European Americans to join. It appears that their three projects did not materialize. As they worked feverishly to publicize their patriotism and precarious position before the larger public, the governmental decisions had already been made that would, in a matter of months, tear them from the social fabric of the West Coast and dispense with any vestiges of their democratic rights.

The Women Speak

Throughout the decade of the 1930s, the Nisei women literati—like their brother writers—eagerly experimented with form and subject. They wrote romantic stories, dramatic fiction, and slice-of-life vignettes, observing rural work, the quirks of humanity, the turn of the seasons, and the pulse of the city. All manner of poetry poured from their typewriters: sonnets, haiku, senryu, free verse, humorous ditties, and lyrical narratives.

Their writing provides glimpses of the many facets of ethnic community life in Los Angeles. To many of the second generation, city life glittered with the allure of modernity and excitement. In a prose poem, Ellen Thun (writing as Ellen Tanna) compared the urban ethnic enclave to a young woman: "Little Tokio stands poised, a modern maid...her arms flung wide to life and the world...eager, facing the sun...alive to the encompassing occidental sophistication...aware and youthfully impatient of aged traditions and hovering elders." In personifying Little Tokyo as a feminine gypsy, jeweled with light, serenaded, "the happiness of her own pulsing and sensuous," she also wove a lively and romantic image of urban Nisei womanhood.[135]

Daily life in the urban enclave offered access to aspects of ethnic culture unavailable elsewhere. Mary Korenaga, who had moved to Los Angeles in 1935, took delight in the amenities of the bustling Japanese American community, noting,

> To those who have not been here, it would seem funny as it did to me to see people ordering rice instead of potatoes at a drug store counter. And nonchallantly [sic] eat okoko [Japanese pickles] and ocha-zuke [rice with tea] with feet dangling half a mile in the air.... And we thought it was funny when one fellow would have a cup of coffee with his osushi.[136]

Ethnic ingredients and food were staple items, and even a small local eatery showed the workings of cultural coalescence.

A young Buddhist woman who wrote under the pseudonym "Poppy Yama" also provided insights into urban life in her column "Lil' Tokio comes to life," chronicling in a mix of reportage and fiction the details of family dynamics, the flavors of the food, and the rhythms of work, including the illicit stills that produced homebrew during Prohibition. In one column she evoked the ambience of a First Street barber shop, from the perspective of the eldest daughter, Masako: "Snip, snip, snip, snip, from morning until night, she heard the snipping of scissors. She has breathed hair in her dreams as they flew about in nightmares of Autumn leaves. Black Autumn leaves which turned red and yellow from American customers who came to the barber shop." In the back of the shop, younger brothers and sisters argued over their homework, and her parents read the Japanese newspapers, while Masako chatted with her girl friend Chiyo in the combined kitchen and dining room. While she washed the dishes, the boisterous Masako reminisced about her family's bootlegging wine before the repeal of Prohibition, and sang lustily, "I love whiskey, I love tea, I love the boys and they love me."[137] Yama's vignettes convey the irrepressible spirit of all the Masakos of Little Tokyo and the color and texture of their world.

Reflecting urban Nisei daughters' resistance to Issei notions of proper feminine expression (particularly as few Issei parents were likely to read their contributions to the ethnic press) as well as the influence of mainstream popular culture, women's writing often addressed heterosexual attraction and love. In a 1937 poem Alice Musashi boldly described how "The eyes of desire like greedy flames / flicker up and down the body / Corroding the dark, secret places."[138] Although they might yearn for romantic happiness, women's poems often

mirrored the more common experience of disappointment in love. As Toyo
Suyemoto wrote:

> I have long sought your heart, your dreams,
> > But you have closed the door
> And barred the way with bitter thoughts
> > That were not there before.
> I stand without, waiting and stilled,
> > Forgetful of the cool
> Wet rain upon my face—and know
> > The beggar is a fool.[139]

Indeed, so many women deluged the newspapers with verses about the pain of
unrequited passion that at least one male journalist grumbled that he wished
they would write something besides dismal love poetry.

The Nisei women literati also examined, with vivid immediacy, female roles
and possibilities in the prewar period. As illustrated by Miwako Yamaguchi's
story, "Appreciation," they were keenly aware of the fragility of their dreams.
Yamaguchi's protagonist is Mary, a Nisei girl who has set her sights on becoming a student at UCLA; her happy anticipation is shaken by her encounter with
another second-generation woman working at a fruit and vegetable stand. When
she learns that the salesgirl's studies at UC Berkeley were cut short by her father's
illness, Mary suddenly realizes her own good fortune in her father's ability and
willingness to fund her education. The work of Nisei daughters also emerged in
second-generation women's writing. Poppy Yama's "Masako" recounts in breezy,
stream-of-consciousness fashion the round of toil: "Pa has to hit me all the time
when I don't help ma with the cooking, washing, ironing and housecleaning.
Whew! Little sister-brother babies' diapers like wet blankets of work, work,
work. Now I sell vegetables, half day."[140] Work, whether wage paid or done within
the family home or business, was a reality for the majority of Nisei women.

Writers like Ellen Thun, chafing against their restrictions and frustrations as
young women, also expressed grand visions. She wrote:

> I know
> How I shall come
> Back again;
> Not the errant beggar
> Cringing for
> Each crumb of Life,
> Nor weeping

To see a little beauty
That another portions me!
No—
I shall come back
Striding down this world—
Life I'll cradle,
Beauty I'll companion,
Careless of one,
And flinging wide the other—
I'll come in glory!
O shining, shining glory![141]

Within the pages of the newspapers and literary journals, women writers wove bonds of community as they poured forth their dreams of glory.

* * *

Considered as an example of prewar second-generation Japanese American organizing, the Nisei Writers Group in Los Angeles and the broader literary movement have left particularly rich, diverse documentation of their goals, interests, anxieties, influences, experimentation, and interaction with each other. Blocked from access to mainstream publishing, they developed a forum in the ethnic press, working to build—like the other Nisei clubs—"a world of their own." The Nisei writers enjoyed a camaraderie forged from a shared passion for creative expression and a strong sense of ethnic and generational identification; their networks spanned geographical distances, meeting within the pages of the English-language sections of the Japanese American newspapers. In 1934, for example, Larry Tajiri noted the international scope of the *Kashu Mainichi*'s literary section: Aiko Tashiro wrote from the Japanese resort city of Karuizawa while Welly Shibata was in Osaka; Mary Korenaga wrote from Provo, Utah; Tooru Kanazawa had moved to Alaska and John Fujii was writing in Texas; Yasuo Sasaki was studying medicine and sending poems from Cincinnati; James Omura and Brownie Furutani were in San Francisco, and Toyo Suyemoto lived in Sacramento; Bill Hosokawa sent columns from Seattle.[142]

Women writers eagerly read each other's work and provided warm support. Lily Yanai, in a 1938 *Kashu Mainichi* column "Telephooie," thanked writer Ayako Noguchi for a gift of orchids, sent perhaps in honor of her restarting the column; she also complimented Noguchi on her column "La Hash Exclusive," which she said (taking Noguchi's food metaphor) was her "favorite dish" on the *Rafu Shimpo* menu. Toyo Suyemoto remarked on the encouragement she received from more senior writers such as Mary Oyama, Ellen Thun, Larry Tajiri, and Yasuo Sasaki. Similarly, Hisaye Yamamoto was influenced and heartened by the

Nisei creative writing that appeared in the ethnic press. Reading their references to each other, playful and admiring, their essays on Nisei literature, and their interviews with each other, conveys their sense of community. Despite occasional squabbles, and no end of brickbats from critics, they were comrades united by the conviction that they had embarked on a worthy and exciting enterprise.

Women such as Mary Oyama Mittwer, Chiye Mori, and Toyo Suyemoto were not only productive writers but also served as leaders in the Nisei literary movement. They sought to educate and stimulate their peers, speaking with authority and spirit. Their works reveal their deep investment in the effort to cultivate second-generation writing. The nascent Japanese American press provided a crucial forum for second-generation efforts; few were ever able to reach a wider audience. Within its pages they experimented with a wide array of forms, reflecting the influence of high art and popular culture; in the weekend literary sections, social-realist fiction rubbed elbows with romance, sonnets, haiku, and free verse. Although most of their dreams of public acclaim went unfulfilled, both their assessments of the realities of life and the possibilities they imagined reveal much about the ways in which second-generation Americans sought to define themselves before World War II.

New themes entered their writing as wartime tensions rose in the United States. Somber images shadowed their imaginings. In 1940, Hisaye Yamamoto asked the "question":

> how can I write of brother love
> of laughter of children in the street
> of pale shoots in the brown of bare earth
>
> how can I speak of casual things
> of the icy cleanness of fresh fallen snow
> of Christmas come wrapped in red ribbon
> how can I sing glad song and smile
> at the soft dusky warmth of a blue, blue song
> or exult in the coolness of smooth rain
>
> when brothers golden like the sun
> and brothers with pale white skin
> hate blindly across the cruelty of steel
> when children hide in darkened cellar
> or flee uncomprehending in sobbing sorrow
> when cold rain beats down unfound ones
> rotting in inglorious muddy death
> with frightened eyes...[143]

The tone of Nisei literature shifted as war abroad and political expediency at home made Japanese Americans increasingly vulnerable. Toyo Suyemoto wrote in 1941:

> Out of the anguish of my heart
>> There must come gentle peace
> That will bid wayward grief
>> And troubled thoughts to cease.
> When one by one, old sorrows pass
>> And I know my own will,
> Let not the spirit fear again
>> Or let my songs grow still.[144]

The vitality of urban cultural activity and organizations such as the Nisei Writers Group, as well as women's roles in shaping them, have been obscured by the uprooting and incarceration of Japanese Americans during World War II. The demands of adjusting to drastically altered circumstances disrupted the Nisei literary movement, as the struggle to meet day-to-day family needs took precedence; some songs grew still. However, Nisei women's organizing skills and resourcefulness would continue to prove important in sustaining families and communities.

Figure 1 The charter class of the Chi Alpha Delta sorority of UCLA pose in front of the Ambassador Hotel in Los Angeles, 1928. "Chi Alpha Delta Sorority," Photographic Files (UCLA University Archives Record Series 100). Library Special Collections. Los Angeles, CA. Courtesy of Aiko Mizue Sugita.

Figure 2 Club membership enabled young Nisei women and men to socialize, as at this Chi Alpha Delta party at Brighton Beach, 1931. "Chi Alpha Delta Sorority," Photographic Files (UCLA University Archives Record Series 100). Library Special Collections. Los Angeles, CA.

Figure 3 Escorted by their teacher and a bus driver, the Toquiwa (Tokiwa) Girls Club of the Chuo Gakuen cool off at the Montebello Plunge on August 4, 1934. Gift of Misuye Sato, Japanese American National Museum (2002.65.5).

Figure 4 The Junior Misses, a YWCA Girl Reserves club, eating watermelon at El Segundo beach, ca. 1941 (?). Left to right: Michi Iwashika Kamon, Grace Oda Tanaka, Miyo Aino (?), Kikuye Misaka (?), Mary Monji Nagahiro, Mary Kamimura Nakaji, and Yoneko Okuda Nakazawa. Courtesy of Mel Nagahiro.

Figure 5 Baby Mildred (Kobata) Yasumura, seated in a high chair, celebrates her first Hina Matsuri (Girls Day), on Terminal Island / San Pedro, March 9, 1935. The inclusion of western dolls in the Girls' Day display reflects the mixing of cultural elements. Gift of Mildred Yasumura, Japanese American National Museum (98.59.1).

Figure 6 Mothers and daughters gather for a Girls' Day celebration in Boyle Heights, with a doll display in the background, ca. 1935. Gift of Ichiroemon Ushiyama Family, Japanese American National Museum (2000.272.3).

Figure 7 Japanese immigrant families began to celebrate children's birthdays in western style. This may have been the birthday party of Minnie Miyatake in Boyle Heights, ca. 1936. Gift of Ichiroemon Ushiyama Family, Japanese American National Museum (2000.272.1).

Figure 8 The Embas, a YWCA club at Roosevelt High School in East Los Angeles, in summer 1940. Left to right: Sumako Miura, Frances Nakano, Tomi Nagao, Midori Mori, Masako Yoshida, Eiko Watanabe, Mary Ann Masuda, Miyeko Onishi, Yae Matsumoto, Rose Ohashi, and Yoshiko Machikawa. Gift of Masako Yoshida, Japanese American National Museum (2000.227.7).

Figure 9 Members of the Embas club and the Japanese Club in the Japanese garden at Roosevelt High School, wearing kimonos for International Day in summer 1940. Gift of Masako Yoshida, Japanese American National Museum (2000.227.3).

Figure 10 The Tartanettes enjoy a beach outing, probably at the YWCA's Eliza Cottage at Huntington Beach. Setsuko Matsunaga Nishi is fourth from the left in the front row. Courtesy of the Nishi Family.

Figure 11 The Tartanettes, a YWCA club, at a 1940 installation dance. Setsuko Matsunaga is second from the left; Maki Ichiyasu (in dark dress), head of the Japanese YWCA, is seated in the middle, with Tartanettes president Fumiko Fukuyama (wearing a patterned skirt) on her right. Courtesy of Fumiko Fukuyama Ide.

Lou-lia—Some terrible things can be caught from kissing.
Dorita—I believe it. You ought to see the poor fish our Aggie
caught.

Figure 12 This Julia Suski drawing appeared in the *Rafu Shimpo* newspaper on August 1, 1926. Courtesy of *Rafu Shimpo*.

Figure 13 Setsuko Matsunaga at center stage in a play directed by Maki Ichiyasu, head of the Japanese YWCA, ca. 1939. Setsuko portrayed a mother whose two sons were fighting on opposite sides in a war. Courtesy of the Nishi Family.

Figure 14 The Nisei dancers of the Dave King and Mae Murray Studios performed at local movie theaters between reels, ca. 1936. Aiko Yoshinaga is the third tap dancer from the left and Helen Matsunaga is second from the right. Courtesy of Aiko Herzig-Yoshinaga.

Figure 15 Lily Arikawa Okura, Cecilia Nakamura, Yoshiye Sato Sanada, and (?) Azuma dance in the Michio Ito revue at the Hollywood Bowl in August 1937. Gift of K. Patrick and Lily A. Okura, Japanese American National Museum (96.321.29).

Figure 16 Lily Arikawa Okura and Kiyoshi Patrick Okura dance at Nisei Week in 1938.
Gift of K. Patrick and Lily A. Okura, Japanese American National Museum (96.321.30).

Figure 17 The 1937 wedding photo of Mary Oyama Mittwer and Frederick Mittwer includes her aunt and uncle on the left; on the groom's left are his father Richard Mittwer and the bride's parents Miyo and Katsuji Oyama. Courtesy of Vicki (Mittwer) Littman, daughter of Mary Oyama Mittwer.

Figure 18 Poet Toyo Suyemoto sent her photo to Mary "Molly" Oyama, ca. 1930s.
Courtesy of Vicki (Mittwer) Littman, daughter of Mary Oyama Mittwer.

Figure 19 Nisei Week Queen Lily Arikawa Okura (standing) and her court ride on the Japanese American community's first and last float in the Pasadena Tournament of Roses Parade, January 1, 1941. Gift of K. Patrick and Lily A. Okura, Japanese American National Museum (96.321.28).

Figure 20 The YWCA Girl Reserves in the Amache camp in Colorado welcome visiting club members from the Tule Lake camp, ca. 1943–1945. Gift of June Hashimoto, Japanese American National Museum (2003.63.14).

Figure 21 Yuri Kochiyama (Mary Nakahara), founder of the Crusaders club, sits with two girls on the steps of a barrack in the Jerome camp in Arkansas. Gift of Yuri Kochiyama, Japanese American National Museum (96.42.5).

Figure 22 Members of Girl Scout Troop #2 of the Rohwer camp in Arkansas pose in front of their clubhouse, a converted barrack where they sang and held meetings on Saturdays. Gift of R. Ruth Shiraishi, Japanese American National Museum (2007.50.17).

Figure 23 Girl Scouts were also active in the Justice Department-run internment camp in Crystal City, Texas, where Issei community leaders and their families were incarcerated, as well as Japanese Peruvians. Gift of Dr. Sumi Shimatsu, Japanese American National Museum (97.89.7).

Figure 24 As before the war, sports proved popular in the camps. Setsu Okada plays first base in a block softball game at the Heart Mountain camp, spring 1944. Gift of Mori Shimada, Japanese American National Museum (92.10.2A).

Figure 25 The Starlettes, the Block 41 girls' basketball team in the Jerome camp, 1944.
Gift of Fumi Mochizuki, Japanese American National Museum (94.30.5).

Figure 26 A Nisei dance in camp, probably held in a mess hall, ca. 1942–1945. Gift of
Jack and Peggy Iwata, Japanese American National Museum (93.102.131).

Figure 27 Friends bid farewell to Fumi Munekiyo, as she departs for Cleveland, Ohio, from the Heart Mountain camp in Wyoming, 1944. Gift of Mori Shimada, Japanese American National Museum (92.10.2DJ).

Figure 28 In 1944 Hugh Anderson, a member of the Friends of the American Way group in Pasadena, went to the Amache camp to talk with Esther Takei and her parents about the possibility of her returning to California to attend college. Esther (between her mother and Anderson) became a test case for the return of Japanese Americans to the West Coast. By courtesy of Esther Takei Nishio.

Figure 29 Staff members of the *Los Angeles Tribune* at a beach party, ca. 1945–1948. Mary Kitano is standing second from left and Hisaye Yamamoto on the far right; the woman sitting in front with legs outstretched is jazz columnist Wilma Cockrell. Courtesy of J. K. Yamamoto.

Figure 30 A club that formed in Manzanar, the JUGS (Just Us Girls) continued to enjoy dancing and sports after the war. Left to right: Yuri Fukushima, Kazu Sakuma, Midori Matsumura, Tada Yamada, Mieko Yada, Mariko Suruki, Sumiko Yoshimoto, and Sumi Fukushima in Boyle Heights in East Los Angeles, ca. 1946. Courtesy of Sumi Hughes.

Figure 31 The Atomettes club formed at the West Los Angeles Community Methodist Church in 1946. Left to right: Susan Hashizume Uemura, Kathi Miyake Yamazaki, Michi Yamaji, Taye Noda Inadomi, Frances Watanabe Yonemori, Sadie Inatomi Hifumi, and Karlene Nakanishi Koketsu, with advisers Rose Honda and Mary Nishi Ishizuka. Gift of Rose Honda, Japanese American National Museum (99.21.7).

Figure 32 The Atomettes, who often wrote and performed their own skits, dressed in costume to provide entertainment at a Japanese American Citizens League event. Club advisers Rose Honda and Mary Ishizuka hold the "Curtain" signs. Gift of Rose Honda, Japanese American National Museum (99.21.5).

Figure 33 The Junior Debs, a girls' club at Roosevelt High School, gather for a dance at the International Institute in Boyle Heights, 1947. Gift of the Shida Family, Japanese American National Museum (2000.232.1).

Figure 34 Flower girl Chrislyn Kei Ito and bride Joyce Teraji with unidentified maid of honor at the YWCA's Magnolia Residence in Boyle Heights, ca. 1950s. The home offered housing to young women like Teraji in the difficult postwar era. Gift of Mrs. Toshiko Nagamori Ito, Japanese American National Museum (2000.370.2).

4

Nisei Women's Roles in Family and Community during World War II

In 2000, when Alice Imamoto Takemoto's son asked about her thoughts on her World War II experiences, after a long pause she said, "If someone ever mentioned internment, I would defend it. I would talk about the positive side. 'Well, I never would have gone to Oberlin or Philadelphia or come to Washington. I never would have been able to do that. I never would have left California.' That was my stock answer."[1]

Takemoto, born in 1926, had grown up in Norwalk, a southern California farming community where her father was the principal of a Japanese-language school and her mother taught the younger pupils. Alice, the last of four daughters, was a piano prodigy, playing concerts at age six. She was 15 years old and the only child at home on March 13, 1942 when her Issei parents—like many other Japanese teachers and ministers—were abruptly arrested by the FBI and jailed. Alice's mother returned to her children in the Santa Anita Assembly Center in June 1942. Her father was imprisoned in Santa Fe, New Mexico, and not allowed to rejoin his family at the Jerome camp in Arkansas until February 1943.

In retrospect, Takemoto told her son, "For fifty years, I never allowed myself to think it was immoral....I kept it out of my mind that an injustice had been done to me. I would not admit that for far too long."

"Why?" he asked.

"It was a defense mechanism," she said. "Otherwise it would have crushed me."

Takemoto's reflections indicate the challenges of delving into and analyzing the wartime experiences of Japanese American women and men. Only decades later did she recount her efforts to bring about her father's return, her sisters' work to improve the family's quality of life in camp, and her involvement with the Crusaders, a Nisei girls' club in Jerome. Consideration of such long-buried memories may now yield a more nuanced understanding of the past.

This chapter examines the experiences of Nisei women during World War II, focusing on Alice Takemoto and 11 other individuals whose lives supply strong connecting threads between the Japanese American family routines of prewar southern California and the years of wartime—and postwar—struggle. Tracing their paths during the war constitutes an effort to re-center women in history, re-examining a turbulent period in which the politics of race overrode gender and class for Japanese Americans. Focusing attention on their everyday experiences reveals how women honed prewar skills and continued to assist their families as much as they could. For those who came of age in camp and in other settings far from their parents and prewar homes, gendered generational networks provided vital support. As they and their families endured forced uprooting and incarceration, young women drew on prewar girls' organizational structures to strengthen social ties and create morale-boosting entertainment amid bleak surroundings. When the government developed clearance procedures for indefinite leave, many Nisei women, like their brothers, moved beyond the barbed-wire perimeter to seek jobs and education in the Midwest and East. As before the war, they again served as highly visible representatives of their families and communities, but did so in regions of the country where few if any Japanese Americans had previously ventured. Their stories show, amid the dislocation and losses of the war, the continuing significance of Nisei women's work, organizing skill, and cultural mediation.

Breaching Women's Silence about Wartime Experiences

As reflected in Alice Takemoto's oral history, recovering Nisei women's experiences of World War II is difficult. In the scholarship on Japanese Americans, the forced removal and incarceration have largely overshadowed everything that came before; at the same time, they have long remained a highly censored if not taboo subject in many Japanese American households. Shedding light on the silence of Takemoto and others, clinical social worker Amy Iwasaki Mass, who was six years old when she and her family were incarcerated, observed in 1978 that "many former camp residents, if asked about their experience, will deny that it was all that bad. They will minimize the negatives and speak of positives that resulted from the whole process."[2] She asserted that Japanese Americans had "used the psychological defense mechanisms of repression, denial, and rationalization to keep from facing the truth"—the truth of betrayal "by the government we trusted, the country we loved...." She likened the incarcerated Issei and Nisei to the "abused child who still wants his parent to love him and hopes to be loved and accepted by 'acting right....'" Thus, she suggested, obedient quiet behavior provided a way of coping with the hostility of a racist America.[3]

Many of the camp newspapers and family letters from which women's wartime observations may be gleaned were subject to official surveillance and censorship. As one Nisei, Katherine Matsuki, said of the Santa Anita Assembly Center newspaper, "Everything in it was happy. All good news."[4] At the start of incarceration, cameras and other items such as short-wave radios were confiscated. Only War Relocation Authority–sanctioned photographers were permitted to take pictures until later in the war. For the most part, these official images presented smiling faces and bustling activity congruent with WRA objectives.

In the face of a powerful, self-justifying government narrative about what happened, reinforced by the Cold War political climate, oral history has proved particularly important in untangling women's wartime experiences. During the 1970s and 1980s, Nisei and Sansei activists involved in the Movement for Japanese American Redress and Reparations began to breach (to quote poet Janice Mirikitani) "the walls of silence" about the war.[5] The public testimony given by previously incarcerated Issei and Nisei about their experiences constituted a crucial aspect of the redress campaign. Since then, a number of Japanese American organizations have undertaken the gathering of oral histories, revealing the linkages between women's roles before and during the war.[6]

Prewar Families

This chapter centers on the wartime experiences of 12 Nisei women, born between 1907 and 1929, who grew up in southern California: Fumiko Fukuyama Ide, Rose Honda, Haruko Sugi Hurt, Mary Nishi Ishizuka, Katsumi Hirooka Kunitsugu, Mary Yuriko Nakahara Kochiyama (widely known as Yuri Kochiyama), Marion Funakoshi Manaka, Mary Oyama Mittwer, Setsuko Matsunaga Nishi, Esther Takei Nishio, Sakaye Shigekawa, and Alice Imamoto Takemoto.[7] Initially they and their families were sent to the temporary Santa Anita Assembly Center, the Pomona Assembly Center, or Manzanar. Subsequently, except for those at Manzanar, some were moved to the Poston Camp in Arizona, others to Rohwer and Jerome in Arkansas, the Heart Mountain Camp in Wyoming, and the Amache Camp in Colorado.[8] All but the youngest, Rose Honda, left the camps during the war to pursue work and education. After the war, three stayed in the east, while the rest returned to California. In fact, Esther Takei Nishio was one of the first Japanese Americans allowed to return to southern California before the official rescission of mass exclusion in 1945. As a student entering the Pasadena Junior College in 1944, she served as a test case for gauging racial climate by U.S. Army officials as they contemplated the return of Japanese Americans to the West Coast.

Fumiko Fukuyama Ide's father owned a hardware store in Little Tokyo; her mother had a dressmaking business upstairs. Until Pearl Harbor day, Fumiko, who had graduated from high school in 1940, did clerical work at the Los

Angeles County General Hospital. After spending six months in the Santa Anita Assembly Center, she was sent to work at the Jerome camp in Arkansas; her sister and one brother had left for college in Nebraska, outside the military zone. When her remaining brother enlisted in the army, she transferred to the Amache camp in Colorado to take care of her father and mother.

Rose Honda grew up in West Los Angeles, the daughter of a gardener. Active in the West Los Angeles Methodist Church, Honda and her family entered Manzanar accompanied by many Japanese Americans from their congregation.

Haruko Sugi Hurt's family farmed in the Central Valley of California before moving to Gardena, where her mother juggled jobs to support the family. Haruko (born in 1915) did sewing and domestic work before the war. They were sent first to Santa Anita, and then to the Rohwer Camp in Arkansas. After leaving camp for work in Chicago, Haruko joined the Women's Army Corps (WACS) in 1945.

Mary Nishi Ishizuka had lived in Hollywood until just before the war, when her family moved to West Los Angeles where her father owned a large plant nursery. On December 7, 1941, he was arrested by the FBI and held in a Justice Department internment camp in Missoula, Montana. The rest of the family was sent to Manzanar. With her sister Midori, Mary left camp for college in Nebraska where she supported herself by doing domestic and food service work.

Born in 1921, Mary Yuriko Nakahara—who later became well known as Yuri Kochiyama, dedicated activist and friend of Malcolm X—grew up in San Pedro, California, a gritty coastal community outside of Los Angeles. Her mother was a graduate of Tsuda College in Japan; her father and his brother-in-law had established the prosperous Pacific Coast Fish Market. She was the only one at home when her father, ailing with diabetes and an ulcer, was seized by the FBI. Denied medical treatment, he was released only shortly before his death several months later. Yuri and the rest of her family were sent to Santa Anita and then to Jerome, Arkansas.

Katsumi Hirooka Kunitsugu, born in Los Angeles in 1925, spent four years in Hiroshima when her family returned to Japan. They moved back to Boyle Heights in East Los Angeles where Katsumi, an aspiring writer, attended Roosevelt High School. She and her family were sent first to the Pomona Assembly Center and then Heart Mountain camp in Wyoming, where she edited the high school newspaper and wrote for the *Heart Mountain Sentinel*. In 1944 she entered the University of Wisconsin to study journalism, doing domestic work to support herself.

Marion Funakoshi Manaka's mother came to the United States as a picture bride for a farmer in Colorado. They moved to Los Angeles, where Marion was born, and then to Santa Ana where the family started a florist shop and nursery. When war broke out, they were sent to Santa Anita and then to Poston in Arizona. After a year, the Funakoshi family left camp for Colorado where they did a range of work and Marion finished high school. At age 17, she went to Chicago where she worked in a defense factory.

Writer Mary Oyama Mittwer (born in 1907) and her husband Fred Mittwer, with two small children, left their home in East Los Angeles to enter Santa Anita.[9] From there they were sent to the Heart Mountain camp in Wyoming. Upon their release in February 1943, they resettled in Denver, Colorado, returning to Los Angeles after the war.

Setsuko Matsunaga Nishi (born in 1921) was in her third year of studying music at the University of Southern California when the war began. Her father worked in real estate and insurance. From Santa Anita, Setsuko went to St. Louis, Missouri, completing BA and MA degrees in sociology at Washington University. She then pursued her doctorate at the University of Chicago.

Esther Takei Nishio grew up in Venice, California, where her parents operated a game concession on the Venice Amusement Pier. Her father was also seized by the FBI and held in a detention camp in Santa Fe, New Mexico, but later joined Esther and her mother at Santa Anita, before they were sent to Amache, Colorado. In September 1944, before the rescission of mass exclusion, Esther returned to California and entered the Pasadena Junior College (which became Pasadena City College).

Sakaye Shigekawa, born in 1913, was the daughter of a gardener and a picture bride in South Pasadena. Her father's ill health catalyzed her interest in medicine, and after graduating from Jefferson High School she became a pre-med student at the University of Southern California. She then attended Loyola Medical School, followed by an internship in Michigan. Shigekawa had begun a residency at the Los Angeles County Hospital when the war started and all Japanese American staff were dismissed. At Santa Anita she became one of seven physicians who provided care for more than 17,000 people. She left Santa Anita for a residency in Chicago and returned to California in 1948.

As these brief biographies indicate, their families were spread across southern California, varying in economic security and the ethnic mix of their neighborhoods. Mary Ishizuka's parents owned a successful plant nursery that catered to an upscale clientele; Rose Honda and Sakaye Shigekawa were both the daughters of gardeners. Most of their families were involved with Japanese American communities, usually through their places of worship. Those young women from more economically comfortable families took part in a range of extracurricular activities; for example, Fumiko Fukuyama Ide, Setsuko Matsunaga Nishi, Esther Nishio, Yuri Kochiyama, and Katsumi Kunitsugu were all active in high school clubs and other youth organizations before the war. As a young adult, Kochiyama also served as an advisor to a number of girls' clubs; unusually, they were not Japanese American, thus reflecting the range of interethnic interaction in different areas and according to class.

After December 7, 1941

For Japanese Americans on the West Coast, the familiar routines of life would be severely disrupted on December 7, 1941 when the bombing of Pearl Harbor by Japan ignited war between the United States and Japan. Esther Takei Nishio was at home when she heard the news on the radio, "and it really frightened me."[10] She was supposed to go help her parents, already at work at the Venice Amusement Pier, but was so shaken that it took her several hours to muster the nerve to join them.

Fumiko Fukuyama Ide was on her way home from a Tartanettes basketball game when "somebody on the streetcar called me a 'Jap'. And nothing like that had ever happened to me. And somebody says, 'Why don't you go back where you came from'. ... I was hurt because I had never had anyone talk to me like that. And then when I went home, I found out about Pearl Harbor."[11]

Japanese Americans felt growing anxiety as the Issei's bank accounts were frozen and the FBI quickly arrested community leaders. Mary Nishi Ishizuka's father was seized on the night of December 7. FBI agents walked into the Nishi home without invitation and into the bedroom of her father, who had already retired for the evening. The family was "afraid to say or do anything." They eventually learned that he had been taken to the police station and then imprisoned in San Pedro. But, as Mary said, "They never let us know where he was. They never gave us any information until later on we found out that he was moved to [Fort] Missoula, Montana" to a detention camp run by the Department of Justice. Similarly, after Esther Takei Nishio's father, the president of the Parent-Teachers Association for the local Japanese language school, was arrested, the family had no idea where he had been taken until months later.

Japanese-language teachers were particularly targeted. Both of Alice Imamoto Takemoto's parents were seized on March 13, 1942, as she recalled, on Friday the 13th. The FBI surrounded the house and arrested her mother, confiscating Japanese teaching materials and handicraft books as evidence. Her mother, one of 44 Issei women arrested, could take only a toothbrush, toothpaste, and a Bible. When Alice's father came home, he too was arrested. Alice, age 15, was the only daughter at home; her sister Marion attended Fullerton Junior College. They spent two weeks alone until their two older sisters cut short their studies in northern California—Grace at UC Berkeley and Lily studying nursing in Oakland—to return home. They never received any notification from the police or FBI regarding the whereabouts of their father. Their mother was first incarcerated in the Norwalk jail, then the Los Angeles jail, and finally sent for three months to the Terminal Island federal prison.

The older Imamoto sisters marshaled what resources they could in an effort to secure their parents' release, asking European American friends—especially in Christian church networks—to write letters vouching for the loyalty of their parents. Their mother's hearing was held in April 1942, and she was allowed to join her daughters in Santa Anita in June. Although their father's hearing board recommended parole, Attorney General Francis Biddle overruled their assessment and he was incarcerated in Santa Fe, New Mexico as a prisoner of war.

This seizure of Issei businessmen, ministers, teachers, and other leaders proved traumatic for individuals and their families and devastating to Japanese American enclaves. The loss of their most experienced leaders deepened the turmoil, confusion, and fear.

Many Japanese Americans found themselves viewed as potential spies. Haruko Hurt, who did domestic work for a Beverly Hills family, recalled her European American employer saying, "I am going to have to look under your bed to see if you have a radio transmitter hidden there." Hurt explained, "You see, this is the kind of reaction that occurred immediately after the war broke out. Every Japanese whether they were born here or immigrants" was under suspicion.[12] Some lost their jobs. Dr. Sakaye Shigekawa, then doing a residency at the Los Angeles County hospital, and Fumiko Fukuyama Ide, who worked in the hospital records department, were both fired. Curfews and travel restrictions increasingly limited Japanese Americans' daily lives.

Few could imagine just how much more circumscribed their lives would become in a matter of months. On February 19, 1942, President Franklin Delano Roosevelt signed Executive Order 9066, arbitrarily suspending the civil rights of American citizens by authorizing the removal of nearly 120,000 Japanese immigrants and their U.S.-born children from the western half of the Pacific Coastal states and the southern third of Arizona. The specter of forced exodus and incarceration began to take concrete form. A new graduate of the Hollywood High at the time, Mary Nishi Ishizuka described the atmosphere of uncertainty: "That was a hectic time, because the rumors were flying, and we knew that we only could take one bag per person. We had no idea what Manzanar was going to be like. The people were saying that there were snakes, and so we were all looking around for boots (chuckles) that would protect us from snakes. We didn't know how cold it was going to be. We didn't have enough warm clothing.... It was hard to decide what to take and what not to take."[13]

Adding to the shock and misery was the urgent need to dispose of businesses and property. The Japanese Americans' material losses were staggering. Esther Takei Nishio's parents left their Venice Amusement Pier game concession and carnival equipment in the hands of trusted employees, but lost everything. Fumiko Fukuyama Ide watched as government agents auctioned off all the stock in her father's hardware store. During the war, metal was needed for the war effort; as she said, "it was very valuable stuff that my father had....So they took everything and he didn't get anything out of it."[14] She and her family "packed like crazy" and stored their personal belongings in a locked part of their house, which they rented to a doctor and his wife; during the war someone broke down the door and took everything. Mary Nishi Ishizuka's parents had established a large, prosperous nursery serving an affluent Westside clientele, including the likes of Will Rogers. After the FBI seized Mary's father, her mother struggled to sell the nursery: "It was a traumatic time. We couldn't sell very much, and we were offered so little for the nursery. It was worth at least $100,000 at the time. My mother was so angry that she was offered so little for the nursery that she decided to just donate it to the government, our neighbors, [and] the Veterans Administration."[15] However, the Nishis were fortunate in that their mail carrier offered to rent their house in their absence and took good care of their belongings. Others, like Katsumi Hirooka Kunitsugu's family, could not store their furniture and had to sell it for a fraction of its value.

Parting with pets was especially wrenching. Esther had to leave behind two beloved dogs: "One was called Shiro [white], and he was a little Skye terrier, and Kuro [black] who was a mixed German shepherd.... I don't know what happened to them."[16] Alice Imamoto Takemoto recalled, "for me the hardest thing was giving away our dog Jerry. He was a little fox terrier."[17] She wrote to her father in April 1942, admitting, "I was so sad that I came home and cried myself sick."[18] Such painful preparations marked the forced departure of Japanese American families from their homes and neighborhoods.

Incarceration: Assembly Centers and Relocation Centers

In the spring of 1942, the U.S. Army's Wartime Civil Control Administration began to remove Japanese American families to 16 assembly centers. Each individual was allowed to bring only as many clothes and personal items as he or she could carry to these temporary camps that had been hastily constructed at fairgrounds, race tracks, and Civilian Conservation Corps camps: 13 in California, one in Washington state, one in Oregon, and one in Arizona.[19]

The streets were jammed, Mary Oyama Mittwer said, near the departure point where the Japanese Americans, under the eyes of military police, boarded buses that would take them to the assembly center. Upon reaching the Santa Anita Assembly Center, she "stared in unbelief at the camp's sentry watchtowers and the barbed wire (looking for all the world like the pictures of Nazi concentration camps in Poland)." An Issei physician said, "I feel sorry enough for us, the Issei, but at least we have a country. I feel sorrier for you Nisei, because it looks as if your own country, the United States, has repudiated you." That, she felt, "was the worst blow of all."[20]

Many Japanese Americans experienced shock when they entered the crude assembly centers, enclosed by barbed-wire fences and under surveillance by armed soldiers stationed in guard towers and patrolling the perimeter. Setsuko Matsunaga Nishi remembered being stunned on the day she and her family went to Santa Anita: "I felt like a zombie, just went through the motions...moving through this like a robot."[21] The barrack living quarters at all the centers were disheartening, but people sent to the assembly center erected at the Santa Anita race track fared worse: Many were housed in hurriedly white-washed stables that stank of manure in the summer heat. Alice Imamoto Takemoto's family had two rooms, "the stall, which was big enough for a horse to stand in, and an inner room. But the walls throughout the building didn't go all the way to the ceiling, so it was open up there. You could hear everything."[22] Katsumi Hirooka Kunitsugu also commented on the lack of privacy in the barracks at the Pomona Assembly Center, where one could "hear people arguing, talking, snoring, fighting."[23]

Standing in lines became a way of life, as everyone adjusted to the primitive communal facilities, waiting to eat in mess halls, use latrines, take showers, and launder clothes. In most of the assembly centers there was a mortifying lack of privacy in the latrines; in Santa Anita, Alice said, "the toilets were in a big room, all in a row, with just a board between them. No door, no curtain."[24] Also in Santa Anita, Esther recalled the humiliation of having to bathe in an unpartitioned round house, previously used to wash the horses, until a shower was built. According to Alice, "The lines were so long I remember getting up at midnight and walking to the grandstand to take one."[25]

Life in the assembly centers was a prelude to the government's removal of the Japanese Americans, completed by November 1942, to 10 permanent relocation centers organized by the War Relocation Authority: the Topaz camp in Utah; the Poston and Gila River camps in Arizona; Amache camp in Colorado; Manzanar and Tule Lake in California; Heart Mountain, Wyoming; Minidoka, Idaho; Jerome and Rohwer, Arkansas. The Jerome and Rohwer camps were located in the swampy lowlands of Arkansas. The other camps were in desolate desert or semi-desert areas subject to dust storms and extreme temperatures reflected in the nicknames given to the three sections of the Poston Camp: Toastum, Roastum, and Dustum. Like the assembly centers, the relocation camps were "primitive prisons."[26]

The standard housing in the camps consisted of spartan tar-papered barracks, each about 20 feet by 100 feet, divided into four to six rooms furnished with steel army cots. Initially each single room or "apartment" housed an average of eight persons; individuals without kin nearby were often moved in with smaller families. Because the partitions between apartments did not reach the ceiling, even the smallest noises traveled freely from one end of the building to the other.

There were usually 14 barracks in each block, and each block had its own mess hall, laundry, latrine, shower facilities, and recreation room.

The flimsy barracks provided little protection from the elements, whether in the desert, mountains, or swampland. At Poston, the scorching summer heat altered previous routines; as community analyst Toshio Yatsushiro, a Nisei researcher working for the WRA, noted, "many housewives did their family washing regularly at midnight or later, largely because it was too hot to do it during the day."[27] During the winter, the uninsulated barracks afforded little comfort. In Jerome, when the winter temperature dropped to 13°F, Alice said it was almost like "living outside."[28] In order to stay warm, her family improvised a makeshift kotatsu (foot warmer), using their toaster: "We put the toaster under the table and a blanket over it, and we'd sit there to keep warm."[29] Regarding the early months in camp, Yatsushiro asserted, "When the emotional ordeal of the evacuation and center confinement were superimposed upon the adverse center conditions, the cumulated strain accruing to the evacuees was immeasurable, indeed by any human standards intolerable."[30]

In the assembly centers and relocation camps, perhaps the hardest adjustment was the loss of privacy, cited over and over by former camp inmates. As Jeanne Wakatsuki Houston recorded in her autobiography *Farewell to Manzanar*, many family members began to spend less time together in the crowded barracks. The even greater lack of privacy in the latrine and shower facilities necessitated adjustments in notions of modesty.[31]

The large communal mess halls, each serving 250 to 300 people, also encouraged family disunity as family members gradually began to eat separately: mothers with small children, fathers with other men, and older children with their peers. Mary Nishi Ishizuka said, "All the hardships we went through, broke up the family," particularly singling out "having to go to mess halls for meals."[32] She remembered the poor food at Manzanar and not being able to sit down with her family because of having to wait in line. Haruko Sugi Hurt, sent to the Rohwer camp, observed, "There was no family life as such in camp, because families didn't eat together, didn't have to. So the kids enjoyed it. It was great freedom for the young people. They just came to their unit to sleep. All the activities was outside of their little unit in the barracks."[33]

The conditions of camp life profoundly altered family relations and affected women of all ages and backgrounds. Family unity deteriorated in the crude communal facilities and cramped barracks. The unceasing battle with the elements, the poor food, the shortages of toilet tissue and milk, coupled with wartime profiteering and mismanagement, and the sense of injustice and frustration took their toll on a people uprooted, far from home. However, the incarcerated Issei and Nisei had no choice but to gaman, to endure.

Life in Camp

Although still numb, Japanese Americans set about making their situation bearable, creating as much order in their lives as possible. In the Santa Anita stable they had christened "Valley Forge," Mary Oyama Mittwer and her husband busied themselves "trying to make the stall more homelike as we unpacked our few belongings, made shelves from salvaged packing crates, laid out straw mats on the asphalt floor, tacked up a few familiar pictures from the home we had just left."[34] Others partitioned their apartments into tiny rooms with blankets and made benches, tables, and shelves as piles of scrap lumber left over from barracks construction vanished. With mail-order fabric, women stitched curtains to afford some privacy in barracks and latrines. Eventually victory gardens and flower patches appeared.

Women as well as men proved adept at contributing to the comfort of their families. Especially in families without Nisei sons or Issei fathers, women shouldered all manner of work, including the kinds of physical labor previously done by men.[35] For example, Alice Imamoto Takemoto's sister Marion became a skillful wood worker in Jerome: "The furniture that we had? She made it. She also made a coffee table—a beautiful hardwood coffee table—and some kind of chest to put our things in."[36]

In this arduous process, women and men alike received mixed messages from the WRA camp administrators. Alexander Leighton, a psychiatrist and WRA community analyst at Poston, pointed out that Japanese Americans who raided government wood piles were able to make needed furniture, whereas those who obeyed the rules and waited for material to be supplied got little or nothing. He concluded that, in some cases, "cooperation served to perpetuate adverse influences while aggressive action got results."[37] This lesson did not go unnoticed.

A few women did act assertively in openly confronting both Issei male authority and government officials. As a teenager Esther Takei Nishio led a successful waitress strike at Santa Anita. She and the other waitresses had to arrive at the mess halls an hour before serving time to set the tables, and it was their unpopular task to dole out the rationed sugar at breakfast. They didn't get to eat until everyone else had been served. "One day they ran out of food, and we didn't get fed," Esther recalled. "And so I led a strike and demanded that from now on the cooks serve the servers before the other people, otherwise we wouldn't work.... Well, we just sat there and wouldn't do anything until they fed us."[38] The grinning chefs agreed. Although Esther recounted this anecdote with humor, it also provides a notable instance of young Nisei women demanding consideration and concrete change from older men of their community.

Others turned to less overt means of resistance to the Wartime Civil Control Administration in charge of the assembly centers. Upon arrival at Santa Anita, Setsuko Matsunaga Nishi started looking for Masamori Kojima, a Nisei college student friend with whom she had been involved in the effort to fight the "evacuation."[39] She found him "sitting on the portable typewriter that Carl Kondo had lent him, having an asthmatic attack on the approach to the Santa Anita grandstand."[40] Wasting no time, they formed a writers group, including Joe Oyama and George Watanabe, and they also began to teach. Setsuko recalled that "people were informally developing classes in whatever they knew that they could share....So Shugo Seno would teach a singing lesson, and someone would teach sewing, and tea ceremony.... There must have been literally hundreds of these informal educational classes that cropped up—with all volunteer work." She and Kojima, along with their Issei friends Joe Koide and Ryoichi Fujii, "set up what we called—so as not to hackle the administration—'citizenship training classes'. That would be a real dull go-away kind of title. But Joe Koide and Ryoichi Fujii discussed current events, and they were fascinating because they came with a left-leaning anti-militarist perspective."[41] Crowds of Issei filled the jockey-stand to listen to Koide's and Fujii's lectures, which were uncensored because they spoke in Japanese. Conducting their class in English, Setsuko and Masamori "could barely get a handful of high school students" to attend. Nevertheless, they were part of an effort to raise morale and perhaps encourage critical thinking.

As they did in the prewar years, Nisei women served as intermediaries and translators for their immigrant parents, utilizing their communication skills on behalf of their families in the camps. Fifteen-year-old Alice Imamoto Takemoto took action in addressing government officials to seek the release of her father, held in a detention camp in New Mexico. Perhaps mindful of her older sisters' earlier letter campaign to win the release of their imprisoned parents, Alice wrote a long letter to the WRA administrators at the Lordsburg Internment Camp. In clear meticulous detail, she recounted the previous efforts made on his behalf, testified to her father's good character and loyalty to the United States, and cited the contributions he had made to the Japanese American and larger Norwalk communities despite his poor health. Her letter voiced the family's hardship, sorrow, and sense of deprivation, while leveling a critique through a series of questions: "Do you know how it is to have your only one dear father be taken away from you when you are only 15? I envy others who have their fathers and mothers with them when our father is as innocent as they are....Do you believe you are doing justice to all of us by breaking up our family and interning a man who is innocent?...Don't you think you have made a grave mistake?"[42] After nearly a year of detention, in February 1943 Zenokichi Imamoto was permitted to return to his family in February. Both parents attributed his release to Alice's letter.

Work

Despite the best efforts of the Japanese Americans to restore order to their disrupted world, camp conditions prevented replication of their prewar lives. Within the limited, artificial environment, family dynamics shifted. Women's work experiences, for example, changed in complex ways during the years of incarceration. Each camp depended on inmate workers to fill a range of jobs, resulting from the organization of the camps as model cities administered through a series of departments headed by European American administrators. The departments handled everything from accounting, agriculture, education, and medical care to mess hall service and the weekly newspaper. The scramble for jobs began early in the assembly centers and relocation camps, and all able-bodied persons were expected to work.

Even before the war many family members had worked, but now children and parents, men and women, all received the same low wages. As WRA community analysts noted, the relationships between parents and children, husbands and wives, were affected by the new framework of life in the camps: "The husband was no longer in the position of main breadwinner in many families, his wife and older children often drawing the same monthly wage."[43] In the relocation camps, doctors, teachers and other professionals were at the top of the pay scale, earning $19 per month. The majority of workers received $16, and apprentices earned $12.[44] In the Amache camp, Esther Takei Nishio's father served as a block manager and her mother worked as a waitress in the block mess hall. Esther got one of her first camp jobs working as an assistant in the dental clinic.[45] Later she worked for the camp newspaper, *The Pioneer*, editing the Sunday-school news and contributing an original one-panel comic featuring a teenaged girl called "Ama-chan."[46] Haruko Sugi Hurt and her sister took jobs as hospital workers in the Rohwer camp. In Jerome, Alice Imamoto Takemoto's three older sisters all had jobs, Lily as the block manager's secretary, Marion as a secretary at the high school, and Grace as a music teacher in the elementary school."[47]

A dearth of resources posed challenges in every arena of camp life and work. In the case of Grace Imamoto, this meant coping with a lack of basic materials: "I had no books," she said, "I had to teach them by rote."[48] Mary Nishi Ishizuka described starting a library in Manzanar, which she remembered as one of her most positive experiences in camp: "First it was a completely empty barrack and headed by two young women.... We had no books at all and started with things from around the environment, like the weeds and snakes, and then people started to donate whatever they had."[49]

Clerical skills proved useful for Fumiko Fukuyama Ide—knowing typing and shorthand meant that she was "never out of a job." In Santa Anita, she worked as a receptionist at the assembly center hospital, using her Japanese language ability to help Issei patients and accompanying the doctors on their rounds, taking stenographic notes for them. In October 1942 she was sent with the medical staff to start a public health office in the Jerome, Arkansas camp. As before the war, a sense of filial duty sometimes took precedence over Nisei plans: Fumiko was preparing to leave Jerome for college when she learned that her mother had fallen ill, so instead she joined her parents in the Amache camp in Colorado, where she got a job as a secretary in the camp attorney's office.[50]

As workers, the Nisei women were viewed favorably by administrators. Psychiatrist and Poston researcher Alexander Leighton commented, "Nisei girls were more compliant to family authority than the boys, and, correspondingly, developed the reputation for being exceptionally conscientious and reliable employees."[51] His observation, although very general, reflects the strict upbringing of second-generation daughters and their continuing awareness of parental expectations. Through their camp jobs, young Nisei women worked to gain resources—however meager—for themselves and their families, and contributed to the well-being of the ethnic community, as they had before the war. Urban girls, joined by their rural cousins, also found relief from the boredom of camp life in a range of social activities that mirrored their prewar networks.

Social Life in Camp and Girls' Clubs

Camp life increased the leisure time of many Japanese Americans. A good number of Issei women, accustomed to long days of work inside and outside the home, found that the communally prepared meals and limited living quarters provided them with spare time. Rose Honda recalled her mother staying busy with sewing, embroidery, and crocheting. Esther Takei Nishio's mother took oil painting classes from a well-known Issei artist living in their block, Tokio Ueyama. Many availed themselves of the opportunity to attend adult classes taught by both Japanese Americans and European Americans. Courses involving handicrafts and traditional Japanese arts such as flower arrangement, sewing, painting, calligraphy, and wood-carving became immensely popular as an overwhelming number of people turned to art for recreation and self-expression. Some of these subjects were viewed as leisure activities by those who taught them, but to the Issei women they represented access to new skills and a means to contribute to the material comfort of the family.

The Japanese Americans also filled their time with Buddhist and Christian church meetings, theatrical productions, cultural programs, talent shows, art exhibitions, athletic events, and visits with friends. All family members spent more time than ever before in the company of their peers. Nisei from isolated rural areas were exposed to the ideas, styles, and pastimes of the more sophisticated urban youth; in camp they had the time and opportunity to social-ize—at work, school, dances, and sports events—in an almost entirely Japanese American environment. Gone were the restrictions of distance, lack of transpor-tation, interracial uneasiness, and the dawn-to-dusk exigencies of field labor. For example, Nisei sisters Chiyoko Hiji Nishimori and Lily Hiji Sawai, who grew up doing grueling farm work with their family in Inglewood and Hawthorne, related how their six months in Santa Anita meant new access to baseball games, talent shows, sumo matches, and movies.[52] Indeed, Chiyoko told her great niece that, although the family left the assembly center after getting a contract to top sugar beets in Colorado, their father's prime motivation was concern that "if we stay here you girls are going to be bad."[53] Some rural Issei must have feared the influence of urban youth and worried that farm daughters might be enticed by the greater range of social activity enjoyed by city girls.

Many of the Nisei young women, drawing on their prewar experiences, revived previous networks and formed new ones. In Manzanar, for example, Sumi Fukushima Hughes and her friends started a club called the JUGS (Just Us Girls), holding dances and playing sports.[54] Alexander Leighton observed the development of social activities in the Poston Camp, remarking, "Very promi-nent at this time were the girls' clubs, which showed a great deal of initiative and organized games, dances, picnics, 'Jamborees', and amateur shows."[55] This roster echoes the urban Nisei social calendars in the ethnic press of the 1930s. Four other WRA community analysts at different camps similarly reported, "They [the younger girls and boys] formed innumerable clubs, the Starlites, the Bombadettes, the Exclusive Blues, the Jayhawks, the Whizzers, the Sagebrush Clan, and carried on their interests in groups, with the help of older people as advisers from both staff and evacuees." Here again, the formation of clubs mir-rors the prewar pattern of Nisei organization, with aid from older advisers. The analysts also remarked that "The WRA encouraged all possible organization [sic] to tie in with national groups—the Girl Reserves, the Girl Scouts, the Boy Scouts, the Brownies, as well as the YWCA and YMCA."[56] It is not clear whether the European American social scientists who served as community analysts knew about the extensive network of Japanese American urban youth groups that existed before the war and their prior linkages with national groups such as the YWCA and YMCA.[57]

The camp newspapers in Manzanar, Poston, and Amache reported the activi-ties of an array of youth groups: co-ed church-related organizations, boys' and girls' athletic leagues, block clubs, and quite a few young women's clubs. Of the last, the YWCA-sponsored groups appear most numerous; the Girl Scouts were also active in the camps. Girls flocked to join Y-related Girl Reserves (GR) clubs; in Manzanar they chose names such as the Chere-ettes, Debonaires, Stardusters, Twixteeners, Subdebs, and Phi Chi Lambda.[58] Rose Honda belonged to both the Twixteeners and the Funsters; her younger sister belonged to the Forget-Me-Nots.[59]

It appears that some prewar YWCA leaders continued their service, as in the case of the popular Maki Ichiyasu, who became director of girls' activities in Poston Unit I.[60] In Amache, former Tartanettes adviser Hana Uno ran a hospitality house, one of the first organizations established to provide a space for youth recreation, made more exciting by visits from Nisei soldiers who had families in the camp. Fumiko Fukuyama Ide recalled that initially "we all kind of hung around outside of our friends' barrack. We had no place really to go, except the hospitality house." Gradually the Japanese Americans organized more activities: "they started to have movies and block parties and dances."[61]

Club activities in camp were clearly patterned on prewar lines—social service, self-improvement, recreation, socializing—with the addition of some preparation for life beyond the barbed-wire fences. Mirroring the welfare dances of the Great Depression, Phi Sigma Kappa held a charity dance on August 15, 1942 with "all proceeds going to needy families in Manzanar."[62] In Poston, the YWCA, in conjunction with its three divisions—the Business Girls, the Inter-Y, and the Girl Reserves—organized a "Shamrock Shag," a St. Patrick's Day-themed benefit dance for 20 March 1943.[63] A Poston Girl Scout troop chose a more hands-on form of community service, aiding in the making of adobe bricks for camp building construction.[64]

Within the drab camp environment, prewar club rituals provided a measure of drama and significance. The appeal of candlelight installation ceremonies persisted. For example, in "a beautiful setting of streamers, carrying out the club colors and flowers," the Colleens' cabinet officers were inducted "in an impressive candlelight ceremonies [sic]" in Poston.[65] A month later, perhaps not to be outdone, or more probably due to the large number of participants, in "impressive bonfire ceremonies, 216 Girl Scouts composed of Brownies, Intermediates and Seniors, plus 31 leaders and their assistants were inducted in a mass investiture rites [sic], first of such held in Poston."[66] In Manzanar, the YWCA Twixteeners held a candlelight installation ceremony to induct their new cabinet officers in June 1943. Other clubs adopted these popular rites: In the same month, the Calico Cats, a women's journalism group, initiated new pledges, followed by a candlelight ceremony to install new officers.[67] And as before the war, Girl Reserves worked to earn the coveted GR ring, also bestowed in a ceremony. In Manzanar it was announced that "girls will receive their G.R. rings from Mrs. Ralph Merritt, wife of the project director and vice-chair of the YWCA board" and that the "Campfire Girls of Lone Pine have been invited as honored guests."[68]

As the invitation to the European American Campfire Girls suggests, girls' clubs within the camps offered ties, however slim, to national organizations and the outside world from which they had been exiled. Camp newspapers document visits to the camps by YWCA and Girl Scout leaders. In March 1943, when Esther Briesmeister, National Secretary of the YWCA's Japanese Project, visited Poston, the *Chronicle* reported that she had "spoken to all of the relocation centers and aided in launching some of the outstanding girls' activities in the various centers."[69] Also in March 1943, a regional representative of the Girl Scouts arrived at Poston "for a series of leadership training courses for Scout leaders in all three units."[70] Club activities sometimes afforded opportunities to leave the camps. In June 1943, for example, 19 Nisei girls from Amache, Heart Mountain, Manzanar, Minidoka, Topaz, and Tule Lake joined 22 "Caucasian delegates" at a Business and Industrial YWCA conference in Utah. The focus of their discussion was "evacuee Japanese"; one night "was devoted to relocation center problems."[71] Although no details of these issues were mentioned, Manzanar delegate Mary Wada said "it was stressed that all nisei girls should relocate and think of their future."[72]

After the WRA developed leave clearance policies for students and workers, YWCA staffers, both in person and through letters published in camp newspapers, encouraged Nisei women to leave the camps and offered the assistance of the Y in their resettlement. The Metropolitan Business and Professional Women's Secretary of the Chicago YWCA wrote a letter to the Manzanar Young Women's Association in February 1943, requesting the names and addresses of Nisei girls coming to Chicago, and assuring them that "they are welcome and that joining one of our clubs would be the quickest way for them to make a normal and happy adjustment to life in Chicago."[73] In April, the *Manzanar Free Press* ran a much lengthier letter from Barbara Abel, the Publicity Director of the Chicago YWCA, explaining, "From the start of evacuation, the Chicago Association has made its services available to evacuees in the same free and friendly footing that it offers to any girl in her search for the normal needs of life—a job, a place to live, interesting things to do, and good friends to do them with." Abel added that, in addition to extending aid in finding work and housing, the Y "has done its level best" in the "more intangible and just as important task of interpreting with intelligence and understanding the problems of these loyal American citizens trapped in a war situation. This interpretation has been made to employers, to housekeepers, church and club women, as well as to the entire YWCA membership...."[74]

Club Activities

Young second-generation women played key roles in reviving prewar groups and shepherding new ones. Esther Takei Nishio was one of the Nisei who stepped in as a club adviser for younger girls. She was joined by Aki Nakagawa, a friend she met while waitressing in Santa Anita. In Amache, they helped organize the Jo-dees, a YWCA Girl Reserves group, as well as holding block dances and starting a theater group.[75] Esther and Aki also began a club for young women of their own age. As before the war, club events facilitated mixed-sex socializing. She recalled, "Oh, I think our main activity was to have a dance so we could meet the guys. [laughs]"[76]

Club activities could also offer girls an opportunity to participate in the war effort. Before the war, Yuri Kochiyama had volunteered with the Girl Scouts, the YWCA, and a settlement house. In Santa Anita, she taught Sunday school, mostly for junior high school girls, and established the Crusaders girls' club: "While waiting to be relocated to the internment camps, I wanted to do something to help the war effort and our boys in the service—especially when I found out that several of my students had brothers in the military. I thought it would be a good idea to write to them."[77] The group grew, as older teenaged girls flocked to join. Beginning with penny postcards, the Crusaders "exchanged thousands of letters with soldiers overseas." Kochiyama recalled, "Our list of soldiers to write grew larger, and even when we were split up to be transferred to different camps, we all promised to continue the work of the Crusaders wherever we were."[78] Nisei soldiers, especially men in the 232nd Engineers (part of the 442nd Regimental Combat Team) responded enthusiastically to the Crusaders' morale-building endeavor, sending contributions "from the front lines" that enabled the girls to switch from mailing postcards to letters in two-cent envelopes.[79]

One of the 30 or so members of the Jerome Crusaders was Alice Imamoto Takemoto, who developed a long friendship with Yuri Kochiyama. Alice spoke of Yuri with appreciation: "She would have been in her early twenties when she started that girls' club. She must have realized there was a need for that kind of thing. She was a very giving person. A ray of sunshine."[80]

Of course, the Crusaders weren't the only Japanese American girls corresponding with soldiers. Esther Takei devoted her inaugural August 16, 1944, column ("dedicated to you girls") in the Pioneer, the Amache newspaper, to GI Joe Nisei's desire for letters from home and the appropriate content of those missives. Her reportage of Nisei men's preferences and her advice to her readers provide a glimpse of gendered and racial dynamics. She quoted a Nisei GI in the Southwest Pacific as saying, "Y'know, I'd rather correspond with 'hakujin [white]' gals than these nisei who are always crying and moaning about racial prejudice, hatred, and injustice."[81] Esther remarked that it was unfair to judge "'hakujin' and nisei lassies on the same basis. After all, the Caucasian girls haven't faced the problems of 'racial prejudice, hatred, and injustice' that we've met since that fateful day in December, 1941." However, perhaps equally mindful of the dangers faced by the soldiers and stung by the comparison to more privileged white women, she urged readers: "Let's show him we aren't all sob-sisters; that we can lift morale along with the best of 'em. It looks like we have a battle on our hands, girls."[82] She advised readers not to burden servicemen "with your own troubles and woes," reminding them that "we are all struggling—for a better, greater America. Let's spur them on to attain that achievement with our moral support and spiritual closeness that letters alone can impart."[83] Letter writing allowed young women to take initiative in supporting their brothers and other Nisei men.

Clubs such as the Jo-dees and the junior and senior Crusaders groups enabled girls to continue to develop organizational skills as well as affording them positive channels for their energies within the stultifying confines of the camps. The Crusaders provided Alice's only memory of pleasure in the camp—she added, "But other than that, we didn't have any fun."[84] Despite their exile in the hinterlands, letter-writing to soldiers gave the Crusaders a way to participate meaningfully in the national war effort and may have reinforced what historian Shirley Jennifer Lim has described as a "feeling of belonging" critical to cultural citizenship.[85] For the younger incarcerated Nisei, the revival of youth organizations may have played a key role in keeping alive a sense of belonging and, like earlier girls' clubs, offering young women a way to demonstrate and claim American identity.[86] Club activities, as before the war, strengthened gendered and generational ties of friendship, facilitated monitored heterosexual socializing, and helped girls exercise a measure of agency even in a restrictive, artificial environment.

Romance, Rituals, and Preparing for Resettlement

The conditions of life in the camps accelerated the changes that had begun before the war with regard to Nisei romance and courtship. Like their non-Japanese American contemporaries, most young Nisei women envisioned a future of marriage and children. They—and their parents—anticipated that they would marry other Japanese Americans, but these women also expected to choose their own husbands and to marry "for love." This mainstream American ideal of marriage differed greatly from the Issei's view of love as a bond that might evolve over the course of an arranged marriage rooted in less romantic notions of compatibility and responsibility. The discrepancy between Issei and Nisei conceptions of love and marriage had sturdy prewar roots; incarceration fostered further divergence from the old customs of arranged marriage.

In the artificial hothouse of camp, Nisei romances often bloomed quickly. As Nisei men left to prove their loyalty to the United States in the 442nd Regimental Combat Team, the 100th Battalion, and the Military Intelligence Service, young couples strove to grasp what happiness they could, given the uncertainties of the future. Mary Yuriko Nakahara, for instance, met a handsome, self-assured

New York Nisei named Bill Kochiyama when he and his 442nd buddies, who were training at Camp Shelby, Mississippi, visited friends at Jerome. "I guess it must have been love at first sight for me because after seeing him on only three quick visits, I knew I was deeply in love with him," she wrote. "It was a common wartime romance, including courtship through mail, but I was fortunate ours had a happy ending. So many of my girlfriends had their hopes shattered with notices that the ones they were waiting for were killed in action."[87] While in camp Fumiko Fukuyama Ide, Marion Funakoshi Manaka, and Esther Takei Nishio also met the men they would later marry.

The announcements of engagements and weddings in the camp newspapers mirrored the prewar format. Echoing the 1930s betrothal celebrations arranged by clubs, the Justameres club in Manzanar held a "miscellaneous shower" on February 16, 1943 for Ayako Muto, the club historian.[88] Despite limited resources, young women strove to make these occasions as festive as possible; as during the Depression years, they exercised their creativity to craft clever decorations and favors, highlighting the importance of the milestone. A description in the *Poston Chronicle* of an afternoon tea organized by three women to celebrate the engagement of Chieko Watanabe and Frederick Tets Kajikawa suggested not only their creative efforts but also the cross-cultural influence of their earlier lives in southern California: "Clever Mexican decorations, flowers, and the pinata, broken by one of the girls, had candies and favors which resembled tamales were tiny lace bags, filled with rice and the scroll, 'Chieko and Tets, 1943.'"[89]

Weddings in camp also reflected some prewar patterns. When Dorothy Yoshiko Ohashi married Mitsuru Kayashima at the Poston III Buddhist Church in March 1943, she "was attired in a traditional white satin gown with finger tip veil and carried a bouquet of gardenias and orchids."[90] Given the straitened circumstances, Nisei brides often wore a suit or an afternoon dress rather than a "traditional" white gown. Prewar musical staples such as "Oh Promise Me" persisted: at the Ohashi-Kayashima wedding, for example, Sakaye Inouye sang "I Love You Truly" and Rosie Takahashi played the wedding march. The bridesmaids' attire, the bouquets carried by the bride and her attendants, and the reception refreshments also received keen attention in wedding announcements. Occasionally reportage included evidence of a Japanese tradition: identifying the baishakunin (match-makers), usually two married couples.[91]

In keeping with this atmosphere, as well as with the earlier offerings of the English-language sections in the prewar ethnic press, camp newspaper columns like the *Poston Chronicle*'s "Fashionotes" and *The Daily Tulean Dispatch*'s "Strictly Feminine" gave their Nisei readers countless suggestions on how to impress boys, care for their complexions and choose the latest fashions. These columns, authored by incarcerated Nisei, mirrored the mainstream girls' periodicals of the time. Such fashion news may seem incongruous in the context of a camp whose inmates had little choice in clothing beyond what they could find in the Montgomery Ward or Sears and Roebuck mail-order catalogs. These columns, however, reflect women's desire to remain in touch with the world outside the barbed-wire fence. Taking a closer look at beauty and fashion practices in the camps, historian Jennifer Malia McAndrew suggests that women adopted a mainstream American aesthetic as one way to maintain a link to the larger culture.[92] The camp newspaper columns also show women's attempt to maintain morale in a drab, depressing environment. "There's something about color in clothes," speculated Tule Lake columnist "Yuri"; "Singing colors have a heart-building effect.... Color is a stimulant we need—both for its effect on ourselves and on others."[93]

These fashion columns addressed practical as well as aesthetic concerns, reflecting the dusty realities of camp life. In this vein, Mitzi Sugita of the Poston Sewing Department praised the "Latest Fashion for Women Today—Slacks," drawing special attention to overalls; she assured her readers that these "digging duds" were not only winsome and workable but also possessed the virtues of being inexpensive and requiring little ironing.[94] Sugita's column mirrored women's cultural adaptation to their crude surroundings. As Nisei artist Miné Okubo observed in the Tanforan Assembly Center (a northern California camp also located at a race track), "Women, from grandmothers to toddlers, wore slacks or jeans."[95]

The columnists' concern with the practical aspects of fashion extended beyond the confines of the camps, as women began to leave for life on the outside—an opportunity increasingly available after 1943 because of changes in the leave clearance process. Sugita told prospective operatives, "If you are one of the many thousands of women now entering in commercial and industrial work, your required uniform is based on slacks, safe and streamlined. It is very important that they be durable, trim and attractive."[96] To the extent that tight budgets would allow, women heading for clerical positions or college might try to heed Marii Kyogoku's admonitions to invest in "really nice things," with an eye to "simple lines which are good practically forever."[97]

The Nisei were reminded that not only their clothing but also their deportment would meet scrutiny when they left the camps. As in the prewar ethnic newspapers, female columnists dispensed advice on how to present themselves to the eyes of "Caucasians [who] will have time only to take the nisei at face value."[98] Esther Takei, who had spent part of 1943 doing live-in domestic work for a Colorado family, began in August 1944 to pen "Confidentially by Esther," a column "dedicated to you girls," for the Granada *Pioneer*. She wrote, "YOUNG PEOPLE with an eye to future resettlement realize the need for social grace and propriety in personal relationships. They realize that in order to win acceptance in any community, a friendly sociable attitude is of primary importance."[99]

She warned that many were not yet ready to face life outside of camp, having developed "rough edges" in the crude, informal environment: "Their speech has become loud, coarse and slangy, their manners sloppy beyond description, and their dressing habits careless." Esther assured her readers, "The young woman with good breeding, a sincere friendliness for those about her and the ability to make friends easily is the one whose absorption into the American scene will be quick and smooth."[100]

Many Nisei, among them a large number of women, were anxious to leave the limbo of camp. With all its work, social events, and cultural activities, camp was still an isolated, limiting environment. As one southern California Nisei woman wrote to a European American friend, it was stifling "to see nothing but the same barracks, mess halls, and other houses, row after row, day in and day out, it gives us the feeling that we're missing all the freedom and liberty."[101] Similarly, Esther Takei wrote in her Amache column, "life in a relocation center is at best a slow process of stagnation for young ideas and aspirations, and will always be foreign to us as long as we are a free people.... And if we are to escape the complete disintegration of our hopes, we must venture forth to establish a new 'beachhead', a new salient on life." Many, like Esther, were eager to "get back to the business of normal living."[102] It was clear that there would be no future for them behind the barbed-wire fences. Significantly, Issei parents, despite initial reluctance, were gradually beginning to sanction their daughters' departures for education and employment in the Midwest and East.

Resettlement

Resettlement—the process of leaving the camps to pursue work and education in the Midwest and East—began slowly in 1942. Among the first to venture out of the camps were college students, many assisted by the National Japanese American Student Relocation Council, a nongovernmental agency that provided valuable placement aid to 4,084 Nisei from 1942 to 1946.[103] Founded by concerned educators and other leaders, this organization persuaded institutions outside the restricted Western Defense zone to accept Nisei students and facilitated their admissions and leave clearances. A study of the first 400 students to leave camp showed that a third of them were women.[104] Because of the cumbersome screening process, few others of the incarcerated Japanese Americans departed on indefinite leave before 1943.[105] In that year the WRA tried to expedite the clearance procedure by broadening an army registration program aimed at Nisei males to include all adults. This poorly conceived process, which included a loyalty questionnaire, had tragic consequences for many families, but the migration from the camps steadily increased.[106]

A large percentage of the relocated students were women (a postwar study showed 40 percent of 1,000[107]), and many, although not all, of these students were helped by the National Japanese American Student Relocation Council (NJASRC). The NJASRC—in accordance with the WRA's aims—carefully selected students who would serve as goodwill ambassadors for the ethnic community, with the ultimate goal that they would lead the way for their families to resettle in the Midwest and East.[108] This reflected WRA head Dillon Myer's objective of dispersing Japanese Americans widely to prevent their reforming prewar enclaves. All of the students leaving the camps, regardless of whether or not they received assistance from the NJASRC, faced tremendous scrutiny and pressure as representatives of a suspect group. Many colleges preferred Nisei women to men, owing to assumptions that they were less likely to be perceived as threatening; this bias may have made available more opportunities for women, but it reflects the persistence of an array of racial and gendered stereotypes.[109] Historian Leslie Ito has likened the role of these women students to that of the Nisei soldiers: "Similar to the decorated 442nd RCT who fought the double battle for America and their community's civil rights, the Nisei students were representing Japanese Americans at home, preparing the nation for the resettlement of thousands of Japanese Americans who were being released."[110]

Mary Nishi Ishizuka, Katsumi Hirooka Kunitsugu, Setsuko Matsunaga Nishi, Esther Takei Nishio, and Alice Imamoto Takemoto were among those eager to leave the camps to pursue higher education.[111] For all of them, it was the first experience of leaving their families and journeying farther than most had ever imagined.

Setsuko Matsunaga Nishi and her sister Helen were among the first students released through the student relocation program. Setsuko explained, "They [the NJASRC officials] were quite open about looking for people who were not only academically strong, but...would be able to withstand what they expected would be a fairly hostile environment." She and Helen had to be cleared by five different government agencies—"At the beginning it was very arduous."[112] Helen was released in September 1942, and in October Setsuko arrived at Washington University in St. Louis, Missouri. There she changed her major: "When the war began, it just seemed unreasonable to try to pursue it [music] as a career. It just seemed...so far fetched to try to pursue a concert career when we had nothing, because we were kicked out." She switched to sociology, which "had always interested me. We heard a lot of sociology and economics around the table."[113] She would complete both her BA and MA degrees at Washington University.

Mary Nishi Ishizuka's well-to-do parents had instilled in her and her five siblings the importance of education. In Manzanar, Mary was also encouraged by two older Nisei students to seek a sponsor so that she could leave camp. After she made inquiries, the YWCA in Lincoln, Nebraska, agreed to find her a domestic-service job, which enabled her to attend Nebraska Wesleyan. Her mother was fearful for her, and Mary had fears too, but she was determined to leave.[114] In Thanksgiving week of 1942, she and her older sister Midori boarded a bus to Reno, Nevada, and from there took a train to Nebraska.

In August 1943, 16-year-old Alice Imamoto Takemoto left Jerome for Oberlin College in Ohio. Her older sisters had already departed for Minnesota where they were doing domestic work to support their university studies. Greatly disappointed by the poor quality of high school education in the camp, Alice wanted to go as soon as possible. She had considered various music schools, but applied to Oberlin for one reason: "When I heard a Nisei [Kenji Okuda] was the student body president I thought, 'That must be a friendly school.'"[115] Because of her prewar performances in numerous Baptist churches Alice knew many ministers, and she received a full scholarship from the Southern Baptist Convention to cover her tuition. Alice had mixed emotions, chafing to leave Jerome, unhappy about parting from her parents, and frightened by the prospect of venturing into the unknown. Her parents, however, had confidence in her: "They never made me fear anything. If they worried about me, they never showed it."[116]

In the summer of 1944 Katsumi Hirooka Kunitsugu was writing for the *Heart Mountain Sentinel* when representatives from the NJASRC approached her. With their encouragement and the prodding of a friend, she applied to journalism schools and was accepted by the University of Wisconsin. The university also found her a schoolgirl job—domestic work in exchange for room and board— with a doctor's family. Katsumi was the first in her family to leave the camp, and found it "very scary, because it was the first time I was on my own."[117]

As the wartime labor shortage opened the way for white and black women to leave domestic service for better paid, more advantageous factory and defense work, the camps received a steady stream of inquiries from employers seeking servants. Before the war, racism had excluded the Japanese Americans from most white collar clerical and sales positions, and domestic service was the largest area of nonagricultural work for Issei and Nisei women.[118] During the war the highest percentage of job offers for both men and women continued to be domestic work. In July 1943, the Kansas City branch of the War Relocation Authority noted that 45 percent of requests for workers were for domestics, and the Milwaukee office cited 61 percent.[119]

Many, if not most, of the relocated women students, like Mary, Alice, and Katsumi, took domestic service jobs to pay for their education. Their experiences provide a sense of the kinds of adjustments Nisei women students faced. Mary and her sister worked in the home of Don Stewart, the lawyer for the governor of Nebraska. Upon arrival, Mary had to begin work immediately, cleaning the stairway. It was a trying experience, because she had done little housework previously and had to learn cooking from her employer. She and her sister stayed there for a year and then moved closer to the campus. Mary preferred to support herself with a part-time job at the Corn Husker Hotel, where she made salads and served desserts.[120] At Oberlin, Alice began doing domestic work in the home of a woman who rented rooms to students—Alice and her sister Grace stayed there too—but her employer was uncongenial, and it proved impossible to work for room and board and still take classes. Fortunately, Grace worked as a cook's helper in a graduate dormitory and paid for her younger sister's room, freeing her from domestic work. To earn her board, Alice washed dishes in a student dining hall. At the University of Wisconsin, Katsumi worked for the large family of a doctor. Because they already had a couple to do the cooking as well as a regular cleaning lady, Katsumi's duties as a schoolgirl primarily entailed washing dishes and diapers and providing general help. During the day she attended classes, working after school.

Juggling the demands of work and study left little free time. As Alice recalled, "It was so hard. My first semester, for example, I took eighteen units. . . . My average was an A-minus. But all I did was work and study. Nothing else. I also practiced [piano] three hours a day."[121]

In the Midwest and East, many Nisei students found themselves navigating race relations within a black/white framework. Living off campus heightened this awareness. Upon arrival at Washington University in St. Louis, Setsuko Matsunaga Nishi was told by the Dean of Women that if, instead of a dorm room, she accepted an offer in a private home for room and board in exchange for doing chores, the program could provide for another student to come out of camp. Setsuko accepted and stayed with the welcoming European American family of Dr. Paul Rutledge, living in the suburbs more than an hour's streetcar ride from the university: "It was as if they had suddenly adopted an older sister. So I did things like babysit for the younger ones and cook meals sometimes." Living with the Rutledges and commuting to school gave Setsuko "an eyeful of race relations in a border city."[122]

As a Japanese American, she occupied an uneasy, variable position in the racial hierarchy, which became evident on the testing ground of public facilities. The Rutledges belonged to a swimming club, and during the "beastly hot and humid" summer, they took Setsuko with them. She said, "The next day, Mrs. Rutledge got a call from the club saying that they didn't want them to bring me back, that I was not welcome there. And when we went to the theatre, neither the Rutledges nor I knew whether we would be permitted to sit in the seats where the tickets were, because blacks had to sit in the balcony. They didn't know where I would be asked to sit. St. Louis was a racially divided city, and Washington University was for whites; no blacks went to Washington University."[123]

The dynamics in public transportation particularly underscored the separation of blacks and whites, as well as the variable status of Japanese Americans. On the streetcar Setsuko took to campus, she said, "I used to try to snooze because it was such a long ride, and I would sit wherever there was a space. A woman came up to me after the person who was sitting next to me left and said, 'You must be new in St. Louis. We don't sit next to colored'. I was just waking up, but I was glad I had the sufficient presence to say, 'I am colored.'" As Setsuko put it, "You get in a situation where things are arranged for black and white.... You have to define what you are again."[124] She defined herself further when she herself became a target. On a bus one day, "a woman was making some loud whispered comments about 'These Japs, what are they doing here'... So I just told her that I'm an American, just as much as she is. Well, it ended up being a real shouting match... I wasn't going to let her get away with it. I was just shouting at her. Everybody was watching. Some people might be willing to take it—not me."[125] Setsuko had defined herself as a person of color and an American entitled to civil rights. Also her gender may have allowed her to confront the two white women openly in a way that would have been more hazardous for a Japanese American male. The stoning of a Nisei man as he waited for a bus in St. Louis also conveys the sense that Japanese American men were perceived by the white public as more threatening. Setsuko's experiences suggest the significance of gender as well as race in the Nisei's negotiation of resettlement.[126]

The reception of the Japanese American students in the Midwest contrasted dramatically with the racial dynamics of the West. "The Nebraskans didn't know whether we were Chinese, Japanese, or whatever," said Mary Nishi Ishizuka. "... it was the first time I felt that people accepted me for what I was, and they didn't have any preconceived notions about Japanese. It was the better feeling than we ever had in California."[127] Mary and her sister Midori were two of the 20 Nisei students at Nebraska Wesleyan. Although the school limited the number of Japanese Americans it would accept, she recalled that the Wesleyan students "bent over backwards to try to befriend us." She was invited to their homes and accorded the honor of being selected to participate in the school May Pole Dance. The only area of racial discrimination that she recalled was exclusion from fraternities and sororities, adding, "But that was true with UCLA, too, or any of the colleges, that Japanese were not included in the sororities and fraternities."[128] During their college years, both Mary and Alice Imamoto Takemoto developed close friendships with non–Japanese Americans.

The relocated students also looked to other Nisei for understanding and camaraderie. There were quite a few Japanese Americans in Madison, Wisconsin, when Katsumi Hirooka Kunitsugu entered the University of Wisconsin school of journalism. She said, "I guess we kind of sought each other out, too, just to support each other."[129] One of the Nisei she came to know there was Sue Kunitomi Embrey—a former editor of the *Manzanar Free Press*, who later became an activist in the Movement for Japanese American Redress and a leader in preserving

Manzanar as a historic site. During the war, however, the Nisei did not discuss their camp experiences with each other. As Katsumi said, "it was just more or less a taboo subject. It was such a painful thing, that we never really dwelled on it."[130] Students such as Setsuko, Katsumi, Alice, and Mary were soon followed by a larger flow of Japanese American men and women workers who also faced a wide range of adjustments.

"Rosie Funakoshi the Riveter": Work Outside the Camps

The trickle of migration from the camps grew into a steady stream by 1943, as the War Relocation Authority developed its resettlement program to aid Japanese Americans in finding housing and employment in the Midwest and East. An April 1943 resettlement bulletin published by the Advisory Committee for Evacuees described "who is relocating":

> Mostly younger men and women, in their 20s or 30s; mostly single persons or couples with one or two children, or men with larger families who come out alone first to scout opportunities and to secure a foothold, planning to call wife and children later. Most relocated evacuees have parents or relatives whom they hope and plan to bring out "when we get re-established."[131]

These resettlers faced new challenges in regions where few if any Japanese Americans had ever ventured.

The European Americans who provided advice about resettlement tended to place the onus of developing positive race relations on the shoulders of the Japanese Americans. In order to accomplish this, and in line with WRA head Dillon Myer's dispersal policy, the Issei and Nisei were counseled against congregating with co-ethnics after relocating. Esther Rhodes, a member of the American Friends Service Committee, cautioned Manzanar inmates interested in relocating "to make some contacts with educational, recreational or religious groups which are NOT predominantly Japanese."[132] The Chicago Advisory Committee for Evacuees "warned Japanese not to segregate themselves by living near each other, going to all-Japanese social affairs, organizing Japanese clubs and associations, and asserted that 'getting together on a racial basis is the first step towards creating another West Coast problem and thus the Japanese are contributing to their own racial segregation.'"[133] This admonition denigrated the prewar networks that had provided vital support to Japanese Americans, especially women. The implication that Japanese Americans were at least partly to blame for their wartime plight resolutely turned a blind eye to the long history of deep-rooted anti-Asian sentiment on the West Coast and segregation enforced by restrictive housing covenants, systemic racial discrimination, and vigilante violence. Instead, Japanese Americans were urged to view relocation as an "individual challenge" by the Chicago Advisory Committee, according to whom "Relocation is being enjoyed by young evacuee men and women who regard themselves as Americans and expect to be treated as Americans."[134] Ironically, those who experienced the greatest shock at forced removal and mass exclusion were Nisei who had indeed regarded themselves as Americans and, as citizens by birth, had expected to be treated as such.

In the effort to develop better race relations, newly relocated Nisei were often expected to serve as active representatives of their families and communities still behind barbed wire. YWCA official Ethel Briesemaster informed an audience of Poston girls that "many resettled Nisei are carrying on as fine 'ambassadors of goodwill'. In many cases, church groups, university clubs, high school core classes [and] other organizations request to hear 'evacuees' speak."[135] Sue Kunitomi, who discovered that people in Wisconsin knew little about the camps, had a busy round of speaking engagements: "Last night I spoke to a Ladies Aid group of the Bethel Lutheran Church.... Next Wednesday I'm speaking to the Women's International League group and a few weeks ago (right after my arrival in Madison) I spoke to a group of service men and their wives."[136] Writing from Bode, Iowa, where she and her husband were working on a farm, Mary Hiraga reported, "Up to date my husband has given a talk to the neighbors here about the Japanese people and I have given two with one more coming up next week.... We hope these talks will give the people here a better understanding of us and our people."[137]

The Nisei speakers for the relocation effort faced scrutiny from the government as well as their audiences. At the request of the Resettlement Committee of the Congregational Churches, Setsuko Matsunaga Nishi gave presentations to hundreds of organizations. "In the beginning when I did that," she recalled, "inevitably somebody would call the FBI, and the FBI would call Mrs. Rutledge... once when the family was out to church, the FBI came and grilled me. I said, 'If you want, I can tell you what I tell them; you can come and listen to me.'" Eventually, after responding to many calls about her, the FBI decided that she needed no further vetting. Setsuko spoke "to all kinds of groups. I'd speak to high school groups and title the talk after a song that was very popular at the time called 'Don't Fence Me In'. And I spoke to the Kiwanis and Lions Club.... What I tried to do was to get them to think, 'Well, she's not much different from us.'"[138]

Resettled Nisei not only educated white audiences about the camps, but also sent back reports of life on the outside to those still incarcerated. Some sent letters to the camp newspapers, encouraging others to follow suit. Claire

Seno, who departed for "points east," described leaving Manzanar in euphoric terms: "When you leave the gate, it's like waking up from a dream. The trip to Reno was swell. Who asked for the malt? I had that and also fried chicken, steak, hamburger and hot dog—Come on, now, aren't your mouths watering yet? Got my divorce from Manzanar at Reno. Now I'm free!" She did not detail the work or study that surely occupied much of her time, but closed with an enticing image: "At present I'm lying in front of a log fire on a nice rug listening to swell music and writing to you. Freeport is a wee town with old-fashioned houses. We live outside the city limits in a modern glass house—just like good old Southern California. People are really nice to me."[139] Similarly, Mary Hiraga declared that "people in this neighborhood have been very friendly and cordial to us at all times," adding that the "Iowa newspapers write up quite a bit on the Japanese people and these reports and editorials are always favorable."[140] Such assurances of a positive reception appeared in many letters.[141] The *Poston Chronicle* observed in May 1943 that resettlers "usually comment on the friendliness of the people they encounter and on the exhilaration they feel at being away from the dust and the drab monotony of tarpaper barracks." The journalist added a cautionary note: "The outside world, of course, is still no bed of roses, but the ones who have gone out report that they are getting along relatively well."[142]

Like the students, resettling workers were often pleasantly surprised by the racial climate outside the West. For example, after arriving at the Women's Army Corps training center in Des Moines, Iowa, Haruko Sugi Hurt discovered that "Away from the West Coast, people were very kind and liberal, because they didn't have the kind of historic experience with Asians." She felt that in the Midwest, Japanese Americans "were treated more like...any other people. So, that was a refreshing experience."[143] Sue Kunitomi echoed this impression in a November 1943 letter, writing, "I can't get over this cosmopolitan attitude in Madison [Wisconsin]." Still, the forced uprooting and incarceration left their mark, as she said, "All the same, I'm expecting somebody to say something anti-Japanese...."[144] With mixed anxiety and hope, Japanese Americans ventured into the Midwest and East.

Chicago was a key destination for resettlers. Togo Tanaka, who worked helping resettlers find jobs and housing, considered Chicago "a staging area, because they landed there and then they went up to Milwaukee or Madison [Wisconsin], or they went further east to New Jersey or New York. They even went South."[145] The magnet that drew them was employment.

For many Japanese Americans, a domestic-service position was often the first step in leaving camp. When Marion Funakoshi Manaka and her family left Amache in 1943, her parents took a job in Englewood, Colorado, working as domestics for the president of the Continental Oil Company; her sister Margaret did domestic work for another family. Later she and her parents moved to

Denver, where her father worked in the stockyards, her mother found a position at the Owens Hotel in housekeeping, and Marion helped during the summer.

Despite the varying conditions of live-in domestic work, it did assure a place to stay, at least temporarily, in cities where war workers had flooded the housing markets. With this in mind, Haruko Sugi Hurt left Rohwer in 1943 to work as a babysitter for a Jewish couple living on the South Side of Chicago. When they no longer needed her service, her kindly employers allowed her to stay with them, charging a minimal amount for room and board until she found another job. Haruko said, "I was treated like a member of the family," recalling how they even made a Christmas dinner for her.[146]

The picture was not always rosy—some Japanese Americans found themselves in exploitative workplaces. "I met one of the Edgewater Beach girls," reported Smoot Katow in Chicago. "From what she said it was my impression that the girls are not very happy. The work is too hard, according to this girl. In fact, they are losing weight and one girl became sick with overwork. They have to clean about 15 suites a day, scrubbing the floors on their hands and knees." He concluded, "The outside world is as tough as it ever was."[147]

For some Nisei women, like their non-Japanese sisters, the wartime labor shortage opened the door into industrial, clerical, and managerial occupations. Nisei women found jobs as secretaries, typists, file clerks, beauticians, and factory workers. Indeed, Haruko's next job, found through the employment listings at the WRA office in Chicago, was as a clerk typist at the Tuberculosis Institute of Chicago and Cooke County. Dissatisfied with this job, she then worked for the federal government at a V-Mail Station in the downtown Loop, processing letters to be sent to soldiers overseas.

The Nisei drew on the support of kin and friends in the process of finding jobs and housing, and adjusting to life in unfamiliar regions. In September 1943, Fumiko Fukuyama Ide's brother Yoshio helped her to leave the Amache camp by getting her a secretarial job at the Congressional Mission Board in Boston, Massachusetts, and a place to live with a minister's family in West Newton, a long bus ride from work. In order to cut the cost of transportation, Fumiko moved in with Mayme Kishi, a Nisei woman who worked at the South End Music School in Boston. She recalled, "The two of us, the only way we could afford to stay there was to work there at the office. At night, after we had our regular jobs during the day, we went to the music school. We took turns at the receptionist desk and doing the housework, so that we could have a room upstairs." They economized on food as well: "Mayme and I, we used to get a can of peaches and a box of something like Bisquick, . . . we'd pour this peach in a pan, and put this biscuit dough over it, and bake it in the school oven. We ate that for days. . . . We made this peach cobbler for weeks at a time!" Fumiko survived that period by focusing on "getting through a day at a time."[148]

Some Nisei women also worked as "Rosie the Riveters" in defense factories. For example, on August 23, 1944 the Amache Camp newspaper, the *Pioneer* announced, "An attractive war-plant job of making parts for rocket ships and bombers was recently opened by a Cleveland concern for nisei girls. At present there are five nisei girls employed by this company."[149] Inexperienced jobseekers were assured that they would receive training in drilling, deburring, assembling, packing, and inspection operations. One of the Nisei to enter defense work was 17-year-old Marion Funakoshi Manaka, who, after finishing high school in Colorado, followed her brother and sister to Chicago where she joined "four other girls that I knew when we were kids in Los Angeles."[150] They rented a room in a converted brownstone house on the South Side, taking a train to work at the Monarch Bicycle Company that had shifted to making parachute buckles during the war; most of the other workers were white women. The young age of Marion and her friends limited their social life, but after work they went to movies or to see performances by entertainers such as Frank Sinatra and Sammy Davis, Jr., at the State Street Theatre.

Professional opportunity drew Dr. Sakaye Shigekawa to the Midwest before large numbers of resettling Japanese Americans had begun to trek there. Unusual both as an early Nisei professional and as a woman physician, in 1942 Shigekawa took a medical residency in Chicago in order to avoid confinement at the Heart Mountain camp. Soon she entered private practice with another doctor, mainly treating Irish, German, and Polish patients. She had pleasant memories of her house calls in the Irish community, where she was known as "Doctor O'Shige."[151] In 1943 and 1944, she also began to see growing numbers of Japanese American patients, as the WRA office directed Chicago resettlers to her.

One of the early Japanese American—and Asian American—social scientists, Setsuko Matsunaga Nishi, also pursued professional training and work in Chicago. Her MA research on early Japanese American resettlement in St. Louis brought her to the attention of sociologists working on the Japanese Evacuation and Resettlement Study under the direction of Dorothy Thomas at the University of Chicago. "Tom Shibutani heard about my work," she said, "and invited me to work for them."[152] She became an assistant research collaborator for the JERS study, submitting her thesis as her contribution. In 1944, in addition to completing both her BA and MA degrees at Washington University, Setsuko married artist Ken Nishi, who was in the army doing information education. She then went to Chicago, where her parents had resettled, to find work.

There Setsuko found a position in the African American community, developing collegial relations that would continue throughout her career. In St. Louis, one of the organizations that had invited Setsuko to speak was the 20th Century Club, a group of black male leaders, including P. L. Prattis, publisher of the *Pittsburgh Courier*. In Chicago she ran into Prattis again while passing out leaflets at the historic meeting that marked the merger of the American Federation of Labor and the Congress of Industrial Organizations. He introduced her to sociologist Horace R. Cayton, Jr., the head of the Chicago Parkway Community House. Cayton hired her to direct his program, the People's Forum—"he had prominent speakers but difficulty publicizing them and drawing an audience." Setsuko learned "that the Chicago Transit Authority would put up posters for free for nonprofit organizations. So I had posters made and we put them all over the city of Chicago. We set up this program and we had standing room only."[153] She also continued her studies, entering the University of Chicago to pursue a doctorate.[154]

An unexpected turn of events initially thwarted Mary Yuri Nakahara's nuptials and led to a job in the South. Accompanied by her mother, Yuri left Jerome in April 1944, intending to marry her fiancé Bill Kochiyama in Hattiesburg, Mississippi, before his unit departed overseas. She was stunned when his father sent a telegram to Bill's captain on the wedding day, denying permission. "We promised to wait for each other until after the war and Bill's discharge," she wrote. "Until then, the chaplain very kindly offered me a job at the Japanese American 'Aloha' USO so I would not have to return to Jerome camp to face curious neighbors."[155]

Because of the U.S. military's racial policies, African American, Asian American, and Latino soldiers were not allowed into white USOs. In response, Hung Wai Ching, a Chinese American member of the Morale Division of the Council on Interracial Unity, had assisted in the establishment of the Aloha USO that served Japanese American and Chinese American soldiers. Yuri later learned that African Americans had not been able to come to the Aloha USO because of its location; a co-worker who, like Bill, had trained at Camp Shelby, told her, "No black soldiers, even in uniform, could walk any major street in Southern towns."[156]

During her two years at the Aloha USO, Yuri mainly assisted the wives of Nisei servicemen, helping them locate housing and, with the skills honed from her prewar and camp activities, organizing regular luncheons and events for them. She also made trips to hospitals in 12 states to visit wounded Nisei soldiers. This period was a pivotal one for Yuri, who said, "It was challenging but very liberating. First, I was on my own, and second, it challenged my thinking. . . . How little I understood about anything in life, and until that time was I indoctrinated with status quo mainstream American ideas, but I now knew it was time to go on my own and think for myself."[157] Like Yuri, many Nisei women drew on past experiences and cultivated new skills as they forged lives outside the camps, becoming more independent in the process.

A Nisei WAC

Although the military service of Nisei men is better known, more than 300 Nisei women volunteered for the Women's Army Corps.[158] Even before Japanese

Americans were eligible to join the WACS, in March 1943 a recruiter visited the Poston camp to address the young women. Lt. Roberta House told a capacity crowd that "the main job is to stand behind the man behind the gun," explaining, "We're not soldiers with guns."[159] She described the range of work for WACS in administration, communication, transportation, and mess management, urging her audience to consider applying when enlistment became possible.[160] On July 27, the newspaper announced that a limited number of Japanese Americans would be accepted in the WAC and pointed out that they would not be assigned to a special unit (in contrast to Nisei men). In September, the *Poston Chronicle* expressed disappointment over the small number of Nisei signing up for the WAC: "From over 1100 single girls in the Center eligible for the WACS, seven have volunteered."[161] The editor attributed the poor showing in part to the fact that many of the women who had initially been interested had already left the camp, and those who remained had family duties and/or disapproving parents. The number of Nisei WACS was relatively small, but, as Mei Nakano reported, they "served at various bases all over the country, in medical detachments, in the Public Information Office, in Military Intelligence School and as typists, clerks and researchers in occupied Germany and Japan."[162] Haruko Sugi Hurt had heard about the Military Intelligence Service Language School and thought it might be more interesting than her work at the V-Mail Station. When she wrote for information, she was invited to join a WAC unit.

Haruko's stint in the military took her across the country. In January 1945 she went to a WAC training center in Des Moines, Iowa, where she was the only Japanese American in the class. After completing basic training, she was sent to Minnesota to work as a typist in the MISLS headquarters office under Major John Aiso at Fort Snelling. There she engaged in intensive study of Japanese language, military terminology, and Japanese geography for eight months. Before she graduated, the war had ended and she was assigned first to the Pacific Military Intelligence Research Section in Maryland and then to the Washington Document Center in Washington, D.C., where she translated materials until her discharge in 1946. Later, her status as a veteran enabled her finally to pursue a long-deferred dream: The GI Bill made possible her college education after she rejoined her family in California.

Paving the Way for Return to California: Esther Takei Nishio

Nisei women played a significant role in the return of Japanese Americans to the West Coast. Aided primarily by a small civil rights group and white veterans of the South Pacific, a Nisei woman college student would very visibly pave the way for the return to California, where intense anti-Japanese hostility lingered. Even though the army had permitted a number of Nisei women to return to California before September 1944, the local newspapers singled out Esther Takei as the first to come back to the Los Angeles region.[163]

In the summer of 1944, Esther Takei and her parents received a visit in Amache from Hugh Anderson, a Quaker auditor from Pasadena who had stored furniture for the Takeis and other Japanese American families before their removal.[164] Anderson, his friend William Carr, a prominent Pasadena realtor, and Carr's wife had formed a group called Friends of the American Way, dedicated to "helping correct the mistakes and heal the wounds of the forced evacuation from the West Coast of all citizens and aliens of Japanese descent."[165] This effort, they believed, would provide "a fruitful and unselfish opportunity for Negro, Jew, Saxon, Catholic, Mexican and Protestant to know and respect each other by working together for the rights of the banished."[166] Anderson and Carr had written to Major General Charles Hartwell Bonesteel, then head of the Western Defense Command, about allowing Japanese Americans to return to the West Coast. According to Anderson, Bonesteel "had us on the telephone almost immediately and said he was willing to open the West Coast if we went ahead and found someone who wanted to return."[167] At Amache, Hugh Anderson talked with the Takeis about the possibility of Esther returning to California to attend college, inviting her to stay with his family. Esther and her parents agreed. Subsequently, the head of the Pasadena Junior College, Dr. John Harbeson, approved her admission, as did Mrs. Hoblitt, the president of the school board. The PJC faculty, staff, and students were polled beforehand and responded favorably to the admission of a Japanese American student.

On September 12, 1944, after a three-day train trip, Esther arrived in Pasadena, her feelings a mixture of "trepidation about my reception and joy at being back." The warm welcome bolstered her: "When I stepped off the train, well-wishers surrounded me—students, the editor of the school newspaper, the Student Christian Association counselor and the Anderson family—and my fears were dispelled."[168] The hope was that Esther "could slip into student body life without too much notice and eventually be accepted by the community-at-large when they became accustomed to my presence."[169]

"Then," Hugh Anderson recalled, "all hell broke loose in Pasadena."[170] The student editor of the PJC newspaper, after meeting Esther at the railroad station, had raced to the Pasadena press with his "scoop" about her arrival, which then made headlines in the Los Angeles newspapers.[171] Said Anderson, "This was the beginning of the effort by the Hearst papers to stop the return of Japanese to the West Coast. The Chamber of Commerce was unhappy with it."[172] A battle of public opinion raged fiercely in southern California.

Six weeks of turmoil ensued, during which groups such as the Daughters of the American Revolution, Native Sons and Daughters of the Golden West,

Gold Star Mothers, and the American Legion heatedly protested Esther's arrival, seeking to pressure the Pasadena Board of Education to expel her. The Board responded that the decision was not theirs to make, being under the jurisdiction of the Western Defense Command and thus the federal government. The Pasadena and Los Angeles newspapers fanned the flames of public furor. The Pasadena *Independent* continually ran the Andersons' address along with its articles, and "streams of cars drove by his house every day to catch a glimpse of 'that girl.'"[173] The Anderson home was barraged by threatening telephone calls; the PJC president also received harassing calls, including a bomb threat to the campus. When the pressure was at its height, Hugh Anderson, fearing for his family's and Esther's safety, sent his wife and children to relatives in another city and Esther stayed with the adviser of the Student Christian Association.

Other groups, including the NAACP, the Friends of the American Way, and an array of churches, rallied to her support. Leaders such as Cal Tech professors Robert Millikan, Linus Pauling, and Robert Emerson offered help, as did the Reverend Herbert Nicholson and J. Frank Burke, owner and publisher of the *Santa Ana Register*. Esther and the Andersons received an outpouring of letters, some hateful but many supportive.

Critical support came from the very group most often invoked as the most opposed to the return of Japanese Americans. Esther's case, which had been reported in the U.S. military newspaper *Stars and Stripes*, particularly struck a chord with servicemen, those abroad as well as some who had returned stateside to recuperate. Observing that those who attacked her often referred to their "relatives in the armed services." USNR Chief Yeoman David C. Munford wrote in a September 1944 letter, "We, in the service, are aware that war is being waged not only upon us as a people, but also upon our form of government, our democracy. We are, therefore, defending not only our geographical boundaries, but our ideals as well. The attack upon our ideals, moreover, is not confined to military theatres alone, but is worldwide, and occurs daily within the United States itself." He expressed the hope that Esther would "be of good cheer and stand fast in your own little battle zone," concluding that "Your importance as a person is as nothing, in a larger sense, to your importance as an example of what can be done or else, *cannot be done to an American citizen*."[174] When the controversy grew most intense, a group of Amvets (an organization formed by veterans who had fought in the South Pacific) at PJC escorted Esther from class to class to protect her. She reported, "Their attitude, and their support, proved very influential in winning over the citizens of Pasadena."[175] Other veterans of the Pacific theater confronted the American Legion, "telling them they had fought to preserve American civil liberties and that they wanted the American Legion to reverse its stand against the return of evacuees."[176] Esther also received visits and encouragement from Nisei veterans of the 442nd Regimental Combat Team who were recuperating at a Pasadena hospital.

In addition to the stress of being a 19-year-old freshman adjusting to the demands of college coursework, not to mention the transition from life in the Amache camp, Esther soldiered on under enormous pressure, not only from those who sought her expulsion, but also from the expectations of supporters who recognized the significance of her return. Just as the Nisei had been expected to represent their families and communities to the larger society before the war, Esther and other carefully selected early returnees knew that on their shoulders rested the hopes of thousands still behind barbed wire or scattered across the Midwest and East. For example, Susumu Kazahaya, a Nisei army sergeant wrote to Esther in September 1944 underscoring the importance of her role: "All I want to say is that since you are the first to come here, you have the most important weapon under your control to impress the people here that there are thousands of other Japanese that are wishing to come back to Southern California. Please utilize that weapon for those that are not so fortunate as you. The impression you leave in your activities will no doubt reflect greatly on the niseis that will return in the future."[177] Another well-wisher, a field secretary for the American Friends Service Committee, wrote, "Although I know you are busy with school work—and I can imagine how many letters you have to write!—I do hope you'll be free enough to give occasional talks to college student Christian groups and to high school church groups.... I know how much it will mean if you can make time for such 'ambassadorial' work."[178]

Esther indeed shouldered this "ambassadorial" role, juggling schoolwork with visits to various churches and speaking on an interracial panel of students. She also encouraged other Nisei to enter or return to college. As corresponding secretary for the Student Christian Association at Pasadena Junior College, she wrote a November 1944 letter that seemed directed to past Japanese American students who perhaps were unable to complete their degrees at PJC because of the war. Extolling the excitement of college life and the role of the SCA in easing her transition, she detailed the anticipated delights of a "Backwards Dance" that echoed prewar Nisei socializing: "I was lucky enough to 'catch' Sgt. John Endo, former L.A. boy, for a date; and eight of us are going to 'double-date'. First, we'll indulge in a turkey dinner at the First Methodist Church, see a movie at the Army Regional Hospital (Hotel Vista del Arroyo), and then to the Civic [Auditorium] for an evening of dancing. Sounds like fun, neh!"[179] The letter ended with her hope that "some day soon, you'll be coming back to see us."[180]

Gradually the furor subsided and the tide of public opinion turned. Esther had stood fast in her own "battle zone" and, with a wide array of support from veterans, civil rights activists, churches, educators, and civic leaders, had prevailed. As the dust settled, she undauntedly encouraged other Nisei to join her, describing the pleasures of activities that evoked prewar Nisei networks and socializing.

According to Hugh Anderson, Esther Takei's successful return was instrumental in convincing General Bonesteel to rescind the mass exclusion of Japanese Americans from the West Coast earlier than expected. Anderson recalled Bonesteel saying, "Well, you know, I wasn't planning to open the West Coast to the returnees for another year. But you proved it was possible, so we are opening the West Coast beginning January 2nd [1945]."[181]

In the fall of 1944 Bonesteel had also issued certificates of exemption to other selected Japanese Americans whose early return would serve to gauge public reaction.[182] These returnees included two women, Kaoru Ichihara, a secretary for the Seattle Council of Churches, and Dorothy Tada, who worked for the YMCA in Los Angeles; Tada remarked that they needed people "who wouldn't scare anybody."[183] For stereotypical reasons of gender, generation, and religious affiliation, Takei, Ichihara, and Tada were ideal in this respect: American-born and -educated, Protestant Christian young women, the least likely to "scare anybody." As in the 1920s and 1930s, during the war young Nisei women served as appealing, nonthreatening, home front representatives of the larger ethnic community.

In the late fall of 1944, by the time the worst of the storm over Esther Takei's return had passed, the Allies appeared to be on the way to winning the war. On December 17, 1944, the day before the Supreme Court ruled on the Mitsuye Endo and Fred Korematsu cases,[184] the Department of War ended the exclusion of the Japanese Americans from the West Coast effective January 2, 1945, and the War Relocation Authority announced that the camps would be closed within the year. By this time, 37 percent of the incarcerated Nikkei of sixteen years or older had already relocated, including 63 percent of the Nisei women in that age group.[185]

Although a number of Japanese Americans, such as Setsuko Matsunaga Nishi, Alice Imamoto Takemoto, and Yuri Kochiyama, chose to stay in the Midwest and East, the majority began to move back to the West Coast after mass exclusion was rescinded. The WRA reported, "the Japanese were cautious in returning to the West Coast and it was not until the last months of 1945 that great numbers came to Los Angeles."[186] By 1946 an estimated 25,000 to 28,000 had resettled in Los Angeles County, as compared with approximately 37,000 before the war.[187]

* * *

Like Alice Imamoto Takemoto, Esther Takei Nishio declined to be interviewed for more than 50 years after World War II. As Alice's son had done, Esther's family and the curators of the Japanese American National Museum finally persuaded her of the importance of telling her story. What emerges from this long-veiled past is how women continued to serve their families and communities—old and new—within the bleak confines of the incarceration camps.

They worked as mess-hall waitresses, nurses' aides, secretaries, journalists, and teachers; they made camouflage nets and harvested crops. Those who had been active in girls' clubs before the war utilized their skills and experience to organize groups within the camps, mentoring younger Nisei and providing positive channels for their energies. Many offered emotional support to their brothers and other Nisei men who entered the military service. They made the most of limited resources, exercising creativity in boosting morale and reviving social networks.

Young women swelled the ranks of those leaving the camps as students and workers heading for the Midwest and East; a few entered the military. They ventured into new arenas and regions of the country unfamiliar to their parents, relying primarily on each other. Some drew on kin for help, like Mary and Alice who went to college with their older sisters; others banded together with friends, like Marion, who joined prewar pals in becoming defense workers in Chicago.

As before the war, young Nisei women students and resettlers also served as highly visible ethnic representatives. This time, it was the War Relocation Authority, the head of the Western Defense Command, and a number of educational leaders who expected that they would prove to be friendly, nonthreatening ambassadors to a larger society immensely suspicious of Japanese Americans. While juggling the demands of coursework and jobs, students such as Setsuko Matsunaga Nishi and Esther Takei Nishio gave presentations at churches and schools on behalf of the incarcerated Issei and Nisei.

The ordeal of uprooting and mass exclusion did not end with the war. For Esther and the other Japanese Americans who returned to the U.S. West, resettlement was a strenuous, difficult process.[188] Starting over with few resources in a place of persisting hostility and a postwar housing shortage challenged the strength of their determination, families, and social networks. Their continuing prewar ties and patterns of organization, as well as shifts in family structure catalyzed by incarceration, would have significant ramifications for postwar developments.

5

Reweaving the Web of Community in Postwar Southern California, 1945–1950

After the dropping of atomic bombs on Hiroshima and Nagasaki in August 1945, the war ended on August 14, sparking celebrations across the country. Mary Nakahara was in Minneapolis, trying to set up a service program for Nisei GIs. She recalled, "On that V-Day, Nisei civilians were calling each other not to go outside, but rather to stay safe and celebrate inside."[1] Rose Honda and her family had returned to Los Angeles from Manzanar by then and happened to be on a streetcar crowded with passengers when the news of V-J Day spread:

> And all the people around us, whatever nationality, they were just throwing their caps, paper, whatever, rejoicing that day. I mean, the people around didn't even notice us as Japanese. I think they were all so jubilant that the war was over. But for me, I thought, oh, I'm Japanese, and surely they'll do something to me—the people around me on the street car...that was one time, I really was scared.[2]

For Japanese Americans, the return to the West Coast and the end of the war presented continuing challenges. Given the traumatic nature of incarceration and the difficulties of postwar rebuilding, historian Kariann Yokota has contended, "The resettlement phase should be acknowledged as an extension of the internment process."[3] In California, hostility lingered—in the form of anti-Japanese signs, housing and job discrimination, vigilante violence, and harassment—compounded by a housing shortage and, with the return of military servicemen, a swelling labor force. Some Issei and Nisei returnees were fortunate to have non–Japanese American friends who helped them find places to live, but the reception they met was mixed. Rose Honda recalled, "[R]ight here in West L.A., many of the stores, shops on Santa Monica Boulevard had signs up, 'No Japs Allowed,' or 'Go Back.'... So that was uncomfortable, not being sure how we were going to be accepted."[4] Nisei like Mary and Rose had good reasons to fear that they would still be perceived as the enemy, as they attempted to find work, rebuild their networks, and interact with the larger society.

This chapter draws primarily on oral history interviews and the ethnic press to trace developments in Nisei women's lives during the least-studied period of Japanese American history and Asian American history.[5] For the Issei and Nisei, the early postwar years were a crucial period in the remaking of families and communities, and southern California persisted as a site of population concentration, although the nature of ethnic enclaves began to shift. Nisei geographer Midori Nishi found in her 1955 study that the size of the Japanese American population of Los Angeles County was less affected by the wartime uprooting than any other region in the United States, as reflected in the substantial rate of postwar return. She reported, "By 1950 eighteen per cent of all Japanese in the United States and thirty per cent of those in California were in Los Angeles City," noting that from "1950 to date there has been a small but continuous movement into the City from many other sections of the country."[6] As articles in the *Rafu Shimpo* newspaper show, Nisei women played active roles in reconstructing community organizations, establishing families, and tackling race relations issues. Girls' clubs proliferated, continuing to provide channels for recreation, socializing, community service, and leadership training and offering a place of belonging and unambiguous acceptance during the rocky postwar period. As it was for many non–Japanese American women, entering the postwar work force was a necessity, and for most Issei and Nisei women, employment was complicated by racial barriers. The experiences of Fumiko Fukuyama Ide, Rose Honda, Haruko Sugi Hurt, Mary Nishi Ishizuka, Katsumi Hirooka Kunitsugu, Marion Funakoshi Manaka, Mary Oyama Mittwer, Setsuko Matsunaga Nishi, Esther Takei Nishio, Sakaye Shigekawa, and Mary Nakahara (Yuri Kochiyama)—central figures in the previous chapter—offer insights into the complex process of rebuilding lives and reweaving the web of community.

Postwar Snapshots

Tracking the migrations of Japanese Americans from the wartime into the 1950s is challenging. It was a time of great flux, and many of the Nisei I have interviewed over the years had difficulty sorting out with precision the comings and goings of their family members: a father heading out of camp on temporary harvest leave, siblings and cousins working and pursuing education across the Midwest and East, a brother returning from army service, a sister who left to join her fiancé and his family. Like a dime store toy in which one creates a picture by using a magnet to attract metal filings to different spots on a page, one can see over time the gradual return of a majority to the West, the magnetic pull of Issei parents particularly drawing children to a new or old location.

Wherever they ended up, most Issei and Nisei faced tremendous hardship and grueling work. Because the struggle for survival consumed so much time and energy, the early postwar organizational landscape of the Japanese American community appears sparse compared with the prewar profusion of groups; however, resilience becomes more and more apparent in the postwar newspaper coverage. Churches were the first institutions to reappear, offering temporary housing and job clearing house services as well as spiritual comfort and fellowship. A Nisei Veterans Association coalesced as GIs returned from service in the 442nd Regimental Combat Team, the 100th Battalion, and the Military Intelligence Service. The Japanese American Citizens League (JACL) grew increasingly visible: The national organization became involved in a variety of legislative battles—from demands for Issei naturalization rights to the entry of war brides. Local JACL chapters reactivated and began efforts to increase voter registration and political participation as well as to promote community well-being through health fairs and other programs. Youth organizations, including vigorous sports leagues, started to spring up, and, continuing a prewar pattern, girls' clubs appeared the most numerous.

The war abroad may have ended in 1945, but fierce battles over civil rights filled the ethnic press in the late 1940s. These included school segregation, fair employment practices, and housing discrimination, as well as issues of particular interest to the Nikkei community. The *Rafu Shimpo* assiduously tracked efforts to overturn the state alien land laws, to gain naturalization rights for the Issei, and to recover their commercial fishing rights, as well as the processing of evacuation claims. The paper also covered the unfolding legal drama as Nisei who had forfeited their citizenship while stranded in Japan during the war[7] and those who had given up citizenship during confinement at the Tule Lake segregation center[8] made appeals to regain U.S. citizenship.

Real estate provides a striking map of the uneven shifts and resistance to change in postwar race relations. In her study of how urban housing markets reflected the changing postwar status of Asian Americans, Charlotte Brooks traces the tenacious battles waged in the 1940s by multiracial coalitions against measures such as Proposition 15, which aimed to incorporate into the state constitution the earlier Alien Land Laws. As Brooks states, "Anti-Asian sentiment was dying in urban areas, but white support for the residential segregation of all nonwhite Californians did not decline nearly so quickly."[9] The fight against restrictive housing covenants was especially arduous, with African American, Asian American, and other racial minority veterans again on the front line. Under the GI Bill they gained access to higher education and home loans, only to discover that military service and FHA support did not guarantee acceptance as a homeowner in many white neighborhoods across the country. In 1948 a landmark Supreme Court case *Shelley v. Kraemer* ruled that restrictive housing covenants were not enforceable, but failed to end them. In southern California, European American realtors who helped minority clients risked reprisals. Lucille A. Swital, a Glendale realtor, received 40 protesting phone calls and then lost her home to a suspected arson fire shortly after announcing that "a fine Japanese American family" would be moving in.[10] In 1950, Pasadena realtor William C. Carr faced threats to drive him out of business because of his aid to Japanese Americans and African Americans.[11]

Real estate proved to be a contested issue for the dead as well as the living. The Westminster Memorial Park in Orange County, for example, would only permit the burial of Pvt. Kazuo Masuda "in a plot where there are no trees or lawn because Masuda was of Japanese ancestry." After protest by the Orange County JACL and after his service in the 442nd was pointed out, Masuda—the posthumous recipient of the Distinguished Service Cross for wartime heroism—was granted "a desirable spot."[12] In 1949, radio commentator Drew Pearson drew attention to Chicago's "after-death race discrimination law" that prohibited the burial of Issei or Nisei; survivors were forced to have their kin cremated or to ship the remains elsewhere.[13] The mayor's Human Relations Commission subsequently learned that all the local cemeteries had "'restrictive covenants' prohibiting burial of persons not of Caucasian ancestry."[14]

For the Nisei and Issei, continuing struggle—in factories and offices, schools, suburbs, cemeteries, and bowling alleys—was a hallmark of the early postwar period. Even in 1950 it was still newsworthy when a major newspaper agreed to eliminate use of the word "Jap."[15] *Rafu Shimpo* editor and columnist Henry Mori assessed the 1940s as "rather a weary decade for most of us....We would like to wrap up the '40s into a small wooden box and chuck it away. May we never encounter another decade of such injustices and unfair dealings."[16] This long taxing struggle remained a pervasive reality in the lives of Japanese American women resettling in southern California.

In their postwar migrations, work, organizational activities, and family formation, the 12 Nisei women profiled here provide a cross-section of Japanese American women's experiences. Three of them—Setsuko Matsunaga Nishi, Alice Imamoto Takemoto and Mary Nakahara (Yuri Kochiyama)—chose to make their lives in the East.

After graduating from Oberlin, Alice went to Philadelphia to study with Olga Samaroff Stokowski, a renowned piano teacher, doing domestic work to support herself. When Stokowski died a year later, Alice moved to Washington D.C., where her parents had resettled, and found a job at the Library of Congress, first answering phones in the information office and then working in the copyright office.[17] She also joined the Friday Morning Music Club. In 1948 Alice met Ken Takemoto, a Nisei veteran from Hawai'i who, with GI Bill support, was pursuing a degree at George Washington University and would later earn a PhD in bacteriology. They married in 1951. Ken embarked on a 32-year career at the National Institutes for Health, and, after their children grew older, Alice returned to performing at concerts; she taught piano for 50 years.

Setsuko Matsunaga Nishi was living in Chicago when her husband artist Ken Nishi was discharged from the army; soon after, because of a training injury, he was hospitalized for almost three years. Setsuko had entered graduate school at the University of Chicago: "At that time, I got a grant with [anthropologist] Bill Caudill to do the Japanese American personality and acculturation study. It was a big project—and with a brand new baby and a near-death husband—but he came through!" She also worked as a research writer for the *Chicago Defender* and in 1948 became acting director of the Chicago Council Against Racial and Religious Discrimination. For a decade she served as director of the research unit of the National Council of Churches. At the time when Setsuko entered academia, "there were very few women at professorial levels. I didn't know of anyone at the time, especially a Japanese American woman."[18] In 1962, she finished her PhD dissertation on Japanese American resettlement in Chicago and in 1965 began her career as a professor of sociology at Brooklyn College and the Graduate Center of the City University of New York.

In October 1945, Mary Yuri Nakahara briefly returned with her family to San Pedro, California, working until January 1946, when she could join her fiancé Bill Kochiyama—newly discharged from the 442nd—in his home town, New York City. There he ran a printing shop and she worked as a waitress in a Chock Full O' Nuts restaurant until she became pregnant in 1947 with the first of six children. Raising their family in Harlem, Yuri and Bill began a lifelong involvement in human rights and social justice efforts, including Malcolm X's Organization of Afro-American Unity.

Like the majority of Japanese Americans, the other nine women returned to the West Coast. The first was Esther Takei Nishio, the poised and spirited "test case" in the fall of 1944; the last was Sakaye Shigekawa, who rejoined her family in 1948, leaving Chicago to establish a medical practice in Los Angeles.

The southern California to which they returned had benefited from the federal government's wartime investment in defense industries and military bases. War contracts had fueled California's rise as a key economic force; by 1944, Los Angeles was second only to Detroit as the largest manufacturing center in the country.[19] This boom attracted thousands of workers, contributing to traffic congestion, smog, and a housing crunch. By 1945 southern California alone had more people than 37 entire states.[20] As southern California defense industries profitably converted to civilian production to meet the enormous postwar demand for consumer goods, workers continued to arrive, seeking sunshine and fortune. According to the U.S. Census, between 1940 and 1950 the population of Los Angeles County swelled 49 percent, from 2,785,643 residents to 4,151,687. The Cold War also ensured the maintenance of military spending, particularly in the aircraft—and later aerospace—industry. But the most notable shift in the urban west occurred with the burgeoning of service jobs in both the public and private sectors.[21]

World War II had increased the entry of women, single and married, into the wage-paid labor force, including the many women who had flocked to the defense industries. At war's end, Rosie the Riveter and her sisters lost their well-paying industrial jobs, while facing pressure from the government, movies, and advertising to pursue domesticity. Particularly for working-class and racial-minority women, leaving the work force was often not an option. Many women moved to lower-paying clerical and sales jobs in the growing service economy; more wives continued their employment. In southern California, a large number of women—often immigrant Latinas and Asians—found low-paid jobs in the growing garment industry.

Housing

Finding housing and work proved the biggest challenges faced by resettling Japanese Americans. The *Rafu Shimpo* reported in January 1946, "Housing costs for returned evacuees who must rent or lease in Los Angeles…are up 50 to 200 per cent over pre-war levels. Inflation in costs of homes for sale are proportionately high."[22] Steep prices were compounded by continuing discrimination in housing:

> Restrictive covenants operate in Los Angeles against Japanese Americans just as they did before the war, we learn. Only it's worse now, if such phenomena can be measured. In 1939–40, The Rafu Shimpo made a survey which indicated that only two out of every ten Los Angeles residences could be occupied by people of Oriental descent. The other eight were restricted.[23]

In October 1946, a *New York Times* journalist reported, "Los Angeles county headed the west coast concentration of Japanese returnees with the count at 23,000," and more than half of "the pre-evacuation 90,000 residents have returned to the west coast."[24] By late December, the *Rafu Shimpo* noted that the number of returnees had nearly reached 25,000.[25] According to reporter Scotty Tsuchiya, "The vital nation-wide housing problem, more than any other factor, imposed the greatest immediate hardship upon the evacuees."[26] A year later, in its 1947 Holiday Issue, the *Rafu Shimpo* reported that the "famous last words" uttered by on-coming returnees were: "We're too busy trying to make a living" and "Let me know if you've got a tip about a good house or an apartment."[27]

Many of the returnees first stayed at hostels run by churches and civic groups. Tsuchiya characterized them as "at best, necessary evils," lacking "adequate sanitary facilities" and "overcrowded to an unhealthy saturation point. Many, no better than flop houses, were condemned by the Public Health Department, but in spite of this, hundreds of returnees were sent to them and to other temporary shelters, pre-fabricated Army barracks set up by the WRA in the outlying areas of metropolitan Los Angeles." Perhaps with some irony, the reporter concluded, "This setup was similar to the relocation camps but without the facilities available in even the centers."[28] The similarities between postwar housing and conditions in camp echo in the words of returnees like Katsumi Hirooka Kunitsugu.

Because of the housing shortage, Katsumi's family could not return to their prewar rented home in Boyle Heights in East Los Angeles, and her father had great difficulty finding a place. Finally an African American woman in Watts agreed to rent a house to them and five Hirookas moved in, together with another Japanese American family of four. Sharing housing and splitting costs in this way became a common strategy for Japanese Americans in many regions as they struggled to build postwar lives. After graduating from the University of Wisconsin, Katsumi could not find a job in the area, so she came back to Los Angeles: "I stayed with my parents for a while, but everything was so crowded. I mean somebody was forever using the bathroom. So I finally moved out to the Evergreen Hostel."[29]

Living conditions at the Evergreen Hostel in Boyle Heights, operated by the Union Church, reminded Katsumi of Heart Mountain. "[I]t was almost like camp in that all we had was a bed and a little stand where we kept our personal belongings, and it was more or less the honor system for everyone. . . . There were some house rules about what time you had to be in by and things like that. But they fed you and it didn't cost very much to live there."[30] In 1949 she got a job covering social news for *Crossroads*, a new Nisei weekly, and was able to leave the hostel for an apartment shared with two women friends.

The crowded conditions and lack of privacy in the hostel also mirrored camp life for Rose Honda and her family, who spent time in two, the first run by friends on Beloit Avenue in West Los Angeles. After the reopening of the West Los Angeles Japanese Methodist Church in which they had been active before the war, they moved to the church hostel where they lived in the parsonage. Rose noted, "[I]t wasn't different from living in camp in one room. But there was much activity going on, because some days downstairs there would be the worship service every Sunday, and people just going in and out....So actually, for everyone there wasn't much privacy."[31]

Because of the continuing gendered division of household duties, shared postwar housing in rentals and hostels particularly called upon the coordinating skills of Issei and Nisei women. In the West L.A. church parsonage, Reverend Susumu Kuwano and his family lived downstairs, with three families residing in the three upstairs bedrooms; 10 more families occupied the social hall, which had been divided into about five rooms. Each family did their own cooking in either the parsonage kitchen or a former garage that was converted into a communal kitchen.[32] Rose said, "I think there was a tremendous amount of coordination and cooperation between the women who had to use the small kitchen they had to take turns to cook for the family."[33]

Even for those who owned property, the process was not easy. When Fumiko Fukuyama Ide's mother returned first, by herself, she discovered that the couple who had rented the Fukuyama house during the war had sublet it. With "grease all over the walls," the house was filthy, filled with tenants, and stripped of the Fukuyamas' belongings. Fumiko's mother "thought the house would be in order, but all the light bulbs were gone; everything was gone." Her son Hiro, who had been in the army, journeyed from the East Coast to help her evict the subletters, and her husband left Amache to aid in the clean up. Then, Fumiko said, "They opened up the house to evacuees who didn't have any place to go, because my mother knew what it was like, not to have any place to go."[34]

The transition back to life in southern California was somewhat smoother for those who had the help of non–Japanese American friends. Haruko Sugi Hurt described as "a saint" her parents' friend Miss Hudson who offered to look after their Gardena home while they were gone, renting it out and paying the property tax and insurance. When she learned they were ready to return, she had their stored furniture moved back, reconnected the utilities, made the beds, and stocked the refrigerator with food.[35] Mary Oyama Mittwer and her family received a warm welcome from Jean and Chester Himes, who had occupied and cared for their home during the war.[36]

The civil rights activists Hugh Anderson and William Carr—founders of the group Friends of the American Way—who had championed Esther Takei Nishio's early return in 1944 to attend Pasadena Junior College also eased her parents' resettlement in spring of 1945. As she recalled, "Mr. Anderson and Mr. Carr found an apartment for us, so then we all moved in together. It happened to be a rooming house right next door to the Pasadena Civic Auditorium."[37] Housing was short and hard to come by, Esther said, "So Mr. Carr, being a real estate broker, aided all the returning families...to find places to live."[38] A major hurdle he and his clients faced was that of the restrictive housing covenants that barred people of color and Jews from living in many areas of southern California.

"[A]t that time, because of the restrictive covenants," Esther remembered, all the racial-ethnic people "whether you were black or Hispanic or Asian had to live on the west side of town. I don't think you could purchase a home beyond Lake Avenue, which is sort of in the center of Pasadena."[39]

Pasadena officials were frank about their efforts to prevent the entry of racial minorities. As Frank Clough, the city manager of South Pasadena, declared in 1946, "We do not have non-white residents living in South Pasadena at the present time, and we hope to insure continuance of this policy."[40] To this end, the city council directed city attorneys to draft restrictive covenant clauses "whereby all properties coming into the city through delinquent taxes would be restricted to only Caucasian residents." However, Clough said that "domestic workers and servants, Japanese and Negroes, are permitted to work in that area."[41] Such entrenched racism, combined with the housing shortage, made finding a home difficult for Issei and Nisei resettlers.

During the war, Little Tokyo had become Bronzeville, as a huge stream of African Americans from the South joined the influx of defense workers. Historic black neighborhoods proved unable to accommodate their numbers, and, greatly limited by restrictive housing covenants and the wartime housing shortage, 70,000 black migrants poured into Little Tokyo, where fewer than 30,000 Japanese Americans had lived. The new arrivals crowded into apartments that were then subdivided into cramped, substandard "kitchenettes" deplored by the Los Angeles County Health Department; however, wartime prosperity temporarily fueled a booming nightlife patronized by both blacks and whites.[42]

After the war, as Japanese Americans began to return to Los Angeles, many of the black sojourners in Bronzeville started to migrate south to Central Avenue and Watts.[43] The transition of Bronzeville back to Little Tokyo was fairly peaceful. Kariann Yokota has attributed the "lack of serious conflict" in large part to "the fact that African American residents did not consider Bronzeville a permanent home, and therefore were not threatened by the return of the Japanese Americans."[44] However, as she documented, the process reveals the influence of the priorities of white property owners as well as the absence of close interethnic relations between the two minority groups, reflecting the persistence of racial hierarchies and stereotyping. Even if "serious conflict" did not erupt, friction did occur, as evidenced by the *Rafu Shimpo*'s steady reportage of a "crime wave" throughout 1946 and 1947, with African American men targeting Japanese Americans for muggings and robberies. After the war, the function and centrality of Little Tokyo shifted. Nisei journalist Katsumi Kunitsugu observed, "the character of Little Tokyo changed from a place where people lived and worked, to...just a business place."[45] Urban redevelopment, beginning soon after the war, hastened this process: Little Tokyo residents—including the *Rafu Shimpo* office—on the northwest side of First and San Pedro faced a "2nd evacuation" in the early 1950s when they were evicted to accommodate the expansion of the police station.[46]

While Little Tokyo dwindled as a residential area, other neighborhoods fared differently. The Seinan-ku or Southwest district grew after the war, still bounded by Vermont on the east and Exposition on the south, while expanding to Adams on the north and Crenshaw on the west. By the end of 1947, the *Rafu Shimpo* reported the presence of 60 Japanese-operated businesses in the area, including grocery stores, gas stations, garages, restaurants, barbers, beauty shops, doctors, dentists, optometrists, and a movie theater. Garden supply stores, lawn mower shops, and nurseries catered to a growing population of Nikkei gardeners. Local realtors estimated that 25 new Japanese American families were moving into the area each month.[47] Housing and jobs proved to be powerful magnets for the resettling Issei and Nisei.

Finding Jobs

As before and during the war, family members scrambled to find employment and struggled to contribute to the family economy. All of the women profiled in this chapter and the previous one sought jobs, including the students. Churches and hostels often served as clearing houses, where employers sent job descriptions. For many Issei and Nisei men and women, domestic service and gardening were the first and main jobs available in southern California. Before the war, Rose Honda's father had worked as a gardener for a European American couple who stored belongings for the family during the war and helped him start over by selling him their Chevrolet Coupe at a low price. Rose and her parents found jobs through listings at the hostel where they were staying:

> So people who lived there, like my dad, would go out and interview for the gardening jobs. There were farms out here [in West Los Angeles], so my mother went out to do day jobs picking string beans or whatever vegetables. Also they asked for domestic jobs. So one day, my friend...Frances Kaji and I, we went out and worked in different homes as a part-time job while we attended school. We laugh about it to this day, because we made seventy-five cents an hour.[48]

Having lost their large successful plant nursery to the war, Mary Nishi Ishizuka's parents also had to start over. Her father began a small nursery and bought an old panel truck so he could do some gardening work. "He didn't seem to harbor really bitter feelings, or he never showed it to us,"[49] Mary reflected, but the huge losses had affected him. She said, "After returning to Los Angeles, my father was not the same man. He gave up on his business. It would be hard to start that kind of business all over again, and he was on in years.... But dad was never the same after he returned."[50]

Esther Takei Nishio's parents also lost their prewar Venice Beach concession business and had to look for whatever work they could find in Pasadena. Esther's mother drew on her prior skills, initially doing domestic work: "She'd board the bus and go to these homes and clean houses for a while. And then because she was a very proficient seamstress, she learned how to operate the power machine."[51] This enabled her to enter southern California's growing garment industry. Esther's father, who had to develop new skills, chose—like many Issei men—to become a gardener, "because that was one job that was easy to find. So my dad bought a few [things], like a trowel...and boarded the bus and went to his different jobs."[52] Eventually he was able to establish the Rose Frozen Shrimp Company with other Issei in Pasadena.[53]

As the *Rafu Shimpo* job listings suggest, for urban Nisei women the most available kind of work was domestic service. For example, a typical set of classified ads in the December 2, 1947 issue included 12 listings for housekeepers, school girls, and mother's helpers, six of them specifying that a "girl" was wanted. Of the two other job ads for that day, one requested a "boy over 18 for delivery," and the ad from the American Chick Sexing Association School in Pennsylvania sought a secretary.[54] Occasionally listings for garment factory work appeared.

Domestic work in private households was a "convenient occupation" for returnees, geographer Midori Nishi observed, "especially among single women who thus secured both housing and employment."[55] This was certainly the case for Midori and her sister Mary Nishi Ishizuka, who both did domestic work while pursuing college education. After returning to Los Angeles from Nebraska, Mary went to UCLA to finish her undergraduate degree. Through the student placement office, she and Midori began working for Sarah Karl of the Karl Shoe Company family. The position entailed more childcare than domestic work. It was "a very lucky break"[56] for Mary, who was fortunate in finding not only an employer but also a friend in Sarah; Mr. Karl, her father, also gave Mary financial assistance through graduate school. The University of Washington faculty members who read Midori's PhD dissertation on "Changing Occupance of Japanese in Los Angeles County, 1940–1950" may not have realized that she was speaking from personal experience as well as research when she said of domestic service, "Issei women tend to remain longer in this line of work than Nisei who were inclined to use it as a stepping stone."[57] By 1955 when she received her doctorate, Nisei women, because of changes in the racial climate, regional economy, and education, had begun to gain access to jobs beyond the reach of most of their Issei mothers.

Outside of domestic positions, finding and keeping jobs in even the lower-paid service industries could be grueling in the early postwar period. Mary Nakahara, who had returned to California at the end of October 1945, met with so much anti-Japanese discrimination that she "periodically used the name 'Mary Wong' to apply for jobs."[58] Because she was waiting to join her fiancé in New York as soon he was discharged from the army, she only applied for waitress jobs that she could leave on short notice. "I must have tried every single restaurant in San Pedro," she recalled, "but no one would hire me. Finally I went to what I remember Walter Winchell said was the roughest place in America: San Pedro's 'Skid Row.' There, they were willing to take chances on hiring a Japanese American, but I never lasted too long (from a couple of hours to maybe a whole night, working night shifts) before I would get identified as a 'Jap' and cause a ruckus."[59] Mary worked the graveyard shifts, "from six o'clock in the evening until three or four o'clock in the morning, if I was lucky. Every time a few people would start complaining, 'Is that a Jap?' the boss would say, 'Sorry, I can't keep you. You're hurting my business.'... Some nice owners would let me stay until I got a cup of coffee thrown at me, at which time the boss would then tell me, 'You'd better go, for your own sake.'"[60]

Within the ethnic community, women found work in beauty salons, one of the avenues for female entrepreneurship and employment before the war.[61] At least three businesses advertised regularly in the daily *Rafu Shimpo* by 1947: the Ozawa Beauty Salon and the Nozaki Beauty Shoppe on First Street in Little Tokyo, and further from the core, May's Beauty Shoppe on 36th Street.[62] The *Rafu Shimpo*'s 1947 Holiday Issue also included ads from six other salons.[63] All of the identified proprietors were female.

Newspaper coverage of beautician work also reveals shifts in the larger racial climate, noticeable in both training and opportunities outside the ethnic community. The significance of this traditional arena of female employment was underscored in the 1946 Holiday Issue of the *Rafu Shimpo* by an article about 21-year-old Margaret Uyemura, a cosmetology student at the Frank Wiggins Trade School who won a second-place prize in a hair styling contest sponsored by the Coiffure Guild of Los Angeles and Hollywood. In a competition that drew 23 local students as well as contestants from other states, Uyemura's upsweep hair-do was commended by the visiting judges for "excellence of workmanship, best moulded [sic] to the contour of the face, with a high degree of originality."[64] In an accompanying photo, the Nisei student beamed from behind her European American model, perhaps suggesting the possibility of future work with a broader clientele. The reporter mentioned that Uyemura had first aimed to become a nurse; presumably wartime incarceration made this dream difficult to realize, as she returned to Los Angeles "from Cleveland via Jerome, Arkansas" and entered cosmetology. Although it is not possible to determine Uyemura's personal preferences, the shorter timeframe (and lower costs) for training and certification may have been a factor: She entered the Wiggins School in March

1946 and would take the state qualifying examination for beauty culturists in January 1947.[65] Prewar work in this field had been largely limited to an ethnic clientele, and even training was affected by wartime anti-Japanese sentiment. On 24 November 1947, the *Rafu Shimpo* gave a large headline to an article announcing that the Bonnie Beauty School in Denver, Colorado, had lifted its ban against Nisei students and admitted Shizue Yamada. The article noted that "Denver beauty institutions have denied Japanese Americans their courses since 1941."[66]

In the early postwar years, Nisei women had begun to find work as factory operatives, particularly in the growing garment industry. Midori Nishi reported, "Prior to the war Japanese were rarely employed as semi-skilled labor in industry and in 1940 'operatives and kindred [similar] workers' represented only six per cent of the Japanese employed in the county. By 1950 this class of workers had increased to sixteen per cent of employed Japanese, compared to the general eleven per cent engaged" in this area.[67] She remarked on the large number of Issei women working in the rapidly expanding garment trade; on the Nisei front, some women had found employment for their "artistic skill...in a number of ceramic factories located within the City" and an estimated 250 worked in phonograph record factories.[68] According to the 1950 U.S. Census, in Los Angeles the major area of work for Japanese women was "operatives and kindred workers," numbering 1,764 individuals.[69]

Coverage of a catastrophic industrial accident at the O'Connor Electro Plating Corporation in the central Los Angeles area south of downtown offers a glimpse of the employment open to returning Japanese American women. On the morning of 20 February 1947, an explosion that could be heard fifteen miles away destroyed the company at 926 East Pico Boulevard, killing at least 17 and injuring 151.[70] Two blocks away, 442nd veteran Buster Suzuki was knocked to the sidewalk by the blast; when he dashed over to help survivors, the gruesome sight reminded him of what he had seen in Europe. The *Rafu Shimpo* reported that "Perchloric acid, being used in secret work for the Government, was cause of the terrific explosion," deemed by city officials to be "the worst blast in the history of southern California."[71] Denying that any secret project was underway, the plant manager insisted that the company was working on a subcontract for a government order to plate aluminum furniture and hospital equipment.[72] The list of the dead and injured reflected a multi-ethnic labor force of women and men. Two Nisei died, and three Nisei and one Issei were hurt, all of them women.

It seems that the electro-plating company had only recently begun hiring Japanese Americans. Alice Iba, age 22, one of those killed, had worked at the plant for a month and a half as assistant to the chief chemist Dr. Robert Magee, who also died. Injured chemist Yoshi Kadota, age 32 (first misidentified as a 24-year-old male, "Yoshio"), had apparently applied and begun working only four days before the explosion. Akiko Otomo, age 20, who lived next door to the plant with her widowed father, died on her first day of work. It appears that Otomo was hired immediately the day she applied; the *Rafu* noted, "If she had been rejected, she was to have had a 'show date with her sweetheart.' "[73]

However, many Japanese American women had already found jobs in the area: Across the street was "a power machine company where many Japanese Issei and Nisei girls are employed," and throughout the vicinity "[h]undreds of Japanese garment workers from other sewing plants were immediately dismissed and ordered to leave the premises."[74] The sister-in-law of injured Fusako Shibuya rushed to the site from her job as a power machine operator a block away. The reports of the accident indirectly reveal that such factory jobs enabled some returning Issei and Nisei women to gain a foothold in the wage paid labor force.

Postwar growth in the southern California service economy, combined with the gradual crumbling of racial barriers owing to the efforts of civil rights groups, made it possible for a modestly larger number of Nisei women to secure clerical and sales positions. This category of labor was second only to that of "operatives and kindred [similar] workers" in size. Midori Nishi found only a slight gain in the number of Japanese women employed as "clerical, sales, and kindred workers," from "1,006 or twenty-one per cent of the employed Japanese women" in 1940 to "1,524 or twenty-five per cent" in 1950.[75] She reported that "Nisei women typists, stenographers, and secretaries are widely distributed in private businesses and government offices."[76] However, the greatest significance of this development may not lie in the number of Nisei clerical workers as much as in *where* they were employed: Increasingly, they were finding jobs outside the ethnic community. Esther Takei Nishio's career provides an illustration of the family pressures Nisei children faced, as well as the barriers and opportunities Japanese American women encountered in the clerical and retail sector.

Concern for her parents, and perhaps exhaustion from the enormous responsibilities she had shouldered as a test case for the return of Japanese Americans to the West Coast, curtailed Esther's college education. During the last semester of her senior year at Pasadena City College, Esther, an only child, felt that "I just couldn't continue going to school anymore, because I could see how hard my parents were working. I wasn't really helping out, you know."[77] She left school and entered the Sawyer School of Business, taking "classes just long enough to learn secretarial skills like typing, stenography, and accounting." She immediately began hunting for a job, answering every ad for a secretarial position listed in Pasadena, "but I was turned down at every point." She recalled, "I would go for an interview and I'd be told, 'Oh, we just filled that opening, so sorry.' And that happened so many times."[78] In Pasadena, the color line in white collar employment, as in housing, was hard to breach. Esther then turned to the Los Angeles newspapers and went to an employment agency. They sent her to a war surplus firm in the flower district downtown and she was hired.

Esther worked there until becoming pregnant soon after her marriage in 1947. Like many of her female peers, she took a hiatus from full-time employment until her son grew older, channeling her energies into the kinds of unpaid work that revitalized postwar Japanese American communities: involvement with the Parent Teachers Association, the Pasonas (a Nisei women's group she had helped found), and church activities. Later she became a secretary at an industrial design firm in Pasadena, working for pioneering designer Henry Dreyfuss; after he retired, she worked for 14 years at the Flying Tiger Airline as secretary to the vice president of law.[79]

The Fukuyama family's housing and work reflect both continuity and shift from prewar patterns. Fumiko Fukuyama Ide returned to Los Angeles from Kansas City around 1947, with "a baby, and a paralyzed father-in-law, and a husband with a collapsed lung." They moved in with her parents, who turned their garage into an apartment for the growing Ide family. Both Issei parents had been entrepreneurs before the war, but were unable to restart their businesses. Having lost his hardware company, her father served as the secretary-treasurer of the Fukuoka Kenjinkai, earning perhaps $25 a month; her mother did domestic work and then used her fine sewing skills at a dress factory in the downtown garment district. When Fumiko's husband Joe recovered, he did some photography for the nearby All People's Center, a multi-ethnic congregation, eventually becoming their playground director and summer camp director. As before the war, Fumiko did both paid and unpaid jobs that could be scheduled around her family duties. When her four sons were little, she worked at home doing clerical piecework as a typist for the Donnelly Corporation, addressing envelopes: "They'd give me the mailing list and I wrote a mile a minute…I think I did 8,000 a week." Placing her typewriter on the kitchen counter, she would sit with her youngest child on her lap, and while she typed, "we would sing nursery rhymes and stories."[80] At the same time, she helped the minister of the All People's church by taking dictation and answering mail. From 1963 until her retirement in 1985, she worked for the A. W. Anderberg Manufacturing Company, starting as a secretary and becoming office manager.

Nisei women also began to move into professional work, and as in the prewar period, two key avenues were teaching and nursing. Rose Honda remembered of her peers, "the immediate friends that I had were going to college. And at that time, they were majoring in either…becoming a teacher, or nurse, or engineers. And many secretarial positions were opened."[81] Moreover, the Nisei were beginning to secure jobs outside the ethnic community. For both men and women, Midori Nishi found that the "number of professional and technical workers almost doubled…in the County, this group representing three per cent of the employed Japanese in 1940 compared to five per cent in 1950."[82] Nishi attributed this development to the large number of Nisei aged 25 to 35 entering the labor force, as well as to the growing number of Nisei who had by 1950 received college education or advanced technical training. The GI Bill and mounting civil rights challenges to racial discrimination also contributed to gradually widening opportunities for Japanese Americans and other people of color in postwar America.

Haruko Sugi Hurt was one of the thousands of returning veterans who entered college under the 1944 GI Bill, which provided government funding for higher education and the purchase of homes. For Haruko, it meant the realization of a long-deferred dream: "Many, many, many years later I'm going to college. But I didn't feel too out of place because there were a lot of male veterans" also attending college under the GI Bill.[83] In 1946 she was discharged from her Women's Army Corps job in Washington, D.C. and rejoined her parents in Gardena. Lacking a car and dependent on bus transportation, she enrolled at the closest school, the University of Southern California. In three years Haruko finished a BA degree in sociology and then spent two more years in the USC School of Social Work, where she met her European American husband. They married in 1951, just three years after the overturning of the California anti-miscegenation law—another sign of postwar change, although it took many years for the larger society to fully accept interracial marriage. Haruko got a job with the Los Angeles Girl Scouts Council and her husband worked for the Veterans Administration Psychiatric Hospital. Eventually, while her children were growing up, she began teaching parent-education courses in adult school and then, after separating from her husband, offered evening classes in English as a Second Language.

Before the war, teachers had comprised the most sizeable professional group among Japanese Americans, and the majority—mainly Issei—had worked within the ethnic enclave, teaching at Japanese language schools or offering classes in Japanese dance, music, and other arts.[84] The Nisei who entered the field of education after the war were able to make new inroads into the public school system, as Rose Honda and Mary Nishi Ishizuka did.

After returning to Los Angeles, Rose Honda, a member of the last graduating class from Manzanar in 1945, had enrolled in the Santa Monica Community College. She first majored in art but realized that she preferred to work with children. When she began to look for a part time job and expressed interest in preschool, she was advised to apply at the Santa Monica Board of Education. "I'll never forget that day," she recalled, "because I was really scared." Nervousness etched in her mind the brick building, the beautiful hardwood floors, and the "staircase I had to go up, and every step seemed to squeak.... I think I was scared in terms of, well, will they really accept me? Or will they hire me? I kind of had that feeling, because I was Japanese."[85] Fortunately, on the strength of her application statement and without an interview, Rose was hired by Mary Alice Mallum, the director of the Santa Monica childcare centers. Rose worked as a student aide and then as a substitute at the McKinley Childcare Center, one of the state-run centers established during the war to provide childcare for women working in defense factories. By the time she graduated, she was hired as a teacher at the center, eventually becoming the director of the John Adams Childcare Center in Santa Monica. Rose would spend 39 years in the Santa Monica Unified School System.

Mary Nishi Ishizuka's path was rockier at first, but the shifting postwar racial dynamics in southern California provided her an entry into the public school system. After completing three years at Nebraska Wesleyan during the war, she returned to Los Angeles and finished her degree at UCLA. Because she wanted to teach, she spent another year getting a secondary education credential. Then, she said, "That's when I felt the discrimination. When I went to the placement bureau, they said they were not accepting Japanese secondary teachers, only in elementary.... That was the biggest blow to me, as far as being discriminated against. I had no place to go, because I had a secondary credential, and no one was going to hire me."[86] Mary then got "a lucky break": A principal from the Lafayette Junior High School in downtown Los Angeles, because of the diversity of the Japanese American, Latino, and African American students, was seeking a "Japanese teacher."[87] Mary became one of the first two Japanese American secondary teachers in Los Angeles.[88]

Meeting the needs of disadvantaged students at Lafayette would open future opportunities for Mary. She taught a special education class that included reading. Because so many of the students entering junior high school did not know how to read, and because of her experience, Mary was asked to become a consultant for the Los Angeles city schools, advising teachers on reading. "After that," she said, "I had my choice of schools to go to."[89] She went to the highly regarded Webster Junior High School and taught there until the birth of her son Kirk, taking a maternity leave. Like the other Nisei women, Mary structured her employment around childrearing duties. She went back to teach for a couple years, then retired after the birth of her daughter Kathy, having spent about 11 years in junior high school education. When her children were grown, she taught for five more years at the Cleveland High School in the San Fernando Valley.

Mary's older sister Midori Nishi was one of the early Nisei women to become a college professor. Midori had started pre-med studies at UCLA in 1941, just before the outbreak of war. Mary recalled, "She was very bitter; she had to leave UCLA and start all over at another university."[90] After receiving her BA in geography from Nebraska Wesleyan in May 1945, Midori decided to pursue graduate work. After a brief postwar return to Los Angeles, she entered the highly ranked geography program at Clark University in Massachusetts with a scholarship, receiving her MA degree in August 1946. She taught for a year as an instructor at Wellesley College and then began doctoral studies at the University of Washington. In September 1950, she became a tenure-track professor of geography at the Los Angeles State College (now California State University, Los Angeles).[91] In 1955 she completed her PhD in geography with a minor in the "Far Eastern and Russian Institute."[92] Her dissertation examined change and continuity in a community she knew well, the Japanese Americans in Los Angeles County, from 1940 to 1950.

Other female professionals, like Dr. Sakaye Shigekawa, also began to move beyond the confines of the ethnic enclave. The prestigious fields of medicine and dentistry drew ambitious Nisei, although in the early postwar years they were largely limited to co-ethnic patients.[93] Shigekawa was a pioneer in establishing a multiethnic practice. When war broke out, she was a resident at the Los Angeles County Hospital, which immediately dismissed all Japanese American staff. She served as a physician in the Santa Anita Assembly Center in 1942, until accepting a medical residency in Chicago. There she soon joined another doctor in private practice, mainly serving Irish, German, and Polish patients, along with a growing stream of Japanese American resettlers. In 1948 she rejoined her family in Los Angeles, where her mother ran a grocery store.

Residential segregation was the first obstacle Shigekawa confronted. In August 1949 she opened an office in Hollywood on Santa Monica Boulevard, a major thoroughfare, starting a practice that would endure for more than five decades. She and her family were not well received at the outset—their white neighbors held meetings and tried to utilize restrictive housing covenants to get rid of them; however, the landmark cases of 1948 and 1953 made this tactic ineffectual. Shigekawa remarked, "[N]eedless to say, most of these people became patients of mine. So in spite of the fact that they tried to get my folks out of there, they became my patients. As a matter of fact, I took care of most of all of them until they died.[94] Over the course of her practice, her area changed from a predominantly European American population to an Armenian and Latino one. She estimated that her patient pool in the beginning was half white and half Asian American (Japanese, Chinese, and Filipinos).

Opening a medical office outside the ethnic community was only one hurdle; whether male or female, Japanese American physicians like Shigekawa also faced entrenched racism within the southern California hospital system. As before the war, she and other returning Nikkei doctors could not obtain hospital privileges. She recounted, "I applied [for privileges] at the Presbyterian Hospital, but once they saw me, they couldn't take me. They didn't even answer my application . . . we had a hard time in Los Angeles in the early days."[95] She and the other Japanese American physicians relied on a crucial prewar institution established by the Issei: "We were very fortunate to have a Japanese Hospital. At least we were able to deliver babies and do our surgery there."[96] In 2000, Shigekawa estimated that she had delivered between 20,000 and 30,000 babies in her career. If it had not been for the Japanese Hospital, which opened in 1929, the Issei and Nisei doctors would have had to refer their patients with surgical and obstetrical needs to white doctors who had privileges at all the other hospitals.[97] Eventually the steadfast efforts of ethnic medical practitioners, in tandem with the impact of the civil rights movement and ethnic consciousness movements, would wear down some of the racial barriers. Shigekawa thought she might have been the first doctor of Asian descent accepted at the Queen of Angels Hospital and believed that she became in 1977 the first woman chief of staff at any Los Angeles hospital.

Shigekawa entered medicine with a clear recognition of the obstacles of racism and sexism. She had "accepted the fact that being Japanese I'll have more difficulty. And being a woman, I knew it wasn't going to be really easy going.... I just felt if anyone did something, I'd challenge them on it."[98] During her prewar internship in Michigan, she did challenge prejudiced co-workers, including a surgeon. Within the Japanese Hospital, Shigekawa was one of several women physicians. She recalled that the male Japanese American doctors treated her well and fairly, perhaps because of their shared experiences of travail in camp: "I was the youngest one in ... Santa Anita. So as far as working with the older Nisei doctors, it was really a privilege. They were very sincere and honest, and they did good work in comparison to some of the doctors I worked with in Chicago. They weren't out to get all that they could get financially. They were really dedicated. They taught me a lot while I was in camp."[99] Although Shigekawa's indomitable attitude was probably a factor, her career also traces slow changes in race relations in southern California medical institutions and practice.

In other professions such as law, persisting racial and gender barriers proved even more difficult to surmount. In February 1947, the *Rafu Shimpo* heralded the return to Los Angeles of attorney Chiyoko Sakamoto, who "passed the California state bar in 1939 and is believed to be the only Nisei woman lawyer in the state. She is one of the three in the United States." Sakamoto, the *Rafu* reported, "is now with the law offices of Hugh E. MacBeth."[100] It is perhaps a sign of efforts by minorities to reach across ethnic lines that Sakamoto was hired by the firm of an African American civil rights lawyer. She appears to have been unusual in finding work in a non-Nisei law firm, although her clientele may still have been primarily co-ethnic. Of the fourteen lawyers listed in the 1953 Japanese Directory of Southern California, 13 (like Hugh MacBeth) were located in central Los Angeles and one in Boyle Heights in East Los Angeles,[101] both areas of population concentration for returning Japanese Americans and other minority groups.

A small number of women journalists covered community and mainstream news for the ethnic press. Mary Oyama Mittwer and Mary Kitano both wrote weekly columns for the *Rafu Shimpo* when it re-started in 1946. Oyama (who wrote under her maiden name in the *Rafu*) signaled her postwar attitude and hopes in the title of her Friday column, first called "New World Coming!" and then "New World A-Coming"[102] —a title borrowed, with the African American author's permission, from a book by Roi Ottley; from January 17, 1947, she renamed it "Reveille," intended as a wake-up call for the Nisei. She discussed how to deal with racism in the workplace and in oneself, reviewed books by Louis Adamic, Sinclair Lewis, Carlos Bulosan, and Nisei war hero Ben Kuroki, mused on whether or not the term "Nisei" was derogatory (she believed it was not), urged university students to consider answering the need for club advisers for the younger Nisei, and pushed her audience to become both more politically active and more interactive with non–Japanese Americans. Mary Kitano, who wrote a Saturday column called "Snafu," often covered political figures and issues like the establishment of a state Fair Employment Practices Committee, as well as reviewing plays, recounting community doings, and offering glimpses of the whirlwind life of reporters on the beat. Notably, Kitano worked for both the mainstream and ethnic press: Before starting her "Snafu" column,[103] she had gotten a job working for the City News Service, "on account of Earl O'Day, former Daily News man now with the War Relocation Authority office here."[104] In her assessment of the attitudes she encountered from other reporters working for the metropolitan papers, she said, "[O]ne finds the majority of fair-minded and liberal reporters on the Daily News."[105] In May 1947 the *Rafu Shimpo* proudly announced that Kitano was "now employed in the library (the 'morgue' in journalistic parlance) of the L.A. Daily News. She thus becomes one of the first Nisei employees of a large local metropolitan daily."[106] Mary Oyama was not paid (at least, not initially) by the *Rafu*, and it is likely that Mary Kitano wrote "Snafu" for free as well, but the latter appears to have been successful in breaking into the then largely male and white ranks of the "Fourth Estate" in Los Angeles.

Katsumi Hirooka Kunitsugu, after graduating from journalism school at the University of Wisconsin, returned to Los Angeles and eventually got a job at *Crossroads*, the "first Nisei Weekly,"[107] established in 1948. Joining the staff in 1949, she recalled, "It didn't pay very much," but it enabled her to leave the hostel where she was living and to share a rental apartment with two women friends. *Crossroads*, an English-language paper, presented a Nisei perspective on news in the Japanese American community, so "there were a lot of articles on jobs and the first Nisei doing this and that and the other," with thorough coverage of the social scene and sports.[108] The newspaper filled an important need by reporting on "what was going on in the community that the big uptown papers [ignored]—the general press never covered the minority communities. So that's what we did."[109] Although they covered the same news, Kunitsugu characterized *Crossroads* as being more liberal than the *Rafu Shimpo*.

Kunitsugu's beat was primarily social news, "So I covered a lot of Nisei weddings. Everyone was getting married [chuckles] in those days. I don't know how many trips I made to the Shatto Chapel of the First Congregational Church where people were always getting married, and I wrote about this wedding or that wedding, and went to all the dances, because being a reporter you'd get in free. [laughs]"[110] Kunitsugu herself soon joined the ranks of the married Nisei, having met her husband Kango Kunitsugu—an engineering draftsman and part-time sportswriter—at *Crossroads*. She left her job in mid-1950 when she became pregnant. However, she then began to write a column with her husband since it didn't require going in to the office but could be composed at home. While raising her children, Kunitsugu wrote off and on for *Crossroads* and also started to do a column "Carousel" for the *Kashu Mainichi*.[111] Like most of the other Nisei women profiled in this chapter, she "stayed home full-time until the kids went to school full-time."[112] In the late-1960s she began to "put in more hours at the *Kashu Mainichi*," always returning home by 3 p.m. and spending considerable time driving her children to and from school.[113] She became the editor of the English section of the *Kashu Mainichi* until 1973.[114] While working as a secretary to a Nisei restaurateur in Little Tokyo, she became involved with the Little Tokyo Business Association and Nisei Week, and in 1975 began a long career as executive secretary for the Japanese American Cultural and Community Center in Little Tokyo. The entire body of her work—starting in the early postwar period—can be seen as a creative effort to strengthen and develop the Japanese American community and several of its core institutions.

A few Nisei women broke into the arts and entertainment in the hardscrabble early years after the war. The *Rafu Shimpo*, like *Crossroads* eager to publicize every possible "Nisei first" or achievement, placed glittering tidbits of news about local and national Japanese American artists, writers, and performers amid the reportage on legal battles waged over escheat cases and restrictive covenants, the fate of wartime renunciants, and sports. Several women dancers and singers provided exciting examples of second-generation accomplishment. Classical Japanese dancer and teacher Fujima Kansuma (also known as Sumako Hamaguchi, her given name), a Los Angeles Nisei who received training in Tokyo from 1934 to 1939, attracted the attention of a War Relocation Authority official by her performances in the Rohwer Camp. After the war he proposed and planned a two-month tour in the summer of 1946 that would allow her to introduce her art form to audiences on the East Coast, including a meeting with Martha Graham.[115] The new media of the era also presented a fresh opportunity: In 1947 the *Rafu* noted, "A dream-come-true in Nisei television was spun last night in Hollywood when one Fujima Kansuma, noted Japanese artist, went under the arc lights," doing a dance and interview for a program sponsored by the Urban League of Los Angeles.[116] She performed frequently within as well as outside the ethnic community, while also continuing to teach; in November 1946 it was reported that 50 of her 136 pupils had returned to Los Angeles. In addition to promoting Japanese dance in the larger society, Fujima Kansuma's school became an institution within the reconstructed Japanese American community. In 2007, she was honored for having taught more than 1,000 dance students.[117]

In this period, a few Nisei women also succeeded in breaking into the world of modern Western dance. For the first time since her incarceration in the Gila Camp in Arizona, Yuriko Amemiya returned to her hometown Los Angeles in March 1946 as a member of Martha Graham's dance company that performed "Appalachian Spring" at the Philharmonic.[118] In what must have been a daringly early public expression of a Japanese American's experiences of wartime uprooting, in October 1946 Amemiya presented a dance recital with Merce Cunningham and John Erdman, performing a solo piece "based on Walt Whitman's 'Shut Not Your Door,' which will express the emotional effects of west coast evacuation in 1942."[119] In 1950 she returned again to Los Angeles with the Martha Graham troupe to perform in a sold-out show, dancing the part of Cordelia in a treatment of King Lear.[120]

A major break from Asian typecasting—perhaps the most monumental— came in 1950 with the news of Nisei soprano Tomiko Kanazawa's acclaimed performance as "Mimi" in the Pacific Opera Company's production of La Boheme in San Francisco. Kanazawa, a "local [Los Angeles] girl who made good in a big way,"[121] the Rafu triumphantly proclaimed, "broke from the traditional casting of all Japanese and Japanese American sopranos in the one role of Cho Cho san in 'Madame Butterfly' by playing Mimi."[122] The newspaper called her casting "a brave step forward" on the part of the Pacific Opera Company—a step vindicated by the lavish praise of all the critics.[123] Perhaps emblematic of both the beginnings of new opportunities and the lingering constraints in postwar race relations, Kanazawa made her 1946 operatic debut as "Cho Cho San" in Philadelphia, reprised the role in an NBC television program in February 1950, and again performed as the lead (to enthusiastic reviews) in the same season as her stint as "Mimi." A model of community spirit as well as Nisei achievement, Kanazawa donated her services for a benefit concert in Little Tokyo in January 1951 to help raise funds for a Japanese community center.

Rafu readers might also thrill to the story ("Farm girl makes good on Broadway") of ballet dancer Dorothy Tomiko Maruki, who grew up in Florin, just south of Sacramento in the central valley of California: "Without any boys in the family, the girl helped with just about everything under the sun; toiled on the farm from dawn to dusk."[124] Despite discouragement by her widowed Issei mother and the uprooting of war, Maruki held fast to her dream. In 1943 she left the Jerome Camp in Arkansas for New York where she entered the Metropolitan Opera School of Ballet; she subsequently auditioned for the San Carlo opera company and was selected out of 15 competitors. The *Rafu* breathlessly reported that the "exotic" Maruki, a "farm girl who, within a short span of five years, has skyrocketed to ballet fame and achievement" would be appearing in the San Carlo opera company at the Philharmonic auditorium in Los Angeles.[125] Amid the harsh realities of postwar resettlement, Nisei readers of the *Rafu* may have nurtured their own hopes of following a version of the script outlined in the reporter's conclusion: "Hard work is ahead for Miss Maruki...but this is a success story. It is something that only God and Fate make for those who have ambitions in getting to the top."[126] Many Nisei and Issei, of course, were preoccupied with the day-to-day struggle to make ends meet.

Compared with their brothers and male cousins, Nisei women appeared to be making more gains in the work force in the early postwar period. At a San Francisco Bay area meeting of the California Council for Civic Unity in October 1947, it was reported that "Japanese American women are the only minority group in California reporting an encouraging employment prospect."[127] According to their findings, "Prospects for Nisei women in clerical and semi-skilled work were termed 'good'; or 'better than before the war.' Issei women too have been able to get more work in fields which were not available to them before the evacuation." By contrast, the CCU stated, Nisei men had been less fortunate, "generally forced to take up manual work in the west coast, though many have migrated to the east for jobs equivalent to their skills and training."[128]

In the late 1940s and early 1950s, continuing larger social trends that began during the war, more married women as well as single women remained in the work force. For many families, the rise in female economic participation proved vital to entering the ranks of the middle class.[129] Wives who could afford to do so tended to leave employment when they had children, and many returned when their children entered school full time. Like their mainstream peers, urban Nisei women like Esther Takei Nishio, Haruko Sugi Hurt, Katsumi Hirooka Kunitsugu, Marion Funakoshi Manaka, and Mary Nishi Ishizuka stayed home to rear children, some caring for elderly parents and in-laws as well; all five re-entered wage paid work when their children grew older. Marion, who juggled childrearing and elder care, later worked in a pearl jewelry store and helped out in a brother-in-law's grocery store, explaining, "I never had a steady job, but just filling in for someone. That was just so I could be home with the children."[130] Sakaye Shigekawa and Rose Honda, who did not marry, pursued satisfying long-term careers that gave them independence and autonomy. The paid and unpaid work of Nisei women provided crucial support for newly returned families in a time of stress and vulnerability, strengthened the recuperating economy of the ethnic community, and enabled them to play a role in the erosion of longstanding racial barriers in a range of fields.

"Up in Atom!": Postwar Girls' and Young Women's Clubs

Amid the disruptions of resettlement and the exigencies of finding work, young Nisei women turned again to peer networks for camaraderie and recreation. Twenty years after a girls' club member wrote the first letter to the editor of the fledgling English-language section of the *Rafu Shimpo*, one of the early letters to the editor of the re-started *Rafu* in April 1946 came from "several groups of high school age (Nisei girls)" seeking the newspaper's help in forming a baseball league: "That is, if any interested person could manage a league for the girls, we feel that with the help of publishing a notice to sign up Nisei girls' teams, a successful league may be obtained. Any suggestions?"[131] The group, perhaps daunted by recognition of the postwar struggle for jobs, housing and family rebuilding that consumed most Japanese Americans' time, signed themselves "Doubtfully yours." The editor replied sympathetically that, although the newspaper was not able to sponsor a league, it would "forward names of interested clubs to the right party who may be able to get the organizations together in competition."[132] In the early postwar years, such Nisei youth athletic organizations and social clubs would stage a remarkable comeback.

From the beginning of 1946 the *Rafu Shimpo* recorded the appearance of old and new Nisei organizations. Perhaps the first mentioned was the L.A. Junior Coeds, a group formed in January by 15 teenage Nisei girls in Hollywood, who met on Saturdays at the Presbyterian Church Manse.[133] Also in January, a local European American Girl Scout leader advertised efforts to start a Nisei troop, and the Moderneers, a girls' club affiliated with the Koyasan Betsuin (a Buddhist temple), elected new officers as well as organizing a softball team.[134] In her *Rafu Shimpo* column "Snafu," Mary Kitano heralded the reappearance of Nisei clubs such as the "glamorous Stardusters and the Manzaknights, formerly of Manzanar," admitting partiality to her own, the Calico Cats—an organization of women journalists that also formed in Manzanar.[135]

Premature and preemptive concern about the small number of postwar youth groups and the related potential for Nisei delinquency prompted a front page editorial on February 1, issuing the call, "Let's get organized!" The writer remarked on the Nisei's prewar delinquency rate having been "the lowest of any racial group according to the police records" and attributed this "splendid record" both to parental control and "the young peoples [sic] organizations such as the Boy Scouts, Girl Scouts, church clubs, and the Y clubs, then in existence in Los Angeles."[136] Having conveniently forgotten the grumbling of Issei parents and older Nisei about the perceived frivolity of the numerous prewar clubs and their jam-packed social calendar, or perhaps having developed renewed appreciation for them in the light of postwar anxieties, the writer sternly urged, "Today with delinquency rates (not Nisei) at a high, steps must be taken to remove our youth from the streets. Now more than ever the leadership and supervision of the youth's organizations are needed. Where dozens of such organizations were once in existence, today a mere handful supply the need for the more than 30 per cent of the pre-war population that has returned to Los Angeles." The writer lamented that, unlike other West Coast Japanese American communities that seemed to be forming young people's clubs, "The Los Angeles area with the greatest number of young people needing guidance seems to be lacking the leadership to provide for this need."[137]

Interest was certainly not lacking among the youth, particularly the girls. Within the next few months the increasing club activities of high school and college-age Nisei women made the news: The Stardusters elected new officers and discussed sponsoring a dance as well as adding bowling and basketball to their calendar.[138] *Rafu* writer Harry K. Honda enthusiastically reported that the Modernaires, another Manzanar group, and the Bambiis, a "group of Roosevelt High School cherubs" would bring "bobby-sox glamour" to the prelims of the Los Angeles Nisei Basketball Tournament in May.[139] Chi Alpha Delta, the first Japanese American (and Asian American) sorority—founded at UCLA in 1929—decided to reactivate the group and held an orientation tea welcoming all Nisei women at UCLA.[140] The J.U.G.s (which stood for "Just Us Girls"), a club for teenagers, elected new cabinet members, and the Maharanias installed their new officers in an "impressive candle-light ceremony" at the All-People's Christian Church, followed by "a semi-formal installation dance."[141] The single page of the *Rafu Shimpo*'s English-language section steadily included more and more news of club meetings, officer elections, wienie bakes, socials, "skate fests," and dances. The patterns set by the prewar clubs clearly retained appeal.

As in the 1930s, postwar clubs enabled young Nisei women to initiate parentally sanctioned socializing with young men. Yukio Kawaratani, a member of the Royal Knights boys club in Long Beach, recalled that his sister and her friends belonged to a counterpart organization, the Hardells: "They said it was short for 'Harbor Girls.' We guys jokingly referred to them as the Hard-ups. . . . Their primary objective seemed to be to hold Saturday night dance parties to which they would invite the guys, including the members of the Royal Knights." The Hardells also organized dance practices, "smaller jam sessions where our family's large portable 78rpm and 33rpm record player was the main source of music. That's where we learned to dance the jitterbug, and then later, the cha cha."[142]

Contrary to the fears of the *Rafu*'s English-section editor, or perhaps partly spurred by his rallying cry, the number of Nisei youth clubs mushroomed at a "brisk" and "startling" pace. In its 1946 Holiday Issue, the *Rafu Shimpo* placed the year-end tally of Nisei social and athletic groups at 85, admitting that its list was not complete.[143] Reporter Harry K. Honda took special note of "the

concentrated numbers of teen-age groups, especially among the girls. This pattern follows the intensity of Nisei clubs prior to evacuation."[144] Of the 85 Nisei
organizations, Honda found only 39 for young men, and 20 of them were
"strictly minor athletic groups." He speculated that male groups were slower to
form, perhaps "due to danger of the draft axing membership." Ten months later,
in October 1947, Mary Oyama likewise noted that "there are numerous girls'
and young women's clubs and organizations but very few groups for boys and
young men. The fair sex declare that they would [be] very glad to invite the boys
to their parties, socials, dances, and doings, but 'where are all the boys?'" Oyama
advised, "For you boys who think that you find life dull and would like to meet
some of the opposite sex, we'd suggest that you get yourselves organized into
some sort of club."[145] She promised to relay news of any new young men's groups
to the girls and two weeks later announced the formation of two boys' clubs at
the All People's Christian Church.

The emergence of interethnic groups was a significant change of the postwar period. Honda noted that about one-eighth of the Los Angeles area clubs
had mixed membership, which he attributed to the sponsoring organizations
being churches "which were the first agencies offering a varied social program
for the returnees this past year."[146] One of the first recorded such groups was
the Intercultural Tri-Y, a YWCA-affiliated girls' club formed at the University
High School in West Los Angeles. Although most of the officers were Japanese
American, the club had two presidents, Gladys Chikazawa and Barbara
Hamilton, and likewise boasted two advisors, Jean Evans and Haru Iwanaga. The
Intercultural Tri-Y's projected activities included sports and service: "Aside from
the basketball games scheduled for the coming semester, the girls are planning to
make decorative plates for the Hospital patients."[147]

The interethnic Tri-Y club would have met with approval from Nisei leaders
who, Harry Honda reported, "have been strong in advising the clubbers to be
more cosmopolitan in their social outlook by actively joining existing Caucasian
or non-Japanese groups in the community. It has been pointed out that Nisei
clubs will only continue to breed the inferiority complex that the Japanese suffered during the earlier days of residence in the city."[148] No mention was made
of the racial discrimination that in the 1920s and 1930s had barred Nisei and
other racial-ethnic youth from extracurricular activities and public facilities in
many districts of southern California. The long shadow cast by the camps made
the ethnic clubs a haven for Nisei youth, but simultaneously heightened anxiety among second-generation leaders who feared that "self-segregation" and
"clannishness" might foster persisting vulnerability. For example, while a student at UCLA, Mary Nishi Ishizuka was approached by a sociology professor
who had sponsored the prewar Nisei Bruin Club and wanted to restart it—she
declined, saying, "This is the reason that we were probably sent to camp, because

people didn't know us, because we stayed in Japanese groups." Although Ishizuka remained active within the Japanese American community, she also joined outside organizations, musing, "If people knew us better, I thought more people wouldn't have been as anti-Japanese as they were."[149] The youth organizations continued to burgeon despite the ambivalence of some senior Nisei.

Indeed, the groundswell of Nisei youth wishing to form clubs quickly surpassed the number of available advisers. In December 1946, the *Rafu* issued a plaintive call for Girl Scout leaders.[150] In her January 17, 1947 column, Mary Oyama begged readers to help out, announcing: "Calling UCLA, USC, LACC, Chapman, and all other colleges and universities—this is an SOS. Wanted: any number of altruistic, social-conscious persons from the social science departments, (graduate or undergraduate) to serve as advisors to Nisei youth clubs and organizations."[151] She stressed the urgency of the need, reporting that "the various Nisei clubs are desperate for lack of leaders to aid them as counsellors [sic] or advisors."[152] In October 1947, Enid Okawara, a social worker at the International Institute in Boyle Heights echoed this plea with an "urgent call for adult advisers." Social workers were sought to work with junior and senior high school groups. Okawara noted, "Many teenage groups have been organized but are not able to 'function fully' because of the lack of adult leadership."[153] In 1949 Oyama issued another call, telling "Reveille" readers that there was "still more than a crying need for more chaperones, more counsellors [sic] and advisors for clubs of all ages and particularly for the under 21 groups."[154]

Rose Honda and Mary Nishi Ishizuka were two of the young adults who stepped in to serve as leaders advising younger Nisei girls. Their joint efforts would nurture one of the liveliest girls' groups to form in the early postwar period, the Atomettes. When she and Mary started the group, Rose said, "[I] thought I knew everything (laughs), but I didn't."[155] The seven girls began as sixth graders. The club had its roots in Rose's Sunday school teaching and her sense of the need for positive activities for the girls, whose families were preoccupied with the struggle to resettle and find work. According to Rose, the Atomettes were the first group formed at the West Los Angeles United Methodist Church, a Japanese American congregation, after the war. Rose Honda recalled that the atom bomb was in the news, and "here were these young girls who were in their very young teens, just as energetic and explosive. They said, 'Let's call ourselves Atomettes.'"[156] The name they chose for their club perhaps reflects the vigor of the late-1940s campaign by the U.S. government, corporations, and media to persuade the public of the potential for peacetime atomic energy uses.[157] It may also reflect the young age of the girls and their lack of a sense of connection to the atomic bombings in Japan.

As for the prewar Nisei girls' clubs, service was an important component of the Atomettes' activities and they had great impact in shaping church traditions after the war. Rose Honda explained:

They printed a newsletter for the church. They were the ones who started the bazaar. They called it May Bazaar, and...they went out to the strawberry fields, and picked the strawberries, and made strawberry jam, and sold it. They were the ones who started the Easter breakfast.... They did all the cooking, and they must have served 50 or 75, or more people—seven girls. And they were the ones who started the choir.[158]

The Atomettes' dedicated advisers strove to provide opportunities for which resettling Issei parents had little time or resources. Busy with her career, other organizations, and her family, Mary modestly downplayed her role, "I was primarily their chauffeur. I was the only one who had a car."[159] However, Rose credited Mary, with her geography background, as the one who "planned trips to go to different museums. And she was the one who introduced us to the Laguna Art Festival, which was very, very new to us. [She] even took us out to Knotts Berry Farm when there was a farm, not just an entertaining park."[160] As before the war, such club outings—including trips to San Francisco and Monterey—greatly expanded the cultural horizons of the Nisei girls. The club also provided an avenue for the girls to express their theatrical creativity. They "got to be very well known for their skits"[161] and every year put on a Christmas play.

Club participation not only introduced the Atomettes to a larger world, but also enabled them to develop leadership skills, to channel youthful energy into creative endeavors valued by their community, and to have a hand in shaping institutional practices. They may have been unusual in the extent of their impact, but they exemplify the ways in which young women's organizations played significant roles in the rebuilding of community during the early postwar period. Their experience and confidence gained from club involvement have continued to benefit the Japanese American enclave. In assessing the Atomettes' recreational and social service activities, Mary said, "They just did all kinds of things. I think that's why they're such great parents and community leaders now."[162] As in the case of many other prewar and postwar club members, the ties forged by the Atomettes would knit a sturdy fabric of lifelong friendship and support. Reflecting the strength of their camaraderie over the course of 50 years, the Atomettes and their advisers Rose and Mary continued to get together several times a year despite residing in different parts of California.[163]

The Nisei social organizations mushroomed so quickly that by January 1947, representatives of more than 20 groups joined to establish an Inter-Club Council to coordinate social activities and avoid overlap. The ICC also stressed "leadership in the community to minimize juvenile delinquency; to serve members in social and group welfare; as well as to solve individual problems."[164] In September 1947, ICC publicity director and Manzaknights member Ralph Lazo accurately predicted that the Nisei social calendar would be filled "to capacity" in the coming months.[165] By December 1950, a Club Service Bureau served as a coordinating organization, with 90 affiliated Nisei groups. As the *Rafu Shimpo* explained, the Bureau "helps arrange dances, programs, parties, etc. It furnishes a listing, advisors, chaperons, entertainers, halls, orchestras." Indicating the presence of lingering anti-Japanese hostility and racial discrimination in some public facilities, the Bureau's role included giving "information about places where Nisei patronage is welcomed."[166] The description of the Bureau's functions hints at the appeal of and need for ethnic social activities during the rocky years of early postwar resettlement.

Japanese American clubs and informal peer networks offered vital support for Nisei youth facing hostility in postwar southern California. After returning to West Los Angeles, Rose Honda's sister "went to University High School, and she said it was not very pleasant. There was still prejudice around. And therefore, the Japanese students just clustered together."[167] Anti-Japanese sentiments persisted at the college level as well. In 1949, as a response to their exclusion from the Greek letter organization system, Nisei women students established Sigma Phi Omega, a group that would become the first Asian American sorority at the University of Southern California. According to Sigma Phi Omega, "Although we did not originate as a sorority, one could speculate that the choosing of Greek letters was a public way of voicing a dissatisfactory opinion about the treatment of Asian American[s], specifically Japanese Americans, by the campus and Greek organizations."[168] As before the war, Nisei youth clubs offered camaraderie and a place of belonging.

By the end of 1950 the extensive *Rafu Shimpo* club directory showed the rapid resurgence of Nisei social organizations, listing more than 200 in the "Southland," half the number at the prewar peak. Of the 170 non-JACL organizations listed in the club directory, at least 78 appear to be girls' or women's clubs; many of the other groups had both male and female members; there were perhaps 28 boys' and men's clubs, including several veterans' associations.[169] As Harry Honda had noted in the 1946 holiday issue, girls' and women's clubs were especially numerous, ranging from YWCA- and church-affiliated groups to International Institute organizations, matrons' groups, high school clubs, and sororities.

Clubs for young single women particularly abounded. For example, Esther Takei Nishio belonged to the Pasonas, for whom she invented the name: "It was 'Pasadena-*onna*,' (laughter) but we shortened it to Pasonas.... And no one knew what it meant, just us."[170] The Pasonas organized activities such as a "Play Nite" at the Pasadena Union Church, offering refreshments and diversion for "bridge fiends, ping pong fans, the parlor game crowd, as well as dance lovers."[171] As their part in the 1947 Summer Frolics Carnival sponsored by a number of Nisei clubs, the Pasonas were in charge of the queen contest.[172] Like most Nisei women's clubs, they also pursued social service, sometimes combining recreation with fund-raising for charity. After they married and had children, they called themselves "Mrs. Pasonas" and took part in a new array of Japanese American community activities.[173]

As before the war, Nisei young women's clubs like the Atomettes and the Pasonas channeled their energies into a range of service projects. Awareness of the economic hardships faced by many of their families and community influenced some of their service choices. As during the Great Depression, some clubs gathered food for needy families at holiday time. In 1947 the enigmatically named Luknes held a successful Thanksgiving drive, collecting 200 cans, a turkey, a box of food, and a $10 contribution.[174] The "Hot Rods," a high school girls' club at the Winona trailer park, sold hot dogs to raise money ($7.40) for the Nisei Fellowship of the local Baptist Church.[175] In 1950, a Christmas Cheer campaign spearheaded by a wide array of Nisei organizations and church groups collected $1,450 in donations as well as toys, canned food, and other presents for the less fortunate in the Japanese American community; young women's clubs such as the Auxiliarettes, Gems, Maharanias, Michiliennes, Silhouettes, and Voguettes raised funds, knitted mittens, and packed and sorted the gifts.[176]

Aiding hospital patients also proved popular. Although southern California hospitals were slow to extend operating privileges to Japanese American doctors, they were not averse to accepting the charitable efforts of Nisei girls. Beginning in March 1947, members of the Miss Teens, a club organized by the International Institute, volunteered to help at the Los Angeles General Hospital, "visiting patients, writing letters for them," and assisting hospital chaplains.[177] In the following month, patients at the hospital received fans made by the Modernaires, with a picture on one side and a poem on the other.[178] The Camilles, a social service club, sponsored a fall benefit recital—featuring local Nisei singer (and YMCA secretary) Sue Takimoto—to raise funds for orphanages, child welfare, and hospitals.[179]

Many young women's organizations set their sights on serving a wider community than ever before. In addition to local projects, groups increasingly took on international causes. For example, the MIY (Members of Intercultural Youths) Club at University High School in West Los Angeles boasted 35 Nisei girl members who, by December 1946, had "(1) sent boxes of food and clothing to needy Dutch girls in Rijivijk, Holland, and to bombed-out Japanese school girl victims of Osaka, Japan; (2) knitted many pairs of bed socks for the Red Cross; (3) made 'tray favors' (Christmas tree decorations) for wounded GI's in hospitals," and had in mind "other worthwhile projects to enrich the lives of their fellow humans."[180] In the same year, the teenage girls' club JUGs began a clothing drive for the needy in Japan.[181] Indeed, Japan relief work motivated many organizations. Rose Honda and Mary Nishi Ishizuka, the busy advisers of the

Atomettes, also helped found the Windsors, a social service organization for Nisei women in West Los Angeles. In October 1949, having raised funds from drives, dances, and other events, the Windsors sent "their third and largest shipment of relief packages" of food and clothing, valued at $300, to typhoon victims in Japan.[182]

As in the prewar days, dances continued to be a favorite recreational and fund raising activity. For example, the Modernaires' Benefit Dance at the Royal Palms Hotel on September 14, 1946, drew a capacity crowd eager to dance to Phil Carreon's orchestra and listen to songs rendered by Mary Kageyama Nomura, the former "Songbird of Manzanar." Delighted by their "grand success," the Modernaires reported they would donate $100 from the sum raised by the dance to the Japan Relief Fund.[183]

International efforts were not limited to Japan. When the YWCA held its second annual bazaar in downtown Los Angeles to benefit the "Round-the-World YWCA Reconstruction Fund which will train 'Y' leaders and help rebuild physically YWCA's throughout Europe and the Orient," two Nisei groups—the Luanans and the Luknes—participated with booths.[184] Many Nisei high school girls also took part in another multi-ethnic YWCA fund raising effort to benefit the same cause, presenting a play based on "the imaginary conversations of persons now living in the displaced camps in many parts of the world."[185] These conversations may have seemed less imaginary to the Japanese American young women, themselves only a few years out of the wartime camps, than to the other cast members.

Young women's organizations also focused their attention on Nisei soldiers at home and abroad. Perhaps no other individual did as much as Mary Nakahara/ Yuri Kochiyama, a dynamo who in 1942 had founded the Crusaders club in camp to send morale-boosting mail to GIs and in 1944 began working at the Aloha USO in Hattiesburg, Mississippi. She herself wrote to more than 15,000 Nisei soldiers and continued to send 200 letters a week in 1946.[186] The saga of the Crusaders—although not Yuri Kochiyama's letter-writing—came to a close in August 1946, when her mother and two other representatives of the group donated the organization's remaining $54 to the Japan Relief Fund.[187]

As injured Japanese American veterans arrived to recuperate in southern California facilities, some of the girls' and young women's clubs tried to lift their spirits. For example, in October 1946, the Pasonas held a social at the Union Church in Pasadena for GI patients and enlisted personnel at the McCormack Hospital, inviting the Inner Circle and Maharanias clubs to join them. The *Rafu* reported, "Dancing, highlighted by the singing of Yukio Ogawa, tenor, and a repast of fried chicken, attracted more than 60 Nisei."[188] The Pasonas also donated $30 to a drive sponsored by Pasadena Nisei to secure a wheelchair for patients at the McCormack General Hospital.[189] In February 1947, members of the newly formed Chere Amis club visited the McCormack Hospital: "Taking sushi and mochi-gashi [sweet confections], the girls, who are also members of the L.A. Buddhist church YBA [Young Buddhists Association], met and cheered each of the nine veteran patients."[190] In December 1950, members of the Bel Sharmeers, Jilts, Luanans, Pandas, Leilanis, Sigma Phi Omega, and the Deenebs piled into an eight-car caravan to take presents to veterans at the Long Beach and San Fernando Veterans Hospitals.[191] The ethnic community's resources were limited in the trying early postwar years, but young women did what they could to provide a taste of home, build morale, and celebrate the return of Japanese American soldiers.

As before the war, joining clubs gave members access to—and experience in organizing—not only self-improvement and social service activities but also a lively round of leisure pastimes: beach outings, wiener roasts, skatefests at roller rinks, parties, dances, talent shows, and athletics. Team sports remained a passion of Nisei youth. In southern California, the Women's Athletic Association re-emerged as an umbrella organization for steadily growing volleyball, basketball, and softball leagues.[192]

Bowling became especially popular among both women and men. From the late 1940s, the *Rafu Shimpo* devoted considerable space to coverage of kegling competitions, which began early in the resettlement period. In November 1946, for example, Mary Kitano proclaimed a historic first in Nisei women's bowling: a tournament in which 12 teams would vie for a championship trophy and cash prizes.[193] At the end of the next year, 14 teams such as Paul's Café, Waikiki Café, Voguettes, and Miss Takes competed in the Women's Bowling League race.[194] A number of Japanese American women bowled professionally and on local television.[195]

In the difficult period of postwar resettlement, young Nisei women continued to serve as representatives of the ethnic community and particularly of selected elements of Japanese cultural heritage. Echoing their prewar participation, in October 1946, Japanese American girls took part in the International Institute's annual pageant featuring the dances, songs and foods of "more than 20 nationalities." The "Three Graces"—Grace Murakami, Grace Masuda, and Grace Kato— announced their willingness to wear the kimono in the "costume parade of all nations."[196] The following year, the *Rafu Shimpo* proudly announced, "As was the case last year, the Japanese community will contribute its talent and culture" to the Institute's global festival.[197] This "talent and culture" would be embodied by at least 14 kimono-clad Nisei girls who served tea and rice crackers in a "Japanese Tea Garden," as well as Nisei dancer Toshiko Nishi, who performed "The Wisteria Maiden," and Sue Takimoto who sang "Kojo no Tsuki."[198] In 1950, 21 Nisei young adults' and teenage clubs, at least 14 of them women's groups, pitched in to help with the International Institute's annual "Little World's Fair."

With the help of their mothers, the girls prepared sushi and chicken noodles; teenagers in kimono again served tea and rice cakes, while others performed "present and the past modes of 'odori' in Japan."[199] Just as the returning Nisei male veterans served as exemplars of loyal red-blooded Americanism, it was young women who were primarily expected to maintain and perform ethnic culture, both within and outside the Japanese American enclave.

The postwar proliferation of beauty contests reflects the popularity of young women as community representatives, within Japanese American circuits and to the larger society. The *Rafu Shimpo* avidly followed queen-contest races throughout California, chronicling the crowning of Lacuanas member Dusty Matsumoto as queen of the 1947 Summer Frolics Carnival in Pasadena as well as displaying the "bevy of Nisei lovelies" vying for the title of Miss Bussei of the Central California Young Buddhists Association.[200] When Nisei Week festivities resumed in Los Angeles in 1949, the Miss Nisei Week queen contest garnered lavish coverage. Such postwar pageants constituted an arena in which Japanese Americans devised their own criteria of appearance and demeanor, drawing on mainstream American and Japanese cultural forms.[201] Emblematic of the complex expectations of the role, the 1949 Miss Nisei Week and her court were shown wearing both contemporary attire and the kimono, embodying stylish modernity as well as ethnic cultural heritage. Like earlier Nisei Week royalty, they (and the 1950 Nisei Week court) were photographed in kimono when greeting Los Angeles mayor Fletcher Bowron.[202]

In the Cold War era, historian Shirley Jennifer Lim has contended, Japanese American and other Asian American beauty contests simultaneously claimed "racial difference while agitating for inclusion into the nation-state."[203] If ethnic beauty pageants served as a barometer of efforts to prove American identity while also celebrating carefully chosen elements of ethnic culture, then 1950 particularly reflected Japanese American anxieties and hopes. The *Rafu Shimpo* called 1950 "the queenest year in Japanese American history," with two national organizations—the Japanese American Citizens League and the Young Buddhists Association—rivaling "the annual search conducted by cities and states for Miss America."[204] The newspaper listed 18 JACL queens of 1950, 12 Bussei (Buddhist) queens of 1950, six Bussei queens of 1951, and nine special events queens ranging from Miss Nisei Week to Miss Nisei Air Race and Queen of the Salt Lake City Invitational Basketball Tournament.[205]

The young women who entered these pageants fulfilled multiple roles for the community, affirming ethnic pride and serving as representatives between generations and among organizations, as well as between the ethnic group and the larger society. Some were already acting as intermediaries through their jobs. For example, profiles of two contestants in the 1950 queen competition for Miss Western Young Buddhist League placed them in the ranks of Nisei women moving into clerical work in mainstream institutions: winner Rosie Moritomo was a stenographer for the Internal Revenue Service in San Francisco, and Fudge Hamasaki of the Southern California YBL worked as a receptionist at the Bundy Engineering Company.[206] The feminist critique of beauty contests, begun in the 1960s, has evolved to recognize the complicated dynamics of racial-minority and postcolonial pageants. In the early postwar period, the Japanese American queen competitions presented non-white models of female accomplishment and glamour, balancing between the values of the ethnic community and the modern feminine ideal promoted by mainstream media.

Courtship and Marriage

Another arena in which postwar Nisei women—and men—negotiated between the expectations of their immigrant elders and the norms of the larger society was that of marriage. As in the 1920s and 1930s, postwar Nisei youth clubs facilitated heterosexual socializing and courtship. Given the median age of the second generation at the outset of war—18—growing numbers were reaching an age at which they (and some anxious Issei parents) expected they would find partners and establish families. It was also expected that those spouses would be co-ethnic: both the immigrant community and the dominant society still disapproved of interracial marriage, forms of which were then illegal in 29 states and in California until 1948.[207] Unsure of their welcome in many mainstream venues, resettling Nisei found camaraderie, understanding born of shared experience, and opportunities to flirt and socialize at club socials and dances. Such group activities offered comfortable, respectable, peer-monitored settings for meeting and getting to know potential partners. When Esther Takei Nishio was later asked why she had not attended school dances at the Pasadena City College, she said, laughing, "probably because I didn't have a boyfriend."[208] However, she recalled, "once we had a lot of returnees from camps, the Nisei would get together and have our own dance party like at the YMCA or YWCA, maybe once every few months."[209] As one of the earliest returnees before the end of the war, and because of the strictures against interracial dating, Esther may have felt uncomfortable about going to PCC dances as a single Japanese American woman. This was clearly not the case with Nisei dances, where she was also more likely to encounter potential partners acceptable in the eyes of the ethnic and mainstream communities.

Mary Oyama certainly viewed club socials and "entertainments" as an ideal way for boys and girls to meet, as she suggested in 1946 to both young women who complained that "the youth organizations are preponderantly feminine in membership" and to older (over 25) Nisei veterans who lamented that the girls they had known before the war were already married or engaged.[210] The young women's seeming hesitation to initiate contact may have stemmed from concerns about propriety. Said one vet, "If we want to meet some new girls, we have to start all over again. We can't very well go down the street saying, 'Hi ya, babe!' and picking them up just like that—at least not the nice Nisei girls, the kind we'd like to know."[211] Although many Nisei met their future spouses through work, school, camp, family and friends, club activities enabled some "nice Nisei girls" to meet "nice Nisei boys" under "appropriate Emily Post circumstances," while they strove to chart romantic marital paths that would differ from the arranged matches of their parents.[212]

As before the war, the urban Nisei retained their love of waltz, tango, and swing dancing. In the early postwar period, dance was their "primary social activity," according to Mary Nishi Ishizuka.[213] When she was dating George Ishizuka, they went to dances organized by the Pioneers and other Nisei clubs. The Windsors, a Japanese American women's group to which Mary Nishi Ishizuka and Rose Honda both belonged, also sponsored dances. Rose recalled, "We were always in formals, and having a dance at the nicest places, like the Santa Ynez Inn.... It was a very exciting time."[214] The dance floor and other club events remained prime settings for budding Nisei romance.

A club service activity eventually led to marriage for one of the Atomettes: The girls baked cookies and sent them to Japanese American men from West Los Angeles who were serving in the armed forces. One recipient, Jack Fukuda, who was stationed in Korea during the Korean War, shared the treat with his buddies. Sid Yamazaki asked who had sent the cookies and thus learned of the Atomettes. As Rose Honda recounts, "when Sid was discharged from the army and decided to attend UCLA, he decided to investigate this West L.A. United Methodist Church. He came and liked the church. He liked the group. He joined the choir. He joined the fellowship, and then he started dating Kathi [Miyake] Yamazaki, and they got married. (chuckles)"[215]

The "fellowship" to which Rose Honda referred was a young adult group of the West Los Angeles United Methodist Church, established to facilitate the socializing together of college-age Nisei. The group's activities included skiing, bowling, picnicking, Bible study, and potlucks. "Through that many of the members met, and they got married in the church," Rose remembered. "So at that time—it must have been in the '50s—I became the church wedding director for 10 years. It was the most wonderful time. Our church was very busy with weddings at least three times a month and at all times during the year."[216]

Marion Funakoshi Manaka, Mary Nakahara/Yuri Kochiyama, Esther Takei Nishio, Katsumi Hirooka Kunitsugu, Mary Nishi Ishizuka, and Haruko Sugi Hurt joined the throngs of Nisei marching to the altar. Marion, Yuri, and Esther married men they had met in camp. Esther was working in a war surplus store when she got a call from Shig Nishio, newly returned from Michigan, who said, "Remember me? I met you in Santa Anita." Esther thought, "Oh sure, he was so cute, you know!" and said, "Of course I remember you." Accompanied by two buddies, he visited one afternoon and then asked her for a date. "It was a lot of fun," Esther remembered, "I think we went to Ocean Park Pier....I was just swooning! (laughter)"[217] Their courtship blossomed as they attended a series of dances sponsored by various Nisei groups. Katsumi and Mary met their husbands through work. While reporting on social news for *Crossroads*, Katsumi met and married a sportswriter for the weekly. A family friend who owned Frank's Nursery asked Mary, then teaching, to help out during the busy seasons, Christmas and Easter; there she got to know George Ishizuka, a widowed floral designer at the nursery.[218] Haruko—the only one of the six women to marry interracially—met her husband, a European American man 11 years her junior, when both were graduate students in the USC School of Social Work.

As the *Rafu Shimpo* reflected, Nisei women continued to support each other through major life stages with bridal showers, assistance with weddings, and baby showers. Women often announced their engagements at club meetings, as Windsor member Elsie Hatago did by passing around "the traditional box of candy."[219] Clubs frequently took the lead in organizing rituals. In November 1946, for example, 15 members of the Sub-Debs Girl Reserve Club gave a surprise bridal shower for their former president in Manzanar. A week later, the Maharanias held a surprise bridal shower for Aiko Oku, a Los Angeles Community College student and vice president of the club, who was to marry Dick Honma, a veteran of the China-Burma-India Theatre.[220] Although the gifts given were less often mentioned, as during the trying years of the Great Depression, such housewares would have been a help to resettling couples. The Pasonas not only honored Esther Takei Nishio and Sunny Asai, their first two members to marry, with an afternoon tea but also helped cater Esther's wedding.[221] Because hers was the first wedding in the group, it proved to be a learning experience for the Pasonas, who made refreshments for the reception.

A steady stream of announcements in the *Rafu's* "Rice and Rings" column mirrored the increase in Nisei weddings mentioned by Rose Honda. The name of the column reflects the second generation's cultural coalescence, referencing both the centrality of rice in Japanese American culture and the popular mainstream practice of throwing rice at departing newlyweds, as well as the exchange of rings in Western nuptials. As before the war, the bride's attire remained a focal point: "Simplicity with formal dignity marked the wedding" of Mary M. Monji, a prewar Junior Misses member, to Masao Nagahiro at the Methodist Nisei Chapel in the summer of 1946. The bride, wearing a "long sleeve white velvet gown with pearl beaded trimmings and finger-tip veil," was attended by a matron of honor and a flower girl.[222] This couple did not appear to have baishakunin (match-makers), who were occasionally mentioned in postwar wedding announcements. As in the 1930s, early postwar receptions were usually held at the church or at a Chinese restaurant such as San Kwo Low, Manshu Low, or Kwo Nan Low—public spaces where the Issei and Nisei could be sure of welcome.

A new feature of quite a few late-1940s wedding announcements was the inclusion of the bride and groom's wartime incarceration, work, and/or military service. Providing what had become common postwar coordinates for Nisei readers, the *Rafu* reported of Mary Monji and Masao Nagahiro that the groom had "served three years in the Pacific combat zones with military intelligence while the bride relocated to Cleveland after being evacuated to Gila Relocation Center before returning here."[223] Similarly, the announcement of Tsuyako Kasai and George Watanabe's wedding informed readers, "The bride had been working for a millinery shop in New York until her return to Los Angeles last fall. George Watanabe had worked as a radio operator in the U.S. merchant marine in the Atlantic during the war."[224] As Mary Kitano observed, "our parents ask one another what prefectures in Japan they come from. We Nisei eager beavers ask each other what other camps we got fenced in. I'm from Manzanar. Where are you from, mate?"[225] Kitano's words and the early-postwar wedding announcements reflect new generational reference points rooted in shared experience.

As the number of wedding announcements mushroomed (and became increasingly brief by 1950), so did the number of baby showers, a female ritual of increasing importance. In July 1946, the Tartanettes held a surprise baby shower for Mrs. May Hamada, celebrating with a steak barbecue at the home of Grace Yamanaka.[226] Originally formed as a prewar Girl Reserves club at the Union Church, the Tartanettes exemplify women's attachment to their networks, continuing as adults to socialize together. Another surprise shower was thrown for Mrs. Ruth Nitake by women friends who presented a "beautifully decorated cake, with stork carrying a baby, the words 'Congratulations Ruth' were inscribed on the frosting."[227]

Young Nisei couples were part of a much larger trend across the country: in 1940, 42 percent of all American women aged 18 to 24 were married, a figure that swelled to almost 60 percent by 1950. The birth of increasing numbers of Sansei (third generation) babies contributed to the national baby boom trend and to the development of a new round of organizational activities for Japanese American women.

Many of the married Nisei women coordinated three-generational households, taking care of aging Issei parents or in-laws as well as Sansei children. After moving back to Los Angeles from Monterey, Marion Manaka and her husband stayed for a while with Marion's sister's family. Then for about seven years they shared a triplex near the Crenshaw area, with Marion's parents living in the front unit, her sister and brother-in-law in the next one, and Marion, her husband, and children in the rear. Because their mother was bedridden, Marion and her sister Gladys did the cooking for and took care of their parents.[228] Esther Nishio's parents retired to Japan in the late 1950s, but Esther and Shig later brought her widowed mother back to Pasadena to live with them. Rose Honda, who did not marry, also served as a caregiver for both her parents.

For young Nisei families, neighborhoods like the Crenshaw area offered a safe, welcoming place with affordable housing. Marion Manaka recalled, "with so many Japanese people there, when you moved in you just felt comfortable, and the kids all enjoyed it, too."[229] Nisei dentists and optometrists offered their services, and the Holiday Bowl was a favorite gathering place for bowling or to enjoy a late-night bowl of noodles. Buying ethnic ingredients required a drive to the nearby Japanese markets on Jefferson, but Chiharu Ikeda, a Japanese "fish man"—a staple figure of many prewar communities—made his rounds through Marion's neighborhood every Monday evening. "The kids would all run out there, and we would buy the fish. The little ones all wanted ame [Japanese candy]." In addition to fresh fish and tofu, Marion recalled, "he carried nori [dried seaweed], candy, and just a few grocery things to hold you over…"[230] The fish man was only one of several popular vendors making door-to-door deliveries: "When the Helm's Bakery truck came, the kids would all run out and want donuts.… Also milk in glass bottles (chuckles) was delivered to your house."[231]

Nisei households largely reflected the sexual division of labor that prevailed in mainstream society and the immigrant community. Whether as daughters or wives, Japanese American women were responsible for the bulk of domestic work. One of their key responsibilities was food preparation. In January 1946, soon after the *Rafu Shimpo* resumed publication, a woman reader suggested the inclusion of a "cooking recipe column," saying, "I know lot of nisei girls will be looking forward to something like that." Mirroring gastronomical preferences, she added, "Try and add variety by printing Chinese, American, and Japanese recipes, whenever possible."[232] Perhaps at her prompting, for about a year, the *Rafu* ran a weekly "Today's Recipe" column, starting on February 5 with directions for a Chinese dish "Celery Chow Yuk," followed on February 9 by simple recipes for a Japanese shrimp concoction and "Nasu no Goma-Shoyu," a minimalist eggplant dish. All of the featured dishes were Chinese or Japanese. The short ingredient lists (two pounds of eggplant were the only ingredient in the "Nasu no Goma-shoyu" recipe) may reflect not only the fledgling skills of novice cooks but also postwar budgets and the need to economize. By 1947, recipes no longer appeared, but notices of cooking classes did.

Community cooking classes similarly reflected Japanese American tastes and economic pressure. In July 1947, Mrs. Matsuo, a "well-known dietician," began teaching classes at the International Institute for young adults and teenagers interested in Italian, American, and Japanese cuisine.[233] Mindful of budgetary concerns and growing families, she demonstrated "new culinary methods of preparing one pound of meat to serve six or eight persons."[234] The American Red Cross also offered cooking classes to Issei and Nisei, with an emphasis on thrift, assuring prospective students, "Careful selections and good cooking can help you win a bout with continued high food prices."[235] Notably, the ARC gently challenged gender divisions in the kitchen by issuing an invitation to "Brides, husbands, and experienced homemakers" to attend the classes.[236]

A new element of popular culture made a splash in postwar Japanese American homes: television. In 1947 Mary Kitano noticed television sets advertised as attractions in local bars. Soon this novelty would transform previous patterns of entertainment and consumer advertising for millions of Americans. In the following year, Mary Oyama noted the impact of this innovation on household routines, remarking on how television "is revolutionizing people's lives. One neighbor serves supper at 4:00 p.m. so that her family and her evening's program can be accommodated to the telecasts."[237] Perhaps speaking from her own experience as a mother, she characterized television as particularly convenient for families with children who could view "the air shows in comfort at home instead of trekking out to the movies or elsewhere. No fussin' and dressin', no long drives or parking worries, no more adults having to sit through hours of: Red Ryder, Tarzan, Gang-busters, and endless Westerns."[238] Similarly, in 1949, *Rafu Shimpo* writer Henry J. Tsurutani declared that television was bringing Japanese American family members together, particularly urban youth who previously went out in the evening to movies or to socialize. He described a prototypical "Yamamoto clan," gathered in the living room, rapt in their favorite programs, and accurately predicted that "before long it may overtake the radio shows."[239]

Television drew together not only family but also friends and neighbors. The first television of Marion Manaka's family was a black-lacquer Stromberg Carlson with green double doors decorated with a gold design of Chinese scenery; this impressive multi-media unit also featured a 45 rpm record player and a radio. Few had televisions in those days, Marion recalled, "So people used to come to our house to watch TV."[240] Her mother's favorite program was wrestling, which she refused to believe was rigged; the children enjoyed programs like the Mickey Mouse Club and Howdy Doody. When Mary Ishizuka's family bought a small black-and-white television, she also invited friends over to watch movies. Rose Honda remembered, laughing, "we were just enthralled on this piece of furniture."[241]

If "togetherness" was becoming a watchword for U.S. society in the early postwar period, for Japanese Americans it meant more than just involvement in the increasingly child-centered family. Although a range of Nisei women's (and sometimes men's) activities began to revolve around Sansei children, they were often ensconced within, and served to reinforce, larger community networks, frequently through the PTA (as in the cases of Marion Manaka and Esther Nishio) and church. Both Esther and Shig Nishio took active roles in the Pasadena Presbyterian Church—he was in the men's social organization and she was president of the Women's Association. For Marion Manaka, the Centenary Church in Crenshaw was a vital social center, offering many age group clubs. The Issei women belonged to the Fujinkai, which cooked and served lunch after church services to raise funds. For a short while, Marion was a member of the Women's Club, a Nisei social and service group that held cooking classes and made handicrafts for church benefits. Her daughter Barbara joined the Pixies group at Centenary; like their mothers, the girls took cooking classes and held bake sales, learning "everyday things."[242] Later Barbara became involved with a Japanese American social club at Dorsey High School. While in high school, she and her friends—like an earlier generation of Japanese American women—also served as leaders for younger girls' clubs at Centenary. Many of the women's activities at Centenary reinforced traditional gender roles, but they also continued to hone women's organizational skills and teach them to the next generation. Through their organizational and domestic skills, Japanese American women sustained churches and other newly re-established ethnic institutions in the early postwar years.

The youth groups they organized for the Sansei reflected both the continuing importance of Japanese American networks and postwar shifts in interracial relations. Mary Nishi Ishizuka served as leader for her elder daughter Karen's Girl Scout troop, an ethnically mixed group of girls who attended the same elementary school. They met weekly at her house, and she helped them work toward earning badges. Mary remembered, laughing, "And I was in charge of the cookie sale, so I had cookies stacked up to the ceiling!"[243] When her younger daughter Kathy reached "Brownie" age, Mary again stepped in to serve as a Girl Scout leader, this time for a mainly Japanese American group from the West Los Angeles United Methodist Church.

Some urban Nisei fathers also played an active role in Sansei youth activities. Also through the church, Mary Ishizuka's husband George and son Kirk became active in the Westside YMCA, which organized basketball games and camping trips. Through Centenary, Marion's husband and son Timmy were involved in the Indian Guides, a father-son program affiliated with the Crenshaw YMCA. Shig Nishio served as a scoutmaster for several years when his son John was a Boy Scout; Esther also helped out, recalling the patrol meetings held at their home: "The backyard would be dug up with big holes and we'd cook beef stroganoff or bake pies in our dutch ovens in the ground. They learned knot tying and all sorts of things. We had a really fun time."[244]

In addition to family-centered activities, some women found friendship and support in informal peer networks. While living in Crenshaw, Marion Manaka and ten other Nisei housewives began meeting for coffee at each other's homes when their children were at school, to talk about "the kids, or the husbands": "Then it kind of dwindled off after the children started growing up. Everybody went to work. And now after they've all retired, we're back together again enjoying each other's company."[245] Several decades later, Marion and the "coffee girls" were still meeting, holding luncheons to celebrate each other's birthdays.

The "coffee girls," the Atomettes, the Tartanettes, the Blue Circles, and many other Nisei women's friendship networks and clubs have continued to meet over the years.[246] The longevity of their group ties reflects the strong roots of urban Nisei youth organizations—established in eras of segregation and exclusion, wartime incarceration, and postwar civil rights struggle—as well as their continued meaning and support.

* * *

Tracing Japanese American women's experiences provides a window into the gritty realities of resettlement, as well as the determination and resourcefulness needed to find jobs, make inroads into new neighborhoods, and claim a place in postwar southern California. Like the initial uprooting and incarceration during World War II, postwar return was a grueling process for the Issei and Nisei, women and men. It is important to remember both the heroism of daily struggle and the better-known legal battles, both of which helped to propel civil rights changes in the 1940s, 1950s, and beyond.

Part of the creative re-weaving of the Japanese American community included the revival of old Nisei groups, some founded in the camps, and the formation of new ones. Young women's clubs, as before the war, were particularly predominant, often affiliated with churches, schools, and the YWCA. Their postwar activities followed many of the prewar patterns, channeling energy into socializing, service projects, education, and sports. In the process they honed leadership and organizational skills that would continue to prove invaluable to their communities. As increasing numbers of Nisei reached adulthood and independence from their parental families, the clubs provided an arena for single women and men to meet and court within a comfortable ethnic space in which they could be sure of welcome—something they could not take for granted outside their peer networks. The racial tensions surrounding their return to the West Coast were amplified in the area of interracial dating and marriage, viewed with disapproval by both Issei parents and the dominant society; even after the California state anti-miscegenation law was overturned in 1948, several decades would pass before a majority of the U.S. public sanctioned such unions. As many Nisei women married and became mothers, they continued to support each other through rituals that had taken root in the 1920s and 1930s. Parenthood often involved them in another layer of organizational activity vital to both the ethnic and mainstream communities.

Details of club activities and Nisei (and Sansei) accomplishments, wherever they might occur, studded the pages of the postwar *Rafu Shimpo*. Every "first" was trumpeted, from the first postwar skating party[247] to the first student of Japanese ancestry to win her nurse's cap from the Queen of Angels School of Nursing.[248] Readers learned not only of Miné Okubo's winning a prestigious James D. Phelan art award in 1949[249] and Miyoko Ito's solo art exhibition in Chicago,[250] but also that teenager Sadako Kawanami's drawings of a saber-tooth tiger and a diplodocus were displayed in a life-science class at the Polytechnic High School.[251] These news items reflect the painstaking work of re-entering a sometimes hostile society and rebuilding a community, and the tenacious effort to make the most of every tiny sign of progress. Every milestone, no matter how small, signaled a step forward in reconstructing brutally disrupted lives and reclaiming a place in the world from which they had been exiled. In this process, girls and women played dynamic roles in regenerating Japanese American families and communities, as well as advancing into new economic, social, and political arenas.

Epilogue

In her award-winning 1999 documentary film "When You're Smiling: The Deadly Legacy of Internment," Janice D. Tanaka lifted a curtain of community silence to reveal some of the postwar casualties among Nisei and Sansei in southern California. The premature deaths of Nisei men like Tanaka's father, her mother's reliance on prescription medication, and a high number of drug-overdose deaths among Sansei—especially young women—in the early 1970s mirrored the persisting pain of World War II forced removal and the difficulties of gaining acceptance in the mainstream.[1]

It is difficult to bring into focus Japanese American urban and suburban family life in the postwar period. The complicated dynamics of resettlement and the pressures faced by the earlier cohort of third-generation children have been overshadowed by the stereotype of Japanese Americans as a model minority. *model minority* The status of Japanese Americans rose in tandem with the importance of Japan as a U.S. ally during the Cold War and the need to solidify America's position as a world leader by countering criticism of domestic race relations.[2] As historian Naoko Shibusawa stated, "The way Americans treated racial minorities—including the recently interned Japanese Americans—became not just a matter of moral conscience, but one of foreign policy and national prestige as the United States sought to win over newly decolonized nations into its orbit."[3] One manifestation of this political shift was the growing residential mobility of Japanese Americans and other Asian Americans in the 1950s; white Californians still viewed them as fundamentally foreign, though now desirable neighbors.[4] Japanese Americans' strenuous efforts to fit in with middle-class mainstream society while rebuilding families and ethnic networks have burnished the picture of postwar recovery. However, beneath the shiny surface of the model-minority image, the aftermath of wartime incarceration affected Janice Tanaka's family and other Japanese Americans in ways that are still being assessed. Nisei writer Hisaye Yamamoto stated, "It is an episode in our collective life which wounded us more painfully than we realize."[5] In analyzing the transgenerational impact of painful histories, literary scholar Gabriele Schwab suggests that "untold or unspeakable secrets,

223

unfelt or denied pain, concealed shame, covered-up crimes or violent histories continue to affect and disrupt the lives of those involved in them and often their descendants as well."[6] Indeed, one of the lessons psychologist Donna Nagata drew from her research on the complex intergenerational effects of Japanese American incarceration was that "Time does not heal all wounds."[7]

Healing from such injuries requires telling and witnessing.[8] In this vein, Sox Kitashima, a pioneering San Francisco activist in the redress movement, says: "As public knowledge and interest about Japanese Americans grows, I feel I shouldn't ignore any opportunity to speak out on issues. Although it recalls such unhappy times when I talk about the war and that part of my life, I feel it is vitally important to educate the public. In turn, talking about the camp experience helps heal some of the pain."[9] Telling her story constitutes one part of the tremendous effort Kitashima has devoted to effecting social change through organizing letter-writing campaigns, attending redress rallies, and lobbying Congress. Her endeavors also include volunteer work for Kimochi, a community organization that serves Japanese American seniors, and fundraising for the Asian American Arts Foundation.

Sox Kitashima is not alone. Donna Nagata's research suggests that, within a range of diverse responses, many Japanese Americans "consider it vital to keep the legacy of the internment alive, noting that the need to remain vigilant about civil liberties, constitutional rights, and racism is as applicable today as ever."[10] Such concerns spurred some urban Sansei to participate in anti-Vietnam War efforts and movements to promote ethnic consciousness and social justice. Evelyn Yoshimura, Merilynne Hamano Quon, Mike Nakayama, and many of the other Sansei interviewed by Janice Tanaka were among those who turned to collective action to address issues such as drug abuse within the ethnic community, forming organizations such as Asian Sisters, Yellow Brotherhood, and Japanese American Community Services-Asian Involvement.[11]

The community organizational experience and drive of the Nisei in southern California may have influenced some of their third-generation children's involvement in the Asian American movement of the late 1960s and 1970s. Wendy C. Mori, a working-class Sansei activist, mused on how, in the postwar period "because of racism, the (Sansei) kids…could not play basketball or baseball at the YMCAs, so our parents created these organizations in the different areas, the Westside, or in East LA, or wherever the Japanese American communities were."[12] They established programs in baseball, basketball, and swimming for their children. "JAs are notorious for organizing groups," Mori said, "and being able to raise funds and then they bought facilities." She speculated on a possible link between this organizational practice and the third generation's activism: "And I don't know, if then the Sansei just kind of kept that going, and then we segue into organizing the whole anti-war thing, Asian American Studies, or whatever it was."[13] Regardless of their motives, Mori and other Sansei women played dynamic roles in the Asian American movement.[14] Although some Japanese American parents may have been dismayed by their daughters' (and sons') political militancy, the patterns and style of Sansei organizing in 1970s Los Angeles may have been at least partially a legacy from the Nisei themselves.

Nisei as well as Sansei women participated actively in the movement for Japanese American redress and reparations during the 1970s and 1980s. Esther Takei Nishio, Mary Nishi Ishizuka, Setsuko Matsunaga Nishi, and many others gave testimony about their experiences at hearings held by the congressional Commission on the Wartime Relocation and Internment of Civilians. Archival researchers, organizers, lobbyists, and educators worked tirelessly, both as individuals and as organizational members, in the long campaign that culminated in the Civil Liberties Act of 1988. For example, after she gave her testimony, the Commission asked Setsuko Nishi to "help them set up a consultation with social and behavioral scientists about the long-term effects of the wartime incarceration."[15] She aided them in organizing a two-day conference, for which she and John Clausen subsequently produced a report, *Papers for the Commission on Wartime Relocation and Internment of Civilians*, presenting an economic-loss analysis as well as covering the long-term impact.[16] The roles of Nisei women were spotlighted in the 2008 program series "Neglected Legacies: Japanese American Women and Redress" organized by anthropologist Lane Hirabayashi at the Japanese American National Museum. The series debuted recent and forthcoming works on Michi Nishiura Weglyn, the author of the landmark work *Years of Infamy: The Untold Story of America's Concentration Camps* (1976); Sue Kunitomi Embrey, a co-founder of the Manzanar Pilgrimage; and Sox Kitashima, a leader in the San Francisco branch of the National Coalition for Redress and Reparations (NCRR).[17] The series also presented stirring first-hand accounts of organizing by Kathy Masaoka, a Sansei leader in the Los Angeles chapter of the NCRR[18], Seattle activist and filmmaker Chizu Omori, and Aiko Herzig-Yoshinaga, whose monumental archival research uncovered evidence crucial to the passage of the Civil Liberties Act of 1988.[19]

Close study of women's contributions in the redress movement offers a deeper understanding of the process of community mobilization as well as providing a wider range of models for bringing about social change. In his research on Aiko Herzig-Yoshinaga, Thomas Fujita Rony emphasizes "the importance of critically analyzing the kinds of labor performed by women in political movements, and how this labor and its recognition might be affected by issues of gender, race, and class." He warns that if women's work is taken for granted and "importance" narrowly defined, "we will not only overlook heroes, we will lose valuable lessons in how the task of achieving freedom and justice for all may be accomplished."[20] Still involved at age 87, Herzig-Yoshinaga serves as an inspiring leader. "I'm very excited to see so many young women active in issues of social justice," she said. "I exhort you to go for it."[21] She also urged, "Don't let age deter you!"[22]

Activists such as Sue Kunitomi Embrey fought hard to memorialize Japanese American wartime incarceration and to ensure that its significance for U.S. civil liberties would become part of the public school curriculum. An educator and writer, Embrey co-chaired the Manzanar Pilgrimage and was a leader of the long campaign that resulted in the state designation of Manzanar as a historical monument in 1973 and as a national historic site in 1992.[23] In such public contestations over historical memory, Nisei women have taken many forms of action, speaking to K–12 and college classes, organizing exhibitions and other commemorative events, conducting research, and rewriting the past.[24]

For Setsuko Nishi, involvement in the redress movement formed part of a larger, ongoing engagement with issues of racial and gender equality. In the 1970s, for example, as a senior fellow at the Metropolitan Applied Research Center, she focused on institutionalized discrimination, working "on projects having to do with concerns beyond compliance with civil rights laws in employment" and conducting major research for class-action discrimination suits. She was also very active on the New York State Advisory Committee to the U.S. Commission on Civil Rights, recalling, "It was a really good organization at the time, and we did groundbreaking reports. It made a difference.... It was the first time that we had an organized approach to the needs of Asian Americans. It was an exciting time to be involved in that."[25] She and Charles Wang served as co-chairs of the Asian American Caucus subcommittee (part of the Pacific Asian Coalition).[26]

For Setsuko Nishi and others, activism has extended into larger communities. Mitsuye Yamada, an educator and organizer as well as poet, began her writing career with poems about wartime incarceration and the struggle to survive the corrosive effect of racism. In 1988 Yamada wrote:

> Imagine there is a future
> where a tight ring of peace
> like Saturn's collar
> holds us all in
> and there is no
> space for war
>
> Imagine there is a future
> where my home town
> this earth
> is no longer
> an experimental station
> for nuclear wars[27]

In this poem she asserts both a claim to a larger inclusive space and the responsibility of ensuring its future. Yamada's vision has fueled and informed her work as a professor of English, a national board member of the human-rights organization Amnesty International, and the founder of Multicultural Women Writers of Orange County.

Other Japanese American women, like Yamada, have channeled energy into multiethnic organizations. The East West Players, one of the oldest Asian American theater companies, furnishes an example of how Nisei women supported fledgling pan-Asian American endeavors in Los Angeles. Mary Oyama Mittwer enthusiastically publicized East West Players productions in her postwar newspaper columns, and Wakako Yamauchi began a career as a playwright by adapting her short story "And the Soul Shall Dance" for the theater company. Writers such as Yamauchi and Hisaye Yamamoto have received national and international attention since the 1970s for their powerful, unsparing depictions of prewar community life, marital relations, and racial tensions, often framed by the southern California landscape. Another generation of writers, including Naomi Hirahara and Nina Revoyr, has also found inspiration for fiction in issues of race, culture, and generational relations in Los Angeles.[28]

Japanese American craft fairs and compilation cookbooks also reflect women's creativity and community spirit. The dazzling profusion of women's engagement in cultural coalescence is exemplified by the handicraft boutiques, run largely by and for women—mostly Nisei and Sansei—for at least twenty years. In fall and spring, special calendars appear in Japanese American newspapers such as the *Rafu Shimpo* (which is still published in both Japanese and English), alerting readers to craft fairs in southern and northern California. Staged in community centers and hotel conference rooms, the boutiques offer housewares, art, jewelry, food, music, literature, clothing and accessories, baby supplies, holiday ornaments, stationery, and more—much of it carrying ethnic cultural references and made by the venders. Shoppers browse through hand towels appliqued with Spam musubi and lucky beckoning cats; cards made with origami paper folded into abstract designs; nondrip soy sauce cruets; pendants inset with washi paper; homemade rice crackers and cookies; felt Christmas tree ornaments whose shapes range from angels to smiling rice balls; t-shirts emblazoned with dragons, sumo bowlers, cranes, and sushi; vests and jackets fashioned from old kimono. Basketball motifs reflect the enduring importance of team sports and ethnic athletic leagues to third-, fourth- and fifth-generation Japanese Americans in southern California. Candles and soap scented with plumeria, pikake, and mango reflect family roots in Hawai'i. Japanese American women in southern California flock with female friends and relatives to these events in search of gifts whose imaginatively adapted cultural elements bespeak appreciation for ethnic heritage. The popularity of the craft fairs also conveys the persistence of women's primary responsibility for organizing holiday celebrations and other occasions that affirm family ties and ethnic cultural practices. Anthropologist Micaela di Leonardo termed this "the work of kinship," pointing out that it is largely women's work.[29]

Another arena of women's cultural adaptation and transmission becomes visible in the vast body of compilation cookbooks that have served as fundraising staples in postwar Japanese American communities from Honolulu to Los Angeles to St. Louis. Explanations of the symbolism and preparation of New Year's dishes and the inclusion of sections devoted to regional specialties show women's efforts to maintain selected aspects of ethnic culture as well as their creativity in making use of local resources. For example, the Orange County Buddhist Church's *Generation to Generation, A Family Cookbook* (1984) includes a chapter featuring an array of strawberry recipes, from beverages and cakes to pies, trifle, soufflé, and jam.[30]

Japanese American compilation cookbooks reflect a range of social, cultural, and technological transformations. *Otoki*, the 2007 cookbook published by the Senshin Buddhist Temple Cookbook in Los Angeles, offers much food for thought as well as for consumption.[31] The preface explains that in "American Jodoshinshu temples, *otoki* became the meal served to everyone after major services by the Fujinkai or women's organization," noting that it is no longer strictly vegetarian and that various temple groups now prepare the food. The range of recipes shows the growing diversity of the congregation as well as their widening circles of kin and friends. Here one can find out how to cook not only Japanese dishes such as makizushi and chawan mushi (a savory custard), but also Korean chap jae (a noodle dish) and soon doo boo (spicy tofu soup), Indonesian nasi goreng (fried rice), Sri Lankan gadju (cashew) curry, Mexican tamales and chilaquiles, Chinese winter melon soup, Eastern European potato latkes, Italian lasagna, Greek baklava, and African American collard greens. Fusion recipes such as Asian coq au vin, tofu salad, cereal senbei (Japanese crackers), and chocolate mochi brownies exhibit the ingenuity of Pacific Rim cooks. A recipe for "Microwave Manju" demonstrates how a previously laborious process has been happily shortened by technology. As writer/farmer David Masumoto observes, "Changing customs can signify that a culture is alive and well. Traditions that don't evolve gradually become acts without meaning; they are like fossils from a dead civilization, relics of a past that only remind us of where we were, not where we are going."[32] Both holiday delicacies and mundane dishes offer a kind of linkage to history as well as exemplifying the imaginative adaptation that characterizes living traditions.[33]

Although the appearance of recipes such as "Jeff's Jambalaya" and "Sam Sato's Azuki Cookies" signal ongoing shifts in gender roles, compilation cookbooks still evidence female authority and primary responsibility in the kitchen.

Although a number of men submitted recipes for *Otoki*, the majority of con-
tributors as well as the cookbook committee are women, mirroring the larger
role women continue to play in familial and communal food preparation.
Women's humor also enlivens such cookbooks via recipes such as the "Next
Best Thing to Robert Redford," a rich dessert included in both the Senshin and
Orange County cookbooks, and the latter's "Watergate Cake with Cover-Up
Icing."[34] Between the covers of these cookbooks lies evidence of the practicality
and artistry with which women have tackled the enormous work of sustaining
families and communities, and also their generosity in sharing knowledge and
experience. Their culinary endeavors have produced deep-rooted legacies in the
Japanese American community.

In August 2010, the 70th Nisei Week Japanese Festival in Los Angeles offered
myriad examples of women's continuing engagement in maintaining, adapting,
and creating ethnic culture, and the ways in which they still represent the community. While men were also active organizers and participants, the visibility
of women's cultural work was particularly striking, signaling both continuity
and change in a festival geared to a shifting constituency. Though the crowds
have "dwindled over the past few years, an influx of non-Japanese Americans
are discovering Nisei Week."[35] An ethnically diverse, multigenerational mix of
locals and visitors circulated past the Japanese American National Museum
and through the Japanese Village Plaza, listening to jazz and taiko drumming,
and enjoying treats like mochi ice cream. A number of the exhibitions at the
Japanese American Cultural & Community Center showcased women's arts
and handicrafts. Viewers admired dramatic ikebana arrangements of palm
fronds, bromeliads, and sunflowers that combined western flora with Japanese
aesthetic principles; watched the painstaking process of kimekomi doll making; and examined intricate sashiko (Japanese needlecraft).[36] An exhibition at
the Union Church by the Little Tokyo Library Quilters showed how Japanese
American women have incorporated Japanese fabric, sewing techniques, and
motifs such as cranes and fans into a quintessential American craft; in keeping
with the community spirit of quilting bees and Nisei women's social service, the
money raised by selling their handiwork was intended to support programming
and resources for the Little Tokyo Branch Library. Gendered cultural performances by women of several generations took place throughout Little Tokyo.
Spectators at the Grand Parade watched elegant kimono-clad dancers from
the school of Madame Fujima Kansuma, the legendary Nisei teacher who cho-
reographed the 2010 Nisei Week odori.[37] Women dancers from the Okinawa
Association of American Geino-bu performed in beautiful traditional dress,
contributing a reminder of complex colonial history and intertwined immigration.[38] Olympic figure skater Mirai Nagasu served as a parade marshal, waving
and tossing gifts. Mirroring the influence of Japanese youth trends, "the Ajuku

Girls, a new American J-Pop group, preened for the cameras"[39] and young women costumed as anime characters roamed through Little Tokyo, striking poses for photographers. Demonstrating facility with both ethnic culture and mainstream popular culture, the candidates in the Nisei Week Queen contest performed two dances: an odori, for which they dressed in kimono and held fans, and later, attired in beach wear, a lively routine "We Love LA!" set to singer Katy Perry's popular hit "California Girls."[40] During the festival, taiko drumming groups vigorously pounded a strong heartbeat heard throughout Little Tokyo, transmitting both tradition and innovation. In Japan, taiko is performed by men; by contrast, in the United States and Canada, since the renewal of interest in ethnic-cultural arts during the 1970s, mixed-sex taiko groups have formed at churches, community centers, and on college campuses. In fact, as a male taiko group member informed a Nisei Week audience, "In America women now predominate in taiko." The range of visual and performing arts displayed during the festival reflects women's involvement in cultural coalescence and the enduring importance of their creative expression for the ethnic community.

Quite a few of the Nisei women's clubs have persisted to the present day, though they are dwindling. The JUGS have continued the friendships they began in Manzanar, still meeting regularly to play cards and making annual trips to Las Vegas. Groups such as the Atomettes and the Pasonas have transformed community institutions and practices as well as providing members with support through the vicissitudes of life. Despite their members' decreasing physical mobility and declining numbers, urban women's networks have maintained their bonds of camaraderie, rooted in gender, generation, ethnicity, and shared history.

A flourishing outgrowth of the earlier Nisei clubs are sororities—Chi Alpha Delta (chartered in 1929) and Theta Kappa Phi (1959) at UCLA, and Sigma Phi Omega (1949) at USC—which were established by Japanese Americans and have over time become pan-Asian American organizations. As the Chi Alpha Delta web site explains, their charter members "recognized a need to promote friendships, communication, and social activity among University women of Asian descent, as well as a desire to encourage school service and school spirit."[41] The sororities' official histories reflect the continuing appeal of sisterhood in the face of lingering anti-Asian discrimination during the 1940s and 1950s. On their web site, Sigma Phi Omega cited postwar anti-Asian sentiment as a context for the formation of the group and thanked their founders for "creating an organization which stood against the prejudices of your time." They not only affirmed the significance of their history, but also linked social consciousness with the preservation of civil liberties: "it is our collective responsibility as Asian-Americans to remember the injustices that occurred only 60 years ago so that history does not repeat itself."[42] The racism faced by charter member Margaret Ohara Shinohara also spurred the inception of Theta Kappa Phi: "After being mistaken for someone of Irish descent (O'Hara), [she] was given a Panhellenic Scholarship upon acceptance to UCLA. After discovering her true Japanese-American identity, Margaret was denied admittance and membership into all of the Greek sororities on the row."[43] In response, Ohara Shinohara and eight friends formed their own sorority. The persistence and growth of Asian American sororities suggests that women's ethnocultural organizations still offer an important network of camaraderie and belonging. That Sigma Phi Omega in 2010 boasted eight daughter chapters in southern California and Texas illustrates this appeal.

From the prewar years through the postwar period, Japanese American women's ethnocultural organizational affinities facilitated their claiming modern American femininity as well as their formation of places of acceptance and support, providing a foundation for their later work in social, service, political, and religious groups within and outside the ethnic community. Women's tireless involvement in all arenas of the redress movement, from grassroots mobilization and educational outreach to congressional lobbying and the implementation of the redress program, serves as a notable example. The imprint of their organizational drive and experience endures in the legacies of this campaign and in the community activities of succeeding generations.

NOTES

Introduction

1. *Rafu Shimpo*, March 28, 1926. The terms "sheiks" and "shebas" reflect the influence of popular movies featuring actors such as Rudolph Valentino and Theda Bara.
2. *Rafu Shimpo*, March 28, 1926.
3. Since Chi Alpha Delta was not established at UCLA until 1929, and due to the satiric pseudonym he used (calling the sorority "U Lambda Stu"), it is not clear to what sorority Sakano was referring. His reference suggests the presence of at least one Nisei sorority and fraternity by 1926. They were founded as alternatives to the European American "Greek letter organizations" that did not then admit racial/ethnic members. Ethnic press reportage also suggests there were other sororities, or versions of sororities, developing prior to or around the same time as Chi Alpha Delta. Regarding Chi Alpha Delta, see Shirley Jennifer Lim, *A Feeling of Belonging: Asian American Women's Public Culture, 1930–1960* (New York: New York University Press, 2006). For more on the JSCA, see David Yoo, *Growing Up Nisei: Race, Generation, and Culture among Japanese Americans of California, 1924–49* (Urbana, IL: University of Illinois Press, 2000), pp. 59–63.
4. *Kashu Mainichi*, April 26, 1936. Joe Oyama and his sister Mary were active writers among the prewar Nisei literati.
5. *Rafu Shimpo*, December 23, 1940, p. 16.
6. *Rafu Shimpo*, April 4, 1926. Satow studied sociology at the University of Southern California and graduated Phi Beta Kappa. For another reference to Satow see *Kashu Mainichi*, January 1, 1932.
7. *Rafu Shimpo*, April 4, 1926.
8. *Rafu Shimpo*, April 4, 1926. An anonymous third writer, who appeared to be a member of the JSCA, also wrote in response to Sakano, welcoming the "new organizations" that heralded a new era in Little Tokyo. It appears that the current of Nisei public opinion ran strongly against Sakano and that this response had a serious effect on him. Three weeks later, his wife wrote a letter to the editor in defense of her husband's character, trying to mollify and enlist the sympathy of those he had offended. She announced that, despite being "a man of great vigor and robust health," "my poor husband is suffering a nervous breakdown because of the terrible criticisms made of him" (*Rafu Shimpo*, April 25, 1926).
9. Nisei youth clubs also formed in San Francisco and Seattle by the 1930s.
10. "Issei" means "first-generation" Japanese immigrants. Their children, the U.S.-born second generation, are called "Nisei;" the third generation are "Sansei." When used as nouns, these terms can be either singular or plural.
11. Noriko Sawada, "Memoir of a Japanese Daughter," *Ms.* 8, No. 10 (1980), pp. 68–70. In 1920, the year Ura Sawada arrived, the Japanese government ceased giving passports to picture brides, because of exclusionist pressure in the United States.

12. Brian Niiya, ed. *Japanese American History, An A-to-Z Reference from 1868 to the Present* (Japanese American National Museum, 1993), pp. 171–172, 282–284. See also Emma Gee, "Issei: The First Women," *Asian Women* (Asian Women's Journal, Berkeley, CA, University of California, Berkeley, 1971), pp. 8–15; Yuji Ichioka, *The Issei: The World of the First Generation Japanese Immigrants, 1885–1924* (New York: The Free Press, 1988); Roger Daniels, *Asian America: The Chinese and the Japanese in the United States since 1850* (Seattle: University of Washington Press, 1988). Filipinos, as U.S. nationals, were able to enter the country until limited by the Tydings-MacDuffie Act of 1934.

13. In 1880 Chinese immigrant men outnumbered women 21:1 in California, so family formation was slow and the population declined after immigration was cut off by the Chinese Exclusion Act of 1882. By 1920 the sex ratio among the Issei was two men to every one woman, and families quickly became the core of Japanese immigrant society. Catherine Lee, "'Where the Danger Lies': Race, Gender, and Chinese and Japanese Exclusion in the United States, 1870–1924," *Sociological Forum* 25, No. 2 (2010): 248–271.

14. The 1922 Supreme Court ruling in *Ozawa v. U.S.* confirmed their ineligibility for naturalization.

15. Having citizen children was a key to property ownership, as title could be held in their names. Some Issei would establish a corporation in which the majority of the owners—stockholders or officers—were their U.S.-citizen children. Setsuko Matsunaga Nishi recalled that as a child, "I was the secretary of the Matsunaga family corporation.... I could barely write, and I was afraid when my father would ask me to sign a document... I would be nervous that I was going to make a mistake." Setsuko Matsunaga Nishi interview by author, September 12, 2009.

16. See Peggy Pascoe, *What Comes Naturally: Miscegenation Law and the Making of Race in America* (NY: Oxford University Press, 2009).

17. *Rafu Shimpo*, Holiday issue, December 23, 1938, p. 12.

18. The reporter noted, "This was especially true of Sundays. Wednesdays and Fridays seemed to be favorite club meeting days; and Fridays and Saturdays were 'dance nights.'" *Rafu Shimpo*, Holiday issue, December 23, 1938, p. 12.

19. "Out of Towners," *Rafu Shimpo*, Holiday issue, December 23, 1940, p. 17.

20. The Modern Girl Around the World Research Group (Alys Eve Weinbaum et al.), "The Modern Girl as Heuristic Device: Collaboration, Connective Comparison, Multidirectional Citation," *The Modern Girl Around the World: Consumption, Modernity, and Globalization*, eds. The Modern Girl Around the World Research Group, Alys Eve Weinbaum, et al. (Durham, NC: Duke University Press, 2008), pp. 1–24.

21. As Sara Evans notes, the first manifestation of the "new woman"—middle class, "college educated, frequently unmarried but self-supporting"—emerged after the Civil War. The independence and individuality of the new woman and the working-class "working girl" alarmed conservative critics. In the early twentieth century, the Victorian sexual code shifted, especially in urban centers where men and women began to enjoy leisure activities in public sites such as movie theaters and dance halls. By 1913, the flapper was a powerful icon, associated with both working-class and middle-class young women's growing autonomy and sexual expression. See Sara Evans, *Born for Liberty, A History of Women in America* (New York: Simon & Schuster, 1989, 1997), pp. 146–147, 160–162.

22. *Rafu Shimpo*, November 29, 1929. See "Q.Q.'s" humorous definitions of Japanese American terms. Regarding the moga in Japan, see Miriam Silverberg, *Erotic Grotesque Nonsense: The Mass Culture of Japanese Modern Times* (Berkeley, CA: University of California Press, 2006), pp. 51–72; "After the Grand Tour: The Modern Girl, the New Woman, and the Colonial Maiden," *The Modern Girl Around the World*, pp. 354–361.

23. *Rafu Shimpo*, April 25, 1926. This "fast living and thirst for excitement," Mrs. Inu noted, was spreading to "all parts of the world." Mrs. Inu did not target girls or identify specific clubs, although she too voiced concern about heterosexual socializing. Her main concern was behavior, rather than appearance.

24. Ibid. Mrs. Inu assured readers that she, too, was fond of dancing.

25. See Alys Eve Weinbaum, "Racial Masquerade: Consumption and Contestation of American Modernity," *The Modern Girl Around the World*, pp. 120–146.

Rafu's estimates purported to cover the "Southland," the actual directory listings included Nisei clubs in Berkeley, the Central Valley of California, and Chicago.

6. The *Rafu Shimpo* holiday issue for December 22, 1939, p. 16, estimated that there were nearly 600 Nisei clubs in southern California; in the December 23, 1940 holiday issue, p. 16, Sadae Nomura referred to "400 active nisei organizations." Four hundred appears to be a reasonable estimate.

7. The Japanese American newspapers did not switch to the spelling "Little Tokyo" until after World War II.

8. *Kashu Mainichi,* January 1, 1941. The 29 members of the Japanese YWCA in 1941 were: In the ABC Kouncil—the Bellamians, Blue Circles, Dot and Dash, Cordelians, Kalifans, Kayans, Phydells, Rho Sigma Rhos, and Toquiwas. In the Inter Y Council were the Archerettes, Chatelaines, Demoiselles, Les Serrelles, Marienettes, Queen Esthers, Pimpernels, Tartanettes, and Trisians. In the Inter-Club Council were the Cub-Bettes, Embas, Loha Tohelas, Sub Debs, Tri-U, Tri-U Juniors, Cardinelles, Kilaueans, and First Nighters. In the Girl Reserves were the Lewas and the Appelachi.

9. In the post-World War II period, Komai's daughter and sons in turn became active in another generation of youth groups sponsored by the Centenary Church and intended to foster lasting friendships among Japanese Americans.

10. Kay Komai recalled several Blue Circles marrying members of Nisei boys' clubs.

11. The California miscegenation law in 1850 banned marriages between "Caucasians" and "Negroes" or "mulattoes;" the law was amended in 1880 to forbid whites from marrying "Mongolians," and in 1931 "Malays." See Peggy Pascoe, *What Comes Naturally: Miscegenation Law and the Making of Race in America.* New York: Oxford University Press, 2009, pp. 21, 84–85, 93.

12. *Kashu Mainichi,* April 26, 1936.

13. *Kashu Mainichi,* April 11, 1937.

14. James P. Allen and Eugene Turner, *The Ethnic Quilt: Population Diversity in Southern California.* Northridge, CA: The Center for Geographical Studies, California State University, Northridge, 1997, p. 125.

15. James P. Allen and Eugene Turner, p. 125.

16. Fumiko Fukuyama Ide interview by author, Los Angeles, California, August 14, 2009.

17. A number of variations appeared, including "Lil' Tokio" and "Little Tokio." For the sake of consistency I have chosen to use "Little Tokyo," the spelling that has become standard usage since the postwar period; it was used in the ethnic press from the 1930s, although less frequently than "Lil' Tokio."

18. See "Village Vagaries," *Kashu Mainichi,* January 1, 1934.

19. See "Lil' Tokio comes to life," *Kashu Mainichi,* October 29, 1933. "Poppy Yama" was the pseudonym of the Buddhist Nisei woman columnist.

20. *Kashu Mainichi,* January 5, 1936.

21. *Rafu Shimpo,* December 10, 1939.

22. *Kashu Mainichi,* May 20, 1934.

23. Eileen H. Tamura, *Americanization, Acculturation, and Ethnic Identity: The Nisei Generation in Hawaii.* Chicago: University of Illinois Press, 1994, p. 34.

24. For more information on Nisei schooling, see David Yoo, *Growing Up Nisei: Race, Generation, and Culture among Japanese Americans of California, 1924–49.* Urbana, IL: University of Illinois Press, 2000.

25. Eileen Tamura deemed the Japanese language schools "ineffective agents of cultural transmission," observing that "...in Hawaii as on the mainland, Japanese schools failed to teach the Japanese language just as they failed to teach Japanese nationalism." (p. 160)

26. Rose Honda interview by author, in Los Angeles, California, July 30, 2009.

27. Setsuko Matsunaga Nishi interview by author, September 12 and 14, 2009.

28. See Brian Masaru Hayashi, Chapter 4, Owe Nothing to Anyone, 1896–1941, in *"For the Sake of Our Japanese Brethren": Assimilation, Nationalism, and Protestantism Among the Japanese of Los Angeles, 1895–1942.* Stanford, CA: Stanford University Press, 1995, pp. 55–72; David K. Yoo, Chapter 2, Keeping the Faith, in *Growing Up Nisei: Race, Generation, and Culture among Japanese Americans of California, 1924–49.* Urbana, IL: University of Illinois Press, 2000, pp.

38–67. Racism complicated religious affiliation, as David Yoo asserts: "Buddhists remained outsiders and Nisei Christians only peripherally benefited from the power and currency of Protestantism within American culture and society." (p. 67)

29. Mary Nishi Ishizuka interview by author, August 4, 2009.

30. David Yoo, p. 42.

31. Eileen Tamura, p. 209.

32. Robert Howard Ross, Social Distance As It Exists Between the First and Second Generation Japanese in the City of Los Angeles and Vicinity. M.A. thesis presented to the Department of Sociology, University of Southern California, September 1939, p. 93. Ross noted that young Nisei Christians faced disillusionment as they matured and faced the hypocritical racism of white Christians.

33. Mary Nishi Ishizuka interview by author, August 4, 2009.

34. Marion Svensrud, Some Factors Concerning the Assimilation of a Selected Japanese Community. M.A. thesis presented to the Department of Sociology, University of Southern California, June 6, 1931, p. 184.

35. Brian Hayashi, Chapter 6, Warm Fellowship with Others, *For the Sake of Our Japanese Brethren*, pp. 95–107.

36. Rose Honda's friends were mostly Nisei peers from the Japanese Methodist church she attended; in the prewar period, the Buddhists and Christians did not socialize together much.

37. Rose Honda interview by author in Los Angeles, California, July 30, 2009.

38. Esther (Takei) Nishio interview, *REgenerations Oral History Project: Rebuilding Japanese American Families, Communities, and Civil Rights in the Resettlement Era*. Los Angeles: Japanese American National Museum, in collaboration with the Chicago Japanese American Historical Society, the Japanese American Historical Society of San Diego, and the Japanese American Resource Center/Museum, 2000, p. 300.

39. Fumiko Fukuyama Ide interview by author in Los Angeles, California, August 14, 2009. She also darned her holey socks to make them last longer and eyed wistfully an affluent friend's dresser full of new ones.

40. Brian Niiya, ed. *Japanese American History, An A-to-Z Reference from 1868 to the Present*. Japanese American National Museum, 1993, p. 201.

41. Chinese American women in Los Angeles similarly contributed to family support through unpaid labor in the home and family business as well as through wage-paid work. See Judy Chu and Susie Ling, Chinese Women at Work, in *Linking Our Lives: Chinese American Women of Los Angeles*, a joint project of the Asian American Studies Center, University of California, Los Angeles, and the Chinese Historical Society of Southern California. Los Angeles: Chinese Historical Society of Southern California, 1984, pp. 65–90.

42. Mary Nishi Ishizuka interview by author, August 4, 2009. While living in Hollywood, Mary biked to the plunge in the nearby Los Feliz area.

43. Fumiko Fukuyama Ide interview by author, Los Angeles, California, August 14, 2009.

44. Rose Honda interview by author, Los Angeles, California, July 30, 2009. Rose loved Shirley Yamaguchi's "tear-jerker" song, "Shina no Yoru" (meaning "China Night").

45. Mary Nishi Ishizuka interview by author, August 4, 2009.

46. Ibid.

47. Fumiko Fukuyama Ide interview by author, August 14, 2009. The Tartanettes were affiliated with the Japanese Union Church.

48. Setsuko Matsunaga Nishi interview by author, September 12 and 14, 2009.

49. Fumiko Fukuyama Ide interview by author, March 27, 2001. Shirley Temple and Judy Garland were both members of the Meglin Kiddies dance troupe.

50. Robert Howard Ross's 1939 survey showed that ikebana was the Japanese art that interested Nisei girls most, followed by the tea ceremony.

51. Some Nisei girls also learned kendo, such as my aunt Dorothy Tsuda Fujii and sculptor Ruth Asawa. In Los Angeles, some Issei parents expected boys—like Setsuko Nishi's and Fumiko Ide's brothers—to become Boy Scouts.

52. Sone, p. 27.

53. Rose Honda interview by author, Los Angeles, California, July 30, 2009.

54. Mary Nishi Ishizuka interview by author, August 4, 2009.

55. Monica Sone, *Nisei Daughter*. Seattle: University of Washington Press, 1953, p. 28.

56. Robert Ross, p. 114.

57. *Hokubei Asahi*, October 11, 1934.

58. Ibid.

59. Setsuko Matsunaga Nishi interview by author, February 11 and 21, 2001 and September 6, 2001.

60. Robert Ross, p. 109.

61. Judy Yung, *Unbound Feet: A Social History of Chinese Women in San Francisco*. Berkeley: University of California Press, 1995, p. 116. Yung drew on research from two studies of Chinese American women in Los Angeles: Kit King Louis' MA thesis, A Study of American-born and American-reared Chinese in Los Angeles. University of Southern California, 1931, and Marjorie Lee's *Hu-Jee: The Forgotten Second Generation of Chinese America, 1930–1950*. Los Angeles, University of California, 1984.

62. Vicki Ruiz, *From Out of the Shadows: Mexican Women in Twentieth-Century America*. New York: Oxford University Press, 1998, p. 52.

63. Setsuko Matsunaga Nishi interview by author, February 11 and 21, 2001 and September 6, 2001.

64. Eiichiro Azuma, *Between Two Empires: Race, History, and Transnationalism in Japanese America*. New York: Oxford University Press, 2005, p. 7. He concluded that "class diversity among them was effectively inconsequential."

65. Eileen Tamura, p. xiv.

66. Fumiko Fukuoka, Mutual Life and Aid Among the Japanese in Southern California with Special Reference to Los Angeles. MA thesis, University of Southern California, May 1937, p. 9.

67. Rose Honda interview by author in Los Angeles, California, July 30, 2009. The majority of early Japanese immigrants came as laborers.

68. Eileen H. Tamura, p. 119.

69. Robert Ross, p. 89.

70. Judy Chu and Susie Ling, "Chinese Women at Work," *Linking Our Lives: Chinese American Women of Los Angeles*, a joint project of the Asian American Studies Center, University of California, Los Angeles, and the Chinese Historical Society of Southern California. Los Angeles: Chinese Historical Society of Southern California, 1984, p. 82.

71. Robert Ross, p. 89.

72. Robert Ross, p. 61. Ross was fluent in Japanese from 16 years of living in Japan.

73. Ross, p. 64.

74. Ross, p. 64.

75. Ross, p. 65.

76. Regarding Issei/Nisei conflict in southern California, see Kanichi Kawasaki, The Japanese Community of East San Pedro, Terminal Island, California. M.A. thesis presented to the Sociology Department, University of Southern California, May 28, 1931, p. 98, and Robert Ross, p. 78; regarding Hawai'i, see Eileen H. Tamura, pp. 173, 179. Although Ross reported conflict between Japanese immigrants and their U.S.-born children, he noted less hostility than in white immigrant homes (p. 35).

77. *Hokubei Asahi*, November 5, 1934.

78. Robert Ross, p. 110.

79. Haruko (Sugi) Hurt interview, *REgenerations Oral History Project: Rebuilding Japanese American Families, Communities, and Civil Rights in the Resettlement Era*. Los Angeles: Japanese American National Museum, in collaboration with the Chicago Japanese American Historical Society, the Japanese American Historical Society of San Diego, and the Japanese American Resource Center/Museum, 2000, p. 130.

80. Mary Oyama was Joe Oyama's sister; both talented writers contributed frequently to the ethnic press. As her diary reveals, Mary and her mother frequently did ironing and other tasks for Issei women friends who fell ill.

81. Haruko (Sugi) Hurt interview, *REgenerations*, p. 126.

82. Mary Nishi Ishizuka interview by author, August 4, 2009.

83. For a discussion of Bruce's Beach and the African American fight against segregation at southern California beaches, see Douglas Flamming, *Bound for Freedom: Black Los Angeles in Jim Crow America*. Berkeley: University of California Press, 2005, pp. 271–275. See also Cecilia Rasmussen, Resort Was an Oasis for Blacks Until Racism Drove Them Out. *Los Angeles Times*, July 21, 2002, p. B-4; Deborah Schoch, Erasing a Line Drawn in the Sand, *Los Angeles Times*, March 19, 2007, p. B-1. For more information on the Inkwell, see Cecilia Rasmussen, In 'Whites Only' Era, an Oasis for L.A.'s Blacks. *Los Angeles Times*, July 3, 2005, p. B-2. These sources give slightly different accounts of the fight against beach segregation, some focusing on the 1927 legal victory that gradually eroded racial barriers at beaches; others focus on the destruction of the Bruce's Beach resort and surrounding black neighborhood. Regarding pool and beach segregation in Los Angeles, see Lawrence Culver, *The Frontier of Leisure: Southern California and the Shaping of Modern America*. New York: Oxford University Press, 2010, pp. 69–74.

84. Douglas Flamming, *Bound for Freedom*, pp. 289–291.

85. Flamming, *Bound for Freedom*, pp. 83–84.

86. Katsumi (Hirooka) Kunitsugu interview, *REgenerations Oral History Project: Rebuilding Japanese American Families, Communities, and Civil Rights in the Resettlement Era*. Los Angeles: Japanese American National Museum, in collaboration with the Chicago Japanese American Historical Society, the Japanese American Historical Society of San Diego, and the Japanese American Resource Center/Museum, 2000, p. 262. There was no school segregation in Los Angeles.

87. The Issei and Nisei patronized both Japanese and Chinese restaurants, but the latter may have been regarded as more novel, serving dishes that Japanese Americans were less likely to prepare at home. Chinese restaurants, which have thrived in the United States since the 1949 Gold Rush, have from their inception served a multi-ethnic clientele.

88. Mary Nishi Ishizuka interview by author, August 4, 2009. Fumiko Fukuyama Ide also said, "Everybody went to Far East to celebrate anything." Interview by author, August 14, 2009.

89. Eileen H. Tamura, p. 191.

90. Mei Nakano, *Japanese American Women, Three Generations, 1890-1990*. Berkeley: Mina Press Publishing, 1990; and San Francisco: National Japanese American Historical Society, 1990, p. 120. As Harry H. L. Kitano states, "It would be difficult to overlook the vast network of services and opportunities available to the Japanese youth." See Harry H. L. Kitano, *Japanese Americans: The Evolution of a Subculture*, 2nd ed. Englewood Cliffs, NJ: Prentice-Hall, 1976, p. 60; David K. Yoo, *Growing Up Nisei: Race, Generation, and Culture among Japanese Americans of California, 1924-49*. University of Illinois Press, 2000, p. 167.

91. "The Typical Nisei Club Girl," *Kashu Mainichi*, January 1, 1941, p. G2.

92. Regarding gendered power dynamics in Little Tokyo, see Lon Kurashige, Rise and Fall of Biculturalism: Consumption, Socialization, and Americanism, in *Japanese American Celebration and Conflict: A History of Ethnic Identity and Festival in Los Angeles, 1934–1990*. Berkeley: University of California Press, 2002, pp. 42–71.

93. The Typical Nisei Club Girl, *Kashu Mainichi*, January 1, 1941, p. G2.

94. *Rafu Shimpo*, November 8, 1926. I suspect that "Katy" may have been Kay Tateishi.

95. Mary S. Sims, *The Natural History of a Social Institution—the Young Women's Christian Association*. New York: The Womans Press, 1936, p. 59.

96. Sucheng Chan, Race, Ethnic Culture, and Gender in the Construction of Ethnic Identities among Second-Generation Chinese Americans, 1880s to 1930s, in K. Scott Wong and Sucheng Chan, eds. *Claiming America: Constructing Chinese American Identities during the Exclusion Era*. Philadelphia: Temple University Press, 1998, p. 143.

97. Nancy Robertson with Elizabeth Norris, "Without Documents No History": Sources and Strategies for Researching the YWCA, in Nina Mjagkij and Margaret Spratt, eds. *Men and Women Adrift: The YMCA and the YWCA in the City*. New York: New York University Press, 1997, p. 276.

98. Japanese Branch Young Women's Christian Association pamphlet ca. 1938, YWCA collection, Special Collections, California State University, Northridge. The pamphlet states, "The first G.R. club was organized in 1918, four years before the Japanese Y.W.C.A. was established here." Note: The information and photos in the undated pamphlet make it

clear that it dates from the prewar period. The pamphlet mentions that its publication coincides with the "sixtieth anniversary" of the GR clubs, founded in 1918; if "sixtieth" is a misprint and it was actually the 20th anniversary, the pamphlet probably appeared in 1938.

99. *Annual Report of the Japanese Y.W.C.A., 1941*, YWCA Collection, Special Collections, California State University, Northridge. This organization initially did case work and sponsored lectures.

100. *Los Angeles Herald*, July 18, 1916.

101. In 1916 the "Japanese Y.W.C.A." in Los Angeles presented a public program that included a pantomime by Japanese girls in the Sunbeam Club and a centerpiece performance, "The Picture Bride," which portrayed "the experiences of a girl who comes to this country as a picture bride and shows how she is taken care of at different stages by the Y.W.C.A." *Los Angeles Times*, November 22, 1916.

102. *Los Angeles Herald*, November 25, 1916.

103. Japanese Branch Young Women's Christian Association pamphlet ca. 1938, YWCA Collection, Special Collections, California State University, Northridge.

104. Sims, p. 64. In YWCA parlance, "industrial" included domestic workers as well as factory operatives; "business and professional" referred to clerical workers, women in middle management, and those in professions such as medicine and education. Nancy Robertson with Elizabeth Norris, "Without Documents No History": Sources and Strategies for Researching the YWCA, pp. 275–276.

105. *Rafu Shimpo*, November 8, 1926.

106. Sims, p. 65.

107. Because of the different (and often cryptic) names of the numerous clubs that appear in the early newspapers, it is sometimes difficult to discern which were YWCA-sponsored organizations. See *Guide Book for Senior High School Girl Reserves*, prepared by the Girl Reserves Department, National Board, YWCA. New York: The Womans Press, 1928, pp. 18, 88.

108. Judith Weisenfeld, *African American Women and Christian Activism: New York's Black YWCA, 1905–1945*. Cambridge, MA: Harvard University Press, 1997, p. 185. I could not ascertain, but think it would be a fruitful subject to pursue, whether the Japanese YWCA staff workers experienced the same struggles as the African American YWCA women in dealing with the larger local and national YWCA.

109. Ibid.

110. *Rafu Shimpo*, August 9, 1926. The ceremony was held at the Beverly Hills home of the parents of adviser Esther Bartlett, a YWCA worker and GR club adviser. "Bill, a small Indian boy" from the Sherman Institute near Riverside, was staying at the Bartletts' home and participated in the ceremony, playing the "Hymn of Lights" on a cornet. Young women participated in candlelight initiation ceremonies and worked to earn GR rings—the highest award that could be bestowed upon a Girl Reserve—throughout the 1920s and 1930s.

111. Raymond A. Mohl, "Cultural Pluralism in Immigrant Education: The YWCA's International Institutes, 1910-1940, in Nina Mjagkij and Margaret Spratt, eds. *Men and Women Adrift: The YMCA and the YWCA in the City*. New York: New York University Press, 1997, p. 113.

112. Mohl, p. 117.

113. Mohl. p. 119.

114. Mohl, pp. 119–120.

115. The programs offered by the Japanese branch—including classes in Japanese literature, Japanese and Western-style cooking, and sewing—reflect efforts to reach Nisei women. *Rafu Shimpo*, March 28, 1927.

116. *Rafu Shimpo*, holiday issue, December 23, 1940, pp. 16–17. Maki Ichiyasu also lived at the Japanese YWCA dormitory with 13 Nisei students and working girls.

117. Fumiko Fukuyama Ide interview by author, March 27, 2001. The Tartanettes' club advisors were also Nisei women: Hana Uno Shepard and Takako Nakajima. Sophie Tajima, a Nisei from Pasadena, California, graduated from Occidental College with a major in sociology. She was an active leader at the Pasadena Union Church where her father was pastor, and also served as president of the Southern California Christian Young People's Federation. Sophie married Reverend Donald Toriumi, who was affiliated with the Union Church. Newspaper

clipping, June 28, 1938, YWCA Collection, Special Collections, California State University, Northridge.

118. Japanese Branch Young Women's Christian Association pamphlet, ca. 1938, YWCA Collection, Special Collections, California State University, Northridge.

119. Joanne Meyerowitz, preface, *Men and Women Adrift*, ed. Mjagkij and Spratt, pp. xii–xiii.

120. Japanese YWCA Christmas booklet, 1940, YWCA Collection, Special Collections, California State University, Northridge.

121. Judy Yung, *Unbound Feet*, p. 152.

122. Fumiko Fukuyama Ide interview by author, March 27, 2001. The Tartanettes, a Girl Reserves group started at the Japanese Union Church, were one of the many GR clubs that came under the umbrella of the Japanese YWCA.

123. Setsuko Matsunaga Nishi interview by author, August 4, 2009.

124. Harry Kitano, *Japanese Americans: The Evolution of a Subculture*, 2nd ed. Englewood Cliffs, NJ: Prentice-Hall, Inc., 1976, p. 50.

125. Vicki L. Ruiz, The Flapper and the Chaperone: Historical Memory among Mexican-American Women, in Donna Gabaccia, ed. *Seeking Common Ground: Multidisciplinary Studies of Immigrant Women in the United States*. Westport, CT: Greenwood Press, 1992, p. 151.

126. Yoshiko Uchida, *Desert Exile: The Uprooting of Japanese American Family*. Seattle: University of Washington Press, 1982, p. 44.

127. *Rafu Shimpo*, November 8, 1926.

128. Alice Asaka, G.R. Choose Name for Organization. *Rafu Shimpo*, December 29, 1930.

129. *Rafu Shimpo*, holiday issue, December 24, 1937, p. 18.

130. Blue Triangle Postpones Snow Hike Until January. *Rafu Shimpo*, December 22, 1930.

131. *Rafu Shimpo*, March 7, 1927. These cooking classes appear to have been geared mainly to Issei women and married Nisei women. Although most were probably already preparing Japanese dishes at home, such classes offered the chance to expand their repertoire.

132. *Kashu Mainichi*, April 15 and May 22, 1932. The Junior Girl Reserves discussion of "It" was doubtless a legacy of Clara Bow, the "It Girl," and the promotion of "sex appeal" in the 1920s.

133. In 1936, the five clubs in the Japanese GR Inter-Club Council invited their mothers to a joint banquet with a "Late Autumn" motif, featuring the staging of two Japanese plays, "Koyaku-neri" and the comedy "Omanju-no-nai-kuni." Omanju-no-nai-kuni means "country without manju," a sweet bean-filled confection. *Rafu Shimpo*, November 15, 1936. In 1937, the A.B.C. Kouncil branched out to hold its first-annual father-daughter banquet. This 1938 event was the second annual banquet, in which clubs such as the Dot and Dash Club and the Debutantes participated. *Kashu Mainichi*, May 16, 1938.

134. *Rafu Shimpo*, January 7, 1929.

135. *Rafu Shimpo*, November 1, 1926.

136. *Rafu Shimpo*, November 8, 1926.

137. *Rafu Shimpo*, December 20, 1926.

138. *Rafu Shimpo*, September 5, 1927.

139. *Rafu Shimpo*, May 9, 1926.

140. *Rafu Shimpo*, September 6, 1926.

141. Ibid.

142. *Rafu Shimpo*, August 1, 1927.

143. *Rafu Shimpo*, August 9, 1926.

144. As Brian Niiya noted, "Formed in part as a reaction to discrimination, the Japanese American women's teams and leagues also served a social function, allowing young Nisei women to meet and socialize with their counterparts in other communities." Brian Niiya, …Introduction, in Brian Niiya, ed. *More Than a Game: Sport in the Japanese American Community*. Los Angeles: Japanese American National Museum, 2000, p. 39.

145. *Rafu Shimpo*, February 7, 1927.

146. Kay Moritani Komai interview by author, Temple City, California, August 9, 2000.

147. The *Rafu Shimpo* reported, "The 5 feet 9 inch Russian center was able to tap the ball where she pleased as she stood above everyone else on the court." This was described as the Blue Triangles' first game against a larger, taller group, which suggests that it may have been their first game with a non-Japanese American team. *Rafu Shimpo*, March 12, 1928.

148. *Rafu Shimpo*, March 12, 1928.

149. *Rafu Shimpo*, March 19, 1928. The reportage of both games shows the perceived linkage of race, height, and athletic advantage.

150. *Rafu Shimpo*, March 14, 1927.

151. Ibid.

152. Kathleen Susan Yep, Slapping back: Mei Wah Hoopsters and the embodied politics of gender, in *They Got Game: The Racial and Gender Politics of Basketball in San Francisco's Chinatown, 1932-1949*. Ph.D. dissertation, Ethnic Studies. University of California, Berkeley, 2002, pp. 43–78.

153. Marjorie Lee, Building Community, contributors Lucie Cheng, Suellen Cheng, et al. *Linking Our Lives: Chinese American Women of Los Angeles*. Los Angeles: UCLA Asian American Studies Center and the Chinese Historical Society of Southern California, 1984, pp. 93, 107–109.

154. Marjorie Lee, p. 107.

155. *Rafu Shimpo*, December 22, 1939, p. 23. The charter members of the group were the Kayans, Queen Esthers, Toquiwas, Nipponettes, Adelphians, Debutantes, and the Tres Arrowians.

156. It also appears that at least a few Nisei girls learned judo—both a martial art and a sport—in the prewar period. See, for example, a *Kashu Mainichi* article (January 3, 1936) about how a Nisei girl and her sisters used judo to foil a would-be robber.

157. *Rafu Shimpo*, December 24, 1937, p. 22.

158. Ibid.

159. Ibid.

160. *Rafu Shimpo*, December 23, 1938, p. 13.

161. *Rafu Shimpo*, November 6, 1938. In the next week, the YWCA Inter-Y Council invited all girls, including the non-affiliated, to attend a "songfest." *Rafu Shimpo*, November 13, 1938.

162. Fumiko Fukuyama Ide interview by author, March 27, 2001.

163. *Kashu Mainichi*, July 25, 1933. See also the detailed description of the North American YWBA's 1931 conference, Delegates of Many Cities Expected at YWBA Conference. *Rafu Shimpo*, July 20, 1931, p. 1; Girls Gather in San Diego for Convention of Y.W.B.A. *Rafu Shimpo*, July 21, 1931.

164. *Rafu Shimpo*, September 20, 1926.

165. In her study of mid-twentieth century beauty culture in the United States, Jennifer Malia McAndrew contends, "Through the performance of minstrel shows, Japanese Americans deflected criticism of their bodies by ridiculing the bodies of another ethnic group—African Americans—in a traditionally American manner." Her analysis of how incarcerated Japanese Americans tried to show their Americanization through wartime cultural performances offers a critical lens for thinking about prewar minstrelsy as well. Jennifer Malia McAndrew, All-American Beauty: The Experiences of African American, European American, and Japanese American Women with Beauty Culture in the Mid-Twentieth Century United States. Ph.D. dissertation, University of Maryland, 2008, pp. 125–126. My research through the prewar ethnic newspapers was not exhaustive, but this is the only reference I found to a Nisei group performing in blackface. Through the 1920s, caricatured imagery of African Americans abounded in popular media and entertainment. One example is the non-speaking black character Impie in Winsor McCay's comic strip "Little Nemo in Slumberland," which ran in the *Rafu Shimpo* as well as in mainstream newspapers; see the *Rafu* comics section for October 8, 15, and 22, 1928. Another example is the popular 1930s radio program "Amos and Andy." For a brief discussion of Chinese American vaudevillians performing in blackface, see Krystyn R. Moon, *Yellowface: Creating the Chinese in American Popular Media and Performance, 1850s–1920s*. New Brunswick, NJ: Rutgers University Press, 2005, pp. 158–159. A striking photo of young Cherokee women students performing in blackface appears in Devon Mihesuah's article, "Too Dark to Be Angels": The Class System among the Cherokee at the Female Seminary, in Vicki L. Ruiz with Carol Ellen DuBois, eds. *Unequal Sisters; An Inclusive Reader in U.S. Women's History*, 4th ed. New York: Routledge, 2008, p. 187.

166. S. Frank Miyamoto, *Social Solidarity among the Japanese in Seattle*. Seattle: University of Washington Press, 1984, p. xvii. *Social Solidarity* was first published in 1939 in the University of Washington Publications in the Social Sciences, Vol. II, No. 2, pp. 57–130.

167. *Rafu Shimpo*, December 20, 1938. The Blue Circles, a group that by this time had graduated from the GR division of the YWCA, were invited to the February 10 social as a guest club. The invited boys' clubs were the Royal Sportsmen, Sequoias, Oliver Cubs, Oliver Tigers, Tartan Juniors, Chuckateers, Golden Bear Juniors, and Cougars.

168. *Rafu Shimpo*, June 20, 1926. "Forfeits" appears to be a version of a Victorian parlor game in which players must answer questions or perform amusing actions in order to recover "forfeited" personal items.

169. Setsuko Matsunaga Nishi interview by author, September 12 and 14, 2009.

170. Box-Lunch social at M.E. Church by Epworth Youths. *Rafu Shimpo*, November 29, 1926.

171. Ibid.

172. Financial Success Marks All Around Lunch Social. *Rafu Shimpo*, February 23, 1931. For more examples of box-lunch socials held by girls' clubs, see: Two Events on Program of Emba Girl Reserves. *Rafu Shimpo*, May 25, 1931; Sea Breeze Plan Idea for Emba's Box Lunch Social. *Rafu Shimpo*, June 8, 1931; Cherry Blossom Club Plan Benefit Box Lunch Social. *Rafu Shimpo*, November 15, 1931.

173. *Rafu Shimpo*, November 29, 1929.

174. *Kashu Mainichi*, April 26, 1936.

175. *Rafu Shimpo*, November 19, 1928.

176. *Rafu Shimpo*, December 23, 1938, p. 14.

177. Kay Moritani Komai interview, Temple City, California, August 9, 2000.

178. *Kashu Mainichi*, November 17, 1931.

179. *Kashu Mainichi*, January 5, 1932. Chi Alpha Delta was the first Japanese American women's sorority at UCLA, founded in 1929. See Shirley Jennifer Lim, *A Feeling of Belonging: Asian American Women's Public Culture, 1930–1960*. New York: New York University Press, 2006.

180. *Kashu Mainichi*, November 28, 1931.

181. *Kashu Mainichi*, July 28, 1933.

182. *Kashu Mainichi*, July 28, 1933.

183. The second generation also had recommendations regarding ideal parental behavior: The polled felt that not only should a girl introduce her escort to her parents, but parents "should be willing to meet the fellow." With an eye to both propriety and the Depression-Era wallet, the poll respondents urged, "If at all possible, it would be a very fine thing if the girl's parents could serve refreshments in the home after the dance. This would mean that the young people would get home earlier, the fellows would be saved some expense, and it would give the parents an opportunity to get better acquainted with the fellows." They also felt that daughters should be permitted to entertain friends at home. The opinions expressed in the poll suggest that the rules of behavior were in the process of negotiation between the urban Nisei youth and their parents. *Kashu Mainichi*, July 28, 1933.

184. *Rafu Shimpo*, December 24, 1937, p. 15. On page 14 of the same issue, a figure of 102 dances is given. The other article included "socials" together with the gatherings formally advertised as dances, raising the number to 130.

185. *Rafu Shimpo*, December 24, 1937, p. 14.

186. *Rafu Shimpo*, December 23, 1938, pp. 12, 14.

187. The *Rafu Shimpo* asserted, When the competition is too stiff, as is the case when there are three dances on a single week-end, then there is driven home the obvious need for some 'Master Calendar' authority.... *Rafu Shimpo*, December 23, 1938, p. 14.

188. *Rafu Shimpo*, December 24, 1937, p. 14.

189. *Rafu Shimpo*, December 23, 1938, p. 12.

190. Toshi Nagamori Ito, *Memoirs of Toshi Ito: U.S.A. Concentration Camp Inmate, War Bride, Mother of Christie and Judge Lance Ito*. Bloomington, IN: AuthorHouse, 2009, p. 35. See *Rafu Shimpo*, December 23, 1938, p. 12; December 24, 1937, p. 14. Nisei also flocked to the Palm Garden Rink, the Long Beach Hippodrome, the Lincoln Rink, the Culver City Rollerdrome, the Mission Beach Rink, the Fifth Street Rink in Pomona, and in El Centro, the Heber Rink.

191. As S. Frank Miyamoto found in Seattle, "Musical and dramatic events" presented by the young people's organizations of the Buddhist and Christian churches "were a means of giving expression to Nisei talent." Miyamoto, *Social Solidarity*, p. xvii.

192. *Rafu Shimpo*, July 25, 1927. It was at this conference that the local YWBAs met to form the North American YWBA.

193. "Japanese 'Nora' Lives in 'Price of Wife' Production," *Kashu Mainichi*, May 7, 1932. This production may have been adapted from a Japanese translation of Ibsen.

194. *Rafu Shimpo*, holiday issue, December 23, 1940, p. 17. Another avenue was the *Peppimist*, the official organ of the Los Angeles Girl Reserves, for which Emba Girl Reserve president Sakiye Yamada served as art editor.

195. The club's stated purpose was "to develop the girl mentally, morally, physically, and spiritually," enabling her "to face life squarely and to find and give the best." *Rafu Shimpo*, April 7, 1926.

196. *Kashu Mainichi*, November 23, 1933.

197. *Kashu Mainichi*, September 21, 1933 and December 13, 1933.

198. *Rafu Shimpo*, December 24, 1937, p. 13.

199. *Rafu Shimpo*, December 23, 1938, p. 12.

200. Ibid.

201. *Rafu Shimpo*, December 17, 1928.

202. For example, in 1934 the Blue Triangles not only gathered toys and useful gifts for a poor family's Christmas, but also contributed clothes to the Japanese Children's Home. *Rafu Shimpo*, December 20, 1934.

203. *Kashu Mainichi*, March 29, 1932.

204. *Rafu Shimpo*, November 13, 1934.

205. Ibid.

206. Annual Report of the Japanese Y.W.C.A., 1941, YWCA Collection, Special Collections, California State University, Northridge.

207. *Rafu Shimpo*, December 23, 1938, p. 15.

208. Ibid. The writer did not elaborate on how the Nisei clubs helped to strengthen "Japanese-American friendship," but this may have been a reference to club members' participation in inter-racial conferences, their involvement in inter-ethnic events such as the International Institute's festivals, and their cultural performances for civic and school programs.

209. Oko Murata Crowned Queen at Blue Triangle Frolic. *Rafu Shimpo*, May 4, 1931. For more on the frolic and queen contest, see *Rafu Shimpo* articles on April 20 and 27, 1931.

210. Large Attendance Rewards Queen Esther Club Dance. *Rafu Shimpo*, July 27, 1931.

211. Chinese, Japanese Invited to Attend Celestian Dance. *Rafu Shimpo*, August 24, 1931.

212. Chinese Invite Japanese to Sport Dance Saturday. *Rafu Shimpo*, July 27, 1931, p. 2.

213. Judy Yung, *Unbound Feet*, p. 152.

214. *Rafu Shimpo*, April 25, 1926.

215. *Rafu Shimpo*, April 11, 1926.

216. *Rafu Shimpo*, January 23, 1928.

217. *Rafu Shimpo*, January 30, 1928. When the Nisei used the term "American," they usually meant European Americans; they often referred to themselves as "Japanese" in the prewar ethnic press.

218. Doings at Asilomar Conference for Co-Eds; Negro Teacher Makes Appeal for Inter-racial Justice, While Dr. Ichihashi Introduces the Orient. *Rafu Shimpo*, July 4, 1926. The conference ran from June 16–26, 1926.

219. Doings at Asilomar Conference for Co-Eds. *Rafu Shimpo*, July 4, 1926. The role of popular northern California Nisei columnist and leader Miya Sannomiya as conference chair may have contributed to Ichihashi's being invited. Perhaps revealing his misgivings about the second generation, Yamato Ichihashi, "anxious to find out whether Japanese college girls were as dumb as the boys," called a meeting of the Nisei attendees one afternoon and "discussed with them the second generation situation." For more information about Yamato Ichihashi, see Gordon Chang, ed. *Morning Glory, Evening Shadow: Yamato Ichihashi and His Internment Writings, 1942–1945*. Stanford: Stanford University Press, 1997.

220. *Rafu Shimpo*, July 4, 1926. The attendees also interacted with the local Japanese American community: The Japanese church in Monterey, "hearing that the girls were homesick for gohan [rice], invited them to a sumptuous nine-course feast of Japanese food."

221. *Rafu Shimpo*, December 23, 1940, p. 16.
222. *Rafu Shimpo*, December 23, 1940, p. 17.
223. *Rafu Shimpo*, December 10, 1939.
224. *Rafu Shimpo*, December 23, 1940, p. 16.
225. Sucheng Chan, Race, Ethnic Culture, and Gender in the Construction of Identities among Second-Generation Chinese Americans, 1880s to 1930s, in K. Scott Wong and Sucheng Chan, eds. *Claiming America: Constructing Chinese American Identities during the Exclusion Era.* Philadelphia: Temple University Press, 1998, p. 128.
226. *Rafu Shimpo*, December 10, 1937. Some groups, such as the Blue Circles and the Tartanettes, have been getting together for more than six decades.
227. *Rafu Shimpo*, December 23, 1940, p. 16.
228. *Rafu Shimpo*, March 10, 1940.
229. *Rafu Shimpo*, holiday issue, December 21, 1941, p. 10.
230. Ibid.
231. Ibid. In the 1920s and 1930s, ethnically segregated clubs were very common, and racial-ethnic youth who attempted to move across racial lines sometimes met painful rebuffs. However, in southern California, the climate of interracial relations varied according to region and neighborhood. Some high schools such as Roosevelt and Belmont, for example, fostered many interethnic clubs and friendships.
232. *Rafu Shimpo*, December 26, 1941. I discuss Mary Oyama and her work in chapter 3.
233. Ibid. I discuss Mary Oyama and the Nisei Writers and Artists League in chapter 3.
234. *Rafu Shimpo*, December 10, 1941.
235. *Rafu Shimpo*, December 22, 1941.
236. *Rafu Shimpo*, December 28, 1941.

Chapter 2

1. *Rafu Shimpo*, December 12, 1928. Louise Suski, the *Rafu Shimpo's* English-language-section editor, was one of the bridesmaids. Rosemary and Justus were fortunate, because her parents planned to give them a store to manage.
2. Regarding the significance of focusing on "the quotidian life," see Martin F. Manalansan IV, ed. *Global Divas: Filipino Gay Men in the Diaspora.* Durham: Duke University Press, 2003, p. 90.
3. "Nadeshiko" is a reference to a flower that symbolized womanhood in Japan.
4. *Rafu Shimpo*, January 12, 1931.
5. David K. Yoo, *Growing Up Nisei: Race, Generation, and Culture among Japanese Americans of California, 1924-49.* Urbana: University of Illinois Press, 2000, p. 79.
6. *Kashu Mainichi*, March 13, 1938. Emiko ruled that girls should not put on makeup in public and that boys should bring refreshments to their female partners at socials.
7. *Kashu Mainichi*, 8 December 1940.
8. Her by-line was So-and-so. *Kashu Mainichi*, Sunday, August 20, 1933. (The newspaper gives the date as August 19, which appears to be a mistake given the sequencing of the previous days' issues.)
9. Ibid.
10. Miss Etiquette Says, *Rafu Shimpo*, November 15, 1936. The Nisei used the term "American" to mean "white."
11. Miss Etiquette Says, *Rafu Shimpo*, October 11, 18, and 25 1936.
12. Miss Etiquette Says, *Rafu Shimpo*, December 6, 1936. Regarding presents for girls, boys were told, "You will always be in good taste if you send books, candy, flower[s] and perfume…." *Rafu Shimpo*, November 29, 1936.
13. See John's Vacation, *Rafu Shimpo*, February 21–April 11, 1926; "The Doctor's Daughter," begins April 18, 1926; "Life's Problems," begins on September 27, 1926.
14. *Rafu Shimpo*, March 10, 1940.
15. Mary Nishi Ishizuka. Interview by author, August 4, 2009.
16. Rose Honda. Interview by author, July 30, 2009.
17. *Rafu Shimpo*, March 28, 1927; *Rafu Shimpo*, March 7, 1927.

83. Kathy Peiss, *Hope in a Jar: The Making of America's Beauty Culture.* New York: Metropolitan Books, 1998, p. 144.
84. *Rafu Shimpo,* 28 November 1937. The Oyama Cosmetics Company was a family business, with the Nisei sons marketing products developed by their Issei father. As Joe Oyama recalled, their products were particularly popular with Issei women; Filipino men were the major customers for the hair pomade.
85. Haru Matsui (pseudonym for Ayako Ishigaki), *Restless Wave, An Autobiography.* New York: Modern Age Books, 1940, p. 229. Reprinted under Ishigaki's real name, as *Restless Wave, My Life in Two Worlds, A Memoir,* with afterword by Yi-Chun Tricia Lin and Greg Robinson. New York: The Feminist Press, 2004.
86. *Rafu Shimpo,* March 16, 1931. "Mrs. Grundy," a character from Thomas Morton's 1798 play *Speed the Plough,* embodied propriety and its censorious impact.
87. Hollywood Madness, A Nisei Melodrama, *Rafu Shimpo,* April 18, 1937. Generally there seemed to be more concern about naive small-town Nisei girls being inflamed with dreams of stardom than about the possible corruption of city girls, who were perhaps presumed to be more sophisticated and worldly wise.

   Buddy Uno's protagonist makes a disastrous marriage with a Chinese American she meets working as an extra on a movie set; she is disowned by her family, and eventually ends up, disillusioned, back in her hometown "Sacraton"—an amalgam of Sacramento and Stockton—working behind the counter in a notorious hash house, rumored to be the local Communist headquarters. This was one of a series of moralistic cautionary tales Buddy Uno wrote for the *Rafu Shimpo.*
88. *Kashu Mainichi,* January 1, 1940.
89. *Kashu Mainichi,* March 20 and April 10, 1938.
90. *Kashu Mainichi,* August 10, 1933. Sugahara's column was titled "The Local Layout."
91. Ibid. Sugahara's commentary may have been tempered by his own enthusiasm for film; he frequently included movie reviews at the end of his column and clearly attended often.
92. *Rafu Shimpo,* December 11, 1938.
93. *Kashu Mainichi,* October 30, 1932.
94. Ibid.
95. *Kashu Mainichi,* March 13, 1938. The story was sarcastically titled "O Glorious Nisei" and appears to be a critique (by an author writing under the pseudonym "Bakarashii," or foolish) of Nisei rowdyism and fights at dances.
96. *Kashu Mainichi,* April 24, 1938. The story, Only the Beginning, was by Les Kirihara.
97. Wakako Yamauchi. Interview by the author, Gardena, California, October 3, 1995.
98. *Rafu Shimpo,* November 24, 1940.
99. *Rafu Shimpo,* December 21, 1941.
100. Vicki L. Ruiz, The Flapper and the Chaperone: Historical Memory among Mexican-American Women, in Donna Gabaccia, ed. *Seeking Common Ground: Multidisciplinary Studies of Immigrant Women in the United States.* Westport, CT: Greenwood Press, 1992, pp. 141–158.
101. In the Meiji Period (1868–1912), while Japanese leaders pursued industrialization and the establishment of broadened education in order to compete with Western nations, they defined the role of women, particularly middle-class women, within the domestic sphere and passed laws to restrict women's rights and political activity. Within this framework, women's status varied according to class and region. See Kathleen Uno, Unlearning Orientalism: Locating Asian and Asian American Women in Family History, in Shirley Hune and Gail M. Nomura, eds. *Asian/Pacific Islander American Women: A Historical Anthology.* New York: New York University Press, 2003, pp. 48–50.
102. Beth L. Bailey, *From Front Porch to Back Seat, Courtship in Twentieth-Century America.* Baltimore: Johns Hopkins University Press, 1988, 1989, pp. 3, 19.
103. See T. Roku Sugahara, So This Is Leap Year…, *Kashu Mainichi,* June 28, 1936.
104. Their idyll was derailed by a car accident on their way home in "the wee small hours" of the morning. When they reached the flapper's home, her boyfriend went with her, "The wrath of her folks to allay / For from experience / He well knew / That she'd have the deuce to pay." *Rafu Shimpo,* April 18 and 25, 1926. The "Venice" referred to in the poem is a community in

southern California; the Venice Pier was a popular amusement site in the 1920s. The poem appears to have been written by a reader.

105. *Rafu Shimpo*, October 8, 1928. Julia Suski's drawings, which appeared regularly from 1926 through 1928, were coupled with sly humor regarding kissing, the romantic foibles of women and men, and the customs of dating. Some of the captions were credited to published sources, often college publications; others were uncredited; some that referred to events within the Japanese American community were clearly generated by Suski or the newspaper staff. Suski depicted both white and Asian/American-looking women and men.

106. *Kashu Mainichi*, July 31, 1933. Mrs. Olds was the bilingual daughter of one of the founders of the Tokyo Doshisha University; she was also giving talks for Issei parents.

107. *Rafu Shimpo*, April 16, 1937. Sometimes the lecturers were female medical authorities like Dr. Nadine Kavinoky, who spoke to two YWCA clubs—the Debutantes and the Alpha Beta Club—and showed a film, "Beginning of Life." *Rafu Shimpo*, November 29, 1937.

108. *Rafu Shimpo*, August 1, 1926.

109. *Rafu Shimpo*, holiday issue, December 24, 1936, p. 20. Male writer Kay Tateishi's short story shows that the "date" had become routine enough to be lampooned.

110. Fumiko Fukuyama Ide interview by author, March 27, 2001.

111. Setsuko Matsunaga Nishi. Interview by author, February 11 and 21, 2001; September 6, 2001. Because her father was educated in the United States, he may have been more liberal about his daughters' dating.

112. Frank Chuman wrote *The Bamboo People*, one of the first legal histories focusing on Asian Americans.

113. Setsuko Matsunaga Nishi. Interview by author, September 12 and 14, 2009.

114. See "Hodge Podge" column, *Rafu Shimpo*, December 16, 1933. Fujii advocated the virtues of going "50-50," with men and women sharing the costs of dates, but it seems that this seldom happened.

115. *Rafu Shimpo*, November 6, 1938.

116. *Kashu Mainichi*, May 3, 1936. The "stag line" referred to the line of men without female partners.

117. *Kashu Mainichi*, holiday issue, January 1, 1941.

118. *Kashu Mainichi*, July 10, 1932.

119. Feminine Interest, *Kashu Mainichi*, October 6, 1935.

120. *Rafu Shimpo*, holiday issue, December 23, 1938, p. 22.

121. From Brewin Typs column by RUS, *Rafu Shimpo*, January 19, 1931. Emphasis added.

122. *Rafu Shimpo*, December 10, 1939.

123. See Editorials, *Kashu Mainichi*, January 21, 1934. To this end, in 1940 the *Rafu Shimpo* offered girls "hints which may help you win your man" and "romance tests" to distinguish between love and infatuation; see *Rafu Shimpo*, January 7, 21, 28, 1940; February 25, 1940.

124. Setsuko Matsunaga Nishi interview by the author, September 12 and14, 2009.

125. For more on the I'm Telling You Deirdre column, see my article, Redefining Expectations: Nisei Women in the 1930s, *California History* (Spring 1994):44–53, 88. Mary Oyama Mittwer was "Deirdre."

126. *Kashu Mainichi*, March 4, 1934.

127. Evelyn Nakano Glenn, *Issei, Nisei, War Bride: Three Generations of Japanese American Women in Domestic Service*. Philadelphia: Temple University Press, 1986, p. 57. In the *Rafu Shimpo* of January 1, 1930, a Nisei man wrote approvingly of "companionate marriage"; other men described an ideal wife as being domestic, good-looking, having sterling character, and serving as an inspiration to them. The one woman who responded said an ideal husband would be intellectual, healthy, frank, and have good character.

128. Christina Simmons, *Making Marriage Modern: Women's Sexuality from the Progressive Era to World War II*. New York: Oxford University Press, 2009, p. 124.

129. Sara Evans, *Born for Liberty, A History of Women in America*. New York: Free Press Paperbacks, 1989, 1997, p. 178.

130. Kristin Celello, *Making Marriage Work: A History of Marriage and Divorce in the Twentieth-Century United States.* Chapel Hill: The University of North Carolina Press, 2009, p. 23.

131. Evans, *Born for Liberty*, p. 179.

132. Robert Howard Ross, Social Distance as It Exists Between the First and Second Generation Japanese in the City of Los Angeles and Vicinity. M.A. thesis, Department of Sociology, University of Southern California, 1939, p. 7. It was also the duty of the baishakunin to investigate the lineage of the prospective partner to ensure suitability. (Ross, who had lived in Japan for about 16 years, was fluent in Japanese.)

133. Ross, p.111–112. A Japanese Christian minister's delineation of three categories of Nisei marriage suggests a range of negotiations among Issei and Nisei: "free love marriage;" the traditional arranged wedding with baishakunin; and unions that were secretly engineered by go-betweens without the awareness of the couple. A fourth permutation combined individual Nisei choice with the appearance of adhering to custom: "A baishakunin is at least nominally selected to help to 'keep the face' of the families and he is allowed to carry out the arrangements of the wedding ceremony, reception, etc., so as to impress those who might be critical of modern romance."

134. Ross, p. 184.

135. *Rafu Shimpo*, August 6, 1928. Kofuji Eto, the daughter of a wealthy Issei agricultural landowner, was engaged to T. Fukunaga, a businessman and secretary of the Pismo Pea Growers Association.

136. *Rafu Shimpo*, April 22, 1937. The prominence of one of the six baishakunin, Sei Fujii—publisher of the *Kashu Mainichi*—may have prompted the inclusion of this detail.

137. It is also possible that the role of the baishakunin had shifted in the United States to involve potential mediation between newlyweds and in-laws, should difficulties arise.

138. See T. Roku Sugahara, Jr., So This Is Leap Year…, *Kashu Mainichi*, June 28, 1936.

139. Ross, p. 184.

140. Peggy Pascoe's insightful work on miscegenation law is especially useful; see her book, *What Comes Naturally: Miscegenation Law and US History*. New York: Oxford University Press, 2009. For a detailed discussion of antimiscegenation laws and their application to Asian Americans, see Megumi Dick Osumi, Asians and California's Anti-Miscegenation Laws, in Nobuya Tsuchida, ed. *Asian and Pacific American Experiences: Women's Perspectives*. Minneapolis: Asian/Pacific American Learning Resource Center and General College, University of Minnesota, 1982, pp. 1–37.

141. Arleen De Vera, The Tapia-Saiki Incident: Interethnic Conflict and Filipino Responses to the Anti-Filipino Exclusion Movement, in Valerie J. Matsumoto and Blake Allmendinger, eds. *Over the Edge: Remapping the American West*. Berkeley: University of California Press, 1999, pp. 201–214; Eiichiro Azuma, *Between Two Empires: Race, History, and Transnationalism in Japanese America*. New York: Oxford University Press, 2005, p. 187.

142. See Village Vagaries, *Kashu Mainichi*, September 17, 1933. Tajiri dismissed nativists' biological arguments against interracial marriage as being "too absurd to oppose."

143. *Rafu Shimpo*, January 6, 1935. Nishida appears to have been male. Given shifts in both the ethnic community and larger society, including the rise of the civil rights movement, the postwar overturning of anti-miscegenation laws, as Nishida predicted, the rate of intermarriage rose among Japanese Americans. By 1990, more than 40 per cent of Japanese Americans had married interracially or interethnically.

144. Lisa See, *On Gold Mountain: The One-Hundred Year Odyssey of My Chinese-American Family*. New York: Vintage Books, 1995.

145. See My Father Was Japanese, *Kashu Mainichi*, holiday issue, January 1, 1935. It is not clear where Uchiyamada and her equally accomplished brother Ambrose grew up, or whether they had any interaction with a Japanese American community in childhood. As young adults, they were well-known members of the Nisei literati. The numbers of mixed-heritage individuals like Margaret Uchiyamada have grown. According to the 2000 Census, Dean Toji reports, Japanese Americans "had the highest proportion of mixed-ancestry members among the dozen largest Asian groups, at 31 per cent." *The New Face of Asian Pacific America: Numbers, Diversity & Change in the 21st Century*, Eric Lai and Dennis Arguelles,

eds. San Francisco: Asian Week, San Francisco with UCLA's Asian American Studies Center Press in cooperation with the Organization of Chinese Americans and the National Coalition for Asian Pacific American Community Development, 2003, p. 77.

146. *Rafu Shimpo*, holiday issue, December 23, 1938, p. 20. The journalist cautiously commented, "How much the baishakunin 'arranged' weddings of Japan have influenced nisei marriage customs in this country is sometimes taken as a partial answer to the favorable low nisei divorce rate."

147. See T. Roku Sugahara, Jr., So This Is Leap Year...., *Kashu Mainichi*, June 28, 1936.

148. *Rafu Shimpo*, November 24, 1940. One of the featured model couples were Thomas and Chiyo Sashihara, whose wedding is discussed in the next section.

149. *Rafu Shimpo*, December 19, 1930.

150. *Rafu Shimpo*, January 17, 1927. Youth adviser Mrs. Lela Leech also took part.

151. *Rafu Shimpo*, December 5, 1927. By contrast, I have seen only one mention of a Nisei "bachelor party" in the press and there were no details as to the format of the celebration.

152. For example, in 1931 May Imai was given "a lovely rose colored glassware shower..." as well as a second "miscellaneous shower." *Rafu Shimpo*, January 5 and 12, 1931. In 1932 Yaeno Sakai was feted with a china shower given by "her feminine acquaintances." *Kashu Mainichi*, June 4, 1932.

153. Because of the distance from family networks in Japan, few Issei couples lived with parents-in-law. However, particularly in farm families, it was usually expected that an eldest Nisei son and his wife would help and care for them, often living with them or close by. In Japan, due to the tradition of primogeniture, the eldest son inherited family land and business, as well as responsibility for parents. In the absence of a son, an eldest daughter and her husband would shoulder key responsibility for aging parents. Generally, daughters-in-law faced much higher expectations than sons-in-law.

154. Postwar weddings show how widespread and deeply engrained many of these practices became. Even Buddhist wedding ceremonies took on much of the look of the Christian white wedding, in terms of dress and attendants.

155. Elizabeth Pleck, *Celebrating the Family: Ethnicity, Consumer Culture, and Family Rituals*. Cambridge, MA: Harvard University Press, 2000, pp. 208, 214–216. As Pleck explained, "The white wedding especially celebrated romantic love, that fairy tale of the prince charming and his young virgin beauty, who chose each other freely because of mutual attraction and then lived happily ever after."

156. *Rafu Shimpo*, June 20, 1927. A best man and ushers accompanied the groom.

157. "Oh Promise Me" and "I Love You Truly" seem to have been the most popular songs at Nisei weddings, judging from the frequency of their mention in newspaper accounts. According to Elizabeth Pleck, "Oh Promise Me" had become popular by the 1880s because of its vision of marriage as a paradise." (Pleck, p. 212.) The reception program also featured entertainments now unfamiliar to present-day wedding guests: Clara Suski and Robert Kuwahara performed a violin and saw duet; a comical story written by Michi Tawa was read; and a European American woman performed a whistling solo.

158. As newspaper reportage reveals, many Nisei newlyweds also visited the Grand Canyon and San Francisco.

159. *Rafu Shimpo*, July 11, 1927. By 1940, Thomas Sashihara was head of the Iwaki Drug company and active in the YMCA, while his wife served on the Japanese YWCA board, and was active in PTA and church circles in Alhambra, California; they had three children. *Rafu Shimpo*, November 24, 1940.

160. The *Kashu Mainichi* reported in a retrospective of 1940 nuptials, "Weddings were less ostentatious, on the whole but many still preferred impressive Buddhist rites, while a few said their 'I do's' in accordance with ancient Shinto ceremonials." *Kashu Mainichi*, holiday issue, January 1, 1941.

161. *Kashu Mainichi*, June 13, 1933.

162. Ibid.

163. Pleck, *Celebrating the Family*, p. 168. Pleck notes that, prior to the 1930s, most people believed it was bad luck to give baby gifts before the child's birth; the development of the baby shower reflects the decline in maternal and infant mortality.

164. Pleck, *Celebrating the Family*, p. 169.

165. *Kashu Mainichi*, April 25, 1938.

166. Kazuo Kawai, Three Roads and None Easy, *Survey Graphic* 9, no.2 (May 1926):165. Kawai, a professor at UCLA, was actively involved with Nisei youth on campus.

167. Judy Yung, *Unbound Feet: A Social History of Chinese Women in San Francisco*. Berkeley: University of California Press, 1995, p. 134.

168. Nisei Girl Interviewed by L.A. Times, *Kashu Mainichi*, April 23, 1933.

169. Ross, p. 163. Ross's survey, also taken by 78 Nisei men, asked, "What vocation do you wish to follow?" His compiled list did not specify which fields were most popular.

170. *Rafu Shimpo*, holiday issue, December 21, 1941, p. 13.

171. In 1939 Mrs. Suma Yokotake noted the racial barriers to Nisei in the Los Angeles City School system. She reported, "At present five nisei are regularly employed in the Los Angeles City School system. Two are in the school building maintenance department, one in the purchasing and distributing of supply and equipment office, one in the teachers personnel office and one in charge of an elementary office. Of these five nisei, four are women." See Be School Teachers, *Rafu Shimpo*, holiday issue December, 22 1939, p. 6.

172. J.J.J., Second Generation Womanhood, *Kashu Mainichi*, December 3, 1933.

173. Ross, p. 127. Women coveted such positions, as Monica Sone recalled from her youth in Seattle: "I knew that the Nisei girls competed fiercely among themselves for white-collar jobs in the Mitsui and Mitsubishi branch firms downtown, local newspaper establishments, Japanese banks, shipping offices and small export and import firms." Monica Sone, *Nisei Daughter*. Seattle: University of Washington Press, 1953, p. 133.

174. Yoshiko Hosoi Sakurai. Interview with Darcie Iki, Sojin Kim, and Valerie Matsumoto, Los Angeles, California, August 28–29, 1996.

175. *Rafu Shimpo*, holiday issue, December 23, 1938, p. 6.

176. *Kashu Mainichi*, January 1, 1940.

177. Peiss, *Hope in a Jar*, p. 91; Ruiz, *From Out of the Shadows*, p. 56. See also Tiffany Gill, *Beauty Shop Politics: African American Women's Activism in the Beauty Industry*. Urbana: University of Illinois Press, 2010.

178. Vicki Ruiz, *From Out of the Shadows*, p. 56.

179. *Rafu Shimpo*, holiday issue, December 23, 1938, p. 6. By 1940, the field was growing crowded and competitive in Little Tokyo, but with bright prospects in smaller enclaves.

180. Evelyn Nakano-Glenn, *Issei Nisei, War Bride: Three Generations of Japanese American Women in Domestic Service*. Philadelphia: Temple University Press, 1986, pp. 69–76.

181. *Rafu Shimpo*, holiday issue, December 24, 1937, p. 11.

182. Gene Gohara, Domestic Employment, *Current Life* (June 1941):6.

183. Fumiko Fukuyama Ide. Interview by author, March 27, 2001. The war ended her mother's plans to send her to Japan for education. In addition to Ide's work at the hospital, Nisei journalist Bean Takeda hired her as a proofreader for an English-language weekly in Little Tokyo.

184. Yung, p. 157.

185. Kawai, Three Roads and None Easy, p. 165.

186. Nisei Girl Interviewed by L.A. Times, *Kashu Mainichi*, April 23, 1933.

187. For information on Sannomiya, see Eriko Yamamoto, Miya Sannomiya Kikuchi: A Pioneer Nisei Woman's Life and Identity, *Amerasia Journal* 23 No. 3 (1997):73–101.

188. "Japanese Y.W. Secretary Warns Second Generation of Pitfalls in Nippon, *Kashu Mainichi*, October 21, 1934.

189. *Kashu Mainichi*, January 20, 1932.

190. *Rafu Shimpo*, November 26, 1937.

191. From the 1920s, utilizing techniques pioneered in Japan, Japanese American men found a niche in chick sexing. See Eiichiro Azuma, Race, Citizenship, and the Science of Chick Sexing: The Politics of Racial Identity among Japanese Americans, *Pacific Historical Review* 78, No. 2 (May 2009):242–275.

192. See Kimi Kanazawa, The Nisei Come of Age, *Kashu Mainichi*, May 24, 1936.

Chapter 3

1. *Kashu Mainichi*, October 28, 1934; see also Larry Tajiri, Village Vagaries. *Kashu Mainichi*, October 8, 1934. Morimoto's name appeared as both "Lucile" and "Lucille" in the ethnic press.
2. Ibid. For more information on Larry Tajiri and his wife Tsuguyo Okagaki Tajiri, see Greg Robinson, ed. and introduction, *Pacific Citizens: Larry and Guyo Tajiri and Japanese American Journalism in the World War II Era*. Champaign, IL: University of Illinois Press, 2011; David Yoo, *Growing Up Nisei: Race, Generation, and Culture among Japanese Americans of California, 1924–49*. Urbana, IL: University of Illinois Press, 2000, pp. 126–148.
3. *Kashu Mainichi*, October 28, 1934. Ellen Thun also wrote under the name Ellen Tanna.
4. *Kashu Mainichi*, January 1, 1934. For more on accomplished poet Toyo Suyemoto, see her memoir, *I Call to Remembrance: Toyo Suyemoto's Years of Internment*, Susan B. Richardson, ed. New Brunswick, NJ: Rutgers University Press, 2007.
5. Kenny Murase, Who's Who in the Nisei Literary World. *Current Life: The Magazine for the American Born Japanese*, October 1940, pp. 8–9. (In November 1941, *Current Life's* subtitle changed to "The Only National Nisei Magazine.") Most of the writers Murase listed lived in southern California, including most if not all of the women: Lucille Morimoto, Molly Oyama, Helen Aoki, Ruth Kurata, Chico Sakaguchi, Lily Yanai, Hisaye Yamamoto, Mary Kitano, and Ayako Noguchi. All but Lucille Morimoto were newspaper columnists; Morimoto regularly contributed poems to the ethnic press.
6. *Shin Sekai-Asahi*, June 23, 1941.
7. The family-run Oyama Cosmetics Company was liquidated in 1942 because of wartime uprooting and incarceration.
8. This information came from Joe Oyama. Family documents also cite the school as the San Francisco National Training School of the Woman's Home Missionary Society of the Methodist Episcopal Church.
9. *Kashu Mainichi*, March 28, 1937. Mary Oyama also wrote as Molly Oyama and Mary Mittwer.
10. See "Letters to the Editor. *Hokubei Mainichi*, August 15, 1990. I am indebted to Joe Oyama, Yasuo and Lillie Sasaki, and Vicki Mittwer Littman for their help with my research on Mary and their talented family.
11. Deep thanks to writer and activist Nikki Sawada Bridges Flynn for doing the detective work to figure out that Mary Oyama was "Deirdre." Oyama's 1934–1938 diary also confirms that she was writing "Deirdre" columns. For more information on her "I'm Telling You Deirdre" column in the *Shin Sekai*, see my article, Desperately Seeking 'Deirdre': Gender Roles, Multicultural Relations, and Nisei Women Writers of the 1930s. *Frontiers* 12, No. 1 (1991):19–32; see also my article, Redefining Expectations: Nisei Women in the 1930s. *California History* (Spring 1994):45–53, 88.
12. *Shin Sekai*, January 12, 1939.
13. *Kashu Mainichi*, July 12, 1936.
14. *Kashu Mainichi*, October 7, 1934.
15. *Kashu Mainichi*, September 29, 1934.
16. *Kashu Mainichi*, May 1, 1938.
17. See Village Vagaries. *Kashu Mainichi*, January 25, 1934.
18. Rhyme-a-Day. *Kashu Mainichi*, July 14, 1932, p. 1.
19. *Kashu Mainichi*, August 14, 1932.
20. Fragment. *Kashu Mainichi*, November 20, 1932.
21. Stan Yogi, Japanese American Literature, in King-Kok Cheung ed. *An Interethnic Companion to Asian American Literature*. New York: Cambridge University Press, 1997, p. 129.
22. *Kashu Mainichi*, November 6, 1932.
23. *Kashu Mainichi*, August 5, 1934.
24. *Kashu Mainichi*, October 28, 1934.
25. Hisaye Yamamoto, …I Still Carry It Around, in King-Kok Cheung, ed. *Seventeen Syllables*, Women Writers, Texts and Contexts series. New Brunswick, NJ: Rutgers University Press, 1994, p. 71.

26. Hisaye Yamamoto, Writing *Seventeen Syllables*, King-Kok Cheung, ed. p. 61.

27. Ibid.

28. *Current Life: The Magazine for the American Born Japanese*, November 1940, p. 11.

29. Ibid.

30. Don't Think It Ain't Been Charmin'. *Kashu Mainichi*, January 1, 1941, G2.

31. Ibid.

32. King-Kok Cheung, Introduction. *"Seventeen Syllables": Hisaye Yamamoto*, Women Writers Texts and Contexts series. New Brunswick, NJ: Rutgers University Press, 1994, p. 5.

33. Teruko Kumei, 'A Record of Life and a Poem of Sentiments': Japanese Immigrant *Senryu*, 1929–1945. *Amerikastudien/American Studies, A Quarterly*, 51, No. 1 (2006):31–32.

34. Teruko Kumei explains that haiku, like senryu, is composed of seventeen syllables, but the subject of haiku is nature, while senryu is about everyday life. Kumei, p. 29.

35. Hisaye Yamamoto, Seventeen Syllables. *Seventeen Syllables and Other Stories*. Latham, New York: Kitchen Table: Women of Color Press, 1988, p. 9.

36. Ibid.

37. Hisaye Yamamoto, Seventeen Syllables, p. 8. For a discussion of the language barrier between Issei and Nisei, see Maire Mullins, Imagining Community: Language and Literacy in Hisaye Yamamoto's 'Seventeen Syllables'. *Journal of Asian American Studies* 13, No. 2 (June 2010): 219–241.

38. Hisaye Yamamoto, *Seventeen Syllables*, p. 8–9.

39. Hisaye Yamamoto, Life Among the Oil Fields. *Seventeen Syllables and Other Stories*. Latham, New York: Kitchen Table: Women of Color Press, 1988, p. 91.

40. Regarding mochi-tsuki, see Hisaye Yamamoto, Las Vegas Charley. *Seventeen Syllables*, pp. 74–75; for her candy memory, see Life Among the Oil Fields, A Memoir. *Seventeen Syllables*, p. 86.

41. Hisaye Yamamoto, Yoneko's Earthquake. *Seventeen Syllables and Other Stories*. Latham, New York: Kitchen Table: Women of Color Press, 1988, p. 52. This story first appeared in 1951.

42. Yamamoto, The Brown House. *Seventeen Syllables and Other Stories*, p. 42. Originally published in 1951.

43. Julia Suski Gives Piano Lessons. *Rafu Shimpo*, September 24, 1928, p. 3.

44. Ibid.

45. Little Symphony Attracts Young Talented Musicians. *Kashu Mainichi*, February 18, 1932.

46. Ibid.

47. Agnes Miyakawa to Present Rich Program of Numbers. *Rafu Shimpo*, June 22, 1931, p. 3. On July 2 she gave a second concert at the Japanese Union church, sponsored by the Japanese Children's Home, which suggests that the second concert was a benefit fund raiser for the orphans.

48. Agnes Miyakawa Wins Honors through Big L.A. Concert. *Rafu Shimpo*, June 29, 1931, p. 1.

49. *Rafu Shimpo*, June 22, 1931, p. 3. In a small deviation from convention, Miyakawa's Madame Butterfly selection was not "One Fine Day," but "Sur la mer calmee."

50. Ibid.

51. *Rafu Shimpo*, June 29, 1931, p. 1.

52. Setsuko Matsunaga Nishi interview by author, September 12 and 14, 2009.

53. *Kashu Mainichi*, January 22, 1933.

54. The Little Tokyo Players struggled in their first year and a playwriting contest sponsored jointly by the northern and southern groups "also failed to click, because of the paucity of serious nisei writers." *Kashu Mainichi*, January 1, 1934.

55. *Kashu Mainichi*, April 26, 1936; May 30, 1936.

56. Setsuko Matsunaga Nishi interview by author, February 11 and 21, 2001; September 6, 2001. Fumiko Fukuyama Ide's brother Yoshio also appeared in this play, portraying one of the sons.

57. *Kashu Mainichi*, September 28, 1934.

58. "Little Girls Win Applause for Perfect Performance," *Rafu Shimpo*, May 16, 1927.

59. Ibid.

60. Interview with Toyoko Kataoka Kanegai by author, Los Angeles, California, August 4, 2000.

61. Lil' Tokyo Shojo Kabuki to Leave Soon on Trip. *Kashu Mainichi*, June 21, 1934, p. 1. The troupe was going to perform in Guadalupe, Salinas, San Jose, San Francisco, and Hawai'i. A drawing of performers in costume included "star" Sumako Hamaguchi, who went on to a long career as a professional dancer and teacher. For more on Hamaguchi, professionally known as Fujima Kansuma, see chapter 5.

62. See Local Layout. *Kashu Mainichi*, August 24, 1933. One exception was Japanese immigrant Sessue Hayakawa, a silent film star of the 1910s. See Daisuke Miyao, *Sessue Hayakawa: Silent Cinema and Transnational Stardom*. Durham, NC: Duke University Press, 2007.

63. Nisei journalist James Omura said, regarding the origins of the Wampus Baby Stars: "Wampus's first name was George. He was a casting critic of considerable note. In 1931, he began his list of the thirteen most promising actresses. The press called the selections Wampus Baby Stars." Toshia Mori was the Wampus Baby Star of 1932. See Frank Chin, *Born in the USA: A Story of Japanese America, 1889–1947*. Rowman & Littlefield, 2002, p. 119.

64. See Review Stand: a cavalcade of the arts. *Kashu Mainichi*, January 1, 1934.

65. See Karen Leong, *The China Mystique: Pearl S. Buck, Anna May Wong, Mayling Soong, and the Transformation of American Orientalism*. Berkeley: University of California Press, 2005; Hye Seung Chung, *Hollywood Asian: Philip Ahn and the Politics of Cross-Ethnic Performance*. Philadelphia: Temple University Press, 2006.

66. See Karin Higa, Hidden in Plain Sight: Little Tokyo Between the Wars, in Gordon H. Chang, Mark Dean Johnson, and Paul J. Karlstrom eds. *Asian American Art: A History, 1850–1970*. Stanford, CA: Stanford University Press, 2008, pp. 30–53.

67. Benji Okubo was the brother of artist Mine Okubo, author of *Citizen 13660*.

68. Setsuko Matsunaga Nishi interview by author, September 12 and 14, 2009. The Ateliers included the Serisawa brothers (Ikuo and Sueo), Chris Ishii, and Ken Nishi. Setsuko, who married Ken Nishi, recalled that the Ateliers were jokingly called "the Eight Liars."

69. Edwin McDowell, Gyo Fujikawa, 90, Creator of Children's Books, obituary, *New York Times*, December 7, 1998.

70. Elaine Woo, Children's Author Dared to Depict Multiracial World, obituary, *Los Angeles Times*, December 13, 1998.

71. *Rafu Shimpo*, January 22, 1940.

72. Woo, Children's Author Dared to Depict Multiracial World. See also Greg Robinson, Prolific Nisei's Work Ranged from Authoring Children's Books to Designing Stamps. *Nichi Bei Weekly*, July 12, 2012, p. 2.

73. News from Schools. *Rafu Shimpo*, February 21, 1926.

74. Tots in Program Thrill Audience with Costumes. *Rafu Shimpo*, April 4, 1927, p. 3. The article does not mention the dance/theatre group to which they belong, but the names are the same as those listed in the theatre performance discussed in the *Rafu* on May 16, 1927. In a 2000 interview, troupe member Toyoko Kataoka Kanegai also spoke about her experiences of both dance and kabuki performance.

75. *Kashu Mainichi*, May 3, 1936.

76. *Kashu Mainichi*, April 26, 1936.

77. *Kashu Mainichi*, January 1, 1935, p. E7.

78. Ibid.

79. *Kashu Mainichi*, January 1, 1937.

80. *Kashu Mainichi*, April 19, 1936.

81. See Village Vagaries. *Kashu Mainichi*, September 28, 1934.

82. *Current Life: The Magazine for the American Born Japanese*. November 1940, p. 11. Wing and Toy are among the featured performers in Arthur Dong's documentary film on early Asian American performers, "Forbidden City U.S.A." The outbreak of World War II prevented them from taking what they had hoped would be a breakthrough opportunity in Hollywood; instead, they had to start over again on the East Coast.

83. *Kashu Mainichi*, October 21, 1933.

84. *Kashu Mainichi*, October 29, 1933.

85. *Kashu Mainichi*, December 13, 1936. *Shukaku* was started in 1936.

86. The writers' group was variously referred to as "The Writers," "The Writers of Los Angeles," and the "Nisei Writers' Group." According to Yasuo Sasaki, it was also called the Nisei Writers and Artists League in its early years, modeled after the League of American Writers.

87. See Viewpoint. *Kashu Mainichi*, November 17, 1935. I have not found any copies of *Leaves*.

88. *Kashu Mainichi*, April 8, 1936; May 20, 1936; June 1, 1936.

89. *Kashu Mainichi*, June 15, 1936. The guests included journalist Charles Leong, Helen Saylor, who had been active in literary activities at Pomona College, and Constance Chandler, a social scientist doing research at USC. I believe the cosmopolitan mix was largely a result of Mary Oyama's influence. It appears that she hosted the social. For information on Shimano, see Bill Hosokawa, A True Story... The Rifle Barked! *Kashu Mainichi*, March 29, 1936.

90. Eddie Shimano, Foreword. *Gyo-Sho, A Magazine of Nisei Literature*. Mount Vernon, Iowa: The English Club of Cornell College, no date given, but the magazine was reviewed in the *Kashu Mainichi* in June 1936, p. 5.

91. Ibid.

92. Ibid.

93. Ibid.

94. Patricia Liggins Hill, ed., *Call and Response: The Riverside Anthology of the African American Literary Tradition*. New York: Houghton Mifflin Company, 1998, pp. 768–795; Alain Locke, Enter the New Negro. *Survey Graphic*, March 1925, pp. 631–634; Nathan Irvin Huggins, *Harlem Renaissance*. New York: Oxford University Press, 1971, pp. 52–83.

95. Eiji Tanabe translated a short story by K. Kawabata for *Gyo-Sho*.

96. "Teru" can be a man's or woman's name—for example, dancer Teru Izumida was a woman and actor Teru Shimada a man. Nisei John McGilvrey Maki was born in Tacoma, Washington, in 1909 to Issei parents and adopted by the white McGilvrey family. In 1936, he adopted a more Japanese name "Maki." With a Harvard Ph.D., he became a professor of political science at the University of Washington and later at the University of Massachusetts, Amherst. See Lewis C. Mainzer, John McGilvrey Maki, in *PS: Political Science & Politics* 40, No. 3 (July 2007): 596–597.

97. Mary Oyama, who was singled out for thanks as a member of the Writers of Southern California who had supported the magazine, also contributed a short breezy poem, "Song of Cynicism."

98. Molly Oyama, Coming of Age. *Gyo-Sho, A Magazine of Nisei Literature*. Mount Vernon, Iowa: The English Club of Cornell College, no date given, but the magazine was reviewed in the *Kashu Mainichi* in June 1936, p. 7.

99. Molly Oyama, Coming of Age, p. 8.

100. Molly Oyama, Coming of Age, p. 10

101. Ellen Thun, Sketch. *Gyo-Sho, A Magazine of Nisei Literature*, p. 20.

102. Ibid.

103. Ibid.

104. Mary Korenaga, Chiyono, *Gyo-Sho*, p. 23.

105. Korenaga, Chiyono, pp. 22–23.

106. *Kashu Mainichi*, June 21, 1936. Carl Kondo's position as a reviewer was somewhat complicated. He was a prolific member of the Nisei literati of southern California and a close friend of Mary Oyama Mittwer. It is impossible to know whether he had submitted any work to Shimano for consideration, but none of his writing was included.

107. *Kashu Mainichi*, June 21, 1936. Together with Izumida and Oyama's works, Kondo also cited Eiji Tanabe's translation of a Japanese story. Kondo reserved a final oblique critique for second-generation readers, not writers, concluding grimly, "When the writings of the Nisei are such that none can mistake it for other than what it is, it will be fulfillment, and the Nisei, I prophecy, will not enjoy its reading."

Kondo himself was one of the writers who came under fire for writing so many stories revolving around white characters. He experimented with a wide range of genres in his fiction, which included hard-boiled mysteries featuring European American detectives and thugs, romance among the Nisei working in a produce market, social-realist stories of white Depression-era job seekers, and even pulp science fiction, with a hero of mixed-race Asian descent. His own work illustrates the tensions in Nisei efforts to foster modes of expression reflecting ethnicity and generation.

108. *Kashu Mainichi*, January 29, 1934; *Rafu Shimpo*, January 1, 1935.

109. *Current Life: The Magazine for the American Born Japanese*, April 1941, p. 10.

110. Ibid.

111. *Current Life: The Magazine for the American Born Japanese*, July 1941, p. 13.

112. According to Kevin Starr, John Fante "immersed himself in the Filipino community of Long Beach in the hopes of writing a novel" about them. He did not finish the novel, but an excerpt, "Helen, Thy Beauty Is to Me," appeared in the *Saturday Evening Post* magazine in 1941. See Starr, *The Dream Endures: California Enters the 1940s*. New York: Oxford University Press, 1997, p. 294.

113. Kevin Starr, *The Dream Endures*, pp. 149–151.

114. Kenny Murase, William Saroyan and the American Short Story. *Current Life: The Magazine for the American Born Japanese*, December 1940, p. 3.

115. Of this Japanese American writer, Saroyan anticipated "that his source of material will be his race, the memory of the old country in his parents, his own personal experience, and the experience of his own kind about him—but—at the same time—I will also predict that everything he writes will be as valid for me as for himself; that while his work will spring from his own inner life, it will be universal." William Saroyan, William Saroyan Salutes Current Life. *Current Life, the Magazine for the American Born Japanese*, May 1941, pp. 8–9.

116. William Saroyan, *Current Life*, p. 8.

117. *Current Life: The Magazine for the American Born Japanese*, 1941, p. 8.

118. Patricia Liggins Hill, ed. *Call and Response*, pp. 794–795.

119. Chester Himes's novel, *If He Hollers Let Him Go*. New York: Thunder Mouth Press, 1945, 1972, 1986, on page 3 mentions "Little Riky Oyana," a thinly veiled reference to Richard "Ricky" Mittwer, the first child of Mary Oyama Mittwer and Fred Mittwer.

120. Mary Oyama, A Nisei Report from Home. *Common Ground* (Winter 1946), p. 26. Emphasis in the original.

121. *Kashu Mainichi*, August 6, 1933.

122. *Kashu Mainichi*, January 1, 1934.

123. *Kashu Mainichi*, January 1, 1935. Suyemoto herself rarely addressed Japanese American issues in her poetry.

124. *Kashu Mainichi*, January 1, 1935.

125. *Kashu Mainichi*, January 1, 1936. Kobayashi cited the names of the Nisei writers' fictional characters as evidence of their failing: "In recent productions, which are pretty sad, Delain, or Margery, or some other Euro-American creature move about in the accepted fiction manner. Could one blame the reader for his rages at such perfidity?" He concluded, "No amount of 'polished dullness', of rehashing other people's ideas in a string of empty words, which sound like a string of empty freight cars rattling over a trestle can be substituted for the free expression of the lyrical ecstasy, the poignancy that comes from life itself."

126. *Kashu Mainichi*, April 5, 1936. See "Medley" by Toyo Suyemoto, who included Kobayashi's critique.

127. *Kashu Mainichi*, April 12, 1936. Aisawa appears to have been a student at Woodbury College at the time.

128. *Kashu Mainichi*, April 5, 1936.

129. See "postscript to whys and wherefores," *Kashu Mainichi*, June 7, 1936. In her list of accomplished writers, Oyama also included Larry Tajiri, Yasuo Sasaki, Aiji Tashiro, and Ambrose Uchiyamada.

130. See continued "postscript to whys and wherefores," *Kashu Mainichi*, June 14, 1936.

131. *Kashu Mainichi*, July 12, 1936.

132. *Kashu Mainichi*, April 18, 1937. It appears that Korenaga and other writers particularly responded to the criticism of a controversial short story "Woman in the Bathrobe," (not published in the Japanese American newspapers) written by Wataru Mori. Mori, a Nisei from Sacramento, in 1938 was a student at the University of California (probably Berkeley). For information on Mori, see "Crumbs" column, *Kashu Mainichi*, April 3, 1938.

133. See Anent Nisei Literature. *Kashu Mainichi*, January 17, 1937.

134. *Kashu Mainichi*, December 23(?), 1941. Note inconsistency in date.
135. *Kashu Mainichi*, October 2, 1932. This excerpt contains no deletions; the ellipses are the author's own punctuation.
136. *Kashu Mainichi*, January 5, 1936.
137. *Kashu Mainichi*, December 31, 1933.
138. *Kashu Mainichi*, January 1, 1937.
139. *Kashu Mainichi*, April 15, 1934.
140. See Lil' Tokio Comes to Life. *Kashu Mainichi*, December 31, 1933.
141. *Kashu Mainichi*, June 4, 1933.
142. *Kashu Mainichi*, October 14, 1934.
143. Excerpt from "question," *Kashu Mainichi*, January 1, 1940.
144. Afterwards. *Current Life: The Magazine for the American Born Japanese* (July 1941), p. 6. For an examination of Suyemoto's wartime poetry, see Susan Schweik, The Pre-Poetics of Internment: The Example of Toyo Suyemoto. *American Literary History* (Spring 1989), pp. 89–109.

Chapter 4

1. Paul Takemoto, *Nisei Memories: My Parents Talk About the War Years*. Seattle: University of Washington Press, 2006, p. 219.
2. Amy Iwasaki Mass, Socio-Psychological Effects of the Concentration Camp Experience on Japanese Americans. *Bridge: An Asian American Perspective* (Winter 1978):62.
3. Mass, Socio-Psychological Effects, p. 63.
4. Takemoto, p. 97.
5. Roger Daniels, *Prisoners Without Trial*, Chapter 5, pp. 88–106.
6. In 1997 the Japanese American National Museum in Los Angeles began the REgenerations Oral History Project, in collaboration with institutions in Chicago, San Diego, and San Jose. Seven of the interviews on which I draw were conducted by the LA REgenerations team, for whom I served as a historical consultant. *REgenerations Oral History Project: Rebuilding Japanese American Families, Communities, and Civil Rights in the Resettlement Era*, Japanese American National Museum in collaboration with the Chicago Japanese American Historical Society, the Japanese American Historical Society of San Diego, and the Japanese American Resource Center/Museum. Los Angeles: Japanese American National Museum, 2000. The Densho Project (www.densho.org) has made available on-line countless documents, photos, and interviews.

In researching Japanese American wartime experiences, another challenge is posed by the problem of government terminology, deeply embedded in the literature, which has shaped and continues to influence the way we think about the mass removal and incarceration of Japanese Americans. Roger Daniels, Aiko Herzig-Yoshinaga, and Yuji Ichioka have all forcefully critiqued the U.S. government's euphemisms with their connotations of benevolent rescue and assistance. In most of the official documentation about the wartime incarceration, the Issei and Nisei were referred to as "evacuees" or "resident colonists," not *prisoners*, and as aliens and "non-aliens," rather than as aliens and *citizens*. Government records depicted them as being "evacuated" rather than *forcibly removed* to "assembly centers" and "relocation centers/camps," not *concentration camps*. The WRA and the army, Greg Robinson reports, agreed to refer to the camps as " 'war-duration relocation centers' and to explicitly forbid the use of the term 'concentration camp' as too negative and coercive." Greg Robinson, *By Order of the President: FDR and the Internment of Japanese Americans*. Cambridge, MA: Harvard University Press, 2001, p. 131. Over time, the terms "internment" and "internment camp" have been uneasily (and with technical inaccuracy) substituted; this is a mistake I have made. The term "internment" applies specifically to enemy aliens who were detained in camps run by the Department of Justice. Thus, Alice Takemoto's father can be said to have been interned, but this would not apply to his family's incarceration in a WRA-run camp. As intended, these insidious euphemisms have played a successful role in shaping public thinking about the mass imprisonment of Japanese Americans during World War II.

Therefore, as much as possible, I refer to "forced removal," "mass exclusion," and "incarceration." See Roger Daniels, "Words Do Matter: A Note on Inappropriate Terminology and the Incarceration of the Japanese Americans, in Louis Fiset and Gail M. Nomura, eds., *Nikkei in the Pacific Northwest: Japanese Americans & Japanese Canadians in the Twentieth Century.* Seattle: Center for the Study of the Pacific Northwest and University of Washington Press, 2005, pp. 190–214; Aiko Herzig-Yoshinaga, "Words Can Lie or Clarify: Terminology of the World War II Incarceration of Japanese Americans" (www.ebookbrowse.com/herzig-yoshinaga-terminology-pdf-d294744945). For a discussion of the debate over usage of the term "concentration camp" in the context of Japanese American wartime incarceration, see Karen L. Ishizuka, *Lost & Found: Reclaiming the Japanese American Incarceration.* Chicago: University of Illinois Press, 2006.

In direct quotations and references to specific locations, I have tried to retain the official terms (e.g., Santa Anita Assembly Center) that any researcher would need to use in order to access relevant material. Because the vast majority of Nisei used, and still use, the term "camp" to refer to the sites in which they were confined during the war years, I include this shorthand form as well. I have also included the camp names commonly utilized by the Japanese Americans whose stories form the backbone of this chapter. Those seeking to conduct further research should bear in mind that "Amache," "Poston," and "Topaz" are not official titles: Amache was the Granada Relocation Center; Poston was the Colorado River Relocation Center, and Topaz was the Central Utah Relocation Center; these are the names by which they are identified in wartime government documents.

7. Setsuko Matsunaga Nishi appeared in the Introduction, and chapters 1, 2, and 3; Fumiko Fukuyama Ide, Rose Honda, and Mary Nishi Ishizuka have appeared in the Introduction and chapters 1 and 2; Mary Oyama Mittwer appeared in the Introduction, and chapters 2 and 3; Haruko Sugi Hurt, Katsumi Hirooka Kunitsugu, and Esther Takei Nishio appeared in the Introduction. Rose Honda and Mary Nishi Ishizuka were interviewed by JANM for the REgenerations project (2000); I interviewed them in 2009.

8. Manzanar at its peak held a population of 10,046; 8,828 came from Los Angeles County. Poston, the largest of the camps, had a peak population of 17,814; 2,750 came from Los Angeles County. Jerome had a peak population of 8,497, with 3,147 from Los Angeles County. Heart Mountain had a peak population of 10,767; 6,448 came from Los Angeles County. Granada (Amache), the smallest camp, had a peak population of 7,318; 3,181 came from Los Angeles County. Rohwer had a peak population of 8,475; 4,324 came from Los Angeles County. Gila River had a peak population of 13,348; 4,952 came from Los Angeles County. See Brian Niiya, ed. *Japanese American History, An A-to-Z Reference from 1868 to the Present.* Japanese American National Museum, 1993, for statistics on each of the camps.

9. Richard was four years old and Eddie not yet one. Daughter Vicki was born in 1944.

10. Esther Takei Nishio interview, *REgenerations,* p. 307.

11. Fumiko Fukuyama Ide interview by author, March 27, 2001.

12. Haruko Hurt, *REgenerations,* p. 131.

13. Mary Ishizuka, *REgenerations,* p. 216.

14. Fumiko Fukuyama Ide interview by author, March 27, 2001. The agents who auctioned off her father's hardware stock said the money was used to pay off his debts.

15. Mary Ishizuka, *REgenerations,* p. 209.

16. Esther Nishio, *REgenerations,* p. 309.

17. Paul Takemoto, *Nisei Memories,* p. 79.

18. Ibid.

19. This number includes the Manzanar assembly center, initially known as the Owens Valley Reception Center, which subsequently became a relocation camp and was renamed.

20. Mary Oyama, My Only Crime Is My Face. *Liberty, The Magazine of a Free People,* August 14 1943, p. 57.

21. Setsuko Matsunaga Nishi interview by author, September 12 and 14, 2009.

22. Paul Takemoto, p. 93. Likewise, Mary Oyama wrote, "At first the crowd noise of 18,500 people jammed in together was so terrific that I thought I could never become accustomed to it.... It was a vast composite roar, an ocean of sound..." (Oyama, p. 57).

23. *REgenerations,* p. 249.

24. Takemoto, p. 96.

25. Ibid. Doing laundry at the former racetrack also required a trip to the grandstand, a mile away from the barracks, "because that's where the hot water was."

26. Tetsuden Kashima, *Judgment Without Trial: Japanese American Imprisonment during World War II*. Seattle: University of Washington Press, 2003, p. 134.

27. Toshio Yatsushiro, Political and Socio-Cultural Issues at Poston and Manzanar Relocation Centers—A Themal Analysis. Ph.D. Thesis, Cornell University (September 1953), pp. 473–474.

28. Takemoto, p. 126.

29. Takemoto, p. 126.

30. Yatsushiro, p. 311.

31. Mary Ishizuka, *REgenerations*, p. 218.

32. Mary Ishizuka, *REgenerations*, p. 214. Rose Honda also recalled that eating in the mess halls became a point of contention between Issei parents and Nisei children who wanted to sit with their friends.

33. Haruko Hurt, *REgenerations*, p. 135.

34. Mary Oyama, My Only Crime Is My Face. *Liberty, The Magazine of a Free People*, August 14, 1943, p. 57.

35. It should be noted that rural women did a range of farm labor, hoeing weeds and harvesting crops, in addition to the domestic tasks delegated to females. However, in the minds of the Japanese American women and men, some chores—such as cutting wood, making furniture, carrying heavy loads—were gendered as masculine duties.

36. Takemoto, pp. 127–128. Marion also made a screen "so when you walked in the room it hid some of the beds."

37. Alexander H. Leighton, *The Governing of Men: General Principles and Recommendations Based on Experience at a Japanese Relocation Camp*. Princeton, New Jersey: Princeton, University Press, 1945, p. 264.

38. *REgenerations*, p. 311.

39. Regarding efforts to oppose forced removal, see Greg Robinson, *A Tragedy of Democracy: Japanese Confinement in North America*. New York: Columbia University Press, 2009, pp. 86–87.

40. Setsuko Matsunaga Nishi interview by author, September 12 and 14, 2009. Masamori Kojima was valedictorian at Roosevelt High School in East Los Angeles, a "brilliant speaker and debater." He became the English editor of the *Chicago Shimpo* newspaper and also editor of *Scene* magazine, and later active in the Japanese American Journalists Association. He would become Los Angeles Mayor Tom Bradley's field representative and then assistant for transportation, parks, and ethnic relations.

41. Setsuko Matsunaga Nishi interview by author, September 12 and 14, 2009. Joe Koide and Ryoichi "Bob" Fujii were Issei liberal antimilitarists and had at one time been members of the Communist Party. Fujii because the editor/publisher of the *Chicago Shimpo*; Setsuko and Masamori, "being citizens, incorporated the *Chicago Shimpo* for them." Later Setsuko and Masamori were involved in the successful effort to stop the deportation of Fujii and Koide.

42. Takemoto, pp. 150–153. The careful crafting of Alice Takemoto's eloquent letter suggests that she would have made a good defense attorney.

43. Edward H. Spicer et al, *Impounded People: Japanese-Americans in the Relocation Centers*. Tucson, Arizona: The University of Arizona Press, 1969, p. 106.

44. As Roger Daniels explains, the WRA set the wage-scale for work within the camps low so that "the wage would not exceed the minimum paid American soldiers" and "to avoid Congressional charges of 'coddling', which came anyway. The analogy was ridiculous. All evacuees, regardless of skills, were permanent privates by WRA fiat; in addition, there were no veterans' benefits for evacuees." *Concentration Camps: North America, Japanese in the United States and Canada during World War II*. Malabar, Florida: Robert E. Krieger Publishing Company, Inc., 1981, p. 93.

45. *REgenerations*, pp. 315–316. Dr. Nagamoto, a pioneer in orthodontics, headed the dental clinic.

46. *REgenerations*, pp. 317–318. "Ama-chan" was a bilingual play on words: because "Amache" was the name of the camp, "Ama-chan" could refer to a camp inmate; at the same time, "-chan" was the affectionate Japanese-language ending sometimes used in addressing close friends or children, rather than the more formal "-san." "Amai" is also the Japanese word for "sweet."

47. Takemoto, p. 130.

48. Takemoto, p. 130.

49. *REgenerations*, p. 217. For more on the Manzanar Library, see Ayame Ichiyasu, "The Manzanar Library…EXPERIMENT IN RESOURCEFULNESS," *Manzanar Free Press*, April 14, 1943, p. 3. Like Ishizuka, Ichiyasu noted the tough beginning, "What we lacked in books we made up by a collection of snake skins, live scorpions, dried brush, bits of odd-colored stones and unusual plants—all objects of interest to 10,000 city people."

50. Just as she had worked to learn medical terms—"which wasn't easy in shorthand"—Fumi then mastered legal terms. She earned $16 a month as a clerical worker in camp. Her mother's health improved. Fumiko Fukuyama Ide interview by author, March 27, 2001.

51. Alexander Leighton, *The Governing of Men*, pp. 75–76.

52. Wendsor Sumie Yamashita, What She Remembers: Remaking and Unmaking Japanese American Internment. M.A. thesis, Asian American Studies Department, University of California, Los Angeles (2010), p. 60. Yamashita's insightful study critiques the dominant narratives of Japanese American wartime experience, revealing how they have obscured a wider range of experiences, including those of her great-aunts Chiyoko Nishimori and Lily Sawai.

53. Wendsor Sumie Yamashita, p. 64.

54. The JUGS club that formed in Manzanar was unrelated to the earlier JUGS club in Norwalk.

55. Alexander Leighton, *The Governing of Men*, p. 108.

56. *Impounded People*, p. 227.

57. The authors of *Impounded People* asserted on p. 227 that the Nisei had greater participation in social activities in camp than in their prewar lives, but the prewar ethnic newspapers suggest that this would not have been the case for many urban youth.

58. *Manzanar Free Press*, October 1, 1942, p. 3; May 5, 1943, p. 3. Girls' sports teams were often organized within these clubs.

59. The YWCA organizations formed early in Manzanar, as evidenced by their planning a first-year anniversary celebration from July 23 to 26, 1943, with Winifred Wygal of the National YWCA staff as honored guest.

60. Colleens Enjoy Folk Dancing. *Poston Chronicle*, Poston Two, February 3, 1943 (no page). Maki Ichiyasu was invited to speak to the Colleens Club of Poston Two on the subject of folk dancing. "A delightful folk dancing session followed under Miss Ichiyasu's able instruction with Kiyo Iwanaga, unit one pianist." The *Chronicle* noted that "Girl Scout leaders were specially invited to the affair," which suggests the sharing of resources and ideas among the leaders of young women's organizations.

61. Fumiko Fukuyama Ide interview by author, March 27, 2001. After marriage, Uno became Hana Uno Shepard. Ide said that the movies shown in camp were old "harmless" films like Abbott and Costello, none of the "current biggies."

62. *Manzanar Free Press*, August 12, 1942, p. 3.

63. *Poston Chronicle*, Poston One, March 19, 1943 (no page). It was noted, "All servicemen visiting in Poston will be admitted free."

64. *Poston Chronicle*, Poston Two, February 4, 1943 (no page).

65. *Poston Chronicle*, Poston Two, January 20, 1943 (no page).

66. *Poston Chronicle*, Poston Two, February 28, 1943 (no page). The Boy Scouts assisted by bringing in logs for the fire.

67. "Social Doings," *Manzanar Free Press*, June 30, 1943, p. 3. The Calico Cats in Manzanar had counterparts in the Brenda Starrs (named after the glamorous comic-strip reporter) of Heart Mountain. As the *Manzanar Free Press* noted on February 17, 1943, "Both of these organizations have memberships consisting wholly of newspaper girls." Both clubs held exclusive dances on the eve of Valentine's Day, and to honor their journalist sisters, the Brenda Starrs dedicated one dance to the Calico Cats.

68. *Manzanar Free Press*, May 29, 1943, p. 3.

69. "YWCA Secretary Addresses Poston Two Girls on 'Y' Activities, Resettlement," *Poston Chronicle*, Poston Two, March 13, 1943 (no page). She is identified as "Ethel Briesemaster" in the *Poston Chronicle* (March 13, 1943), and as "Esther Briesmeister" in the *Manzanar Free Press* (October 1, 1942, p. 3). She and a National Girls Reserve staff member arrived to begin a series of Y Council activities at Manzanar in October 1942.

70. "Regional Girl Scout Representative Here to Give Leadership Courses," *Poston Chronicle*, Poston Two, March 21, 1943, no page.

71. "Nineteen Japanese Present at 'Y' Meet," *Manzanar Free Press*, June 30, 1943, p. 1.

72. Ibid., p. 3.

73. "Club Activities," *Manzanar Free Press*, February 27, 1943, p. 2.

74. "YWCA Services Open to Everyone, Writes Barbara Abel," *Manzanar Free Press*, April 17, 1943, p. 2. The YWCA in Des Moines, Iowa, and Omaha, Nebraska also offered assistance. "Opens Des Moines Hostel for Women," *Manzanar Free Press*, June 23, 1943, p. 3; "Camp Brewster Open to Girls," *Manzanar Free Press*, July 21, 1943, p. 1.

75. Granada *Pioneer*, "Y's Way," August 30, 1944, p. 4.

76. *REgenerations*, p. 318.

77. Yuri Kochiyama, p. 13

78. Ibid.

79. Ibid.

80. Takemoto, p. 129.

81. "Confidentially by Esther," Granada *Pioneer*, August 16, 1944, p. 5.

82. Living in a society in which interracial matches were prohibited by law as well as by the preferences of immigrant elders and the ethnic community, and in which the idealized female was white, shaded in complicated ways relations between Nisei women and men.

83. "Confidentially by Esther," Granada *Pioneer*, August 16, 1944, p. 5.

84. Takemoto, p. 129.

85. Shirley Jennifer Lim, *A Feeling of Belonging: Asian American Women's Public Culture, 1930–1960*. New York: New York University Press, 2006, p. 7. Drawing on Renato Rosaldo's notion of cultural citizenship—"the need to prove and claim Americanness"—Lim examines young, single Asian American women's participation in and adaptation of leisure practices as a way to create new bases for social inclusion (p. 10).

86. Offering another perspective on how Japanese Americans tried to contest marginalization, historian Jennifer Malia McAndrew cites minstrel shows performed by a Santa Anita girls' club and a Denson (Jerome) drama club as illustrations of how Japanese Americans attempted to define themselves "against black stereotypes to enhance their similarities and thus cultural ties to whites." Jennifer Malia McAndrew, All-American Beauty: The Experiences of African American, European American, and Japanese American Women With Beauty Culture in the Mid-Twentieth Century United States. Ph.D. dissertation, University of Maryland, College Park (2008), p. 132.

87. Yuri Kochiyama, *Passing It On—A Memoir*, p. 15.

88. *Manzanar Free Press*, February 17, 1943, p. 4.

89. Watanabe-Kajikawa Engagement Revealed. *Poston Chronicle*, December 31, 1942 (no page).

90. Marriage Vows Exchanged. *Poston Chronicle*, Poston III, March 28, 1943 (no page).

91. For example, see Mizokami Weds Manzanar Girl. *Poston Chronicle*, Poston three, March 23, 1943 (no page); "Masumoto-Tsurutome United in Wedlock," *Poston Chronicle*, Poston III, March 30, 1943 (no page).

92. Jennifer Malia McAndrew, All-American Beauty, pp. 128–129.

93. "Yuri," Strictly Feminine. *The Daily Tulean Dispatch*, September 29, 1942, p. 2.

94. Mitzi Sugita, Latest Fashion for Women Today—Slacks. *Poston Chronicle*, June 13, 1943, p. 1.

95. Miné Okubo, *Citizen 13660*. Seattle: University of Washington Press, 1946, 1983, p. 52.

96. Ibid.

97. Marii Kyogoku, "a la mode," *Topaz Trek*, February 1943, p. 38.

98. "Confidentially by Esther," Granada *Pioneer*, August 30, 1944, p. 5.

99. Ibid.

100. Ibid.

101. Shizuko Horiuchi to Henriette Von Blon, December 27, 1942, Henriette Von Blon Collection, Hoover Institution Archives, Stanford University, Stanford, California.

102. Confidentially by Esther. Granada *Pioneer*, August 23, 1944, p. 5.

103. From 1942 to the end of 1945 the Council allocated about $240,000 in scholarships, most of which were provided through the donations of churches and the World student Service fund. The average grant per student was $156.73, which in that era was a major contribution toward the cost of higher education. See: National Japanese American Student Relocation Council, Minutes of the Executive Committee Meeting, Philadelphia, Pennsylvania, December 19, 1945. According to Robert O'Brien, 5,522 Nisei students in total attended college in the Midwest and East between 1942 and 1945.

104. Robert O'Brien, *The College Nisei*. Palo Alto: Pacific Books, 1949, pp. 73–74.

105. Roger Daniels reports that in 1942 alone, some 10,000 Japanese Americans were released to do agricultural labor and the majority of the releases were temporary. *Prisoners Without Trial*, pp. 74–75.

106. There is a large literature dealing with the WRA's efforts to separate perceived "loyal" from "disloyal" Japanese Americans and to send those deemed disloyal to a segregation camp, and ultimately for many, repatriation to Japan. For example, see Michi Weglyn, *Years of Infamy: The Untold Story of America's Concentration Camps*. New York: Morrow Quill Paperbacks, 1976; Tetsuden Kashima, *Judgment Without Trial: Japanese American Imprisonment during World War II*. Seattle: University of Washington Press, 2003; Roger Daniels, *Prisoners Without Trial: Japanese Americans in World War II*. New York: Hill and Wang, 1993; Audrie Girdner and Anne Loftis, *The Great Betrayal: The Evacuation of the Japanese-Americans During World War II*. Toronto: Macmillan, 1969.

107. O'Brien, p. 84.

108. Leslie Ito, "Japanese American Women and the Student Relocation Movement, 1942–1945," *Frontiers: A Journal of Women Studies* 21, No. 3 (2000):2–3.

109. Ito, pp. 3–4; Thomas James, *Exile Within: The Schooling of Japanese Americans 1942–1945*. Cambridge, MA: Harvard University Press, 1987, pp. 127–128.

110. Ito, p. 16.

111. Esther left camp and took a domestic-service job, intending to gain residency in Colorado and attend college. However, her father called her to come back to the family before the residency year was completed and she did not go to college in Colorado.

112. Setsuko Matsunaga Nishi interview by author, September 12 and 14, 2009.

113. Ibid.

114. Mary's father was still incarcerated in Missoula, Montana, at this time.

115. Takemoto, p. 174.

116. Takemoto, p. 177.

117. *REgenerations*, p. 251.

118. Evelyn Nakano Glenn, The Dialectics of Wage Work: Japanese-American Women and Domestic Servants, 1905–1940. *Feminist Studies* 6, No. 3 (Fall 1980), p. 432.

119. Advisory Committee for Evacuees, *Resettlement Bulletin* (July 1943), p. 3. Institutions also sought Japanese Americans to do service-industry work: For example, the August 23, 1944 issue of the Granada *Pioneer* carried an ad from the Cranbrook Academy of Arts in Michigan seeking a head cook, a second cook, a head waitress, and a general kitchen assistant.

120. *REgenerations*, p. 220.

121. Takemoto, p. 187.

122. Setsuko Matsunaga Nishi interview by author, September 12 and 14, 2009.

123. Ibid.

124. Ibid.

125. Ibid.

126. Setsuko Nishi recounted the stoning incident in her interview.

127. *REgenerations*, p. 220.

128. *Regenerations*, p. 222. Chi Alpha Delta, the first Japanese American sorority was established at UCLA in 1929 in response to the exclusion of Asian Americans from the Greek system. See Shirley Jennifer Lim, *A Feeling of Belonging*, pp. 11–46.

129. *Regenerations*, p. 252.

130. *Regenerations,* p. 254.
131. Advisory Committee for Evacuees, *Resettlement Bulletin* (April 1943), p. 2.
132. Esther Rhodes Visits. *Manzanar Free Press,* July 21, 1943, p. 2.
133. Making Right Impression Up To Evacuees, Is Advice. *Manzanar Free Press,* June 30, 1943, p. 1.
134. Ibid.
135. YWCA Secretary Addresses Poston Two Girls on 'Y' Activities, Resettlement. *Poston Chronicle,* Poston Two, March 13, 1943 (no page).
136. Letters from the Public. *Manzanar Free Press,* November 17, 1943, p. 2.
137. Letters from the Public. *Manzanar Free Press,* July 21, 1943, p. 2.
138. Setsuko Matsunaga Nishi interview by author, September 12 and 14, 2009.
139. Letters from the Public. *Manzanar Free Press,* September 22, 1943, p. 2.
140. Letters from the Public. *Manzanar Free Press,* July 21, 1943, p. 2.
141. Some critical letters did appear; they seem fewer in number and appear to come mainly from temporary harvest workers, many of whom were cheated by exploitative employers.
142. 500 Indefinite Leaves Issued. *Poston Chronicle,* May 23, 1943, p. 1.
143. *REgenerations,* pp. 150–151.
144. Letters from the Public. *Manzanar Free Press,* November 17, 1943, p. 2.
145. *REgenerations,* p. 439. Many of the *REgenerations* interviews reveal the popularity of Chicago as a destination for resettlers.
146. *REgenerations,* p. 140.
147. 500 Indefinite Leaves Issued. *Poston Chronicle,* May 23, 1943, pp. 1, 4.
148. Fumiko Fukuyama Ide interview by author, March 27, 2001.
149. The Road Back. Granada *Pioneer,* August 23, 1944, p. 4.
150. *REgenerations,* p. 272.
151. *REgenerations,* p. 367.
152. Setsuko Matsunaga Nishi interview by author, September 12 and 14, 2009.
153. Ibid. Setsuko Nishi directed the People's Forum 1944–1945. Among his publications, Horace Cayton co-wrote with St. Clair Drake *Black Metropolis* (1945). Later he and Nishi co-wrote *The Changing Scene,* Volume II of *Churches and Social Welfare.* New York: The National Council of Churches, 1955.
154. For a study of early Asian American social scientists—such as Setsuko Nishi—at the University of Chicago, see Henry Yu, *Thinking Orientals: Migration, Contact, and Exoticism in Modern America.* New York: Oxford University Press, 2001.
155. Yuri Kochiyama, p. 16.
156. Kochiyama, p. 40.
157. Kochiyama, p. 17.
158. Brian Niiya, ed. *Japanese American History, An A-to-Z Reference from 1868 to the Present.* Japanese American National Museum, 1993, p. 345.
159. Life of WAACS Extolled by Lt. Roberta L. House Before Unit II Women. *Poston Chronicle,* Poston Two, March 5, 1943 (no page).
160. Life of WAACS Extolled.... *Poston Chronicle,* Poston Two, March 5, 1943 (no page); see also Yoshiye Takata, An Interview... Meet Lt. House. *Poston Chronicle,* March 7, 1943 (no page).
161. Editorial, Issues in the WAC Recruitment. *Poston Chronicle,* City Page, September 8, 1943, p. 2.
162. Mei Nakano, *Japanese American Women, Three Generations, 1890–1990.* Berkeley: Mina Press Publishing, 1993, p. 170.
163. Kevin Leonard, *The Battle for Los Angeles; Racial Ideology and World War II.* Albuquerque: University of New Mexico Press, 2006, p. 237. Leonard cites a *Los Angeles Times* report that 39 Japanese American women with their children had been allowed to return to the West Coast since December 1943; these women were all married to non-Nikkei men or to U.S. servicemen. (p. 235)
164. Hugh Harris Anderson is one of the unsung heroes of wartime and postwar civil rights efforts. Taking his family with him, he voluntarily spent a year working with the Japanese Americans at the Poston camp in Arizona until he contracted poliomyelitis there. In addition to helping Esther Takei and Japanese Americans in southern California, he also tried to assist

the Hagiwara family in claiming their rights to the Tea Garden they had created and tended at the Golden Gate Park in San Francisco.

165. Letter from William Carr to Dr. Harold Kingsley, December 12, 1944, Hugh H. Anderson Papers, Japanese American Research Project, Box 41, Special Collections, Young Research Library, UCLA.

166. Ibid.

167. Hugh Harris Anderson, "Recollections," unpublished manuscript in the collection of Esther Takei Nishio (1990), p. 117.

168. Esther Takei Nishio, testimony before the Commission on Wartime Relocation and Internment of Civilians (CWRIC), August 6, 1981.

169. Ibid.

170. Hugh Harris Anderson, "Recollections," p. 117.

171. Esther Takei Nishio testimony before the CWRIC, August 6, 1981.

172. Anderson, "Recollections," p. 118.

173. Esther Takei Nishio testimony before the CWRIC, August 6, 1981.

174. David C. Munford letter to Esther Takei, received September 23, 1944, Hugh H. Anderson Papers, Japanese American Research Project, Box 41, Special Collections, Young Research Library, UCLA.

175. Esther Takei Nishio testimony before the CWRIC, August 6, 1981.

176. Ibid.

177. Copy of letter from Sgt. Susumu Kazahaya to Esther Takei, September 7, 1944, Hugh H. Anderson Papers, Japanese American Research Project, Box 41, Special Collections, Young Research Library, UCLA.

178. Copy of letter from Helen Brill to Esther Takei, no date, Hugh H. Anderson Papers, Japanese American Research Project, Box 41, Special Collections, Young Research Library, UCLA.

179. Letter from Esther Takei, addressed to "Dear Friend," November 21, 1944, Hugh H. Anderson Papers, Japanese American Research Project, Box 41, Special Collections, Young Research Library, UCLA. Esther's first sentence shows that the letter is aimed at former PJC students: "Being back in sunny California…is wonderful and attending P. J.C. just as you did not so very long ago, is doubly exciting." Esther's final phrase ends with "neh!", a Japanese ending that indicates or asks, "isn't that so." This suggests that the letter was geared to other Nisei.

180. Ibid.

181. Hugh Harris Anderson, "Recollections," p. 119. See also Audrie Girdner and Anne Loftis, *The Great Betrayal: The Evacuation of the Japanese-Americans during World War II.* Macmillan, 1969, p. 380. The army rescinded the exclusion orders on December 17, 1944, effective January 2, 1945. See Kevin Leonard, p. 246.

182. Girdner and Loftis, *The Great Betrayal*, p. 380.

183. Ibid.

184. For information on the cases of Mitsuye Endo and Fred Korematsu, both Nisei, see Peter Irons, *Justice at War: The Story of the Japanese American Internment Cases.* New York: Oxford University Press, 1983.

185. Leonard Broom and Ruth Riemer, *Removal and Return, The Socio-Economic Effects of the War on Japanese Americans.* Berkeley: University of California Press, 1949, p. 36.

186. U.S. Department of the Interior, War Agency Liquidation Unit (formerly War Relocation Authority), *People in Motion: the Postwar Adjustment of the Evacuated Japanese Americans.* Washington, D.C.: U.S. Government Printing Office, 1947, p. 85.

187. *People in Motion*, p. 82. As families reunited and young adult Nisei formed their own households, the numbers grew: The 1960 Census enumerated 82,261 persons of Japanese descent in Los Angeles County; by 1970, the number had risen to 104,994.

188. Kariann Yokota, From Little Tokyo to Bronzeville and Back: Ethnic Communities in Transition. MA thesis, University of California, Los Angeles, 1996, pp. 5–6.

Chapter 5

1. Yuri Kochiyama, *Passing It On—A Memoir.* Los Angeles: UCLA Asian American Studies Center Press, 2004, p. 18.

2. Rose Honda, *REgenerations Oral History Project: Rebuilding Japanese American Families, Communities, and Civil Rights in the Resettlement Era.* Los Angeles: Japanese American National Museum in collaboration with the Chicago Japanese American Historical Society, the Japanese American Historical Society of San Diego, and the Japanese American Resource Center/Museum, 2000, p. 109.

3. Kariann Yokota, From Little Tokyo to Bronzeville and Back: Ethnic Communities in Transition. MA thesis, University of California, Los Angeles, 1996, p. 6.

4. Rose Honda, *REgenerations*, p. 96.

5. The *Rafu Shimpo*, established in 1903 and forced to close in April 1942, was the first Los Angeles Japanese American newspaper to re-open, resuming publication of its Japanese- and English-language sections on January 1, 1946. The *Kashu Mainichi*, whose publisher Sei Fujii was not released from a detention camp until after the war, reopened later and only published in Japanese in the early postwar era.

6. Midori Nishi, Changing Occupance of the Japanese in Los Angeles County, 1940-1950. Ph.D. dissertation, University of Washington, 1955, p. 9.

7. On February 3, 1948, the *Rafu Shimpo* reported that of about 15,000 Nisei who became stranded in Japan during World War II, an estimated 7,000 forfeited their U.S. citizenship because of "ignorance or circumstances beyond their control." A February 18, 1948 article listed those circumstances: "About 1700 were drafted in the Japanese Army; another 1500 had to work under Nipponese nationality status; while more than 700 (mostly girls) voted in Japan's first postwar election in April, 1946, not knowing their citizenship statuses were at stake." The first strandee case filed in the Federal District Court on February 10, 1948 was that of a Nisei woman, Etsuko Arikawa, who was taken to Japan for education in 1938; see *Rafu Shimpo*, February 10, 1948, p. 1. In 1949, Federal Judge Charles C. Cavanah in Los Angeles ruled that Etsuko Arikawa and Miyoko Tsunashima "voted under mistake and misunderstanding and therefore did not lose their U.S. citizenship." *Rafu Shimpo*, October 5, 1949, p. 1.

8. "Renunciants" were Nisei who gave up their citizenship during World War II at the Tule Lake segregation center. In a 1949 action with ramifications for an estimated 4,000 Nisei, the U.S. Circuit Court of Appeals affirmed the earlier restoration of citizenship to three Japanese American women residing in southern California. Miye Mae Murakami, Tatsuko Sumi, and Mutsu Shimizu (along with Albert Inouye) had been the test case for the ACLU, which argued that they had renounced their citizenship "under pressure and coercion." See *Rafu Shimpo*, January 28, 1949, p. 1; August 27, 1949, p. 1; and October 27, 1949, p. 1.

9. Charlotte Brooks, *Alien Neighbors, Foreign Friends: Asian Americans, Housing, and the Transformation of Urban California.* Chicago: The University of Chicago Press, 2009, p. 176.

10. Suspect racial flare in burning. *Rafu Shimpo*, August 1, 1949, p. 1.

11. Realtor receives threat for selling to minorities. *Rafu Shimpo*, February 6, 1950, p. 1.

12. GI burial plot issue settled as DSC winner funeral set. *Rafu Shimpo*, November 27, 1948, p. 1. The request was granted after the memorial park head learned that Masuda had served in the 442nd RCT. It is not clear that nonmilitary Issei or Nisei would receive any such consideration.

13. Columnist Pearson Decries Nisei Burial Ban in Chicago. *Rafu Shimpo*, January 6, 1949, p. 1.

14. Burial Bias Issue Studied. *Rafu Shimpo*, January 10, 1949, p. 1. On March 18, 1949, the *Rafu* reported, "More than one [Chicago] cemetery is expected to amend its policy concerning its racial restrictions." Barred from white cemeteries by these restrictive covenants, African Americans and other racial minorities had to establish and maintain separate cemeteries. By this time, the small Japanese cemetery serving the Chicago area was full and had no room for more bodies.

15. The *San Francisco News* announced it would refrain from using the word "Jap" in headlines on May 6 and the *Minneapolis Morning Tribune* did likewise in June. Word 'Jap' to be eliminated. *Rafu Shimpo*, June 13, 1950, p. 1; Metropolitan dailies avoid use of 'Jap.' *Rafu Shimpo*, 1950 Holiday Issue, December 20, 1950, p. 5.

16. Henry Mori, Making the Deadline. 1949 Holiday Issue, *Rafu Shimpo*, p. 21.

17. Paul Howard Takemoto, *Nisei Memories: My Parents Talk About the War Years.* Seattle: University of Washington Press, 2006, pp. 213, 217–219. In order to remain close to

their daughter Lily, her husband Ken, and two grandchildren in Virginia, Alice's Issei parents moved to Washington, D.C. where they found domestic service jobs.

18. Setsuko Matsunaga Nishi interview by author, September 12 and 14, 2009.

19. Richard White, *It's Your Misfortune and None of My Own: A New History of the American West.* Norman, Oklahoma: University of Oklahoma Press, 1991, p. 498.

20. Richard White, *It's Your Misfortune and None of My Own,* p. 508.

21. White, p. 517.

22. Togo Tanaka, Post Script. *Rafu Shimpo,* January 24, 1946, p. 1. This reportage appears to have been sent to columnist Tanaka by English-language section editor Henry Mori for inclusion in the "Post Script" column.

23. Ibid.

24. Highlights of 1946 on Parade. *Rafu Shimpo,* 1946 Holiday Issue, December 21, 1946, p. 1.

25. Scotty Tsuchiya, 25,000 resettled in L.A. *Rafu Shimpo,* 1946 Holiday Issue, December 21, 1946, p. 1.

26. Tsuchiya, p. 1.

27. News Nuggets of '47. *Rafu Shimpo,* 1947 Holiday Issue, December 22, 1947, p. 7.

28. Tsuchiya, pp. 1, 2, 15.

29. Katsumi Kunitsugu, *REgenerations,* p. 255.

30. Katsumi Kunitsugu, *REgenerations,* p. 256.

31. Rose Honda, *REgenerations,* p. 71.

32. Rose Honda, *REgenerations,* p. 70.

33. Rose Honda, *REgenerations,* p. 71.

34. Fumiko Fukuyama Ide interview by author, March 27, 2001.

35. Haruko Hurt, *REgenerations,* p. 134.

36. See chapter 3 for Mary Oyama's description of their homecoming.

37. Esther Takei Nishio, *REgenerations,* p. 340.

38. Esther Takei Nishio, *REgenerations,* p. 342. In 1950 angry white homeowners demanded that the realty board revoke William Carr's license, but were ignored. Carr received support from the ACLU, the PTA, and the Pasadena JACL chapter. See *Rafu Shimpo,* 1950 Holiday Issue, p. 3.

39. Esther Takei Nishio, *REgenerations,* p. 342. As Josh Sides recounts, "The landmark Supreme Court decisions *Shelley v. Kraemer* and *Barrows v. Jackson,* handed down in 1948 and 1953, respectively, effectively abolished racially restrictive housing covenants, the most entrenched barrier to neighborhood integration." Sides, *L.A. City Limits: African American Los Angeles from the Great Depression to the Present.* Berkeley: University of California Press, 2003, p. 95.

40. 'Whites only!' But domestic workers O.K. *Rafu Shimpo,* September 20, 1946, p. 1.

41. Ibid., p. 1.

42. Josh Sides, *L.A City Limits,* pp. 45–47.

43. Sides, p. 98. For an insightful analysis of African American and Japanese American relations in Los Angeles, see Scott Kurashige, *The Shifting Grounds of Race: Black and Japanese Americans in the Making of Multiethnic Los Angeles.* Princeton, New Jersey: Princeton University Press, 2008.

44. Kariann Yokota, p. 72.

45. Katsumi Kunitsugu, *REgenerations,* p. 259.

46. 2nd Evacuation for Part of Li'l Tokio. *Rafu Shimpo,* 1949 Holiday Issue, December 20, 1949, p. 2. For the impact of redevelopment on Japantowns in the 1950s–1970s, see the entry on "redevelopment," in Brian Niiya, ed. *Japanese American History, An A-to-Z Reference from 1868 to the Present.* Los Angeles: Japanese American National Museum, 1993, pp. 288–289.

47. Southwest: Businesses, homes of Japanese flourishing. *Rafu Shimpo,* 1947 Holiday Issue, December 22, 1947, p. 2.

48. Rose Honda, *REgenerations,* pp. 67–68.

49. Mary Ishizuka, *REgenerations,* p. 225.

50. Mary Ishizuka, *REgenerations,* p. 241.

51. Esther Nishio, *REgenerations,* p. 344.

52. Esther Nishio, *REgenerations,* p. 344.

53. Esther Nishio, REgenerations, p. 344. Esther believes that her father's enterprise may have been the first frozen food company operated by Issei.
54. Classified Ads. *Rafu Shimpo*, December 2, 1947, p. 1.
55. Midori Nishi, p. 138.
56. Mary Ishizuka, REgenerations, p. 215.
57. Midori Nishi, p. 138.
58. Yuri Kochiyama, p. 19.
59. Ibid.
60. Ibid.
61. Midori Nishi also mentions the prewar to postwar continuity of the barbershops and beauty salons located in Japanese American enclaves. Nishi, Changing Occupance, p. 138.
62. For example, see ads in the *Rafu Shimpo* on January 15, 1947, January 30, 1947, February 18, 1947, and March 22, 1947.
63. The other salons included in the 1947 Holiday Issue were the Camellia Beauty Salon, the Futaba Beauty Salon, the Mary J Beauty Shop, the June Beauty Salon, the Originelle Beauty Studio, and the Seinan Beauty Salon. The Moderne Beauty Salon on Sawtelle in West Los Angeles—listed in 1946—either had gone out of business or did not run an ad in the 1947 issue.
64. 'Unassuming' Coiffure Makes Big Hit. *Rafu Shimpo*, 1946 Holiday Issue, December 26, 1946, p. 11.
65. Ibid.
66. Beauty School Lifts Nisei Ban. *Rafu Shimpo*, November 24, 1947, p. 1. Colorado had a small but significant Japanese American population before World War II, and they were not incarcerated. The establishment of the Amache Camp brought more Japanese Americans to Colorado; many of them resettled, often temporarily, in Denver and other parts.
67. Midori Nishi, p. 139.
68. Ibid.
69. See Table 22.—Social and Economic Characteristics of the Japanese Population for Selected States, Urban and Rural, and for Selected Metropolitan Areas: 1950—Con. *United States Census of Population: 1950*, Vol. IV, *Special Reports*, Part 3, Chapter B, Nonwhite Population by Race. Washington, D.C.: U.S. Government Printing Office, 1953, pp. 3B–79. The third largest area of work was private household work (domestic service), with 821 women.
70. Accounts vary from day to day in the estimate of how many workers were killed or injured. The *Los Angeles Times* reported on February 21, 1947, that at least 15 persons were killed and 151 injured. It seems that, according to the *Rafu Shimpo*, at least two more died.
71. Many Japanese Injured in E. Pico Plant Holocaust; Expect 44 Death Toll to Rise. *Rafu Shimpo*, February 20, 1947, p. 1; 1 Nisei Dead, Another Missing; Scores Hurt in Yesterday's E. Pico Plant Blast. *Rafu Shimpo*, February 21, 1947, p. 1. The *Rafu* made no further mention of the cause of the accident.
72. Marvin Miles, Factory Disintegrates; Houses Near by Collapse; Wreckage Traps Victims. *Los Angeles Times*, Part I, February 21, 1947, pp. 1, A. According to the *Times*, the appearance of two armed soldiers at the plant after the blast spurred rumors of secret military work. "The Army inspectors called at the plant after the blast, the spokesman said, to determine if there was any salvage value to the furniture, which included hospital beds, chairs and davenports."
73. *Rafu Shimpo*, February 21, 1947, p. 1.
74. *Rafu Shimpo*, February 20, 1947, p. 1.
75. Midori Nishi, p. 140.
76. Midori Nishi, p. 143. Nishi also notes that Nisei women were working as stock clerks and sales clerks in department stores and retail shops.
77. Esther Nishio, REgenerations, p. 345.
78. Esther Nishio, REgenerations, p. 345.
79. Esther Nishio, REgenerations, p. 355.
80. Fumiko Fukuyama Ide interview by author, March 27, 2001.
81. Rose Honda, REgenerations, p. 107.
82. Midori Nishi, p. 144. According to the 1940 and 1950 Censuses, the number of Japanese women professional and technical workers in Los Angeles grew from 123 in 1940 to 320 by 1950.

83. Haruko Hurt, *REgenerations*, p. 155.

84. Midori Nishi, p. 144.

85. Rose Honda, *REgenerations*, p. 100.

86. Mary Ishizuka, *REgenerations*, p. 214.

87. Mary Ishizuka, *REgenerations*, p. 215.

88. Barbara Takahashi, a "comely young school marm" with an MA from Columbia University, was identified by the *Rafu Shimpo* as the first Nisei to teach junior high school in the Los Angeles City system. See Teaches at Kern Jr. High. *Rafu Shimpo*, February 7, 1948, p. 1.

89. Mary Ishizuka, *REgenerations*, p. 237.

90. Mary Ishizuka, *REgenerations*, p. 214.

91. Midori Nishi, p. 144.

92. Midori Nishi, p. 207.

93. Midori Nishi, p. 149.

94. Sakaye Shigekawa, *REgenerations*, p. 371.

95. Sakaye Shigekawa, *REgenerations*, p. 373.

96. Sakaye Shigekawa, *REgenerations*, p. 373.

97. For information on the prewar rise of Japanese American hospitals and the Issei doctors' legal battle to found one in Los Angeles, see the entry on "Japanese hospitals" in Brian Niiya, ed. *Japanese American History, An A-to-Z Reference from 1868 to the Present.* Los Angeles: Japanese American National Museum, 1993, pp. 188–189.

98. Sakaye Shigekawa, *REgenerations*, p. 376.

99. Sakaye Shigekawa, *REgenerations*, p. 374.

100. *Rafu Shimpo*, February 27, 1947, p. 1.

101. Midori Nishi, pp. 152–153.

102. The title of Mary Oyama's column—which began on March 1, 1946—shifted subtly from "New World Coming!" to "New World A-Coming" with Roi Ottley's permission, given the understanding that she was writing the column for free, which she announced in her May 3, 1946 column. The May 10 column appeared under the revised title.

103. Mary Kitano's "Snafu" column in the *Rafu Shimpo* began on February 2, 1946.

104. Mary Kitano, guest writer for Henry Mori's column, "Making the Deadline," *Rafu Shimpo*, January 25, 1946, p. 1. In this column Kitano breezily described what it was like to be a Nisei woman journalist in Los Angeles. By October 1946, Kitano had taken a job as a "rewrite man" on the staff of the California News Service. As the *Rafu* reported on October 1, 1946, "Miss Kitano, secretary of the Coordinating Council and Organizing Committee, still dead-locked in strike with the local Evening Herald, is also doing reportorial work for a Hollywood columnist."

105. Ibid.

106. 'Snafu' Writer Now With the Daily News. *Rafu Shimpo*, May 22, 1947, p. 1.

107. Katsumi Kunitsugu, *REgenerations*, p. 256.

108. Katsumi Kunitsugu, *REgenerations*, p. 257.

109. Katsumi Kunitsugu, *REgenerations*, p. 257. Unfortunately, there seems to be no surviving complete set of *Crossroads* (1948–1971). Longtime editor (1953–1969) W. T. Wimpy Hiroto sadly reported that he had had the only full file, which deteriorated; in 2012 he donated the remaining 31 editions to the UCLA Asian American Studies Center Library. The Japanese American National Museum has one 1955 issue of *Crossroads*.

110. Katsumi Kunitsugu, *Regenerations*, pp. 256–257.

111. The *Kashu Mainichi* was one of the two main prewar Japanese American newspapers in Los Angeles. Its postwar comeback was much slower than that of the *Rafu Shimpo*, which is now the only surviving Japanese American newspaper in Los Angeles.

112. Katsumi Kunitsugu, *Regenerations*, p. 258.

113. Katsumi Kunitsugu, *REgenerations*, p. 260.

114. Katsumi Kunitsugu left the *Kashu Mainichi* after a local Japanese American businessman threatened to sue the publisher over an article that she wrote—and believed to be truthful—and the publisher did not support her. See *REgenerations*, p. 262.

115. Dick Honma, Danseuse to tour midwest, may perform in New York. *Rafu Shimpo*, June 5, 1946, p. 1.

116. Dancer Performs for Television Show. *Rafu Shimpo*, March 27, 1947, p. 1.
117. Stepping Out with Sensei. *Rafu Shimpo*, December 6, 2007, p. 1.
118. Mary Oyama, New World Coming! *Rafu Shimpo*, April 12, 1946, p. 1.
119. Nisei Dance Star in Gotham Recital. *Rafu Shimpo*, October 24, 1946, p. 1.
120. Talented Dancer Appears Here with Martha Graham Troupe. *Rafu Shimpo*, March 11, 1950, p. 1. Amemiya, who was married to Charles Kikuchi and had a 17-month-old girl, not only performed but also taught a Martha Graham dance class in Manhattan.
121. Opera Singer Tomiko Kanazawa Here for Benefit Performance. *Rafu Shimpo*, December 22, 1950, p. 1.
122. Tomiko Kanazawa Acclaimed for Role of Mimi in La Boheme. *Rafu Shimpo*, December 2, 1950, p. 1.
123. Opera Singer Tomiko Kanazawa Here for Benefit Performance. *Rafu Shimpo*, December 22, 1950, p. 1.
124. Up the Ladder of Ballet Fame ... Farm Girl Makes Good on Broadway. *Rafu Shimpo*, February 25, 1947, p. 1. The urban reporter may have not been aware that both rural Nisei girls and boys often did the same farm labor.
125. Ibid.
126. Ibid.
127. Tell Job Opportunities for Nisei Girls. *Rafu Shimpo*, October 14, 1947, p. 1.
128. Ibid.
129. William H. Chafe, *The Unfinished Journey: America Since World War II*. New York: Oxford University Press, 1986, p. 127.
130. Marion Manaka, *REgenerations*, p. 293. Immediately after the war, Marion and her husband joined his family in Monterey, California. He fished on his brother-in-law's boat, and Marion worked with her sisters-in-law packing sardines in the Monterey Canning company. They moved to Los Angeles in 1946 or 1947 when her husband got a job as cook on another Nisei-owned fishing boat. See *Regenerations*, pp. 276–279.
131. Reader's Open Forum. *Rafu Shimpo*, April 10, 1946, p. 1.
132. Ibid.
133. Girls' Club Organized. *Rafu Shimpo*, January 22, 1946, p. 1.
134. Plans to Organize Girl Scouts Group. *Rafu Shimpo*, January 30, 1946, p. 1; Moderneers Elect Irene Kusayanagi as Their President. *Rafu Shimpo*, January 31, 1946, p. 1.
135. Mary Kitano, Snafu. *Rafu Shimpo*, May 4, 1946, p. 1.
136. Editorial ... Let's Get Organized! *Rafu Shimpo*, February 1, 1946, p. 1.
137. Ibid.
138. Stardusters to Meet at Advisor's Home This Sunday. *Rafu Shimpo*, March 26, 1946, p. 1.
139. Harry K. Honda, Bobby-Sox Glamour to Feature Tourney Prelims. *Rafu Shimpo*, April 29, 1946, p. 1.
140. Chi Alpha Delta Sorority to Reorganize Club. *Rafu Shimpo*, April 5, 1946, p. 1; Alpha Delta Sorority. *Rafu Shimpo*, May 3, 1946, p. 1; Uclans Honored at Sorority Tea. *Rafu Shimpo*, May 6, 1946, p. 1.
141. J.U.G. Girls' Club in Election Meet. *Rafu Shimpo*, June 18, 1946, p. 1; Installation of Cabinet Members. *Rafu Shimpo*, June 18, 1946, p. 1.
142. Yukio Kawaratani, *Reluctant Samurai: Memoirs of an Urban Planner, From Tule Lake to Bunker Hill*, Yukio Kawaratani, 2007, pp. 84–85.
143. Harry K. Honda, 85 Nisei Clubs Geared for Busy '47. 1946 Holiday Issue, Rafu Shimpo, December 21, 1946, pp. 1–2.
144. Harry K. Honda, 85 Nisei Clubs Geared for Busy '47. *Rafu Shimpo*, Holiday Issue, December 21, 1946, pp. 1–2.
145. Mary Oyama, Reveille. *Rafu Shimpo*, October 31, 1947, p. 1.
146. Ibid.
147. Girls' Tri-Y Group Holds Election at University High. *Rafu Shimpo*, January 25, 1946, p. 1.
148. Harry K. Honda, *Rafu Shimpo*, Holiday Issue, December 21, 1946, p. 2.
149. Mary Ishizuka, *REgenerations*, p. 226.
150. Wanted: Girl Scout Leaders! *Rafu Shimpo*, December 7, 1946, p. 1.
151. Mary Oyama, Reveille. *Rafu Shimpo*, January 17, 1947, p. 1.

152. Ibid.

153. Need Advisers. *Rafu Shimpo*, October 24, 1947, p. 1.

154. Mary Oyama, Reveille. *Rafu Shimpo*, March 3, 1949, p. 1.

155. Rose Honda, *REgenerations*, p. 82.

156. Rose Honda, *REgenerations*, p. 80. See also Mary Nishi Ishizuka, *REgenerations*, pp. 232–233. As listed in the 1950 Holiday Issue of the *Rafu Shimpo*, December 20, 1950, p. 7, the Atomettes were: Frances Watanabe, Susan Hashizume, Karleen Nakanishi, Michi Yamagi, Tayeko Noda, Sadie Inatomi, and Kathy Miyake.

157. Paul Boyer, *by the Bomb's Early Light: American Thought and Culture at the Dawn of the Atomic Age*. Ew York: Pantheon Books, 1985, pp. 294, 302. Boyer places these efforts to assuage public fears and promote the sense of the "friendly atom" within the context of an intensifying Cold War and nuclear arms race.

158. Rose Honda, *REgenerations*, p. 80. The newsletter was titled "Up in Atom," echoing a popular phrase, "Up and at 'em." See Mary Ishizuka, *REgenerations*, pp. 232–233.

159. Mary Ishizuka, *REgenerations*, p. 231.

160. Rose Honda, *REgenerations*, p. 80.

161. Mary Ishizuka, *REgenerations*, p. 231.

162. Ibid., p. 231.

163. Mary Ishizuka, *REgenerations*, p. 232. At the time of the interview in 1998, the six surviving Atomettes—then becoming grandmothers—and their advisers were still getting together several times a year.

164. "Reveal Inter-Club Council calendar," *Rafu Shimpo*, September 16, 1947, p. 1.

165. Ibid. Ralph Lazo was a Chicano youth who had, as a matter of principle, joined his Nisei friends in Manzanar for two years. He remained active in both ethnic communities after the war, and in 2007 was the subject of a Visual Communications film, "Stand Up for Justice: The Ralph Lazo Story."

166. What Is the Club Service Bureau? *Rafu Shimpo*, 1950 Holiday Issue, p. 7.

167. Rose Honda interview by author, July 30, 2009.

168. Sigma Phi Omega Sorority Inc., "history of sigma phi omega" (http://www.sigmaphiomega.com/y8n_about_history.htm). See also Gwen Muranaka's column about Sigma Phi Omega, of which her mother Julia Taniguchi Uriu was one of the founders: Why Not, USC? *Rafu Shimpo*, May 27, 2010, p. 5.

169. 1950–51 Club Directory," *Rafu Shimpo*, 1950 Holiday Issue, pp. 7, 26–30. Judging from the geographical spread of clubs included, the *Rafu* defined the "Southland" as ranging from as far south as San Diego, to as far north as Fresno in the Central Valley.

170. Esther Takei Nishio, *REgenerations*, p. 347. "Pasadena-onna" means "Pasadena woman" or "women."

171. Pasonas to Sponsor 'Play Nite' Aug. 8. *Rafu Shimpo*, August 1, 1947, p. 1.

172. Queen Candidates. *Rafu Shimpo*, June 10, 1947, p. 1; Chosen Queen. *Rafu Shimpo*, June 16, 1947, p. 1.

173. Esther Takei Nishio, *REgenerations*, p. 349.

174. Luknes Thanksiving Food Drive a Success. *Rafu Shimpo*, December 1, 1947, p. 1.

175. Donate to Church. *Rafu Shimpo*, September 9, 1947, p. 1.

176. Christmas Cheer Campaign Nets $1450; Toys & Foods. *Rafu Shimpo*, December 20, 1950, p. 1.

177. Miss Teens Girls Help at Hospital. *Rafu Shimpo*, March 22, 1947, p. 1.

178. Fans for Patients. *Rafu Shimpo*, April 23, 1947, p. 1.

179. Camilles to Sponsor Recital in September. *Rafu Shimpo*, August 9, 1947, p. 1. The Camilles club formed in March 1947, as reported in the *Rafu* on March 14, 1947.

180. 'Worthy!' Say Girls of MIY Club. *Rafu Shimpo*, December 7, 1946, p. 1.

181. J.U.G.'s to Begin Clothing Drive. *Rafu Shimpo*, October 9, 1946, p. 1. The J.U.G.s worked in conjunction with the International Institute and the American Friends Service Committee.

182. Windsor's [sic] Relief Work. *Rafu Shimpo*, October 27, 1949, p. 1. The Windsors sent "dry soup, sugar, cocoa, raisin[s], rice, hash, powdered milk, clothing, and shoes" valued at $300.

183. Capacity Crowd at Modernaire Dance. *Rafu Shimpo*, September 16, 1946, p. 1; see also Mary Kitano's "Snafu" column, *Rafu Shimpo*, August 31, 1946, p. 1.

184. Nisei Girls Clubs Will Have Booths at YWCA Bazaar. *Rafu Shimpo*, February 1, 1947, p. 1. Some of the funds also went to support members' travel to conferences.

185. Tri-Y Girls in Play. *Rafu Shimpo*, March 12, 1947, p. 1. A Nisei woman, Betty Wakamatsu, past president of the Tri-Y club at Polytechnic High School was "bestowed the honor of presiding over the entire program."

186. 200 Letters per Week to GIs is USO Girl's Record. *Rafu Shimpo*, July 10, 1946, p. 1.

187. Crusaders Give to Japan Relief. *Rafu Shimpo*, August 19, 1946, p. 1. The club representatives were Mrs. Tsuya Nakahara, Peggy Kumamoto, and Kay Tagami.

188. Pasonas Hold Social for Soldiers, Clubs. *Rafu Shimpo*, October 17, 1946, p. 1. Esther Takei was one of three women in charge of the dance program. The Pasonas' next event was a benefit dance on October 26 to support the Japan Relief Fund.

189. Pasonas Set Date for Benefit Dance. *Rafu Shimpo*, September 11, 1946, p. 1.

190. Club Visits Army Hospital. *Rafu Shimpo*, February 28, 1946, p. 1. The girls were escorted by a Nisei soldier from Oregon, and the injured men they visited—veterans of the 100th Battalion and the 442nd Regimental Combat Team—were mainly from Hawai'i. Regarding the formation of the Chere Amis, see *Rafu Shimpo*, January 24, 1947, p. 1. In 1946 the Dot and Dash club for over-21 Nisei women also made plans to take gifts to Nisei GI patients at an army hospital in Van Nuys, *Rafu*, November 28, 1946, p. 1.

191. Vet Patients Visited by Southland Clubs. *Rafu Shimpo*, December 23, 1950, p. 1.

192. Brian Niiya, More Than a Game: Sport in the Japanese American Community—An Introduction, in Brian Niiya, ed. *More than a Game: Sport in the Japanese American Community*. Los Angeles: Japanese American National Museum, 2000, p. 39.

193. Mary Kitano, Snafu. *Rafu Shimpo*, November 30, 1946, p. 1. Kitano's paragraph on "Bowling Belles" appears to have been mangled by a typesetter, so it is not entirely clear whether the "first" was a Nisei women's tournament or the inclusion of a large number of women's teams in a Nisei bowling tournament.

194. Paul's Café Drawing Clear in Women's Bowling Race. *Rafu Shimpo*, December 8, 1947, p. 1.

195. Niiya, *More Than a Game*, p. 39.

196. Japanese to Participate in International Pageant. *Rafu Shimpo*, October 9, 1946, p. 1.

197. Gala 2-Day International Festival Slated at Institute. *Rafu Shimpo*, September 29, 1947, p. 1.

198. Japanese Girls Will Serve Tea at Institute. *Rafu Shimpo*, October 9, 1947, p. 1. "Kojo no tsuki" may be translated as "Castle Moon."

199. Nisei Clubs Help Make Institutes' [sic] All-Nations Festival. *Rafu Shimpo*, October 14, 1950, p. 1.

200. Bevy of Nisei Lovelies in Queen Race. *Rafu Shimpo*, July 15, 1947, p. 1. Sumiko Nakagawa of Reedley, a commerce major at Reedley College, won the contest; see *Rafu*, July 26, 1947. (Dusty Matsumoto is not related to the author.)

201. Rebecca Chiyoko King-O'Riain, *Pure Beauty: Judging Race in Japanese American Beauty Pageants*. Minneapolis: University of Minnesota Press, 2006, pp. 63–64.

202. *Rafu Shimpo*, Nisei Week Special Number, August 11, 1949, pp. 1–2. The Nisei Week queens were not the only ones to meet with civic officials—for example, Blanche Jikaku, Queen of the 442nd Regimental Combat Team, visited Los Angeles from Hawai'i in 1947 and also met the mayor. For an analysis of the postwar revival of Nisei Week, see Lon Kurashige, *Japanese American Celebration and Conflict: A History of Ethic Identity and Festival in Los Angeles, 1934-1990*. Berkeley: University of California Press, 2002.

203. Shirley Jennifer Lim, *A Feeling of Belonging: Asian American Women's Public Culture, 1930-1960*. New York: New York University Press, 2006, p. 147.

204. Are Queen Contests Overdone? *Rafu Shimpo*, 1950 Holiday Issue, p. 3.

205. Ibid, pp. 3, 6.

206. Bussei Hold 8th Annual WYBL Parley. *Rafu Shimpo*, May 1, 1950, p. 1. A photo shows the new queen wearing a tiara and receiving a ceremonial cup.

207. The court decision was split 4-3, reflecting the conflicted views regarding interracial marriage. See Peggy Pascoe, *What Comes Naturally: Miscegenation Law and the Making of Race in America*. New York: Oxford University Press, 2009, pp. 205–223. For a detailed discussion of anti-miscegenation laws and their application to Asian Americans, see also Megumi Dick Osumi, Asians and California's Anti-Miscegenation Laws, in Nobuya Tsuchida, ed. *Asian*

and Pacific American Experiences: Women's Perspectives. Minneapolis: Asian/Pacific American Learning Resource Center and General College, University of Minnesota, 1982, pp. 1–37.

208. Esther Takei Nishio, *REgenerations*, p. 344.

209. Esther Takei Nishio, *REgenerations*, p. 343.

210. Mary Oyama, New World A-Coming. *Rafu Shimpo*, December 6, 1946, p. 1.

211. Ibid.

212. Mary Oyama, New World A-Coming. *Rafu Shimpo*, December 6, 1946, p. 1.

213. Mary Nishi Ishizuka interview by author, August 6, 2009.

214. Rose Honda interview by author, July 30, 2009.

215. Rose Honda, *REgenerations*, p. 81.

216. Rose Honda, *REgenerations*, p. 83.

217. Esther Takei Nishio, *REgenerations*, p. 347.

218. Mary Nishi Ishizuka, *REgenerations*, pp. 234–235. Mary's parents opposed her marrying George because he already had a three-year-old child, but the couple eventually married, and Mary's sister Midori served as maid of honor.

219. "Engagements," *Rafu Shimpo*, April 20, 1950, p. 1. Hatago was engaged to Jerry Endo. Among clubs like the Windsors, it was the custom that the sharing of candy accompanied engagement announcements. Another Windsor member announced her engagement to a Quixotics member by passing out Uno candy bars, as reported on August 25, 1949.

220. Bridal Shower. *Rafu Shimpo*, November 18, 1946, p. 1.

221. Pasadena Group to Hold Tea. *Rafu Shimpo*, August 27, 1947, p. 1.

222. Wedding Bells for Nisei. *Rafu Shimpo*, July 1, 1946, p. 1.

223. Ibid, p. 1.

224. Wedding Bells Ring for Two Nisei Couples Here. *Rafu Shimpo*, February 20, 1946, p. 1.

225. Mary Kitano, Snafu. *Rafu Shimpo*, May 4, 1946, p. 1.

226. Baby Shower to Tartanette Member. *Rafu Shimpo*, July 30, 1946, p. 1.

227. Stork Shower. *Rafu Shimpo*, June 19, 1947, p. 1.

228. Marion Funakoshi Manaka, *REgenerations*, pp. 280–281. After Marion's mother died, her father lived for a while with a son and daughter-in-law, eventually returning to live with Marion and her husband until his death at 102.

229. Marion Manaka, *REgenerations*, p. 287.

230. Marion Manaka, *REgenerations*, p. 288.

231. Marion Manaka, *REgenerations*, p. 288.

232. *Rafu Shimpo*, January 31, 1946, p. 1. Her letter to the editor was signed "Miss T.K."

233. Cooking Lessons. *Rafu Shimpo*, July 25, 1947, p. 1; Cooking Class. *Rafu Shimpo*, October 18, 1947, p. 1. Mrs. Matsuo also offered a class on making varieties of chop suey; see *Rafu*, September 6, 1947.

234. Cooking Class. *Rafu Shimpo*, October 18, 1947, p. 1.

235. Reports Cooking Classes by ARC. *Rafu Shimpo*, September 20, 1947, p. 1. Unfortunately there was no follow up reportage of who signed up for the classes.

236. Reports Cooking Classes by ARC. *Rafu Shimpo*, September 26, 1947, p. 1.

237. Mary Oyama, Reveille. *Rafu Shimpo*, September 9, 1948, p. 1. See also *Rafu*, August 26, 1948, p. 1.

238. Mary Oyama, Reveille. *Rafu Shimpo*, September 9, 1948, p. 1.

239. Henry J. Tsurutani, Thinking Verbally. *Rafu Shimpo*, 1949 Holiday Issue, p. 23. Although mostly in favor of television, Tsurutani noted a downside: "It's hard to get the youngsters to bed" and "the school-aged children won't do their homework."

240. Marion Manaka, *REgenerations*, p. 282.

241. Rose Honda, *REgenerations*, p. 111.

242. Marion Manaka, *REgenerations*, p. 284.

243. Mary Nishi Ishizuka interview by author, August 6, 2009.

244. Esther Nishio, *REgenerations*, p. 349.

245. Marion Manaka, *REgenerations*, p. 285.

246. Some men's clubs such as the Cougars have also continued to meet. Veterans' organizations have remained particularly active.

247. It was held by the Lacuanas girls' club on August 18, 1946. *Rafu Shimpo*, August 9, 1946, p. 1.

248. *Rafu Shimpo*, May 29, 1950, p. 1. Chiyoko Yamamoto was the first Nisei to graduate from the Queen of Angels School of Nursing and Yoshiko Sakaguchi was the first to graduate from the Bishop School of Nursing for the Good Samaritan Hospital.

249. Phelan Award Won by Okubo. *Rafu Shimpo*, September 21, 1949, p. 1.

250. Art Show. *Rafu Shimpo*, October 21, 1949, p. 1.

251. Prehistoric Life Drawings on Exhibit. *Rafu Shimpo*, March 15, 1947, p. 1.

Epilogue

1. In her film, Janice Tanaka noted that in 1971 alone, 31 young Sansei women died from what appeared to be drug overdoses.

2. Lon Kurashige, *Japanese American Celebration and Conflict: A History of Ethnic Identity and Festival in Los Angeles, 1934-1990*. Berkeley: University of California Press, 2002, pp. 123–125.

3. Naoko Shibusawa, *America's Geisha Ally: Reimagining the Japanese Enemy*. Cambridge, MA: Harvard University Press, 2006, p. 7.

4. Charlotte Brooks, *Alien Neighbors, Foreign Friends: Asian Americans, Housing, and the Transformation of Urban California*. Chicago: The University of Chicago Press, 2009, pp. 221–222.

5. Hisaye Yamamoto, I Still Carry It Around, originally published in *Rikka* 3, No. 4 (1976); reprinted in King-Kok Cheung, ed. *Seventeen Syllables, Hisaye Yamamoto*, Women Writers Texts and Contexts series. New Brunswick, NJ: Rutgers University Press, 1994, p. 69.

6. Gabriele Schwab, Writing against Memory and Forgetting. *Literature & Medicine* 25, No. 1 (Spring 2006):95–121.

7. Donna Nagata, Echoes from Generation to Generation, in Erica Harth, ed. *Last Witnesses: Reflections on the Wartime Internment of Japanese Americans*. New York: Palgrave, 2001, p. 70.

8. Schwab, p. 102.

9. Tsuyako "Sox" Kitashima and Joy K. Morimoto, *Birth of an Activist: The Sox Kitashima Story*, San Mateo, CA: Asian American Curriculum Project, Inc., 2003, p. 142.

10. Nagata, p. 68.

11. Laura Pulido, *Black, Brown, Yellow, and Left: Radical Activism in Los Angeles*. Berkeley: University of California Press, 2006, pp. 109–110.

12. Mary Uyematsu Kao, Three-Step Boogie: Japanese American Women in the 1970s Asian American Movement in Los Angeles. MA thesis in Asian American Studies, University of California, Los Angeles, 2007, p. 58.

13. Ibid.

14. For a shorter published form of Mary Uyematsu Kao's thesis, see Three-Step Boogie in 1970s Los Angeles: Sansei Women in the Asian American Movement. *Amerasia Journal* 35, No. 1 (2009):112–138; Susie Ling, The Mountain Movers: Asian American Women's Movement in Los Angeles. *Amerasia Journal* 15, No. 1 (1989):51–67.

15. Setsuko Matsunaga Nishi. Interview by the author, September 12 and 14, 2009.

16. The Nishi and Clausen report, *Papers for CWRIC*, was published separately from the Commission report *Personal Justice Denied*.

17. See producer/director Sharon Yamato's documentary film "Out of Infamy: Michi Nishiura Weglyn." See Tsuyako "Sox" Kitashima and Joy K. Morimoto, *Birth of an Activist: The Sox Kitashima Story*. San Mateo, CA: Asian American Curriculum Project, Inc., 2003. See Diana Meyers Bahr, *The Unquiet Nisei: An Oral History of the Life of Sue Kunitomi Embrey*. New York: Palgrave Macmillan, 2007.

18. The Los Angeles branch of the National Coalition for Redress and Reparations has continued their civil rights activism, in 2000 changing their name to Nikkei for Civil Rights and Redress.

19. Alice Yang Murray's 2008 study *Historical Memories of the Japanese American Internment and the Struggle for Redress* (Stanford: Stanford University Press, 2008) includes the contributions of Nisei women activists in the movement and in community constructions of historical memory. For more on Aiko Herzig-Yoshinaga, see Thomas Fujita-Rony, 'Destructive Force': Aiko Herzig-Yoshinaga's Gendered Labor in the Japanese American Redress Movement, *Frontiers* 24, No. 1 (2003):38–60.

20. Thomas Fujita-Rony, 'Destructive Force', pp. 53–54.

21. Gwen Muranaka, Women Recall Fight for Redress. *Rafu Shimpo*, April 12, 2008, p. 1.

22. Author's notes from attending the panel presentation "Organizing the Community," Part 2 of the program series Neglected Legacies: Japanese American Women and Redress, sponsored by the Japanese American National Museum and the UCLA Asian American Studies Center, April 5, 2008. Aiko Herzig-Yoshinaga, born in 1925, says that she became an activist and researcher at age 55 or 56, learning by trial and error.

23. See Alice Yang Murray's *Historical Memories of the Japanese American Internment and the Struggle for Redress*. Stanford: Stanford University Press, 2008, pp. 239, 267–275; and Sue Kunitomi Embrey, From Manzanar to the Present: A Personal Journey, in Erica Harth, ed. *Last Witnesses: Reflections on the Wartime Internment of Japanese Americans*. New York: Palgrave, 2001, pp. 167–85. See also Diana Meyers Bahr, *The Unquiet Nisei: An Oral History of Sue Kunitomi Embrey*. New York: Palgrave Macmillan, 2007.

24. Alice Yang Murray, *Historical Memories of the Japanese American Internment and the Struggle for Redress*. Stanford: Stanford University Press, 2008). Yang Murray presents a sophisticated examination of the efforts of scholars, activists, Japanese Americans who were incarcerated during World War II, and government officials to shape public interpretations of the causes and ramifications of the wartime incarceration of Issei and Nisei. Her discussion of Aiko Herzig-Yoshinaga's impact in rewriting history is instructive.

25. Setsuko Matsunaga Nishi. Interview by the author, September 12 and 14, 2009.

26. At the time of her death in 2012, Setsuko Nishi was writing a landmark national study begun in 1998, *Recovery and Hidden Injuries: Wartime Incarceration and the Life Course of Japanese Americans*.

27. Mitsuye Yamada, My Home Town This Earth, in *Desert Run: Poems and Stories*. Latham, NY: Kitchen Table: Women of Color Press, 1988, p. 84. Yamada's archive is at the University of California, Irvine.

28. Naomi Hirahara is the creator of a mystery series featuring Japanese gardener Mas Arai, who made his debut in *The Summer of the Big Bachi*. Hirahara won an Edgar Award for *The Snakeskin Shamisen* in 2007. Nina Revoyr is the author of three novels, including *Southland*. New York: Akashic Books, 2003, a mystery that delves into Japanese American and African American histories in the Crenshaw area; and *The Age of Dreaming*. New York: Akashic Books, 2008, which explores race in early Hollywood via the life of a Japanese star of the silent film era.

29. Micaela di Leonardo, The Female World of Cards and Holidays: Women, Families, and the Work of Kinship. *Signs* 12, No. 3 (Spring 1987):440–453. In her study of Seattle Japanese Americans, Sylvia Yanagisako observed that Issei and Nisei women were delegated the task of maintaining kin networks.

30. This cookbook, first printed in 1984 and 1985, can be ordered from the OCBC Cookbook Committee, Orange County Buddhist Church, 909 South Dale Street. Anaheim CA 92804. Nine women served on the cookbook committee.

31. The *Senshin Buddhist Temple Cookbook Otoki* is sold by the Senshin Buddhist Temple, 1311 West 37th Street, Los Angeles, CA 90007; telephone 323-731-4617.

32. David Masumoto, Of Turkey and Sushi. *Eating Well* Nov/Dec (1995):54–56.

33. For more on Asian American foodways, see Robert Ji-Song Ku, Martin Manalansan, and Anita Mannur, eds. *Eating Asian America*. New York: New York University Press, 2013. See also my essay Teaching Asian American History and Foodways. *Amerasia Journal* 32, No. 2 (2006):75–78.

34. Next Best Thing to Robert Redford. *Generation to Generation*, p. 263; and *Otoki*, p. 157. Watergate Cake with Cover-Up Icing. *Generation to Generation*, p. 270.

35. Ryoko Onishi and Jordan Ikeda, Cool Weather, Good Times at Nisei Week Festival. *Rafu Shimpo*, August 17, 2010.
36. Women were also well represented in exhibitions of ceramics, sumie brush painting, and other art forms.
37. See Chapter 5 for more about acclaimed Los Angeles dancer and teacher Fujima Kansuma (Sumako Hamaguchi), who studied odori in Japan before World War II.
38. The inclusion of Okinawan dance may have been a milestone for Nisei Week. On the last weekend, a member of the Okinawa Association of America, Yuko Yamauchi, said, "I don't know if it's the first time, but they're including an Okinawa obon dance in this year's street ondo dancing, so it's exciting." Gwen Muranaka, One Final Dance for Nisei Week. *Rafu Shimpo*, August 24, 2010.
39. Ryoko Onishi and Jordan Ikeda, Cool Weather, Good Times at Nisei Week Festival. *Rafu Shimpo*, August 17, 2010.
40. Gwen Muranaka, Nishiyama Crowned Nisei Week Queen. *Rafu Shimpo*, August 17, 2010.
41. See http://www.chialphadelta.com
42. See http://www.sigmaphiomega.com See also Gwen Muranaka's "Ochazuke" column, Why Not, USC?. *Rafu Shimpo*, May 27, 2010. Muranaka's mother Julia Taniguchi Uriu was one of the founders of Sigma Phi Omega.
43. See http://www.thetakappaphi.com/about.html

BIBLIOGRAPHY

Government Documents

Nishio, Esther Takei. Testimony before the Commission on Wartime Relocation and Internment of Civilians (CWRIC), August 6, 1981.

U.S. Bureau of the Census. *United States Census of the Population: 1940.*

U.S. Bureau of the Census, *United States Census of the Population: 1950.*

U.S. Bureau of the Census, *United States Census of the Population: 1960.*

U.S. Bureau of the Census, *United States Census of the Population: 1970.*

U.S. Department of the Interior, War Agency Liquidation Unit. *People in Motion: the Postwar Adjustment of the Evacuated Japanese Americans.* Washington, D.C.: U.S. Government Printing Office, 1947.

Newspapers and Magazines

Current Life: The Magazine for the American Born Japanese
Granada *Pioneer*
Hokubei Asahi
Kashu Mainichi
Los Angeles Times
Manzanar Free Press
New York Times
Nichi Bei Weekly
Poston Chronicle
Rafu Shimpo
San Francisco News
Shin Sekai-Asahi
The Daily Tulean Dispatch
Topaz Trek

Interviews

Herzig-Yoshinaga, Aiko. Typed responses to interview questions from author, August 2007.

Honda, Rose. Interview by Valerie J. Matsumoto, July 30, 2009; August, 6 2009. Los Angeles, CA.

Honda, Rose. Interview in *REgenerations Oral History Project: Rebuilding Japanese American Families, Communities, and Civil Rights in the Resettlement Era*, Japanese American National Museum, Chicago Japanese American Historical Society, Japanese American Historical Society of San Diego, and Japanese American Resource Center/Museum. Los Angeles: Japanese American National Museum, 2000.

Hurt, Haruko Sugi. Interview in *REgenerations Oral History Project: Rebuilding Japanese American Families, Communities, and Civil Rights in the Resettlement Era,* Japanese American National Museum, et al. Los Angeles: Japanese American National Museum, 2000.

Ide, Fumiko Fukuyama. Interview by Valerie J. Matsumoto, March 27, 2001; August 14, 2009. Los Angeles, CA.

Kanegai, Toyoko Kataoka. Interview by Valerie J. Matsumoto, 2000. Los Angeles, CA.

Ishizuka, Mary Nishi. Interview in *REgenerations Oral History Project: Rebuilding Japanese American Families, Communities, and Civil Rights in the Resettlement Era,* Japanese American National Museum, et al. Los Angeles: Japanese American National Museum, 2000.

Ishizuka, Mary Nishi. Interview by Valerie J. Matsumoto, August 4, 6, and 14, 2009. Los Angeles, CA.

Kunitsugu, Katsumi Hirooka. Interview in *REgenerations Oral History Project: Rebuilding Japanese American Families, Communities, and Civil Rights in the Resettlement Era,* Japanese American National Museum, et al. Los Angeles: Japanese American National Museum, 2000.

Komai, Kay Moritani. Interview by Valerie J. Matsumoto, August 9, 2000. Temple City, CA.

Manaka, Marion Funakoshi. Interview in *REgenerations Oral History Project: Rebuilding Japanese American Families, Communities, and Civil Rights in the Resettlement Era,* Japanese American National Museum et al. Los Angeles: Japanese American National Museum, 2000.

Nishi, Setsuko Matsunaga. Interview by Valerie J. Matsumoto, February 11 and 21, 2001; September 5 and 6, 2001; August 4, 2009; and September 12 and 14, 2009. Telephone conversation with Setsuko Matsunaga Nishi, September 6, 2001.

Nishio, Esther Takei. Interview in *REgenerations Oral History Project: Rebuilding Japanese American Families, Communities, and Civil Rights in the Resettlement Era,* Japanese American National Museum, et al. Los Angeles: Japanese American National Museum, 2000.

Shigekawa, Sakaye. Interview in *REgenerations Oral History Project: Rebuilding Japanese American Families, Communities, and Civil Rights in the Resettlement Era,* Japanese American National Museum, et al. Los Angeles: Japanese American National Museum, 2000.

Yamauchi, Wakako. Interview by author, October 3, 1995. Gardena, CA.

Books and Articles

Allen, James P. and Turner, Eugene, *The Ethnic Quilt: Population Diversity in Southern California.* Northridge, CA: The Center for Geographical Studies, California State University, Northridge, 1997.

Azuma, Eiichiro, *Between Two Empires: Race, History, and Transnationalism in Japanese America.* New York: Oxford University Press, 2005.

——, Race, Citizenship, and the 'Science of Chick Sexing': The Politics of Racial Identity among Japanese Americans. *Pacific Historical Review* 78, No. 2 (May 2009):242–275.

Bahr, Diana Meyers, *The Unquiet Nisei: An Oral History of the Life of Sue Kunitomi Embrey.* New York: Palgrave Macmillan, 2007.

Bailey, Beth L, *From Front Porch to Back Seat, Courtship in Twentieth-Century America.* Baltimore: Johns Hopkins University Press, 1989.

Boyer, Paul, *By the Bomb's Early Light: American Thought and Culture at the Dawn of the Atomic Age.* New York: Pantheon Books, 1985.

Brady, Marilyn Dell, Organizing Afro-American Girls' Clubs in Kansas in the 1920's. *Frontiers: A Journal of Women Studies* 9, No. 2 (1987):69–73.

Brooks, Charlotte, *Alien Neighbors, Foreign Friends: Asian Americans, Housing, and the Transformation of Urban California.* Chicago: The University of Chicago Press, 2009.

Broom, Leonard, and Riemer, Ruth, *Removal and Return, The Socio-Economic Effects of the War on Japanese Americans.* Berkeley: University of California Press, 1949.

Celello, Kristin, *Making Marriage Work: A History of Marriage and Divorce in the Twentieth-Century United States.* Chapel Hill: The University of North Carolina Press, 2009.

Chafe, William H, *The Unfinished Journey: America Since World War II.* New York: Oxford University Press, 1986.

Chan, Sucheng, Race, Ethnic Culture, and Gender in the Construction of Ethnic Identities among Second-Generation Chinese Americans, 1880s to 1930s, in K. Scott Wong and Sucheng

Chan, eds. *Claiming America: Constructing Chinese American Identities during the Exclusion Era*. Philadelphia: Temple University Press, 1998, pp. 127–164.

Cheng, Lucie, Cheng, Suellen, Chu, Judy, Lee, Feelie, Lee, Marjorie, and Ling, Susie, *Linking Our Lives: Chinese American Women of Los Angeles*. Los Angeles: Chinese Historical Society of Southern California and the Asian American Studies Center, University of California, Los Angeles, 1984.

Cheung, King-Kok, ed., *Seventeen Syllables: Hisaye Yamamoto*. Women Writers: Texts and Contexts. New Brunswick, NJ: Rutgers University Press, 1994.

Chuman, Frank F, *The Bamboo People: The Law and Japanese-Americans*. Del Mar, CA: Publisher's Inc., 1976.

Chung, Hye Seung, *Hollywood Asian: Philip Ahn and the Politics of Cross-Ethnic Performance*. Philadelphia: Temple University Press, 2006.

Culver, Lawrence, *The Frontier of Leisure: Southern California and the Shaping of Modern America*. New York: Oxford University Press, 2010.

Daniels, Roger, *Asian America: The Chinese and the Japanese in the United States since 1850*. Seattle: University of Washington Press, 1988.

——, *Concentration Camps: North America, Japanese in the United States and Canada during World War II*. Malabar, FL: Robert E. Krieger Publishing Company, Inc., 1981.

——, *Prisoners Without Trial: Japanese Americans in World War II*. New York: Hill and Wang, 1993.

——, Words Do Matter: A Note on Inappropriate Terminology and the Incarceration of the Japanese Americans, in Louis Fiset and Gail M. Nomura, eds. *Nikkei in the Pacific Northwest: Japanese Americans & Japanese Canadians in the Twentieth Century*. Seattle: Center for the Study of the Pacific Northwest and University of Washington Press, 2005, pp. 190–214.

De Vera, Arleen, The Tapia-Saiki Incident: Interethnic Conflict and Filipino Responses to the Anti-Filipino Exclusion Movement, in Valerie J. Matsumoto and Blake Allmendinger, eds. *Over the Edge: Remapping the American West*. Berkeley: University of California Press, 1999, pp. 201–214.

di Leonardo, Micaela, The Female World of Cards and Holidays: Women, Families, and the Work of Kinship. *Signs* 12, No. 3 (Spring 1987):440–453.

——, *The Varieties of Ethnic Experience: Kinship, Class, and Gender among California Italian-Americans*. Ithaca: Cornell University Press, 1984.

Embrey, Sue Kunitomi, From Manzanar to the Present: A Personal Journey, in Erica Harth, ed. *Last Witnesses: Reflections on the Wartime Internment of Japanese Americans*. New York: Palgrave, 2001, pp. 167–186.

Evans, Sara, *Born for Liberty, A History of Women in America*. New York: Simon & Schuster, 1997.

Fante, John, Helen, Thy Beauty Is to Me. *Saturday Evening Post* 213, No. 5 (March 1, 1941):14.

Fass, Paula, *The Damned and the Beautiful: American Youth in the 1920's*. New York: Oxford University Press, 1977.

Fischer, Michael M. J, Ethnicity and the Post-Modern Arts of Memory, in James Clifford and George E. Marcus, eds. *Writing Culture: The Poetics and Politics of Ethnography*. Berkeley: University of California Press, 1986.

Flamming, Douglas, *Bound for Freedom: Black Los Angeles in Jim Crow America*. Berkeley: University of California Press, 2005.

Fujita-Rony, Thomas, 'Destructive Force': Aiko Herzig-Yoshinaga's Gendered Labor in the Japanese American Redress Movement. *Frontiers* 24, No. 1 (2003):38–60.

Garcia, Matt, *A World of Its Own: Race, Labor, and Citrus in the Making of Greater Los Angeles, 1900-1970*. Chapel Hill: The University of North Carolina Press, 2001.

Gee, Emma, Issei: The First Women, in *Asian Women*, University of California, Berkeley, 1971: 8–15.

Gill, Tiffany, *Beauty Shop Politics: African American Women's Activism in the Beauty Industry*. Urbana: University of Illinois Press, 2010.

Girdner, Audrie, and Loftis, Anne, *The Great Betrayal: The Evacuation of the Japanese-Americans During World War II*. Toronto: Macmillan, 1969.

Glenn, Evelyn Nakano, The Dialectics of Wage Work: Japanese-American Women and Domestic Servants, 1905-1940. *Feminist Studies* 6, No. 3 (Fall 1980):428–471.

——, *Issei, Nisei, War Bride: Three Generations of Japanese American Women in Domestic Service.* Philadelphia: Temple University Press, 1986.

Gohara, Gene, Domestic Employment. *Current Life: The Magazine for the American Born Japanese,* June 1941.

Gordon Chang, ed., *Morning Glory, Evening Shadow: Yamato Ichihashi and His Internment Writings, 1942-1945.* Stanford: Stanford University Press, 1997.

Hayashi, Brian Masaru, *'For the Sake of Our Japanese Brethren': Assimilation, Nationalism, and Protestantism Among the Japanese of Los Angeles, 1895-1942.* Stanford: Stanford University Press, 1995.

Herzig-Yoshinaga, Aiko, *Words Can Lie or Clarify: Terminology of the World War II Incarceration of Japanese Americans.* http://www.ebookbrowse.com/ herzig-yoshinaga-terminology-pdf-d294744945.

Higa, Karin, Hidden in Plain Sight: Little Tokyo Between the Wars., in Gordon H. Chang, Mark Dean Johnson, and Paul J. Karlstrom, eds. *Asian American Art: A History, 1850-1970.* Stanford: Stanford University Press, 2008, pp. 30–53.

Hill, Patricia Liggins, ed., *Call and Response: The Riverside Anthology of the African American Literary Tradition.* New York: Houghton Mifflin Company, 1998.

Huggins, Nathan Irvin, *Harlem Renaissance.* New York: Oxford University Press, 1971, pp. 52–83.

Ichioka, Yuji, *The Issei: The World of the First Generation Japanese Immigrants, 1885-1924.* New York: The Free Press, 1988.

Irons, Peter, *Justice at War: The Story of the Japanese American Internment Cases.* New York: Oxford University Press, 1983.

Ishigaki, Ayako [pseudonym Haru Matsui], *Restless Wave, My Life in Two Worlds, A Memoir.* New York: The Feminist Press, 2004.

Ishizuka, Karen L, *Lost & Found: Reclaiming the Japanese American Incarceration.* Chicago: University of Illinois Press, 2006.

Ito, Leslie, Japanese American Women and the Student Relocation Movement, 1942-1945. *Frontiers: A Journal of Women Studies* 21, No. 3 (2000):1–24.

James, Thomas, *Exile Within: The Schooling of Japanese Americans 1942-1945.* Cambridge, MA: Harvard University Press, 1987.

Japanese American National Museum, Chicago Japanese American Historical Society, Japanese American Historical Society of San Diego, and Japanese American Resource Center/ Museum, *REgenerations Oral History Project: Rebuilding Japanese American Families, Communities, and Civil Rights in the Resettlement Era.* Los Angeles: Japanese American National Museum, 2000.

Kao, Mary Uyematsu, Three-Step Boogie in 1970s Los Angeles: Sansei Women in the Asian American Movement. *Amerasia Journal* 35, no.1 (2009):112–138.

Kashima, Tetsuden, *Judgment Without Trial: Japanese American Imprisonment during World War II.* Seattle: University of Washington Press, 2003.

Kawai, Kazuo, Three Roads and None Easy. *Survey Graphic* 9, No. 2 (May 1926):164–166.

Kawaratani, Yukio, *Reluctant Samurai: Memoirs of an Urban Planner, From Tule Lake to Bunker Hill.* Yukio Kawaratani, 2007.

King-O'Riain, Rebecca Chiyoko: *Pure Beauty: Judging Race in Japanese American Beauty Pageants.* Minneapolis: University of Minnesota Press, 2006.

Kitano, Harry H. L., *Japanese Americans: The Evolution of a Subculture,* 2nd ed. Englewood Cliffs, NJ: Prentice-Hall, Inc., 1976.

Kitashima, Tsuyako "Sox," and Morimoto, Joy K., *Birth of an Activist: The Sox Kitashima Story.* San Mateo, CA: Asian American Curriculum Project, Inc., 2003.

Kochiyama, Yuri, *Passing it On—A Memoir.* Los Angeles: UCLA Asian American Studies Center, 2004.

Ku, Robert Ji-Song, Manalansan, Martin F., IV, and Mannur, Anita, eds., *Eating Asian America.* New York: New York University Press, 2013.

Kumei, Teruko, *'A Record of Life and a Poem of Sentiments':* Japanese Immigrant *Senryu,* 1929-1945. *Amerikastudien/American Studies, A Quarterly* 51, No.1 (2006):29–49.

Kurashige, Lon, *Japanese American Celebration and Conflict: A History of Ethnic Identity and Festival in Los Angeles, 1934-1990.* Berkeley: University of California Press, 2002.

Kurashige, Scott, *The Shifting Grounds of Race: Black and Japanese Americans in the Making of Multiethnic Los Angeles.* Princeton, NJ: Princeton University Press, 2008.

Lai, Eric, and Arguelles, Dennis, eds., *The New Face of Asian Pacific America: Numbers, Diversity & Change in the 21st Century.* San Francisco, CA: Asian Week with UCLA's Asian American Studies Center Press in cooperation with the Organization of Chinese Americans and the National Coalition for Asian Pacific American Community Development, 2003.

Lee, Catherine, 'Where the Danger Lies': Race, Gender, and Japanese Exclusion in the United States, 1870-1924, *Sociological Forum* 25, No. 2 (June 2010):248–271.

Leighton, Alexander H. *The Governing of Men: General Principles and Recommendations Based on Experience at a Japanese Relocation Camp.* Princeton: Princeton, University Press, 1945.

Leonard, Kevin, *The Battle for Los Angeles; Racial Ideology and World War II.* Albuquerque, NM: University of New Mexico Press, 2006.

Leong, Karen, *The China Mystique: Pearl S. Buck, Anna May Wong, Mayling Soong, and the Transformation of American Orientalism.* Berkeley: University of California Press, 2005.

Levenstein, Harvey, *Paradox of Plenty: A Social History of Eating in Modern America,* rev. ed. Berkeley: University of California Press, 2003.

Lim, Shirley Jennifer, *A Feeling of Belonging: Asian American Women's Public Culture, 1930-1960.* New York: New York University Press, 2006.

Ling, Susie, *The Mountain Movers: Asian American Women's Movement in Los Angeles. Amerasia Journal* 15, No. 1 (1989):51–67.

Locke, Alain, Enter the New Negro. *Survey Graphic,* March 1925.

Mainzer, Lewis C, John McGilvrey Maki. *PS: Political Science & Politics* 40, No. 3 (July 2007):596–597.

Maki, Mitchell T., Kitano, Harry H. L., and Berthold, S. Megan, *Achieving the Impossible Dream: How Japanese Americans Obtained Redress.* Champaign: University of Illinous Press, 1999.

Manalansan, Martin F., IV. *Global Divas: Filipino Gay Men in the Diaspora.* Durham, NC: Duke University Press, 2003.

Mass, Amy Iwasaki, Socio-Psychological Effects of the Concentration Camp Experience on Japanese Americans. *Bridge: An Asian American Perspective* (Winter 1978):61–63.

Masumoto, David, Of Turkey and Sushi. *Eating Well* (Nov/Dec 1995).

Matsui, Haru, *Restless Wave, An Autobiography.* New York: Modern Age Books, 1940. [See also Ishigaki, Ayako]

Matsumoto, Valerie J, Desperately Seeking 'Deirdre': Gender Roles, Multicultural Relations, and Nisei Women Writers of the 1930s. *Frontiers* 12, No.1 (1991):19–32.

——, Redefining Expectations: Nisei Women in the 1930s. *California History* (Spring 1994):44–53, 88.

——, Teaching Asian American History and Foodways. *Amerasia Journal* 32, No. 2 (2006):75–78.

Meyerowitz, Joanne, Preface to *Men and Women Adrift: The YMCA and the YWCA in the City,* Nina Mjagkij and Margeret Spratt, eds. New York: New York University Press, 1997, x–xii.

Mihesuah, Devon, 'Too Dark to Be Angels': The Class System among the Cherokee at the Female Seminary, in Vicki L. Ruiz with Carol Ellen DuBois, eds. *Unequal Sisters: An Inclusive Reader in U.S. Women's History,* 4th ed. New York: Routledge, 2008, pp. 183–96.

Miyamoto, S. Frank, *Social Solidarity among the Japanese in Seattle.* Seattle: University of Washington Press, 1984.

Miyao, Daisuke, *Sessue Hayakawa: Silent Cinema and Transnational Stardom.* Durham, NC: Duke University Press, 2007.

Mohl, Raymond A, Cultural Pluralism in Immigrant Education: The YWCA's International Institutes, 1910-1940, in Nina Mjagkij and Margaret Spratt, eds. *Men and Women Adrift: The YMCA and the YWCA in the City.* New York: New York University Press, 1997, pp. 111–137.

Moon, Krystyn R, *Yellowface: Creating the Chinese in American Popular Media and Performance, 1850s-1920s.* New Brunswick, NJ: Rutgers University Press, 2005.

Mullins, Maire, Imagining Community: Language and Literacy in Hisaye Yamamoto's 'Seventeen Syllables.' *Journal of Asian American Studies* 13, No. 2 (June 2010):219–241.

Murase, Kenny, Who's Who in the Nisei Literary World. *Current Life: The Magazine for the American Born Japanese,* October 1940.

—— William Saroyan and the American Short Story. *Current Life: The Magazine for the American Born Japanese*, December 1940.

Murray, Alice Yang, *Historical Memories of the Japanese American Internment and the Struggle for Redress*. Stanford: Stanford University Press, 2008.

Nagata, Donna, Echoes from Generation to Generation, in Erica Harth, ed. *Last Witnesses: Reflections on the Wartime Internment of Japanese Americans*. New York: Palgrave, 2001, pp. 61–74.

Nakano, Mei, *Japanese American Women, Three Generations, 1890-1990*. Berkeley: Mina Press Publishing, 1990.

Niiya, Brian, ed., *Japanese American History, An A-to-Z Reference from 1868 to the Present*. Los Angeles: Japanese American National Museum, 1993.

——, *More Than a Game: Sport in the Japanese American Community*. Los Angeles: Japanese American National Museum, 2000.

Nishi, Setsuko, *The Changing Scene*. New York: The National Council of Churches, 1955.

O'Brien, Robert, *The College Nisei*. Palo Alto: Pacific Books, 1949.

Okubo, Miné, *Citizen 13660*. Seattle: University of Washington Press, 1983.

Orange County Buddhist Church Cookbook Committee, *Generation to Generation, A Family Cookbook*. Orange County Buddhist Church, 1984.

Osumi, Megumi Dick, Asians and California's Anti-Miscegenation Laws, in Nobuya Tsuchida ed. *Asian and Pacific American Experiences: Women's Perspectives*. Minneapolis: Asian/Pacific American Learning Resource Center and General College, University of Minnesota, 1982, pp. 1–37.

Oyama, Mary, My Only Crime Is My Face. *Liberty, The Magazine of a Free People*, August 14, 1943.

——, A Nisei Report from Home. *Common Ground* (Winter 1946):26–28.

Pascoe, Peggy, *What Comes Naturally: Miscegenation Law and the Making of Race in America*. New York: Oxford University Press, 2009.

Peiss, Kathy, *Hope in a Jar: The Making of America's Beauty Culture*. New York: Metropolitan Books, 1998.

Pleck, Elizabeth, *Celebrating the Family: Ethnicity, Consumer Culture, and Family Rituals*. Cambridge, MA: Harvard University Press, 2000.

Pulido, Laura, *Black, Brown, Yellow, and Left: Radical Activism in Los Angeles*. Berkeley, CA: University of California Press, 2006.

Richardson, Susan B., ed., *I Call to Remembrance: Toyo Suyemoto's Years of Internment*. New Brunswick, NJ: Rutgers University Press, 2007.

Robertson, Nancy, with Norris, Elizabeth, 'Without Documents No History': Sources and Strategies for Researching the YWCA, in Nina Mjagkij and Margaret Spratt, eds. *Men and Women Adrift: the YMCA and the YWCA in the City*. New York: New York University Press, 1997, pp. 271–298.

Robinson, Greg, *By Order of the President: FDR and the Internment of Japanese Americans*. Cambridge, MA: Harvard University Press, 2001.

——, ed., *Pacific Citizens: Larry and Guyo Tajiri and Japanese American Journalism in the World War II Era*. Champaign, IL: University of Illinois Press, 2011.

——, *A Tragedy of Democracy: Japanese Confinement in North America*. New York: Columbia University Press, 2009.

Ruiz, Vicki L, The Flapper and the Chaperone: Historical Memory among Mexican-American Women, in Donna Gabaccia, ed. *Seeking Common Ground: Multidisciplinary Studies of Immigrant Women in the United States*. Westport, CT: Greenwood Press, 1992, pp. 141–158.

——, *From Out of the Shadows: Mexican Women in Twentieth-Century America*. New York: Oxford University Press, 1998.

Saroyan, William, William Saroyan Salutes Current Life. *Current Life, the Magazine for the American Born Japanese*, May 1941.

Sawada, Noriko, Memoir of a Japanese Daughter. *Ms.* 8, No. 10 (April 1980):68–76, 110.

Schwab, Gabriele, Writing against Memory and Forgetting. *Literature & Medicine* 25, No.1 (Spring 2006):95–121.

Schweik, Susan, The Pre-Poetics of Internment: The Example of Toyo Suyemoto. *American Literary History* (Spring 1989):89–109.

See, Lisa, *On Gold Mountain: The One-Hundred Year Odyssey of My Chinese-American Family.* New York: Vintage Books, 1995.

Shibusawa, Naoko, *America's Geisha Ally: Reimagining the Japanese Enemy.* Cambridge, MA: Harvard University Press, 2006.

Shikagi, Doris, *Senshin Buddhist Temple Cookbook Otoki.* Los Angeles, Shenshin Buddhist Temple, 2008.

Shimano, Eddie, Foreword. *Gyo-Sho, A Magazine of Nisei Literature.* Mount Vernon, IA: The English Club of Cornell College, n.d. (ca. 1936).

Sides, Josh, *L.A. City Limits: African American Los Angeles from the Great Depression to the Present.* Berkeley, CA: University of California Press, 2003.

Silverberg, Miriam, After the Grand Tour: The Modern Girl, the New Woman, and the Colonial Maiden, in The Modern Girl Around the World Research Group, Alys Eve Weinbaum, Lynn M. Thomas, Priti Ramamurthy, Uta G. Polger, Madeleine Yue Dong, and Tani E. Barlow, eds. *The Modern Girl Around the World: Consumption, Modernity, and Globalization.* Durham, NC: Duke University Press, 2008, pp. 354–361.

Silverberg, Miriam, *Erotic Grotesque Nonsense: The Mass Culture of Japanese Modern Times.* Berkeley: University of California Press, 2006.

Simmons, Christina, *Making Marriage Modern: Women's Sexuality from the Progressive Era to World War II.* New York: Oxford University Press, 2009.

Sims, Mary S, *The Natural History of a Social Institution—the Young Women's Christian Association.* New York: The Womans Press, 1936.

Sone, Monica, *Nisei Daughter.* Seattle: University of Washington Press, 1953.

Spicer, Edward H., and United States War Relocation Authority, *Impounded People: Japanese-Americans in the Relocation Centers.* Tucson, AZ: The University of Arizona Press, 1969.

Starr, Kevin, *The Dream Endures: California Enters the 1940s.* New York: Oxford University Press, 1997.

Takemoto, Paul Howard, *Nisei Memories: My Parents Talk About the War Years.* Seattle: University of Washington Press, 2006.

Tamura, Eileen H, *Americanization, Acculturation, and Ethnic Identity: The Nisei Generation in Hawaii.* Urbana and Chicago: University of Illinois Press, 1994.

The Modern Girl Around the World Research Group, Alys Eve Weinbaum, Lynn M. Thomas, Priti Ramamurthy, Uta G. Polger, Madeleine Yue Dong, and Tani E. Barlow, The Modern Girl as Heuristic Device: Collaboration, Connective Comparison, Multidirectional Citation, in The Modern Girl Around the World Research Group, et al., eds. *The Modern Girl Around the World.* Durham, NC: Duke University Press, 2008, pp. 1–24.

Uchida, Yoshiko, *Desert Exile: The Uprooting of Japanese American Family.* Seattle: University of Washington Press, 1982.

Uno, Kathleen, Unlearning Orientalism: Locating Asian and Asian American Women in Family History, in Shirley Hune and Gail M. Nomura, eds. *Asian/Pacific Islander American Women: A Historical Anthology.* New York: New York University Press, 2003, pp. 42–57.

Weglyn, Michi, *Years of Infamy: The Untold Story of America's Concentration Camps.* New York: Morrow Quill Paperbacks, 1976.

Weinbaum, Alys Eve, Racial Masquerade: Consumption and Contestation of American Modernity in The Modern Girl Around the World Research Group, et al., eds. *The Modern Girl Around the World.* Durham, NC: Duke University Press, 2008, pp. 120–146.

Weisenfeld, Judith, *African American Women and Christian Activism: New York's Black YWCA, 1905-1945.* Cambridge, MA: Harvard University Press, 1997.

White, Richard, *It's Your Misfortune and None of My Own: A New History of the American West.* Norman, OK: University of Oklahoma Press, 1991.

Wong, Jade Snow, *Fifth Chinese Daughter.* Seattle: University of Washington Press, 1989.

Wong, K. Scott, and Sucheng Chan, eds., *Claiming America: Constructing Chinese American Identities during the Exclusion Era.* Philadelphia: Temple University Press, 1998.

Young Women's Christian Association of the U.S.A. Girl Reserve Department, *Guide Book for Senior High School Girl Reserves.* New York: The Womans Press, 1928.

Yamada, Mitsuye, *Desert Run: Poems and Stories*. Latham, NY: Kitchen Table: Women of Color Press, 1988.

Yamamoto, Eriko, Miya Sannomiya Kikuchi: A Pioneer Nisei Woman's Life and Identity, *Amerasia Journal* 23, No. 3 (1997):73–101.

Yamamoto, Hisaye, *Seventeen Syllables and Other Stories*. Latham, NY: Kitchen Table: Women of Color Press, 1988.

Yogi, Stan, Japanese American Literature, in King-Kok Cheung, ed. *An Interethnic Companion to Asian American Literature*. New York: Cambridge University Press, 1997, pp. 125–155.

Yoo, David K, *Growing Up Nisei: Race, Generation, and Culture among Japanese Americans of California, 1924-49*. Urbana: University of Illinois Press, 2000.

Yu, Henry, *Thinking Orientals: Migration, Contact, and Exoticism in Modern America*. New York: Oxford University Press, 2001.

Yung, Judy, *Unbound Feet: A Social History of Chinese Women in San Francisco*. Berkeley, CA: University of California Press, 1995.

Dissertations and MA Theses

Fukuoka, Fumiko, Mutual Life and Aid Among the Japanese in Southern California with Special Reference to Los Angeles. MA thesis, University of Southern California, 1937.

Kao, Mary Uyematsu, Three-Step Boogie: Japanese American Women in the 1970s Asian American Movement in Los Angeles. MA thesis, University of California, Los Angeles, 2007.

Kawasaki, Kanichi, The Japanese Community of East San Pedro, Terminal Island, California. MA thesis, University of Southern California, 1931.

Lee, Marjorie, *Hu-Jee*: The Forgotten Second Generation of Chinese America, 1930-1950. MA thesis, University of California, Los Angeles, 1984.

Louis, Kit King, A Study of American-born and American-reared Chinese in Los Angeles. MA thesis, University of Southern California, 1931.

McAndrew, Jennifer Malia, All-American Beauty: The Experiences of African American, European American, and Japanese American Women With Beauty Culture in the Mid-Twentieth Century United States. Ph.D. dissertation, University of Maryland, College Park, 2008.

Nishi, Midori, Changing Occupance of the Japanese in Los Angeles County, 1940-1950. Ph.D. dissertation, University of Washington, 1955.

Ross, Robert Howard, Social Distance As it Exists Between the First and Second Generation Japanese in the City of Los Angeles and Vicinity. M.A. thesis, University of Southern California, 1939.

Svensrud, Marion, Some Factors Concerning the Assimilation of a Selected Japanese Community. M.A. thesis, University of Southern California, 1931.

Yamashita, Wendsor Sumie, What She Remembers: Remaking and Unmaking Japanese American Internment. M.A. thesis, University of California, Los Angeles. 2010.

Yatsushiro, Toshio, Political and Socio-Cultural Issues at Poston and Manzanar Relocation Centers—A Themal Analysis. Ph.D. dissertation, Cornell University, 1953.

Yep, Kathleen Susan, They Got Game: The Racial and Gender Politics of Basketball in San Francisco's Chinatown, 1932-1949. Ph.D. dissertation, University of California, Berkeley, 2002.

Yokota, Kariann, From Little Tokyo to Bronzeville and Back: Ethnic Communities in Transition. M.A. thesis, University of California, Los Angeles, 1996.

Manuscript Collections

Esther Takei Nishio Collection, private collection.

Henriette Von Blon Collection. Hoover Institution Archives, Stanford University, Stanford, CA.

Hugh Harris Anderson Papers. Special Collections, Charles E. Young Research Library. University of California, Los Angeles, CA.

Mitsuye Yamada Papers. Special Collections and Archives. University of California, Irvine, CA.

Yoshinaga Family history compilation, private collection.

YWCA Collection. Special Collections. California State University, Northridge, CA.

Fiction and Poetry

Himes, Chester, *If He Hollers Let Him Go*. New York: Thunder Mouth Press, 1986.

Hirahara, Naomi, *Snakeskin Shamisen*. New York: Delta Trade Paperbacks, 2006.

——, *Summer of the Big Bachi*. New York: Bantam Dell, 2008.

Kim, Ronyoung, *Clay Walls*. Sag Harbor, New York: The Permanent Press, 1987.

Korenaga, Mary, "Chiyono." *Gyo-Sho, A Magazine of Nisei Literature*. Mount Vernon, IA: The English Club of Cornell College, n.d. (ca. 1936).

Oyama, Molly, Coming of Age. *Gyo-Sho, A Magazine of Nisei Literature*. Mount Vernon, IA: The English Club of Cornell College, n.d. (ca. 1936).

Thun, Ellen, Sketch. *Gyo-Sho, A Magazine of Nisei Literature*. Mount Vernon, IA: The English Club of Cornell College, n.d. (ca. 1936).

Yamada, Mitsuye, My Home Town This Earth, *Camp Notes and Other Writings*. New Brunswick, NJ: Rutgers University Press, 1998.

Yamamoto, Hisaye, *Seventeen Syllables and Other Stories*. Latham, NY: Kitchen Table: Women of Color Press, 1988.

Visual Media

McCay, Winsor. "Little Nemo in Slumberland." Comic Strip.

"Mary Ann Gay." Comic Strip. *Rafu Shimpo*.

Out of Infamy: Michi Nishiura Weglyn. DVD. Directed by Nancy Kapitanoff and Sharon Yamato. 2010.

Stand Up for Justice: The Ralph Lazo Story. DVD. Directed by John Esaki. Los Angeles: Visual Communications. 2007.

When You're Smiling: The Deadly Legacy of Internment. Directed by Janice D. Tanaka. 1999.

Web Sites

Chi Alpha Delta. http://www.chialphadelta.com

Densho Project. www.densho.org

Sigma Phi Omega Sorority Inc., History of Sigma Phi Omega. www.sigmaphiomega.com

Theta Kappa Phi. History. www.thetakappaphi.com/about.html

Correspondence and Miscellaneous Documents

Advisory Committee for Evacuees. *Resettlement Bulletin*, April 1943.

Advisory Committee for Evacuees. *Resettlement Bulletin*, July 1943.

Japanese American National Museum and UCLA Asian American Studies Center. Part II: Organizing the Community. Panel presentation, *Neglected Legacies: Japanese American Women and Redress* program series, Los Angeles, CA, April 5, 2008.

National Japanese American Student Relocation Council. Minutes of the Executive Committee Meeting. Philadelphia, PA, December 19, 1945.

INDEX

Oral history interviews / memoirs
Japanese American newspapers

CPSIA information can be obtained
at www.ICGtesting.com
Printed in the USA
BVOW01s2251281016
466281BV00003B/5/P